TOURING
NEW
MEXICO

POLLY ARANGO

KATHY CHILTON

LANCE CHILTON

JAMES DUDLEY

PATRICIA McENEARNEY STELZNER

TOURING
NEW
MEXICO

University of New Mexico Press

Albuquerque

Dedicated to our parents, who
helped give each of us a love of
travel.

© 1995 by the University of New Mexico Press
All rights reserved.
First Edition

Illustrations © 1995 Katherine Chilton
Maps by Carol Cooperrider

Library of Congress Cataloging in Publication Data

Touring New Mexico / Polly Arango . . . [et al.],
        p.   cm.
Includes bibliographical references (p.   ) and index.
ISBN 0-8263-1622-0.
1. New Mexico—Tours.
2. Automobile travel—New Mexico—Guidebooks.
I. Arango, Polly, 1942–
F794.3.T68 1995
917.8904'53—dc20
94–16724
CIP

CONTENTS

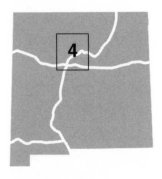

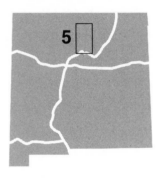

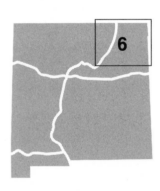

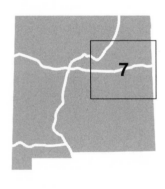

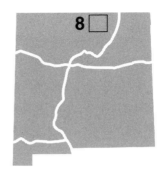

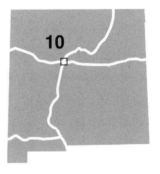

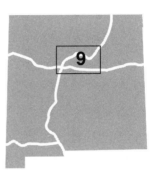

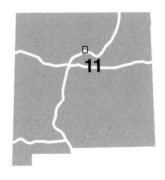

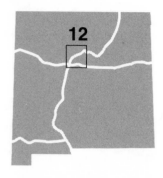

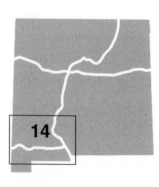

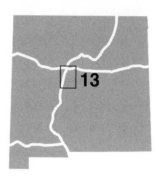

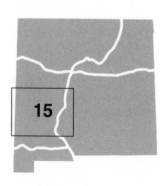

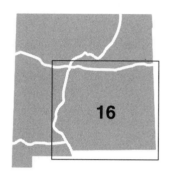

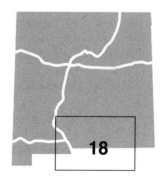

INTRODUCTION

Jigsaw puzzles of the United States usually show New Mexico as a large yellow piece to be squeezed in between pink Arizona and lavender Texas. The simple geometric aspect of a map of New Mexico shows a big rectangle with a small, squarish bootheel in the lower left, a triangular tooth at El Paso, and two tiny deviations from the straight lines in the upper right corner, giving no hint of the convoluted complexity, colors, and life of the land within those borders. We intend that this book will introduce you to those dimensions by guiding you through damp caverns and sunburned deserts, to lush mountainsides and black lava flows, into red sandstone canyons, and along rushing rivers in a land that is populated by a wonderful mixture of people who have given the state a lively spirit. We begin with some suggestions about how to travel in New Mexico, both physically and philosophically. Our guide does not always stop at the state line but makes forays into Colorado, Texas, and Mexico as we feel you would when in that area.

Getting Around—Physically

Take this book and its more detailed companion, *New Mexico: A New Guide to the Colorful State,* and a new highway map. Use the larger guide to plan your own side trips and to learn more about the people, history, economy, and arts of New Mexico. Road maps are free at ports of entry, highway rest areas, tourist information centers, and from the New Mexico Tourism and Travel Division, 1100 Saint Francis Drive, Santa Fe, New Mexico, 87503 (827-0291 in New Mexico or 1-800-545-2040 out of state). The "Indian Country Map" by the AAA of southern California and the *Roads of New Mexico* atlas provide details of each region and are for sale locally. New Mexico has recently changed all its state highway numbers, so old road maps and roadside signs may not agree. We have not discerned any logic to the new highway numbering system except that the road to the Alamogordo Space Hall of Fame is State Highway 2001.

We assume that most of you will journey to or in New Mexico by car. The possibilities for train travel are few but delightful and will be discussed later in the book. Buses tend to ply limited routes. Travel by airplane gives you an extraordinary geological perspective but is generally impractical for the tourist. And extensive travel by boat, as you can see by the amount of blue on your map, is not feasible.

WEATHER

New Mexico weather is difficult to predict. We can say that you will probably encounter fierce winds in the spring, dramatic thunderstorms with rainbows in the late summer, freezing temperatures and snow in the winter, but warm sunshine most of the time. The only places in the state where you might see an umbrella are at Pueblo summer corn dances, where they are used to protect elders from the heat, or at rainy Albuquerque Dukes baseball games when the fans refuse to quit. The lightning that accompanies summer storms should be respected both for its beauty and its danger. New Mexico has few snowplows and seldom uses sand or salt on its roads. Because of the possibility of severe weather, we recommend preparedness for yourselves and your car, including rental cars. Call the State Highway Department at 1-800-432-4269 for road conditions before you start. Flash floods cover some roads in the summer, and snowdrifts obscure others in the winter. To be prepared, take these things with you: water, snack food, a blanket, a small shovel for sand and snow, a first-aid kit, a flat tire inflater, matches, chains in winter, bug repellent, a flashlight, sunscreen, and a repertoire of songs and stories. Fill up the gas tank before heading out, and take an extra quart of oil, because the distances between service stations can be great. Be aware that New Mexico often leads the nation in an unenviable statistic: highway fatalities due to drinking drivers. Driving on small rural roads on weekend evenings warrants special care.

ALTITUDE   Allow yourself time to become accustomed to New Mexico's relatively high altitude. It is common to feel tired or short of breath when you have come to New Mexico from a lower altitude. New Mexicans have learned to blame the altitude for baking failures, car troubles, and peculiar behavior.

COVERING LONG DISTANCES   New Mexico is sparsely populated, but most of its 1.6 million inhabitants are willing and eager to answer any questions you may have. You will find it worthwhile to shop in trading posts, village groceries, and general stores, where you can ask about local events, places to eat, picnic possibilities, town characters, and where the fish are biting. Nearly every town has a library and at least one park that provides cool respite or room to run, and perhaps a bandstand for impromptu performances by the backseat travelers. New Mexico's town libraries are superb places to take a break because they exhibit local art; display children's books and magazines to be read in one sitting; provide comfortable chairs, local newspapers, and phone books; and have knowledgeable librarians. The telephone yellow pages are an excellent source of information for travelers. They list accommodations and restaurants, and will mention the carousel repair shop, tortilla factory, or rock shop that you might want to visit. The yellow pages also reflect the character of a place by the quantity of certain listings: the oil-drilling equipment suppliers in Hobbs, the Indian jewelry stores and pawn shops of Gallup, the acupuncturists in Santa Fe, and the scuba instructors in Santa Rosa. Tourist Information Centers in Tucumcari, Gallup, Chama, Albuquerque, Santa Fe, Las Vegas and Taos are prepared to help you plan your journey.

New Mexico's highway rest areas are usually handsome and clean and provide some tourist information. We recommend that you move around at parks and rest areas—play Frisbee or catch, jump rope, or play tag. Snack and talk in the car and exercise in the "rest" areas, or you and your children may become restless. Our many college campuses are also good places to refresh yourself after a long drive. The extensive lawns, cool buildings, and friendly students can put a different perspective on a visit to a town or city.

Children do not usually care about most scenery or museums. They prefer scenery they can climb on or dig into and museums that allow some kind of interaction. Fortunately, New Mexico is rich in places that combine spectacular scenery and hands-on fun. Bandelier's spindly ladders into Anasazi cliff dwellings, White Sands' great gypsum dunes, Carlsbad Caverns' long descending trail, and Fort Union's historic pathways are made for young explorers. The Santa Fe and Albuquerque Children's Museums, Explora, and the Museum of Natural History in Albuquerque, the New Mexico Museum of Mining in Grants, and the Living Desert State Park in Carlsbad invite youngsters to experience their exhibits with hands-on displays. New Mexico also prizes the many unique museums that in size and scope are easily tolerated by children. Smokey Bear Museum in Capitan, My House of Favorite Things in Ancho, or the Jemez State Monument in Jemez Springs just might pique their interest.

Beyond the scenery and museums, children may like to ride a horse, milk a goat, watch puppeteers, scrounge in a flea market, soak in a hot spring, put hands and feet in four states at once, listen to a fiddler, or watch a small-town rodeo. Standard car games like finding license plates from all the states or travel bingo with points awarded for sighting steeples, barns, fountains, and traffic lights would take months to play in the great expanses of New Mexico. Instead, try counting telephone poles or antelopes, finding animal forms in clouds and hills, or identifying birds and flowers. Let the kids ask some of the questions when you visit a museum; encourage them to buy the picnic supplies or bait (children under twelve may fish without a license). Children love to keep a record of a journey—whether spoken into a tape recorder, drawn on a map, written in a journal, snapped with a camera, or collected in a jar.

In New Mexico, you will probably sample foods that are new to you. "Red or green?" is the first question asked in many New Mexican restaurants. Do you prefer rich, red chile sauce made from ground, dried chile pods or tangy green chunks of the fresh pod swimming in a sauce? Then it will be your turn to ask, "Which is hotter?" Hot in New Mexico is HOT. Try *sopaipillas* and fry bread, which are Hispanic and Indian variations of fried bread dough; everyone likes these delicacies. With honey, they are the perfect counter to the burning heat of New Mexican chile. And for dessert . . . we may be the only state in the country with an official state cookie, the *bizcochito,* a cinnamon sugar cookie with a hint of anise. Other local specialties include *posole*; *carne adovada*; the cowboy favorite, chicken fried steak; and varieties of tortillas and beans, which are always present in a true New Mexican meal.

ACCESSIBILITY   Like many states, New Mexico is realizing the importance of assuring access to its public places for people with disabilities. In most of the state, parking areas, building entrances, restrooms, campgrounds, and museums have been built or remodeled so that travelers with a range of impairments can use them with ease. However, there seems to be little consistency about universal accessibility in New Mexico, and at this time, there are no statewide publications to guide the tourist (or citizen of the state) to especially accessible places. With the passage of the Americans with Disabilities Act, more and more of New Mexico will meet access standards. In the meanwhile, we think you will discover that New Mexico welcomes all visitors to explore and enjoy its treasures. Call the Governor's Commission on Concerns of the Handicapped about access issues before you come to New Mexico.

Getting Around—Philosophically

As you travel here, we ask you to respect the plants, the pots, the pterodactyls, and especially the people of New Mexico. Here are some guidelines.

PLANTS   All roadside plants—including the lush growth of wild asters, sunflowers, and an occasional spiky buffalo gourd—are protected by law and are important for erosion prevention. The variety of plants in New Mexico is great, but you will observe that the quantity is low. Unique climatic conditions allow for the growth of many endangered species. Indeed, somewhere in the state is a secret preserve for a cactus that exists only in that two-acre plot.

Naturalist John Muir said, "The first rule of tinkering is that you save all the pieces."

ANIMALS

The state's variety of wildlife is also great, greater than anywhere else on earth except for a Central American rain forest and a portion of California. You can see a real roadrunner outside of the cartoons, a howling coyote not carved of wood, or a jackrabbit without antelope horns. A few words of caution: Livestock on the highway pose a significant danger to travelers, and yellow caution signs mark unfenced grazing areas. Deer and elk routes are also unpredictable in mountain areas. Mountain lions in the New Mexican mountains are shy, but some of the bears are not. Campers should not leave food in tents, and shutterbugs must keep their distance from these handsome wild animals. Rabies and plague (yes, plague) exist in the state, so you must resist the temptation to feed cute little prairie dogs and chipmunks. We do not need to warn you to stay away from porcupines and skunks. Do protect your dog or cat from fleas. Some poisonous snakes are native to all areas of the state, so be careful about where you put your hands and feet. The hairy tarantulas you might see on the road in the southern or western part of the state will not hurt you unless you provoke them.

POTS

Because plunderers have come before you, we will not list any of the many archaeological sites that do not have full-time protection. Federal and state laws strictly prohibit the removal of archaeological specimens. If you are lucky enough to find ancient potsherds, arrowheads, or stone tools, you may take pictures or make sketches, but then put them back where you found them so that future scientists will be better able to piece together the puzzles of previous civilizations. If you wish to volunteer for an archaeological dig, contact one of the state universities and ask for information from the anthropology department.

FOSSILS

New Mexico has a state fossil, the Coelophysis. Several of these small, fast dinosaurs were found in the Ghost Ranch area of northwestern New Mexico, and their remains can be seen in the New Mexico Museum of Natural History in Albuquerque and at the small museum at Ghost Ranch. If you want to collect and keep any fossils for yourself, you must get written permission from the land-holder. Only the Bureau of Land Management lets you collect on its land and keep fossil invertebrates and plants without a permit. Do not, however, collect more than 250 pounds of petrified wood per person per year.

RESPECT FOR PEOPLE   It is the people of New Mexico that make our state such a wonderful place to live and to visit. Here are some suggestions about how best to show them your respect. Obey "no trespassing" signs. Ask questions, ask permission. It is courteous to leave a donation in the churches you may visit and to tip the person who has opened a building especially for you. You may visit all of New Mexico's twenty-two Indian reservations if you adhere to tribal laws. These laws are posted at the entrances to the reservations, and further inquiries may be made at tribal governors' offices. Most tribes prohibit or restrict photography, sketching, and recording devices; most restrict visits to daylight hours; and most have some ceremonial days during which areas are closed to non-Indians.

You may have the pleasure of hearing native languages of some of New Mexico's people—for example, Navajo, Keres, Spanish, or Zuni. Words from all of New Mexico's languages have become part of our speech, so we have included a glossary at the back of this book to help you understand such words, which are italicized when they appear in the text.

SHOPPING   The quality of light and an appreciation of fine craftsmanship have made New Mexico a place that has attracted artists and encouraged the artistic capabilities of its people. It is also an excellent place to shop for arts and crafts. New Mexican specialties include paintings and drawings of the land and people, Navajo rugs, Hispanic and Pueblo weavings, traditional embroidery, Pueblo pottery, Apache and Navajo basketry, silver and turquoise jewelry, glass bead and handmade bead jewelry, Zuni stone carving, carved wooden kachina dolls, wrought iron, horse tack and saddles, contemporary arts of all kinds, and delicious examples of the culinary arts. The popularity and expense of authentic handwork, especially Native American handwork, have resulted in a proliferation of factory-made copies; we suggest that you ask questions before purchasing items. A rug may be a Navajo design made of cotton instead of wool by Indians in Mexico instead of Navajos. Perhaps that is what you want. If you want a true Navajo rug, inquire about who wove it and where and with what yarns. Likewise, ask if silver is sterling, if turquoise is natural, stabilized, or plastic, if pottery is hand built or poured ceramic and who made it, if *heishi* beads are hand or machine polished, and who carved the *kachinas*. New Mexico is also the right place to buy custom clothing and furniture, handmade and recycled papers, unusual flower and vegetable seeds, and salsas and sodas. Small workshops, studios, vineyards, and galleries all around the state also offer information and warm welcomes. "Buy New Mexico", a local organization, is a good source for informed shopping for New Mexican goods.

BOOK ORGANIZATION

The *entradas* section, which precedes the tour descriptions, will welcome you to New Mexico with a little information about your specific point of entry. We have tried to give you an idea of the amount of time you may need for each tour and the highlights along the route. The calendar and activities section will help you plan your trip to coincide with some wonderful festivals, fiestas, or fairs. You may prefer to travel with a theme in mind. If, for example, your special interest is space travel, New Mexico has many sites that should interest you.

At the beginning of each tour we have listed places where accommodations are available—motels or hotels or bed-and-breakfast inns and youth hostels. We suggest that you get a current listing of these and of campsites from the state tourism division in Santa Fe. Many historic hotels in small towns have been restored, and a variety of interesting homes have become bed-and-breakfast inns. The transient nature of phone numbers, accommodations, and restaurants has precluded our listing them in this guide. Write your favorites in the margins, in pencil.

You have come to a place that is extraordinary. Even the license plates tell you that it is the Land of

Enchantment. However, New Mexico is not a theme park. You cannot pay your money at the entrance and expect to be continuously entertained. Here you create your own adventures and fantasies. We invite you to come along with us as we tour our favorite state.

THANKS   Thanks to Elizabeth Hadas, Barbara Guth, Emmy Ezzell, Carol Cooperrider, Octavia Fellin, to Susan Bennett, Sam Cata, Theodore Church, Martha Egan, Juan Flores, Inez Gabaldon, Debra Garcia, Placido Garcia, Larry Goodell, Sherri Gosdin, Kathy Heyman, Tim and Patty Jennings, Martha Liebert, Barbara MacPherson, Roger Madalena, Don McAlavy, Reuben Miera, Bob Phillips, Sylvia Ruiz, Ann Rustebakke, Helen Sandoval, Alex Stelzner, Cathy and Tod Stevenson, Rose Tafoya, Trish Thomas, Karin Vallo, Roy and Shirley Wheeler, Cindy White, Judith White, Corinne Wolfe, and all those who helped us with *New Mexico: A New Guide to the Colorful State.*

CALENDAR

Dates may change for any of these events. Please contact chambers of commerce, visitor and convention bureaus, individual pueblo tribal offices, or the Indian Pueblo Cultural Center in Albuquerque for more specific information.

JANUARY

mid-January: New Mexico Legislature convenes—floor sessions and hearings in the Roundhouse are open to the public

1 Taos Pueblo: Buffalo or Deer dance
Other pueblos: Ceremonial dances

6 Most pueblos: Installation of new governors
Cochiti, Picurís, San Felipe, San Juan, Santa Ana, Santa Clara, Santo Domingo, Taos, and Tesuque pueblos: Three Kings Dances
San Ildefonso Pueblo: Eagle Dance
Taos Pueblo: Buffalo Dance

7 Many pueblos: Ceremonial dances

8–10 Laguna Pueblo: Green Corn Dance

15 Albuquerque, Santa Fe: Martin Luther King, Jr., celebrations

22-23 San Ildefonso Pueblo: San Ildefonso Feast Day— vespers and procession on January 22; fiesta, Buffalo Dance, Comanche Dance, and Deer Dance on January 23

25 Picurís and Taos pueblos: Dances honoring Saint Paul

| Dates to be announced: | Santa Fe: Los Tres Reyes Magos ("The Three Wise Kings," a medieval folk play) |

FEBRUARY

mid-February	Albuquerque, Las Cruces: Black Heritage Week celebrations
	Bosque del Apache: Departure of sandhill cranes and their adopted whooping cranes for summer homes in Idaho
2	Grants: Mount Taylor Winter Quadrathlon
	Cochiti, San Felipe, and Santo Domingo pueblos: Candlemas Day dances

MARCH

18	Belen: Annual Fiesta de San José—Mass, procession, and food at San José Church
19	Laguna Pueblo: Feast Day of Saint Joséph at Old Laguna; Harvest Dance
Dates to be announced:	Several pueblos: Opening of the irrigation ditches, accompanied by festivities
	Deming: Rockhound Roundup, rock swap, free agates, jaspers, and opals

APRIL

Easter	Cochiti, Jemez, San Felipe, San Ildefonso, Santa Ana, Santa Clara, and Santo Domingo pueblos: Spring Corn Dance, Basket Dance, ceremonial foot races, and pole shinnying
	Ranchos de Taos: Blessing of the Animals at St. Francis Church
	Santuario de Chimayó: Pilgrimages
	Tomé: Religious procession
early April	Alamogordo: Twice-a-year-only tour to Trinity Site, test site of first A-bomb explosion

mid-April	Albuquerque: Rio Grande Valley Bicycle Tour
	Albuquerque: American Indian Heritage Week; Gathering of Nations Pow-wow, dance competition, crafts exhibit
	Deming: Old-timers' Celebration
	Farmington: Apple Blossom Festival—dance, parade, and melodrama
late April	Albuquerque: Founders' Day Celebration and Parade, Old Town
Dates to be announced:	Truth or Consequences: Ralph Edwards Fiesta—parades, races, carnival, art show, rodeo, river race, fishing derby, and fiddlers' contest

MAY

early May	Albuquerque ¡Magnifico!—Art Festival
	Albuquerque: Mother's Day concert by New Mexico Symphony Orchestra at Rio Grande Zoo
	La Cienega: El Rancho de las Golondrinas Spring Festival—Spanish Colonial arts, food, demonstrations, and entertainment
	Tularosa: Rose Festival—banquet, coronation, parade, carnival, talent show, and food
mid-May	Deming: Fiddling contest
	Pilar: Rio Grande white-water canoe-kayak-raft race
	Farmington: Rodeo
	Tularosa: San Francisco de Paola Festival—Mexican dances and food
late May	Albuquerque: The Great River Race from Corrales Bridge to San Gabriel Park in anything that floats
	Albuquerque: Fiesta de San Felipe de Neri in Old Town
	Farmington: Four Corners Hot-Air Balloon Rally—competition, races, and other events
	Santa Rosa: Santa Rosa Day Celebration—parade, barbecue, street dances, arts and crafts show, fishing contest, stock car show
Date to be announced:	Taos: Spring Arts Celebration
1	San Felipe Pueblo: San Felipe Feast Day—fiesta and spring Corn Dance

3 Cochiti and Taos pueblos: Santa Cruz Day—Corn Dance, ceremonial races, and the blessing of the fields

5 Albuquerque, Artesia, Deming, Las Cruces, Las Vegas, and Mesilla: Cinco de Mayo (May 5, the day of a victory of Mexico over France) celebrations, concerts, and dances

29 Tesuque Pueblo: Blessing of the fields and Corn Dance

JUNE

early June   Albuquerque: June Music Festival—chamber music
Albuquerque: Summerfest series of weekend ethnic festivals throughout the summer
Clovis: Pioneer Days and Rodeo—parade, Miss New Mexico Rodeo Pageant, horse sale
Raton: Rodeo

mid-June   Albuquerque: Juneteenth—celebration of black culture and history
Farmington: San Juan Sheriff's Posse Rodeo at rodeo grounds
Fort Sumner: Old Fort Days—parade, barbecue, staged bank robbery, arts and crafts sale, fiddling contest, bluegrass music, and horse show
Los Cerrillos: Fiesta de la Primavera—art, entertainment, games, food

late June   Albuquerque: New Mexico Arts and Crafts Fair—exhibits of works by over 200 artisans; entertainment, demonstrations, and lectures, at State Fair Grounds
Albuquerque: Arts in the Parks—dramatic, musical, and variety entertainment in several city parks
Farmington: Rodeo
Farmington: Air show
Gallup: Indian Capital Amateur Rodeo in Red Rock State Park
Gallup: Lion's Club Rodeo, at Red Rock State Park
High Rolls: High Rolls Cherry Festival—cherry cider, cherry butter, jelly, cakes, pies, hay rides, arts and crafts

Pecos National Monument: Trade fair—demonstrations by Indian and Hispanic artisans
San Jon: Caprock Amphitheater, "Billy the Kid" through late August
Taos: Taos Music Festival
Tesuque: Opening of Shidoni Gallery outdoor sculpture show, with several acres of sculpture garden
Tucumcari: Piñata Festival—pageant, rodeo, food, bicycle tour, and road races

12–13　Zuni Pueblo: Rain Dance

24　San Ildefonso, Sandia, Santa Clara, and Taos pueblos: San Antonio Feast Day—Corn dances

Cochiti, San Juan, and Taos pueblos: San Juan Feast Day— Buffalo and Comanche dances, arts and crafts at San Juan, Corn Dance at Taos, Grab Day at Cochiti

29　Acoma, San Felipe, Santa Ana, and Santo Domingo pueblos: San Pedro Feast Day—Corn Dance, Grab Day, and rooster pull

Date to be announced:　Aztec: Fiesta Day celebration—pet parade, candle-light parade, burning of Zozobra (Old Man Gloom), coin dig, bicycle race, carnival, and junior rodeo

JULY

early July　White Sands: Full Moon Tours
Deming: Butterfield Trail Days—parade, fiddling contest, dances, trading post, and barbecue
Española: Fiesta de Oñate—vespers, torch relay, street dancing, food, parade, entertainment, and fireworks
Santa Fe: Opera season begins and continues through August
Santa Fe: Rodeo de Santa Fe

mid-July　Dulce: Jicarilla Apache Little Beaver Roundup Rodeo
Farmington: Aquacade at Brookside Pool
Magdalena: Old Timers' Reunion—parade, fiddling contest, dancing, hot air ballooning, rodeo, and barbecue

Raton: Jaycees Rodeo and Parade

Santa Fe: Santa Fe Chamber Music Festival—concerts, open rehearsals featuring visiting composers

late July One of the northern pueblos: Eight Northern Pueblos Arts and Crafts Show—traditional and contemporary crafts, dances, and food (call Indian Pueblo Cultural Center in Albuquerque for current site)

Chimayó: Los Moros y Cristianos Pageant—Spanish medieval pageant of Moors and Christians, at the Holy Family Church

Estancia: Old-timers' Day—parade, fiddling contest, junior rodeo, and barbecue at the Country Fair Grounds

Eunice: Old-timers' Fiddling Contest

Raton: Rodeos

Ruidoso: Art Festival

Santa Clara Pueblo: Puye Cliffs Ceremonial—dances by various tribes in ancestral cliff ruins, arts and crafts, and food

Santa Fe: Spanish Market, at the Palace of the Governors— artisans displaying and selling paintings, retablos, bultos, weavings, and tin work; dances, food

Taos: Fiesta—Dances and coronation of queen

Tucumcari: Rodeo

2–4 Grants: Fourth of July Celebration—large parade, arts and crafts show, and fiddling contest

3–6 Mescalero: Mescalero Apache maidens' puberty rites—dances and rodeos

3–4 Clayton: Fourth of July Rodeo

Las Vegas: Fourth of July Fiesta—parade, arts and crafts fair, music, food, and fireworks

Roswell: Country Music Festival—music and fireworks

4 Albuquerque, Carlsbad, Cimarron, Eunice, Gallup, Lordsburg, Lovington, Moriarty, Santa Fe, Santa Rosa, Socorro, Springer and numerous other communities: evening fireworks

Cimarron: Maverick Rodeo

Nambe Pueblo: Nambe Waterfalls Ceremonial—dances by visiting tribes, arts and crafts, and food

Santa Fe: Los Compadres street breakfast
Silver City: Frontier Days Celebration—parade, dances, and fireworks

4–5   Tucumcari: Rodeo

4–6   Red River: Fourth of July Celebration—parade, shoot-out, tug of war, horseshoe-pitching contest, and tennis tournament

5   Roswell: Birthday Shindig—Fiddling contest at the County Historical Museum

14   Cochiti Pueblo: San Buenaventura Feast Day—Corn Dance

25   Acoma Pueblo: Santiago Day—rooster pull
Cochiti, Laguna, San Felipe, and Santa Ana pueblos: Santiago Day; Grab Day

26   Acoma Pueblo: Santa Ana Feast Day—Grab Day
Santa Ana and Taos pueblos: Santa Ana Feast Day—Corn Dance

Date to be announced: Carlsbad, Galisteo, and Silver City: Rodeos

AUGUST

early August   Lincoln: Old Lincoln Days—reenactments of Lincoln County War, parade, Pony Express run, arts and crafts fair, ghost town tours, and fiddling contest
Pecos National Monument: Pecos Feast Day and Folk Mass
Pie Town: Polo tournament, barbecue, and dance
Melrose: Old-timers' Days and Rodeo
Socorro: Socorro County Fair and Rodeo

mid-August   Albuquerque: La Luz Trail Run up the Sandia Mountains
Belen: Our Lady of Belen Fiesta—parade, carnival, dances, arts and crafts fair, and burning of the devil
Bosque Farms: Bosque Farms Fair—parade, fiddling contest, horse show, and dance

Chama: Chama Days—parade, rodeo, arts and
    crafts, dances, and food
Clovis: Music Festival
Datil: Rodeo
Española: Rio Arriba County Fair
Farmington: Connie Mack World Series baseball
    tournament, San Juan County Fair
Gallup: Intertribal Indian Ceremonial—parades,
    dances of many tribes, rodeos, arts and crafts
    exhibit, and foods, at Red Rock State Park
Hillsboro: Black Range Art Exhibit
Las Vegas: San Miguel County Fair
Los Alamos: Los Alamos County Fair and Rodeo—
    parade, exhibits, band concert, rodeo, dance,
    and ice cream social
Lovington: Lea County Fair and Rodeo—carnival,
    parade, and horse and livestock shows
Santa Fe: Indian Market—hundreds of artisans
    displaying and selling jewelry, pottery, sculpture,
    weaving, and paintings; dances and food

late August Capitan: Lincoln County Fair
Carlsbad: Carlsbad Cavern Bat Flight Breakfast—
    flight of hundreds of thousands of bats returning
    to Carlsbad Cavern at dawn
Clayton: Union County Fair
Deming: Great American Duck Race—dance,
    parade, duck costume contest, and races
Gallup: North American Indian Rodeo Champion-
    ships—rodeo, dances, fiddling contest, barbe-
    cue, and parade at Red Rock State Park
Las Vegas: Jaycees Rodeo
Tucumcari: Quay County Fair
Zuni Pueblo: Zuni Fair and rodeo—arts and crafts,
    food

2 Jemez Pueblo: Old Pecos Bull Dance—celebration of
    Feast of Our Lady of Angels, patron of aban-
    doned Pecos Pueblo, whose survivors moved to
    Jemez in 1838; Corn Dance

4 Santo Domingo Pueblo: Santo Domingo Feast
    Day—Corn Dance

4–10 Bloomfield: Salmon Ruins Barbecue, at Salmon
    Ruins

8–10 Carrizozo: Santa Rita Fiesta—vespers and dance

Socorro: Fiesta de San Miguel—coronation, dance, games, food, Mass, and procession, at San Miguel Mission

9–10 Picurís Pueblo: San Lorenzo Feast Day—sunset dance, foot races, and pole climb; Corn Dance

9-11 Bernalillo: Fiesta de San Lorenzo—Los Matachines and Mass; procession, food and dance

10 Acoma, Cochiti, and Laguna pueblos: San Lorenzo Feast Day—Corn Dance, Grab Day

11–12 Santa Clara Pueblo: Santa Clara Feast Day—Corn and Harvest dances

15 Laguna and Zia pueblos: San Antonio and Our Lady of the Ascension Feast Days—various dances at Laguna and Corn Dance at Zia

28 Isleta: San Agustin Fiesta—fiesta, carnival, and concessions

Date to be
announced: Chama: Chama Days—parade, rodeo, barbecue

SEPTEMBER

early
September Alamogordo: Otero County Fair and Rodeo

Albuquerque, South Valley: Harvest Festival, burning of Old Man Gloom

Belen: Valencia County Fair—fiddling contest, parade, exhibits, music, rodeo, and carnival

Bernalillo: New Mexico Wine Festival

Clovis: Curry County Fair—largest county fair in the Southwest

Shiprock: Northern Navajo Nation Fair and rodeo—dances, arts and crafts

Fort Sumner: DeBaca County Fair—exhibits, horse and livestock show, and barbecue

Grants: Bi-County Fair—rodeo and fiddling contest

Hatch: Chile Festival—music; art; hot, medium, and mild food; *ristra* contest

Hillsboro: Apple Festival—cider, pie, arts and crafts, and fiddling contest

Navajo Nation: Fair, rodeo, dances, food, at Window Rock, Arizona

Socorro: Socorro County Fair and Rodeo

Springer: Colfax County Fair—parade, exhibits, livestock show, tractor pull, and cow-chip throwing contest

mid-September   Aztec: Pioneers' Picnic

Las Vegas: Annual People's Fair—arts and crafts, music, puppet and magic shows

Mesilla: Pan-American Fiesta—parade, folk dancing, frontier ballads, mariachi bands, and barbecue

Santa Fe: Fiesta de Santa Fe—celebrating the 1692–1693 reconquest of New Mexico by Don Diego de Vargas; burning of *Zozobra* (Old Man Gloom), parades, arts and crafts, street singing, dancing, and food

mid-September to late September   Albuquerque: New Mexico State Fair—midway, hobbies, crafts, livestock, produce, art, auto shows, cooking displays, rodeo, concerts, horse racing, parade, Indian Village, Spanish Village, dances, and food

late September   Chama, Cloudcroft, Eagle Nest, Grants, Los Alamos, Raton, Red River, Ruidoso, Santa Fe, Silver City, Springer, and Truth or Consequences: Fall color tours and celebrations

Las Cruces: Vaquero Days, Southern New Mexico State Fair— parade, arts and crafts, hot air balloons, sports, and food

Red River: Aspencade—outdoor events, bicycle tour, dances, arts and crafts, and food

Ruidoso: Aspencade Festival—parade, motorcycle convention, band concerts, arts and crafts, and mule races

Silver City: Cliff-Gila-Grant County Fair

Socorro: San Miguel Feast Day—fiesta and rodeo

Taos: Old Taos Day Fair

2   Acoma Pueblo: San Esteban Feast Day—fiesta, Corn Dance

8   Laguna and San Ildefonso pueblos: Nativity of the Blessed Virgin Mary Feast Day—dances

15   Dulce: Jicarilla Apache annual feast—rodeo, foot
        races, and pow-wows, at Stone Lake

19   Laguna Pueblo: San José Feast Day—dances, rodeo,
        and barbecue

25   Laguna Pueblo: Saint Elizabeth Feast Day—dances

29–30   Taos Pueblo: San Geronimo Feast Day—sundown
        dance, other dances, races, fair, and pole climb

OCTOBER

early October   Alamogordo: International Space Hall of Fame
        Induction and Open House
        Alamogordo and Socorro: Twice-a-year-only tour to
        Trinity Site, test site of first A-bomb explosion
        Albuquerque: International Hot Air Balloon Fiesta—
        races, mass ascensions, parade, and food
        Albuquerque: Greek Festival—Greek food, dancing,
        and church tours at St. George Church
        Cloudcroft: Aspencade and Oktoberfest
        Deming: Southwestern New Mexico State Fair and
        Rodeo—parade, exhibits, and livestock judging
        Eagle Nest: Paul Bunyan Days
        Farmington: Four Corners Cultural Heritage Festival
        Gallup: Heritage Day—celebration for people of
        various ethnic backgrounds
        La Cienega: El Rancho de las Golondrinas Fall
        Festival—exhibits, demonstrations, food, and
        entertainment, in museum of Spanish Colonial life
        Santa Fe: Festival of the Arts—numerous art shows
        and demonstrations
        Shiprock: Northern Navajo Fair
        Taos: Festival of the Arts—art, music, and dance

mid-October   Deming: Kolbase Festival—Bohemian sausage
        barbecue
        Socorro: Forty-niners Celebration—mining con-
        tests, parade, dances, chile cookoff, fiddling
        contest, and jalapeño-eating contest
        Truth or Consequences: Fiddling contest

late October   Alamogordo: Frontier Fiesta—arts and crafts,
        fiddling contest

Bosque del Apache: Sandhill cranes and a few whooping cranes return to the sanctuary for the winter

High Rolls and Mountain Park: Apple festival, hayrides, food, and drinks

Portales: Peanut Valley Festival—arts and crafts, entertainment, and Peanut Olympics

3–4 Ranchos de Taos: Fiesta de San Francisco—candle-light procession and fiesta

4 Nambe Pueblo: San Francisco Feast Day—dances

12 Albuquerque: Columbus Day Celebration in Old Town Plaza

15 Laguna Pueblo: Saint Mary Margaret Feast Day—dances

Dates to be announced: Las Cruces: Whole Enchilada Festival—food, entertainment, contests, and sporting events

NOVEMBER

early November Albuquerque: Southwest Arts and Crafts Festival
Carlsbad: Fall color tours, Guadalupe Mountains
Las Cruces: Renaissance Arts and Crafts Fair

late November Eagle Nest: High Altitude Glider and Soaring Festival
Farmington and Albuquerque: Christmas parades
Roswell: Wool Bowl—national junior college championship football game
Zuni Pueblo: Shalako dance (or early December)

1
12 Taos Pueblo: Dances
Jemez and Tesuque pueblos: San Diego Feast Day—early afternoon Corn Dance, all-day trade fair at Jemez; Buffalo, Comanche, Deer, and Flag dances at Tesuque

DECEMBER

early December	Alamogordo, Belen, Bernalillo, Cloudcroft, Clovis, Portales, Santa Rosa: Christmas tree lighting, parade
	Tortuga: Our Lady of Guadalupe Fiesta—evening torchlight ascent of Mount Tortuga, and fiesta
mid-December	Albuquerque, Artesia, Ranchos de Taos, Silver City, Santa Fe: Spanish Christmas folk drama, *Las Posadas*
	Las Cruces: Spanish folk drama, *Los Pastores*, in several local churches
	Raton: City of Bethlehem Christmas exhibit in Climax Canyon
11–12	Jemez Pueblo: Our Lady of Guadalupe Feast Day— dance and drama, *Los Matachines*
	Nambe Pueblo: Deer Dance
	Pojoaque Pueblo: Bow and Arrow, Buffalo, or Comanche dances
	Taos: Our Lady of Guadalupe candlelight procession
24	All around the state: *farolito* and *luminaria* displays
	Albuquerque: City bus tours of *luminarias*; hot air balloons in Country Club area
	Carlsbad: Parade of boats and lights on the Pecos River
	Ranchos de Taos: Torchlight procession, Midnight Mass at St. Francis of Assisi Church
24–29	Acoma, Cochiti, Isleta, Jemez, Laguna, Picurís, San Felipe, San Ildefonso, San Juan, Santa Ana, Santa Clara, Santo Domingo, Taos, Tesuque, and Zia pueblos: evening masses, dances; Los Matachines at Picurís and San Juan; Turtle Dance at San Juan
Date to be announced:	Alamogordo: Christmas Fair
	Aztec: Festival de los Farolitos—illuminated ruins

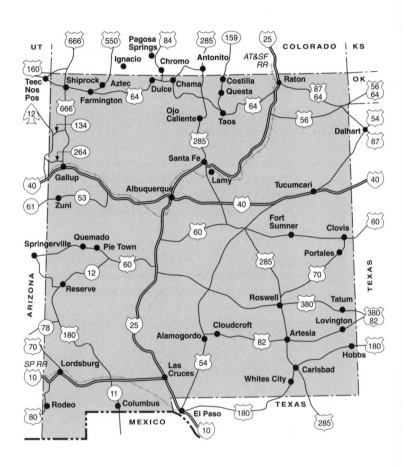

ENTRADAS

The first visitors to New Mexico were big game hunters, descendants of the earliest Americans who had migrated from Siberia across the Bering Strait to North America. Later, groups of desert dwellers moved in from the west, gradually adapting to a sedentary lifestyle. The Athapascans from Canada also found homes in New Mexico but continued their nomadic ways until the 1800s, long after the Anasazi had built permanent dwellings. These multi-storied apartments were called 'pueblos' by the Spanish colonizers when they arrived in the new or "other" Mexico in the sixteenth and seventeenth centuries. Called *entradas* or entrances, these expeditions began with Coronado's long march in 1540. Finally came the settlers from the eastern and middle sections of the United States to put down their roots in the new territory. Modern travelers, while not always pioneers or colonizers, certainly are adventurers. It is in this spirit of adventure that we suggest some routes over which you might make your *entrada* into the Land of Enchantment, moving clockwise from El Paso.

ENTRADAS FROM THE SOUTH

INTERSTATE-10

I-10 enters New Mexico via El Paso, Texas, and parallels, as far as Las Cruces, the Camino Real, the principal trade and supply route between Mexico City and the capital of the remote province, Santa Fe. Tour Eighteen ("Oases") traces this entrada for you—from Juárez, Mexico, up into the cool mountains and hidden springs of southern New Mexico. A new border crossing near Santa Teresa, New Mexico, allows you to enter Mexico at the eastern edge of the El Paso metropolis, near the Sunland Park racetrack.

N.M. 11

Pancho Villa raided across the border into Columbus during the Mexican Revolution. The state park dedicated to this event and to the display and preservation of desert wildlife greets you just inside the international boundary. Travelers going to or from Mexico can use the Columbus border crossing, which is less crowded than the El Paso area entry points, and more convenient if you are heading for western New Mexico. This might be the perfect place to step over into Mexico for a few hours or to begin a tour of Chihuahua, Mexico's largest state. On the American side, it is thirty miles to Deming, the gateway to Rock Hound State Park, the Mimbres Valley, and the overland route to Hatch via N.M. 26. Deming, on Tour Fourteen, offers tourist facilities, whether you are returning from a camping trip or an international excursion from Mexico.

U.S. 80

In the days when United States highways closely followed railroad routes, U.S. 80 abruptly turned south near the Arizona line to follow the Southern Pacific tracks to smelters in Douglas, Arizona. The tracks are gone now, but you can still take U.S. 80 north between oddly shaped peaks and lonely desert towns. New Mexico's "bootheel" fascinates naturalists, because it serves as a living laboratory to which strange animal relics from the Pleistocene Age have retreated. "Island populations" that survive in the unusual conditions there include the grasshopper mouse, the gray checkered whiptail lizard (which reproduces strictly by cloning), and the Chihuahuan ridge-nosed rattlesnake, a subspecies found only atop Animas Peak. As you enter New Mexico at Rodeo, the Chiricahua Mountains loom on your left and the grassy hills of the Gray Ranch straddle the Continental Divide on your right.

ENTRADAS FROM THE WEST

I-10

Travelers entering New Mexico from San Diego and Tucson usually take Interstate 10, approximating the route of the California Column, those Union troops sent to New Mexico to drive out Confederate soldiers who had occupied the state.

Just across the state line, after driving many miles through the high Chihuahua desert, you can stop for a cold drink in the old railroad town of Steins and visit the remains of the once elegant hotel. Past Steins the highway parallels the railroad. On both sides are alkali flats, distinctively white, sometimes after a rainfall looking like shallow lakes.

Even Lordsburgers admit that summer days there get hot, but at their 4,250-foot elevation, half encircled by the Continental Divide, the nights are cool. Begun as a rail stop on the Southern Pacific, Lordsburg is now sustained by cotton, a grape-growing and wine-bottling industry, thermally heated greenhouses and vegetable dryers, mining, and tourism. It offers comfortable accommodations for travelers, as well as unusual attractions in every direction: for hunters exotic game like javelina and Mexican bighorn sheep, birds, and Sonoran white-tailed deer; for fishermen trout and bass. Rock-hounds hunt desert roses, fluorspar, manganese, and volcanic glass and would-be miners more precious metals. Hiking and camping enthusiasts head for nearby National Forests—Gila to the northeast or Coronado to the southwest.

Shakespeare, south of Lordsburg, is one of New Mexico's more renowned ghost towns. Carefully preserved by the Hill family, Shakespeare's buildings look much as they did in the late 1800s when miners and others worked the mines and played raucously.

U.S. 70

U.S. 70 is the direct route into New Mexico from Phoenix and Globe, Arizona, cutting diagonally across the dry southwestern corner of the state to connect with I-10 at Lordsburg. You can then drive straight across the southern route on I-10 or head up to Silver City (Tour Fifteen) on N.M. 90. Just before Silver City is the new suburb of Tyrone that replaced the fabulous old Phelps-Dodge town of the same name. Designed to look like a Spanish city, old Tyrone was swallowed up by Phelps-Dodge mining operations.

ENTRADAS FROM U.S. 666

Travelers who prefer the vast spaces of Catron County to mountainous driving should leave U.S. 666 just before Clifton and enter New Mexico on N.M. 78. The only outpost you will pass through on this lovely route through ranching and farm country is tiny Mule Creek, named by the first white settler for a muletrack which crossed his land.

U.S. 666 is a scenic road for much of its length. The section between Clifton and Alpine, Arizona, is also known as the Coronado Trail to commemorate portions of Francisco Vasquez de Coronado's route as he sought the fabled Seven Cities of Gold. The modern Trail was begun in 1926 as a tourist route, its two lanes winding like a corkscrew through the high peaks of the Blue Range and the Apache-Sitgreave Forest, with spectacular views comparable to the Swiss Alps. If you are heading north or southeast, you can take U.S. 180 at Alpine through the Apache National Forest. Just west of Reserve, a friendly Western town with all the amenities for travelers, you will link up with N.M. 12. Another *entrada* runs from Springerville past Quemado (named for the burned brush along the creek) and Pie Town (no longer famous for its pies), and through beautiful White Horse Canyon before getting to Datil. This scenic route follows the Magdalena Livestock Driveway, along which thousands of cattle were moved in years past from Springerville to Magdalena before being sent east.

N.M. 53

New Mexico Route 53 meets Arizona 61 west of
Zuni. Straight and level, the road roughly follows
the route taken by Indians, Conquistadors, U.S.
Army squadrons, and early adventurers. Zuni
Pueblo and the water supply at nearby El Morro
attracted travelers, many of whom carved fascinating messages into the soft sandstone "Inscription
Rock." Viewing the calligraphy on Inscription Rock
and camping in the national monument's campground are experiences to be savored. In the late
nineteenth century, this route diminished in
importance. The railroad chose a route that went
north of the Zuni Mountains because of the ample
coal supplies in what became the Gallup area, and,
as usual, the highways followed the railroads.

I-40

Many travelers from the west enter New Mexico
on Interstate 40, a major freeway that follows the
Rio Puerco (Dirty River). Huge billboards herald
souvenir shops selling postcards, the "coldest beer
and soda for miles," and goods that may have been
made either on the reservation or in Asian factories.

It may then come as a surprise that the heavily-
traveled Interstate passes through beautiful scenery,
weaving its way between Jurassic sandstone cliffs of
orange, tan, beige, rose, red, and yellow. The cliffs
were cut by the Rio Puerco, which when not dry,
runs through Gallup on its way to the Little
Colorado River in Arizona. There is fine natural
sculpture in these cliffs where river-edge stone has
dropped away for lack of support, leaving behind
towering arches and small caves and alcoves.

ENTRADAS FROM THE NAVAJO NATION

Several roads through the Chuska Range
connect Tribal Route 12 with U.S. 666 east of the
mountains. Some of these roads, like those connecting Lukachukai and Red Valley, and Navajo and
Tohatchi, require a real love for adventure, a check
locally for condition of the mud surfaces, and often
a four-wheel-drive vehicle. The roads through the
Chuskas are beautiful; tall trees and small lakes
along the way are a refreshing change after miles of

desert driving. The Navajo tribe operates several campgrounds in the Chuskas, and fishing is available with a tribal fishing permit. Two other routes, Navajo Tribal Route 32 (N.M. 134) over Narbona Pass, and Tribal Route 3 (N.M. 264), the main road into Gallup from the reservation, are well paved. N.M. 264, is heavily traveled and dusty and is not particularly scenic, but it avoids the high mountain passes in the Chuskas to the north. Careless drivers make nighttime travel hazardous.

The northernmost entrada from the reservation, U.S. 64, passes through Teec Nos Pos just before entering New Mexico. At this point you have the opportunity to visit unique Four Corners Monument, 15 miles to the north. One of New Mexico's shortest state highways, N.M. 597, carries visitors just a half mile from the main road to the monument. Many a tourist has lain spread-eagled with one extremity in each of the four states at the marker denoting the exact spot where the four meet. Children will find this real life geography lesson worthy of a visit.

The desolate and windswept Navajo town of Teec Nos Pos stands among mesas and red rock monoliths. Beklabito, two miles east of the border, is also a Navajo settlement. Both are the homes of chapter houses, the Navajo nation's equivalent of precincts, where local policy is debated. Delegates from each chapter are sent to the Tribal Council in Window Rock, Arizona. As you close in on the raw edges of Shiprock, the largest town on the Navajo Reservation, the Shiprock itself looms to your right. The core of an old volcano, Shiprock is more poetically named "winged rock" by the Navajo, referring to a myth about a rock that sprouts wings to rescue the tribe.

ENTRADAS FROM THE NORTH

U.S. 666

Visitors from Colorado and Utah or New Mexicans who have been visiting Mesa Verde, Hovenweep, and other Four Corners attractions, can enter New Mexico on Highway 666, the north-south highway that cuts through the Navajo Reservation. Just before the border, a short detour on U.S. 160 leads to the Four Corners Monument (see U.S. 64 Entrada). However, you need to return to U.S. 666 to continue into New Mexico. With the giant Sleeping Ute Mountain to the right, the sweeping sails of Shiprock ahead, and the blue Chuska Range farther off to the south and west, this is a magical way. On the way to Farmington, the highway crosses the San Juan River at Shiprock, a small town part of which still looks much the way it did when it was established in 1903 to serve the Navajo Reservation. From here U.S. 666 continues straight south to Gallup (Tour One). Driving this road at night can be dangerous; there are few lights and many bad drivers. An alternative route heads east from Shiprock on U.S. 64 to Farmington (Tour Two).

U.S. 550

Colorado's southern Rockies provide the backdrop for the entrance into New Mexico via U.S. 550. The road parallels the Animas River much of the way, traversing high ranchlands and winding through canyons, and this route is a lovely introduction to the northern section of the state. You pass through the Southern Ute Reservation just before crossing the state line; signs invite you to visit the Ute capital, Ignacio. The tiny communities of Riverside and Cedar Hill and scattered ranch homes break up your trip through the high desert. It is fourteen miles from the state line to Aztec, with its Anasazi ruins and Victorian homes.

U.S. 84

While U.S. 84 winds into shady canyons and faithfully follows the Navajo River through foothills and beneath mountain ridges, it cannot offer the magnificent vistas of the routes farther east. On the other hand, because of its lower altitude and the amount of traffic it sustains, this route tends to stay open when others have closed because of snow. The first town over the Colorado border, Chromo, is small and does not have a gas station, but Pagosa Springs, 24 miles north, has many services for the traveler. Once you have entered New Mexico, Dulce (on the Jicarilla Reservation) and Chama are each about one-half hour apart on Tour Three ("Rio Arriba").

N.M. 17

Choose this paved mountain pathway, which originates to the east in Antonito, Colorado, only if the road is open (it sometimes is closed after a winter snowstorm) and only if you enjoy driving in the mountains and being surrounded by snowy peaks. On your drive south over Cumbres Pass (10,022 feet), you will be rewarded with an unforgettable panorama—rugged, white-capped mountains on all sides. The 10-mile drive from Cumbres Pass into the town of Chama takes you along the Chama River Valley, where cattle graze in the summer and cottonwoods and aspens shimmer in the fall. N.M. 17 connects with U.S. 64/84 in Chama, and Tour Three ("Rio Arriba") proceeds south or west from there.

U.S. 285

This route seems to tilt you southward, almost spilling you across the high plains of Colorado into New Mexico. The border town in Colorado, Antonito, is also the northern terminus of the Cumbres and Toltec Scenic Railroad. Though small, this historic Hispanic community offers several tourist services and boasts the oldest Catholic church in the state. The railroad yard includes a random collection of narrow-gauge train cars and engines. U.S. 285 follows the original path of the Denver and Rio Grande Railway all the way south to Española. Only the communities of Tres Piedras (about midway between Antonito and Española) and Ojo Caliente (a little farther south) have gas and food. Ojo Caliente, however, offers mineral baths and restful massages at the hot springs in town. Once you reach Tres Piedras, you will be on Tour Three ("Rio Arriba").

CO. 159/N.M. 522

If you have just come from the Great Sand Dunes north of Fort Garland, Colorado, or want to get to Taos or Red River without driving through too many mountains, this route is a good alternative. As you drive south on Colorado 159 across the high Colorado Plateau into New Mexico, Ute Peak, a prominent extinct volcano just across the state border, can be your guide. Almost straddling the state line, Costilla offers a restaurant, gas station, small grocery store, and access to a ski area and mountain lakes. Questa, fifteen minutes south on N.M. 522, provides a range of travel services, as well as access to the Rio Grande Gorge National Recreation site. If you would like to connect with Tour Sixteen, you can pick it up in Taos.

I-25

I-25 begins way up north in Wyoming and ends in the southern New Mexico city of Las Cruces, near the Mexican border. Its route through New Mexico is historic. The northern portion follows the Santa Fe Trail. South of Santa Fe, the Interstate parallels the Rio Grande and the path of the Camino Real, the royal road that connected Mexico City with the colony of New Mexico in the seventeenth and eighteenth centuries.

I-25 introduces you to the state by winding up the Sangre de Cristo Mountains in Colorado to Raton Pass, where, at almost 8,000 feet, you can look down and see the old highway and the Santa Fe Railway tracks immediately below you. Like any mountain pass, this one is sometimes closed by snowstorms, even in late May or early September. Heavy, fast-moving rainstorms can also slow you down. If the weather looks bad, or if you are in need of a walk, a map, a meal, or a night's lodging, then visit Raton, about 8 miles south of Raton Pass. I-25 connects you with Tour Seventeen at Raton.

ENTRADAS FROM THE EAST

ENTRADAS VIA CLAYTON

Tour Six describes the attractions in Clayton and some of its historical personalities. Any of the three U.S. highways that come into Clayton from Oklahoma (U.S. 56, 64, or 87) will connect you to Cimarron, Eagle Nest, and Taos and to all the camping, skiing, hiking, fishing, and hunting sites that northern New Mexico offers.

U.S. 54

U.S. 54 links Chicago with El Paso, Texas. It enters New Mexico from Liberal, Kansas, the Oklahoma Panhandle, and Dalhart, Texas, following the Chicago, Rock Island, and Pacific tracks. In the first decades of this century, thousands of head of cattle were shipped east along this railroad. Once passenger service used these tracks. Now freight trains and trucks connect the Midwest, Mexico, and the Pacific, while the well-contoured pavement carries automobile tourists and "Snowbirds" back and forth from the northern states. Much of this traffic stops at Ute Lake State Park near Logan, where the waters of Ute Creek and the Canadian River provide irrigation and recreational areas.

I-40

Route 66 is probably the best known of all entrances into New Mexico. I-40 follows old Route 66, which once linked Chicago to Los Angeles, slicing southwesterly across the Midwest before crossing the "desert" states of New Mexico, Arizona, and California. In many places you can see the old pavement and the tourist cabins, gas stations, and curio shops from another age, in varying states of decay or recovery.

By the time you approach the state line on I-40, you might already have noticed vegetation characteristic of New Mexico—cholla cactus (with bright magenta blossoms in early summer)—and a mix of wildflowers, chamisa, and other hardy bushes. Windmills mark the sites of scattered ranches and watchful travelers will note that wiser soil conservation practices have helped heal the scars of the disaster of the dustbowl years. Billboards advertise the musical drama of Billy the Kid at the Caprock Amphitheater south of San Jon, the pleasures of Ute Lake to the northeast, and the countless motels and eating establishments in Tucumcari, described in Tour Seven.

U.S. 60

The "Ocean to Ocean Highway," the first numbered transcontinental automobile route, opened in 1917 and linked Norfolk, Virginia, and Los Angeles, California. Its right-of-way here in Texas and eastern New Mexico followed the Belen Cutoff of the Santa Fe Railroad, built mainly so that transcontinental freight traffic could avoid the steep grades of the main line via Raton. The first stop is

Clovis, the livestock, grain, and railroad capital of the high plains, described in Tour Seven. The roads branch here; U.S. 70 turns south to Portales and Roswell, while U.S. 60 continues west past the string of "cutoff towns" to Fort Sumner, scene of many events in the life and death of Billy the Kid.

U.S. 380

U.S. 380 is best known as the road that connects the Lubbock, Texas, area to recreational sites in Ruidoso, Sierra Blanca, and the Capitan Mountains, described in Tour Seventeen. Your first stop in New Mexico might be Tatum, home of the creator of whimsical signs that proclaim hundreds of ranches and businesses all over the high plains. U.S. 380 also takes you to Bottomless Lakes State Park, through Roswell's downtown, across sheep ranching country, to historic Lincoln State Monument and the Valley of Fires State Park, finally crossing the Jornada del Muerto to link up with I-25.

ENTRADAS VIA LOVINGTON AND HOBBS

Lovington, seat of Lea County, awaits visitors entering the state on U.S. 82. Begun as a dugout homestead, it is intimately associated with neighboring Hobbs because of their common origins in dry farming on the high plains and their common dependence upon the huge underground Hobbs Oil Pool, which has supplied jobs and wealth to the area since its discovery in 1928. Lovington-Hobbs also boasts one of the first paved highways in the state (well-traveled N.M. 18 joins the two cities) as well as New Mexico Junior College, the first such two-year institution in the state. After Lovington, U.S. 82 makes its descent through the Caprock near Maljamar, and it crosses the Pecos at the oil-drilling and processing center of Artesia. The entire stretch of U.S. 82 via Cloudcroft through the scenic and recreation areas of the Sacramento Mountains is included in Tour Sixteen.

U.S. 180, pathway to Carlsbad Caverns, arrives in the oil boom and livestock city of Hobbs as a scenic back road between Fort Worth and El Paso. Hobbs welcomes travelers three miles inside the state line. It is a twentieth-century place rich in lore, from early homesteaders' dugouts to a teeming shack city of brothels, pool halls, and oil-slickened streets during the first boom in 1930. The town nearly vanished when the price of crude plummeted, but later picked up again with the advent of new drilling techniques. Hobbs has continued to grow, its prosperity fluctuating with the price of oil, and it still supplies agricultural, petrochemical, and oil extraction needs over a wide area. The former air base here is the home of the Confederate Air Force Museum, a collection of obsolete World War II aircraft salvaged by airmen under the command of mythical Colonel Jethro Culpeper. Because of the old air base and the high open plains, flying, gliding, air shows, and competitions attract aviation enthusiasts from far and wide to Hobbs.

MORE ENTRADAS FROM THE SOUTH

U.S. 285 enters New Mexico from Pecos and Ft. Stockton, the heart of West Texas, where several routes lead into Big Bend National Park. It is known to vacationers in the Southwest as a route usually safe for winter travel between Big Bend and Carlsbad Caverns. This highway forms the main eastern leg of Tour Sixteen and meets Tour Eighteen at Whites City, the entrance to Carlsbad Caverns.

U.S. 285 here ascends the Pecos River, parallels the return of the Rodriguez-Chamuscada Entrada, and follows a branch of the Santa Fe Railroad, which was originally built as part of a plan to promote irrigated farming and to lure settlers to the lower Pecos. You will see little evidence of farming until you near Carlsbad.

The entrada on U.S. 180 between Carlsbad Caverns and the Guadalupe Mountains National Park takes you past stark mountains that hide historic caves, rustlers' hideouts, verdant springs and isolated ranch homes. The entrance to Carlsbad Caverns' New Cave is a few miles north of the Texas border.

The eastern edge of the El Paso metropolis also offers you the U.S. 54 entrada that connects you directly to Dog Canyon and Alamogordo (Tour Eighteen) and to White Sands (Tour Sixteen). The last entrada, I-10, returns to where you began, on the old Camino Real up the Rio Grande toward Santa Fe.

ENTRADAS VIA AMTRAK

Amtrak, the national passenger railway system, traverses New Mexico on two routes. The Southwest Limited (Trains 1 and 2) skirts the southern part of the state between El Paso and Lordsburg. The Southwest Chief (Trains 3 and 4) carries passengers to depots all along the former route of the famous Santa Fe Chief, entering near Raton and exiting west of Gallup.

THE SOUTHWEST LIMITED

Amtrak passengers in southern New Mexico follow the right-of-way of the old Sunset Limited between New Orleans and Los Angeles. Now comfortable Amtrak service between New Orleans and Los Angeles makes the 2,500-mile trip three times a week in about forty-three hours. The route serves Houston, San Antonio, Tucson, Phoenix, and intermediate cities and towns. Both trains (eastbound and westbound) stop in El Paso, Deming, and Lordsburg during daylight hours.

THE SOUTHWEST CHIEF

Westbound, you board the train in Chicago in the late afternoon, sleep your way across the Great Plains, and swing into New Mexico at Raton Pass early the next afternoon, arriving in Albuquerque a few hours later. The entire trip is about twenty-four hours long. From central Kansas on, you follow the historic path of the Santa Fe Trail, watching prairie dogs and jackrabbits, and trading the green landscape of midwestern trees and grasses for a horizon of mountains that really do look purple from a distance. Just past Trinidad, Colorado, your train will begin the arduous climb up to Raton Pass in the Sangre de Cristo Mountains, descending to Las Vegas.

Immediately outside Las Vegas, the train begins another long, slow ascent to Lamy, where Santa Fe passengers disembark at a clean, white station that seems to be in the middle of nowhere. From Lamy to Albuquerque, the train descends past ancient pueblos and the small communities of the Rio Grande Valley to modern Albuquerque.

Eastbound visitors arrive in Albuquerque after a sixteen hour trip from Los Angeles with stops in

Needles, Flagstaff, Gallup, and smaller cities along the route. If the train is on time, it will probably cross the New Mexico state line around breakfast, stopping in Gallup to pick up passengers and a guide who will describe the high points of the trip through Indian Country, explaining the history and customs of the Navajo and Pueblo Indians whose reservations you will cross. The railroad tracks follow I-40, diverging from the highway to provide you with different views of the settlements and scenery along the way: a close up look at the red bluffs near Gallup, Mt. Taylor, Laguna Pueblo and its farming villages. Closer to Albuquerque, the train dips south towards Los Lunas before pulling into the station.

Of the major New Mexico towns served by Amtrak, only Albuquerque is equipped to provide regular taxi or car rental service at the depot. But arrangements can be made with Amtrak ahead of time so that in Raton, Las Vegas, Lamy, Grants, and Gallup, as well as Deming and Lordsburg, a vehicle will await your arrival.

ALBUQUERQUE AIRPORT ENTRADA

Unlike most airports, New Mexico's international airport greets its passengers with a definite sense of the uniqueness of the state. There are magnificent, hand-carved vigas in the "great room," patterned brick floors, and an art collection that serves as an excellent introduction to the state. Framed murals painted by Taos artist Pop Chalee were salvaged from Albuquerque's first airport; the *santos* of Hispanic *santeros;* and modern Indian, Hispanic, and Anglo pottery and paintings make up the marvelous collection that enhances the airport's sun-filled rooms and hallways. As you wait for your baggage, take time to explore this unique gallery or allow extra time to walk the halls before your departure. Transportation from the airport into Albuquerque is by taxicab, rental car, or city bus. Commuter airlines and scheduled limousine services provide transportation to other New Mexico towns.

TOUR ONE
MINES,
HOGANS,
AND
PUEBLOS

Places:	Albuquerque, Chaco Canyon, Gallup, Zuni, Grants, Albuquerque
Mileage:	Approximately 320 miles, excluding side trips
Suggested travel time:	A weekend to four days
Highways:	I-40, N.M. 124, N.M. 23, N.M. 605, N.M. 509, Tribal 9, N.M. 57, N.M. 371, N.M. 602, N.M. 53, I-40
Accommodations:	Albuquerque, Grants, and Gallup
Camping:	Albuquerque, in the mountains near Grants, Bluewater Lake, Chaco Canyon, McGaffey and Red Rock State Park (both near Gallup), and El Morro

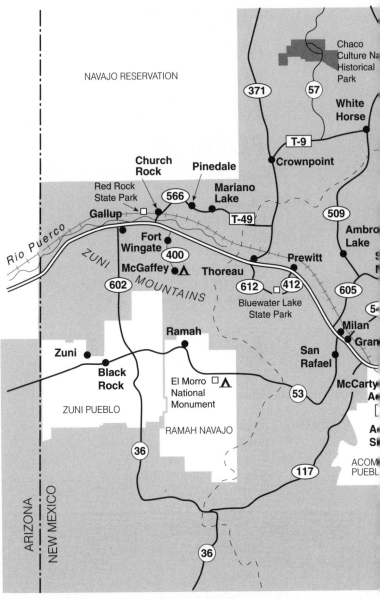

NOTE: Numerous campsites in Jemez Mountains (Santa Fe National Forest), and in Zuni Mountains (Cibola National Forest)

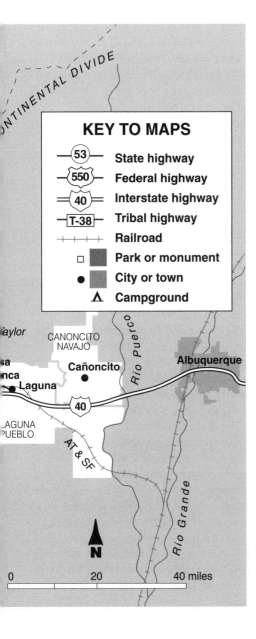

KEY TO MAPS

—(53)— State highway

—(550)— Federal highway

=(40)= Interstate highway

—| T-38 |— Tribal highway

++++++ Railroad

☐ ▉ Park or monument

● ▉ City or town

▲ Campground

CONTINENTAL DIVIDE

aylor

CANONCITO
NAVAJO

Cañoncito
●

Rio Puerco

Albuquerque

a
nca
Laguna

(40)

LAGUNA
PUEBLO

AT & SF

Rio Grande

N

0   20   40 miles

1

This tour has a focus as broad as its landscape: it encompasses and embraces the vast array of colors and forms of this part of the earth and the rich variety of its inhabitants. The long drive will take you past forests of deep or bright green as well as dominant geological formations of brilliant red, soft beige, and intense volcanic black. Veins of coal and uranium run underneath this colorful panorama.

People and cultures of the ancient and historical past have left evidence of their presence here. For hundreds of years sandstone mesa tops have been home to Pueblo people at Sky City on the Acoma reservation and, long ago, to Anasazi Indians at Chaco Canyon. The valleys below have sheltered other Pueblo people, as well as Navajos, Anglos, and Hispanics. Each group forms a vital part of the current cultural mix. The coal mining that brought many European immigrants to the area and the uranium mining that brought prosperity to the economy of Gallup and Grants from the 1950s to the 1980s have faded now, yet the heritage of mines and miners still infuses this region.

You will climb Nine Mile Hill on Interstate 40 out of Albuquerque and push west, passing gear-grinding trucks on the slow lanes of the expressway and new home developments to either side. Looking back you see a spectacular view of the Rio Grande Valley and the Sandia and Manzano mountains to the east. After topping out, you descend steeply into the valley of the Rio Puerco. If you are alert to geography, you may notice later in this tour that the Rio Puerco appears to have crossed the Continental Divide; in actuality, the Rio Puerco near Gallup is an altogether separate "filthy" or "muddy" river. A third New Mexico Rio Puerco is, mercifully, not on this tour. As you continue west, find the next freeway exit, marked Cañoncito, where a small band of Navajos live apart from the main tribe in the hilly country north of the highway. Time has eased old enmities between the Cañoncito Navajos and those of the "Big Reservation," though by tradition this group has been known as the Diné Ana'i, the "People who are enemies." The Cañoncito band derives from a group of Navajos who were settled under Spanish protection in 1818, when their leader, Joaquin, betrayed a planned Navajo raid to Spanish authorities. Cañoncito consists of homes and flocks of sheep scattered among the hills and mesas, and of a well–appointed day school at the end of the eight–mile paved road.

Twelve miles west of the Cañoncito exit, the main east–west line of the Santa Fe Railroad crosses the Interstate. The little Laguna town of Mesita lies just beyond this crossing. It dates to the 1870s when a religious schism occurred among the Laguna Indians. The conservative faction moved to Mesita; some of them later moved on to Isleta Pueblo, where a small group, the Laguna Fathers, remains.

Unlike most New Mexico pueblos, Laguna and Acoma, which lie just ahead, consist not of a single large village, or pueblo, but of a series of settlements grouped around the original village, and Mesita is one of these, lying just a few miles east of the center, Old Laguna. The links between Laguna and Acoma have continued—some rivalry, some intermarriage, some competition, and some cooperation. The Laguna/Acoma high school is evidence of that cooperation. In northwestern New Mexico, when someone is "going to LA", it usually means that they are heading for Laguna and Acoma. Huge red sandstone rocks seem to guard the entry to Laguna from the east; a freeway exit to N.M. 124 allows entry into Old Laguna and other Laguna villages north of the Interstate.

Old Laguna sits on a rocky knoll above a dry lake bed. The lake, which was formed by a beaver dam on the Rio San José, existed when the Spanish gave the name *Laguna* (lake) to the village of Kawaika and the tribe that lived there. The Laguna people have used dry–farming methods and ditch irrigation for centuries to grow crops of beans, squash, chile, wheat, and corn. These crops are still the staple favorites in Laguna homes. Although a rainwater cistern sits next to the new Tribal Community House, the tall green tank near the Interstate holds the water used by the tribe.

The Laguna people are respected for their knowledge of wild plants, and for centuries they have gathered and eaten wild potatoes, wild onions, yucca fruit, and piñon nuts, which were at one time used as a medium of exchange. Collections of antlers on the roofs of Laguna homes bespeak the expertise of Laguna hunters, and deer are still plentiful on the large reservation. Laguna maintains its herding tradition in many ways. The tribal governor used to have the role of assigning grazing areas to families with sheep. In spite of management efforts, the number of sheep rose to 52,000 in the 1930s, which contributed to the denuding of the surrounding land that had been covered with tall grass only a few decades before. The flocks have decreased in size but sheep still graze right up to the edge of another immense denuding of the earth—the Jackpile open–pit uranium mine, the largest of its kind in the world. Although the Laguna people are also expert pottery makers, artists, and entrepreneurs, most tribal members commute to regular jobs in Albuquerque or Grants.

Built after the Pueblo Revolt of 1680, Old Laguna is new by Pueblo standards. A group of people originating in the Mesa Verde area traveled south and joined with dissidents from the Rio Grande pueblos to found a new tribe at Laguna. Some or all of the group may first have sought a haven at Acoma and brought some Acomas with them when they established their own home fourteen miles north of the Acoma mesa top in 1697. This small splinter group has become the

Laguna Church

second largest of the New Mexican pueblos.

Lagunas used markers and shrines to claim the surrounding territory for hunting and farming. Despite the markers, in the 1800s the Navajo and Apache made frequent raids upon the Laguna lands. Spanish settlers "borrowed" land to protect the area from these raids but later claimed the land as their own. Anglo settlers also encroached upon the Laguna territory. Several Protestant Anglos moved into the village, married Laguna women, and became leaders in the tribe. The resultant confusion of Catholics, Protestants, Zuni cult members, Spanish, and Anglos created tensions that led to what is called the "Laguna Break." It was then that the more conservative tribe members moved to Mesita and eventually to Isleta.

During this break, burros were kept in the church, and the handsome adobe building was nearly torn down. You will be glad that it was left standing when you enter the stark white structure on the top of the hill. The thick stone walls maintain cool temperatures even in the heavy heat of summer. Delicate depictions of the stations of the cross are complemented by bold black, green, red, and yellow border designs on the white walls. Walk along the adobe floor between simple pews to the elaborate altar. Four twisted columns, a folk echo of Bernini's columns at St. Peter's in Rome, visually support an animal hide canopy painted with rainbows, the sun, moon, and stars, along with various Christian symbols.

If now you wish to visit Acoma Pueblo, take N.M. 124 to Casa Blanca, or Interstate 40 west to the exit for N.M. 23 (there is an excellent view of tranquil Old Laguna and its ancient hilltop church from a scenic turnout on the busy freeway). At the exit, you will find a modern Acoma marketing center that is open to the public, and tribal offices and services.

New Mexico 23 winds southwest among the steep mesas to Acoma Pueblo. According to legend, one of these buttes, Enchanted Mesa, not far from the Acoma Sky City itself, is the ancient home of the Acoma tribe. Tribal tradition holds that a daytime storm destroyed the paths from the surrounding farms to the homes at the top of Katzimo, or Enchanted, Mesa, stranding those on the top and forever separating them from their relatives, who were farming below. The remainder of the tribe eventually set up housekeeping at what is one of the longest–occupied settlements in the United States, Acoma Pueblo, or Sky City.

From a distance you can see the rectangular adobe houses and the massive church of San Estevan Rey atop the steep–sided mesa, but you may not be able to differentiate them from the rock formation until you draw near. Acoma homes have clung to the windy mesa top for more than a thousand years. Although most of the Acoma tribe lives on the reservation, only a few families live right on the mesa, alternating custodial and religious responsibilities among tribal members. Many Acoma families have ceremonial homes in Sky City.

To go to the top, you must first stop at the Acoma Cultural Center and Museum. After paying for a tour, you will ride in a van on the short, paved, ascending road, constructed by a movie company in the 1950s. Agile and adventurous visitors may ask permission to descend, after the tour, by way of a steep sandstone staircase that was once the primary route between the valley floor and mesa top. The tours of the village are led by knowledgeable Acoma guides and last about an hour, with time for stops to admire or purchase some of Acoma's fine pottery or fresh bread. The pueblo is occasionally closed to outsiders and tour hours might vary. It is best to call ahead for information.

While information given by the guides some-times omits the unhappy or desperate times suffered by the tribe, population statistics over the last few centuries give some clues about Acoma's past. The Acoma numbered about 6,000 in 1599. That number plummeted to about 2,000 in 1630, to 760 in 1700, 1,000 in 1790, 350 in 1850, and regained the 2,000 mark only in the 1960s. These figures reflect great losses as a result of encounters with the Spanish that led to disease and then war, losses in the Pueblo Revolt (1680–1692) when Acoma joined with other Pueblo tribes to success-fully expel the Spanish, and a disastrous smallpox epidemic. The first contacts between the Spanish explorers and the Acoma were wary but peaceful.

Then in 1598 some Acoma tribesmen killed Juan de Zaldivar and all but five of his accompanying soldiers. The Spanish and Acoma accounts of precipitating events vary. Spanish soldiers sought revenge for the killing by hauling up a cannon and firing it through the village streets, by burning homes, by killing eight hundred of the tribe, by taking some girls as slaves, and by cutting off one foot of all men over twenty–five years old. All surviving males between the ages of twelve and twenty–five were required to give twenty years of personal service to the Spanish. After the Pueblo Revolt some Spanish troops destroyed Acoma's crops, forcing many tribespeople to move to outlying villages and to what is now Laguna.

While you walk with the guide, you may be greeted by the smell of piñon smoke (wood is hauled up to warm homes and to bake bread), the sound of spring peepers (tadpoles and frogs fill the natural cisterns), the muffled sound of drums on a feast day, or the pleasure of a cold soda purchased on a hot summer day. Take time to notice the adobe guardians of the cemetery, the first school used by Spanish missionaries to teach Acoma children, the glorious intricacy of designs applied to Acoma pottery with a chewed yucca brush, the patterns of farming in the valley below, and the broad vistas afforded by the mesa's height.

Return from Acoma to the Interstate either by backtracking along N.M. 23 or by heading north-west on Tribal Route 38 to McCartys, one of the main villages of the Acoma tribe. In McCartys and Acomita, which lies just east of McCartys, Acoma tribe members pursue their traditional occupations of farming and pottery making, in addition to occupations of all types that often make them commuters into Grants or Albuquerque. The delicate white Acoma pots can often be purchased at the potters' homes. The pots' carefully smoothed surfaces have been painted with remarkably fine geometric designs and/or the bird, mammal, and insect motifs reminiscent of ancient Mimbres Indian pottery. In McCartys, under the cliffs of the Sunhouse Peaks, you will also find a striking church built of local stone in the twentieth century, a half–size replica of the church on the Acoma mesa top.

Eleven miles west of McCartys, an Interstate exit leads to Grants. Grants is the seat of Cibola County, the most recent of New Mexico's thirty–three political subdivisions. Cibola, named for the ephemeral "city of gold," was described by Fray Marcos de Niza on his exploratory trip of 1539. Fray Marcos reputedly saw the sun glinting off straw roofs of the pueblo of Zuni, concluded without further exploration that the town was made of gold, and hurried home to Mexico to tell of his great find. Coronado's subsequent *entrada* of 1540 failed to find gold but discovered many of the Rio Grande pueblos before he and his men were led on to what is now Kansas, still looking for gold. Cibola County split off from Valencia County in 1982 when the promise of great wealth from uranium seemed ready to support the county government, but the uranium boom proved almost as short–lived as Cibola's gold. Gradual closure of the county's uranium mines has occurred over the past ten years, leaving Grants with many boarded––up buildings and homes, and putting some Grants residents, and the Laguna, Acoma, and Navajo miners, out of work.

To commemorate the mining boom, Grants opened the New Mexico Museum of Mining. A small, well–displayed history of mining in the area is supplemented by a hands–on experience: By climbing into what looks like a standard elevator, you descend into a simulated working mine. Retired miners–turned–guides accompany some tours; on others, you may be handed a tape recording to listen to on your tour. You have to imagine the heat, damp, noise, and danger, but the realistic setting and informative guide make that easy. This tour is a gem. The town hall and library in Grants adjoin the museum, which is near the west end of the town's strip on old Route 66, now N.M. 53 and Santa Fe Avenue. Much of modern Grants now lies north of the strip; motels, restaurants, and shut-tered businesses are almost all that remain of the main street's palmier days.

Near the east end of Main Street, in a converted gas station, is a National Park Service visitor center for El Malpais National Monument and Conserva-tion Area, one of the newest units of the Park Service, set aside to preserve the lava flows and unusual surrounding scenery south of the Interstate. Bureau of Land Management (BLM) land is also part of the area set aside; the BLM maintains a visitor center on N.M. 117, on the way to Quemado. Both the Park Service and the BLM visitor centers are slated to be replaced by a joint visitor center on Interstate 40.

At the present Park Service visitor center, displays and helpful rangers point the way to this convoluted country. Numerous hiking trails and a loop road wind through this area. To take the loop, head east from Grants to the first exit, N.M. 117. The road skirts the huge prehistoric lava flow before taking you to a magnificent sandstone arch, La Ventana, well marked by the side of the road. A dirt road, County Road 42, passable but difficult in a passenger car, makes up the middle third of the loop. Toward the end of this section of the loop, a rough road leads to short trails up to two of the cinder cones responsible for the lava. New Mexico 53 then takes you along the west edge of the lava flow back through the small Hispanic community of San Rafael to the freeway. (The total distance of this loop is 93 miles; because the dirt road makes driving slow, plan at least four hours just for the driving.)

At the northern edge of Grants, on N.M. 547 about 1.5 miles west of Main Street, the employees at the Grants Ranger Station of the Cibola National Forest stand ready to help, offering information about the forest's terrain, which includes the lofty forests of Mount Taylor and the extensive, lower Zuni Mountains southwest of Grants. New Mexico 547 continues northeast onto the slopes of Mount Taylor, which rises to 11,301 feet. Not quite as high as Mount Taylor, but with a forest lookout tower with a stupendous 360–degree view, is nearby La Mosca. You can drive to the top of La Mosca, but the road is extremely steep and rocky, recommended only for four–wheel drive vehicles. Take your passenger car a good distance up the mountain, however, to campgrounds and hiking and cross–country skiing trails. If you do not mind a little more effort, and after checking at the ranger station, take the long drive that traverses the mountain to San Mateo. The drive is beautiful, and the long–isolated village of adobe houses surrounding a chapel is interesting, and includes evidence of uranium–mining sprawl on the outskirts of the settlement. Mount Taylor is the backdrop for San Mateo, for Grants, and for vistas in all directions. The extinct volcano dominates the landscape; it is a sacred mountain for Navajos, Lagunas, and Acomas.

If you must complete this tour in only a weekend, you may have to skip the Chaco Canyon detour (but plan to return on another occasion to one of New Mexico's most revered and fascinating spots). From Grants, you ascend Interstate 40 slowly to the Continental Divide, the dividing line between eastern and western river drainages, accompanied by chains of red sandstone cliffs, which become more vivid as you approach the divide from either direction. One consolation for those forced to bypass Chaco: You can see the little jewel of Bluewater Lake by taking a short drive south from the highway, either on the seven–mile stretch of N.M. 412 southwest from Prewitt, or on N.M. 612, twelve miles on a narrow road southeast from Thoreau. A small village and a campground are on opposite shores of the lake, but the roads do not connect: To get from one settlement to the other, it will take you five minutes if you have a boat, but an hour driving by car. Bluewater Lake is the result of an early dam on Azul Creek built to provide irrigation to the surrounding Tusas Valley. Little farming is carried on here today, but the sparkling lake, nestled against the Zuni Mountains, draws a small crowd of fishermen, campers, and boaters to its shores.

Those taking the Chaco Canyon loop should leave the freeway on N.M. 605 just beyond Milan, the small suburb west of Grants. You will rejoin the freeway later at the town of Thoreau, just east of the little village of Continental Divide. New Mexico 605, a paved road, connects San Mateo with the outside world. At the uranium mining district of Ambrosia Lake, turn left on recently completed N.M. 509, which climbs up and then parallels the Continental Divide. You will travel through a sweep of space north to the Navajo settlement of White Horse. Drive west on Tribal Route 9 and then north on N.M. 57 to the Chaco Canyon National Historic Park, thirty miles from White Horse, from groceries, and from gas.

As you bump north on this unpaved section of N.M. 57, you may wonder why you have strayed so far from modern civilization. At any time of year, the browns and yellows of the dry hills and the blue of the sky remain unchanging from one hilltop to the next wash bottom. The long road gives little hint of the riches to come, even as you approach the gap in Chacra Mesa, the formation that lies at the southern edge of the valley known as Chaco Canyon.

You have probably come to marvel at the remnants of a mysterious ancient civilization, the secrets of which are only now slowly yielding to painstaking scientific study. Or perhaps you have come to camp in the quiet campground under the cliff of the mesa, or to hike on one of the many trails connecting features in the park. Maybe you have come to study the Chacoans' astronomical wonders, the waterworks that irrigated fields in this dry land, or the miles of roads connecting

Chaco with Chaco outliers, settlements with cultural links to Chaco, in the distance. Surely you will want to visit some of the earliest and most remarkable communal dwellings in North America. Pueblo Bonito, Chetro Ketl, Pueblo del Arroyo, and Kin Kletso are among the largest of these, and are situated close to the National Park Service's visitor center.

Stop at the visitor center first, to pay the entrance fee, obtain information on the nearby campground, and to see well-designed exhibits or a movie on the people of Chaco Canyon. You will find that the Anasazi, the "Old Ones," inhabited Chaco Canyon for about seven hundred years, until they abruptly left early in the thirteenth century. The Anasazi, who may be ancestors of the present-day Pueblo Indians, might have fallen victim to the sixty–year drought from 1130 to 1190, the erosion of the river bottom, and the exhaustion of their soil. Many of them may have moved to more fertile ground, easier to irrigate, along the Rio Grande. They left behind their massive dwellings, their roads, their water system, and rooms full of belongings—carefully formed and decorated pottery, turquoise beads, and surprisingly, shells and feathers indicating that the Anasazi traded with Indians living in what is now Mexico. Their *kivas* were left filled with ceremonial objects, which leaves visitors with what is probably an unanswerable question: Why was the disappearance of the great civilization so sudden?

The main park road will take you to some of the major ruins: the great, D–shaped Pueblo Bonito, with its hundreds of rectangular rooms and thirty round kivas arrayed in five stories around a large plaza under the cliff; the smaller Chetro Ketl, with its Great Kiva, sixty feet in diameter and roofed with logs dragged in from miles away; Pueblo del Arroyo and the mysterious "Tri–wall" (a round structure with three concentric rings of wall), which has given rise to much speculation about the nature of Chaco religion and the relationships of Chaco inhabitants with the inhabitants of Mesa Verde to the northwest. You may now have explored three ruins; there are 2,200 more in the immediate vicinity, dating from thousands of years before Christ to Navajo settlements of the last century. At Kin Kletso, just west of Pueblo Bonito, a narrow path allows hikers to ascend to the top of the mesa, affording them a magnificent view of the ruins arrayed under its rim. From there, a trail heads north to Pueblo Alto, a large ruin recently excavated in part and the convergence point of the remarkable network of roads that led to tributary villages farther to the north.

In the rock near the edge of the mesa, you will find numerous natural pools, called *tinajas*, which may have supplied some of the large population's water needs in this dry environment. As the Chaco

River cut its course deeper and deeper into the valley floor, the irrigation system designed by the Chacoans became more and more important for those caring for the crops that fed the five to six thousand people who lived in the area at its height in the eleventh and twelfth centuries. At the top of Fajada Butte, just to your right as you descend into the valley, lie huge stones close enough together to allow light to enter only in specific small places, considered part of an ancient process for measuring cycles of the sun and the moon.

Among the 2,200 sites discovered in the Chaco area, some give evidence that other peoples attempted to join the "Chaco phenomenon." Toward the end of the classic Chaco period, natives of the Mesa Verde area moved into several of the great houses on the periphery of the canyon. Their pottery, distinctively different from that of the Chacoans, indicates their long–ago presence. Navajos found the dry canyon in about 1700, setting up a few sheep camps along the Chaco River.

Chaco's wonders have captivated many new-comers, beginning with Spaniards traveling west from Jemez Pueblo in the middle of the seventeenth century. Later visitors included other Spaniards, Indian tribes, Mexicans, and Americans. Written and pictorial description of the site began with the expedition of Lieutenant James Simpson, of the U.S. Army Topographical Engineers, in 1849. The picture of Chaco's ancient people that you will gain through books, movies, the self–guided ruin tours, and the exhibits at the visitor center comes from the work of thousands of archaeologists, amateur and professional, who have sifted the soil, pieced together the potsherds, dated the tree rings, and pored over the infrared aerial photos to assemble an idea of this highly advanced prehis-toric people.

Fifteen people toured Chaco in 1906, its first year as a National Monument; the number of annual visitors is now in the thousands. Perhaps the washboard road leading in or the simplicity of the campground engenders a feeling that you have accomplished something when you get there, and a sense that Chaco now belongs to you as well as to those Anasazi of long ago.

The Chaco Canyon loop is completed by returning to N.M. 57, on which you head west to Crownpoint, taking N.M. 371 south to Thoreau and the Interstate. Crownpoint is best known for its semimonthly rug auctions, which have grown to be the biggest anywhere in Navajo country. Weavers from all over the reservation exhibit their wares on tables piled high, a Navajo taco dinner is served, and then professional and amateur bidders up the ante on the magnificent multicolored creations long into the night. The auction is held in the Crownpoint Elementary School. The town includes several other day and boarding schools, the administrative center of the Bureau of Indian Affairs' Eastern Navajo Agency, and a recently constructed Public Health Service hospital. Thoreau, named after Henry David, but pronounced "threw" by New Mexicans, is twenty–four miles south and also an education center for children of Navajo and Anglo ranchers.

Navajo Chief Blanket

You may continue on this tour either by way of Thoreau and then taking Interstate 40 past the red cliffs west toward Gallup, or by detouring briefly via a parallel road north of the cliffs. Tribal Route 49, which turns off ten miles south of Crownpoint, not far after Satan Pass, is a well–paved replacement for earlier dirt roads that jolted inhabitants of the Navajo towns of Mariano Lake and Pinedale as they came from their homes to buy supplies. These communities, once so isolated, lie in a long, dry valley, given to the grazing of sheep, goats, and cattle and to the hogans, trailers, and frame houses of the Diné. At its end, Tribal 49 meets N.M. 566; turn left on this road through the spectacular red, white, and green rocks to the village of Church Rock, to Red Rock State Park, and to Interstate 40 just east of Gallup.

A hogan is the traditional house of the Navajos. A door that faces east opens onto one large circular room, often with a heater or stove in the center and a cribwork log ceiling. The most common building materials are wood and mud, but in other areas hogans are built of stone or brick. Many families maintain a hogan for ceremonial purposes, while living in modern homes.

If you travel through Thoreau after your Chaco Canyon detour, turn west again on Interstate 40. You will pass several highly advertised emporia constructed to entice visitors to buy Indian or pseudo–Indian souvenirs. These may temporarily distract you from the beautiful red rocks to your north. The wind–and–water–sculpted red cliffs in which the houses of Iyanbito nestle are particularly notable. Shortly afterward, the splendid monuments of Church Rock and Pyramid Rock are easily visible from the highway beyond the town of Fort Wingate.

Fort Wingate, a small munitions dump until 1933, has a long history. Founded after the Civil War, it had moved twice before coming to its present location. Kit Carson's troops left from Fort Wingate when attempting to deal with Navajos in the 1870s. "Black Jack" Pershing and Douglas MacArthur have been two of the more notable inhabitants since Carson's time. The fort is now closed.

At Fort Wingate you may choose to remain on the Interstate, but there are other interesting alternatives: You can head south on N.M. 400 through the little village of Fort Wingate to the cool piney heights, the refreshing mountain scenery, and the campgrounds of McGaffey Lake, or you can parallel the Interstate on a frontage road that will take you to the modern Navajo settlement of Church Rock and to Red Rock State Park just outside the village, and then into Gallup. The park, set at the bottom of red sandstone cliffs, has a large campground, which is filled to capacity every August during the world–famous Gallup Intertribal Ceremonial, held in the park's amphitheater.

Local Anglos, Hispanics, and Indians have poured into Gallup for the Ceremonial in August for more than sixty years. Many Navajos don traditional dress complete with magnificent silver and turquoise jewelry and come to town to see old friends, to see or show what's new in Indian arts, and to watch the programs at the Red Rocks. Tourists, anxious to partake of the week's events, also come from all fifty states and around the world and fill every motel room in town.

1

There are many Gallup Ceremonial events, but four in particular draw the most interest. A parade of groups of Indian dancers, marching and riding groups, and bands winds through downtown Gallup, the Ceremonial Queen and her court smiling as they gaze down from their richly decorated horses. In the Red Rock exhibit hall, a wonderful sale and display of Indian rugs, jewelry, pottery, and other arts takes place. A daily Indian Cowboy Rodeo with bull riders, clowns, ropers and barrel racers brings clouds of dust and crowds of spectators to the amphitheater beneath Pyramid Rock. And finally, the Ceremonial presents a nightly program of Indian dances, put on by groups from all over North America, representing some of their tribes' ceremonial and social dances. During the rest of the year, Red Rock State Park is quieter, a good place to camp, with a small museum of Anasazi, modern Pueblo, and contemporary Navajo exhibits. Indian dance programs, concerts, and rodeos are offered regularly in the park amphitheater during the summer.

These red rocks have been the scene of many Western movies. In the 1940s and 1950s especially, Western stars rode through the red rocks by day and bedded down in Gallup at night, usually at the historic El Rancho Hotel. El Rancho has been lovingly restored in rambling Rustic style, its walls covered with autographed photos of the stars who once stayed there. The stars' names are also given to the rooms: You can stay in the Humphrey Bogart, the John Wayne, or the Ronald Reagan rooms, among many others.

Gallup calls itself the "Heart of Indian Country," but it is mostly an Anglo town of many nationalities south of the Santa Fe railroad, and a largely Hispanic settlement north of the tracks. Navajos and Zunis come to town, primarily from the surrounding reservations, to shop, to sell their livestock or art, and to use health, education, and recreation facilities. A combination of "dry" reservations and plentiful bars in Gallup has resulted in excessive drinking in town. Community members from Gallup and the reservations are working together courageously on the problems of alcoholism in the area and are providing some model solutions for the rest of the state.

Many tourists say, "Oh, I've been *through* Gallup," but fewer say, "Oh, I've been *to* Gallup." Going through Gallup is faster and more superficial now than it was only a decade ago, before the I–40 bypass, when travelers had to drive through the city on 66 Avenue or Coal Avenue. Many of the buildings on the main streets across from the train station served tourists on the once frequent trains or on cross–country driving adventures. Hotels occupied the second stories, and businesses operated below. In the early twentieth century an opera house, some saloons, and a bordello (now a police substation) beckoned travelers. Richly decorated doorways were often placed at the corners of buildings to entice people to enter. The Drake Hotel at 216 East 66 Avenue is said to have been controlled by bootleggers, who ran wine through the building's pipes in place of water.

Fifteen trains stopped here each day between 1900 and 1948. Today, travelers on Amtrak stop only once a day on trains heading east and west for less than five minutes, enough time only to notice the decorative brickwork of the many trading companies and other businesses fronting the track or to catch a glimpse of the statue in the wall of the C.N. Cotton Warehouse. The statue depicts Manuelito, a great Navajo chief who governed during the era of the Long Walk of the Navajo tribe. Passengers were sometimes startled to see saguaro cactus in front of the station. A Hollywood film crew in 1989 was working on a story about a small New Mexican town and decided that Gallup didn't look "New Mexican" enough, so they imported these giant cactus that are not native to any part of the state. Saguaro cannot survive the sometimes fierce Gallup winters, and the city has sought a wintertime baby–sitter in a warmer climate for these Hollywood gifts. When last seen, they were in a motel at the west end of town.

Tourists are still served in Gallup, as evidenced by the plethora of motels and restaurants. We recommend exploring the city beyond the highway and tracks, discovering the riches behind the facades of the more than two hundred trading companies. Fine Navajo and Zuni jewelry, Navajo sand painting, and exquisite Navajo weaving are the specialties of this area. C.N. Cotton opened a trading company in 1894 to sell Navajo rugs to Easterners through a catalog and thus established Gallup as a commercial center for Native American crafts.

In the area south of the railroad tracks, the Ford Canyon Recreation Area offers a playground, picnic tables, and athletic fields. The public library is a relaxing spot for children and adults. Its Southwestern collection and frequent art exhibits are notable. Across the street in the McKinley County Courthouse are a set of handsome historical murals by Lloyd Moylan. Ask permission to visit the courtroom, which displays the restored murals. You can take a walking tour of historic buildings, guided by the brochure available at tourist information centers.

If you happen to be in Gallup on a Saturday, you may better understand its economy. The sidewalks are crowded, the new shopping centers are full of shoppers, and the streets are bumper to bumper with brand–new, well–used, and antique pickup trucks. The pickups may hold huge water drums to be filled, alfalfa bales and salt blocks, livestock, groceries, or entire families. The population of the city explodes just for the day, and repair garages, movie theaters (including the Spanish colonial revival–style El Morro on Coal), the excellent library, and the stores are all very busy.

Head south from Gallup on N.M. 602, which now bypasses the downtown area to the west before joining the old road south, close to the imposing Gallup Indian Medical Center building on a hill south of town. This hospital addresses the everyday medical needs of local Native Americans and serves the population of a much larger area for more specialized care.

The road to Zuni rises and falls as it crosses hilltops and usually dry wash bottoms. As you travel you might listen to the Navajo language programs on the local radio stations to hear the tonal quality of this rich, complex language. Hogans and less traditional dwellings dot the hillsides. Sheep, goat, and cattle herds are occasionally seen; several small trading posts front the road. Where N.M. 602 meets N.M. 53, turn right for the short drive into Zuni Pueblo. The community of Black Rock, largely a government center and home to those who work in the Zuni Indian Hospital and the Bureau of Indian Affairs, soon comes into view on the right. Houses now appear all along the route from Black Rock into the heart of Zuni, blending the two communities into one.

Zuni, the largest of the Pueblo tribes, has been geographically isolated from the other New Mexico pueblos and has developed a unique Zunian character within the traditional Pueblo religion and arts. The Zuni language has no close relatives. The religion, although related to Rio Grande Pueblo beliefs, includes its own complex ritual organization. Many Zuni people make jewelry and pottery, and the Zuni excel in stone inlay work, especially the fine, lacy silver fingers that embrace tiny pieces of turquoise and coral to form "needlepoint" designs. Zuni alone is known for elaborate beadwork dolls, certain styles of *kachina* figures, and carved fetishes. The design motif of black deer with a red arrow heart prances only on the white slipped background of Zuni pottery.

Zuni people have lived in the area for hundreds of years, first in pit houses and later in multitiered community apartments and now in a great variety of homes, including portions of the original stone and adobe structures, new adobe, stone, frame, brick, and aluminum. The Zuni home has played an important role in religious rites as well as in the social structure of the Zuni. The grandest ceremony of the year is Shalako, during which six new homes, chosen to represent all homes, are blessed.

The selected homes are decorated with bright blankets and animal trophies draped with turquoise necklaces. Floors are sometimes excavated to accommodate dancers, guests, and the tall, clacking figure of Shalako, a birdlike presence. The intricacy of the long series of events leading up to the final night–long dance and morning races invites further reading about Shalako. Zuni tradition has welcomed visitors to the last stage of the Shalako ceremony, and thousands have come to experience the penetrating cold, the sounds, and the rhythms of the December dance. The generosity of the host families is shown by the dozens of fresh sheepskins drying along the barbed–wire fences near the chosen homes and by the aroma of mutton stew emanating from the kitchens within.

Unfortunately, abuse of Zuni hospitality by some visitors in recent years has caused the tribe to restrict its invitation of the general public.

Initial contact between the Zuni tribe and Europeans—the Spanish—was sporadic and violent. The first "Spanish" visitor was actually a former slave from the Barbary Coast, Estevan, who was seeking rich cities in the north for Spain. He was killed by the Zunis after transgressions of Zuni law. Fray Marcos de Niza saw Zuni villages from a distance and reported back to Mexico City that they were worthy of further exploration, told stories of gold and gems, and an expedition was sent out from Mexico in 1540.

Coronado's expedition fought a brief battle against Zuni warriors and occupied the village of Hawikuh. The Zuni people later made peace with Coronado, who then left Zuni in search of gold and the Seven Cities of Cibola. Three other Spanish expeditions followed in the sixteenth century. These also sought gold, as well as converts to Christianity, and found cultivated corn, salt, and domesticated flocks of turkeys. The Spanish in turn brought European diseases that periodically devastated the population and livestock. The Spanish settlements that were established after the expeditions were located along the Rio Grande, allowing the Zuni tribe continued relative isolation, although some European priests remained at Zuni. Catholic missionaries were killed during the Pueblo Revolution of 1680, but reestablished a mission in Zuni Pueblo in 1692. The Zuni people have consistently observed traditional religious practices and farming methods complementary to the newer European ways.

It had been the custom of the tribe to live in many villages, farming, hunting, and collecting plants and minerals in a large area of what is now Arizona and New Mexico, but the population was consolidated into a single pueblo after the Pueblo Revolt. The Zunis then lived in outlying villages only to do seasonal farming or for religious celebrations. The huge multistoried pueblo gave way to individual homes and roads atop the mounded remains of village structures. However, *kivas*, religious pathways, and dance plazas remain at the core of the pueblo that has adjusted housing patterns to accommodate water, electricity, cars and trucks, businesses, school and health centers. The mission church, with its twin bells, is a center of the pueblo. A graveyard and small plaza are adjacent to the church. You should visit the church, if possible, to see the remarkable murals that show the elaborate dress of the Zuni dancers, who depict *kachinas* and Shalako.

East of the N.M. 602–N.M. 53 junction, N.M. 53 proceeds along the more or less level ground of the shallow valley of the Rio Pescado. About ten miles east of the junction, the road passes out of the Zuni Reservation and into that of the Ramah Navajos. Like the Cañoncito band, the Ramah Navajos are separated from the "Big Reservation," but send representatives to its tribal council. The large Ramah reservation is sparsely populated, but in the town of Ramah, just beyond the reservation line, the band has set up its own schools, radio station, and clinic.

Ensconced within the center of the Ramah Navajo Reservation, El Morro National Monument has beckoned travelers for centuries. The base of the towering rock mesa has consistently held a pool of clear water, a necessity and a luxury for those traveling in the desert. This site was once on the busy main trails east and west through northern New Mexico, but the throngs have disappeared since the days of the railroad, and the highways now bypass it thirty miles to the north. Travelers have visited El Morro and left marks, pictographs, and petroglyphs of their passing since well before Coronado's time. The mesa of Inscription Rock was home to Indian villages many years before the rock became a repository of inscriptions and then a national monument. "Pasó por aquí," wrote Don Juan de Oñate, who stopped there in 1605, after establishing the first permanent European settlement in the Southwest near Santa Fe. Other Spaniards, Mexicans, and then Americans painstakingly inscribed their names on the rock as they paused by the cool pond, some with better and more flourishing penmanship, if less historical importance. There are drinking fountains in the visitor center now, so the water is left in the pool, and visitors are encouraged to inscribe their names only in the visitors' log or on a designated rock outside the building. They may also enjoy the peacefulness of the lovely setting, imagining what it might have been like to visit with Oñate, or with U.S. Army artist R. H. Kern, or Lieutenant Edward Beale of the Camel Brigade, all of whom inscribed El Morro. A guided trail leads visitors to the signatures on the rock and then up to the pueblo ruins on top, and a pleasant campground lies east of the visitor center.

The drive from El Morro to San Rafael is beautiful, with the Ponderosa–covered slopes of the Zuni Mountains to the left and rolling rangelands to the right. About thirty–five miles east of El Morro, the road turns northward, skirting the western edge of the lava flows of El Malpais National Monument. One remarkable feature of the lava flows—an ice cave near the road—seems a haven on hot summer days. The cave is on private land, though most of the surrounding area has been assimilated into the national monument. After paying an admission fee, you can walk the well–maintained, shaded paths to the ice cave and nearby Bandera Crater, a spectacular cinder cone responsible for some of the Malpais's lava flows. If you did not take the Malpais National Monument loop earlier on this tour, you may wish to detour via County Road 42, which circles the south side of Bandera Crater on its forty–three–mile passage to N.M. 117 and La Ventana Arch. Check road conditions first.

If you continue north on N.M. 53, you will pass through the small Hispanic village of San Rafael before reaching Interstate 40 on the outskirts of Grants. If you can read in the car, try Tony Hillerman's mystery novel *People of the Darkness,* which is set in part in this area. Interstate 40 will be your route back to Albuquerque. Perhaps Mount Taylor will have snow on the top. The sacred peak of the Navajo should still be in the rear view mirror when you arrive back in Albuquerque about seventy miles later. The sky on your journey may have been as colorful as the land, and Mount Taylor is a dramatic link between the two.

TOUR TWO
FOUR
CORNERS

Places: Farmington, Bloomfield, Aztec,
Mesa Verde, Cortez, Shiprock,
Farmington

Mileage: Approximately 214 miles,
excluding side trips

Suggested
travel time: Three or four days

Highways: U.S. 64/550, N.M. 544, N.M. 574,
N.M. 170, CO. 140, U.S. 160, U.S.
666

Accommodations: Farmington, Bloomfield, Aztec,
Mancos, Mesa Verde National
Monument, and Cortez

Camping: Farmington, Angel's Peak, Aztec,
and Mesa Verde National Park

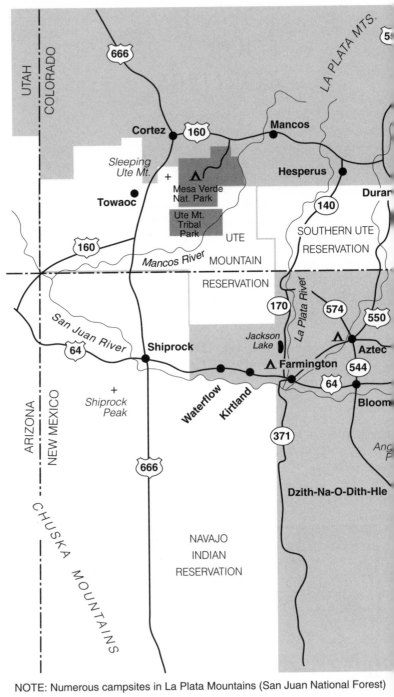

NOTE: Numerous campsites in La Plata Mountains (San Juan National Forest)

2

160

72

San Juan River

COLORADO

NEW MEXICO

Navajo
Lake
State
Park

Navajo
Lake

△ ☐ Navajo Lake
State Park

64

N

10   20 miles

2

Like any trip in New Mexico, Tour Two takes you through New Mexico's past, but this one is a journey extending way back into prehistory, into an age when the San Juan Basin was washed by a huge, inland sea; into the more recent past when the Anasazi developed Chaco Canyon and its "outliers"; into the near–present, when pioneers settled this corner of New Mexico; until you arrive at the modern age of huge power plants and refineries. Since this route takes you to the fabled Mesa Verde Ruins, you begin in Farmington and go through southern Colorado on the way to Mesa Verde National Park and the Four Corners region, returning to New Mexico via Shiprock, and back to Farmington. Along the way, you will drive through landscapes reminiscent of the Grand Canyon, past rocks carved into bizarre shapes by wind and sand, past alpine meadows and snow–packed mountains, and, perhaps most interesting of all, to ruins of ancient towns mysteriously abandoned.

Farmington is called "To tah" by the Navajo, for the three rivers that converge here—the Animas and La Plata run south from Colorado, the San Juan east from the Continental Divide. The rivers drew settlers in the 1870s and led to the name "farming town." Real growth didn't come to the area until the 1950s, when the energy industry discovered that Farmington is situated in the basin of an ancient sea and is the beneficiary of vast coal, oil, and gas reserves. Since then, Farmington has endured the boom periods and unplanned growth that follow the oil and gas industry. But beyond the businesses that line the approaches to Farmington, Main Street is wide and prosperous looking; pleasant tree–lined neighborhoods and parks welcome you.

Start your day in Farmington at the Farmington Museum on North Orchard Street, where you can quickly learn some geology and history about the region from the exhibits of rocks, tools used by early peoples, and mementos of the pioneers. A special children's section allows your kids to dress up, work a giant puzzle, and try other hands–on activities. Changing exhibits may focus on the beginnings of the oil and gas industry in Farmington or on the weaving expertise of the Navajo. The museum has published a "slightly

Navajo basket

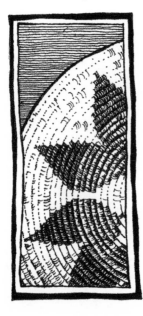

gossipy" architectural walking tour through Farmington's historic core, which will acquaint you with the builders of the town's original homes and businesses. Meet the Hubbards, who owned the town's first automobile and a charming Victorian house; the Bowman brothers, who built a drugstore in 1912; and Mrs. Sammons, the first female bank president in New Mexico, who presided at the old brick and stone building at 101 West Main.

As you are discovering Farmington's roots along Main Street, stop in at the Chamber of Commerce for up–to–date information on Farmington and at the Carson–McKee museum, a privately owned venture run by three generations of collectors. Because of the different interests of the museum's owners—and those of others who send their collections here—you will encounter an eclectic mixture of exhibits: bows and arrows and other weapons of the Plains Indians, very old Chinese dolls, and ancient rocks and fossils, including several dinosaur eggs and a nest. On a commercial note, Farmington's location encourages the sale of Indian art; there are a couple of traders on Main Street. Keep following the walking tour if you do not want to miss one gossipy fact. The tour highlights homes, churches, businesses, and a park, all within a concentrated area. When you are done, drive—or keep walking—to San Juan College Kokopelli Valley Cultural Center at 615 West Main. The Center, very user–friendly, focuses on past and present peoples and cultures of the Four Corners. It sponsors archaeology classes, hosts art shows by area residents, features traveling exhibits from other institutions in the Southwest, and serves as a conduit for information on the archeology and native cultures of the Four Corners.

For the lunch hour you can join area residents who head up to the airport restaurant for a meal and expansive views from the mesa. Another option is to take Main Street east out of town and follow it north to the turnoff—left—to Farmington Lake. A hard–packed dirt road leads to picnic spots overlooking the brilliant blue lake, or down to the shore, where fishermen try to catch breakfast or lunch. There are other picnic sites in town. Turn west at Thirtieth Street for the Kiwanis Park. Farther west turn onto College Boulevard past the striking campus of San Juan College, the state's largest independent two–year college, to Lion's Wilderness Park for shaded picnic spots and views of Angel's Peak to the east and Shiprock to the west. The park's natural amphitheater is the setting for an annual musical pageant celebrating the contact between Indian and Anglo. At the south end of the city, near Scott Avenue and East Main Street, Berg Park runs along the Animas River, with wide paths on both sides of the river for walking and riding, playgrounds and cool spots under trees for river watching and eating lunch.

In the fall, when the cottonwoods display their brilliant colors, the Bolack B–Square Ranch just east of town is an attractive after–lunch stop. State Fair–goers know the B–Square for its spectacular vegetable displays. The Bolacks are also known for their efforts to preserve the natural wildlife of the area. Two museums on the ranch highlight other family interests—antique farm machinery, electricity–generating equipment, and former governor Tom Bolack's hunting trophies and souvenirs. Tours of the museums are by appointment only.

The fame of the San Juan River as a premier fishing spot lures fishermen from all over the country to try their skill in the river, especially below Navajo Dam. Before you leave Farmington, spend some time on the river, with or without a guide. Above the dam, the deep blue waters of Navajo Lake, which is reached from U.S. 550 via N.M. 173 or from U.S. 64 via N.M. 511 or 539, attract visitors interested in boating and fishing. Campsites, a large marina, a special site for people with disabilities at Cottonwood Campground, and facilities for hunters make Navajo a popular recreation spot. The dam also stores water for the huge Navajo Indian Irrigation Project south of Farmington. Five miles northwest of Farmington, along La Plata River, the Jackson Lake State Water-fowl Area allows fishing and picnicking and a chance to view some wildlife. Seasonal horse racing at San Juan Downs and newly developed mountain biking trails offer plenty of activity before you set off to the Four Corners area.

The tour out of Farmington will take three or four days, which will give you enough time to explore Anasazi ruins, wilderness areas, and pioneer museums along the way. Twelve miles east of Farmington pull into the parking lot for the Salmon Ruins. The ruins take their name from the farsighted farming family that homesteaded the land and kept looters from the site. In 1969 members of the San Juan County Museum Association saved the site from a developer and persuaded San Juan County to purchase the property. The museum association built the research center and library, which sit at the entrance to the ruins.

At the museum examine the exhibits—pots, sherds, utensils of daily living—only a fraction of those recovered from the site. Pick up a guidebook before proceeding to the new Heritage Park and ruins below the museum. Examples of the different types of dwellings used in the San Juan Valley give youngsters the opportunity to experience the difference between a Jicarilla Apache tepee and a Ute wickiup, and to learn how a Navajo sweat lodge and hogan are built. Next to the orchard, the original Salmon homestead and outbuildings— a root cellar and barn—provide a glimpse into pioneer family life.

Follow the path to the ruin, which is still only partially reconstructed. Here you can introduce younger members of your party to Anasazi civilization within a compact and visitor–friendly site. Children can walk along the walls and peer down into the tiny living quarters and larger kivas. Your guidebook will explain that Salmon Pueblo is related to Chaco Canyon (see Tour One for a description of Chaco). Salmon Ruin is one of the two largest of the Chacoan outliers built in the eleventh century. One of the main highways out of Chaco Canyon, the great "North" road, led to the Salmon settlement. Like the builders at Chaco, the Salmon people brought in from far away the heavy timbers and sandstone used in constructing the pueblo. The Salmon area experienced two periods of settlement, one in the eleventh century and one in the thirteenth. You can see where the later residents divided up the rooms built by their predecessors, making small rooms even smaller. Those who arrived in the latter period probably came from Mesa Verde, judging from their pottery and architecture. Neither settlement lasted more than a century; the pueblo was abandoned by 1299. It lay covered by vegetation for centuries

Side Trip to Nacimiento Badlands

After leaving the ruin, drive on to Bloomfield, a couple of miles down the road, and turn right at the intersection with N.M. 44 for a trip to the Nacimiento Badlands. Soon you pass the Navajo Indian Irrigation Project, where rows of green fields contrast with the uncultivated acres of sage on your right. The project has not been the success the Navajo Nation hoped for, a greening of the desert which would provide jobs and cash, but it is a continuing venture. The Project (daa'ak'eh nitsaa, or large farm) grows potatoes for chips and french fries, as well as onions, beans, exotic shiitaki mushrooms, and pumpkins.

A sign soon indicates the Angel Peak Recreation Area. A well–maintained dirt road leads to Cliffview picnic area and Angel Peak campground overlooking canyons layered in shades of violet, gray, yellow, charcoal, and sage. As the

Sparrow on four-wing saltbush

road winds along the cliff, you can view the "angel" from different angles, until you reach a lookout directly facing the rock. The angel or "rock on top of two prongs," as the formation is called in Navajo, was formed from the hard caprock that covered softer shale and sandstone left behind when the inland sea receded. Apparently, there was never enough water in the area to support humans; however, signs of modern civilization intrude in the form of gas company installations. Weather and time willing, plan a picnic here. The Sage picnic area shelters will protect you from the summer sun.

After you return to the highway, head south for about ten miles until you notice the imposing buildings of Dzilth–Na–O–Dith–Hle, a Navajo health center and school. You may wonder why the center is located off the reservation, but this is "checkerboard country," where land is owned by the federal government or private individuals as well as by the Navajo Tribe or individual members. Across the way, where the Berea Mission and Navajo school hug the road, a gravel road (County Road 7500) takes you twelve miles to the De-Na-Zin Wilderness Area, and the Bisti Badlands farther on. *De-Na-Zin* is Navajo for "standing crane"; perhaps cranes rested here on their migrations. Visitors who detour to the wilderness area (few do—you are likely to be the only one) find themselves in a lonely landscape fashioned of sandstone and shale. Hardy vegetation, including yucca and juniper, sprouts in the sand. One section, the Logjam, consists of petrified logs. The fossil remains of dinosaurs, mammals, and the reptiles that slithered through the ancient swamp, can be found—but not removed. Because De-Na-Zin is so remote, take lots of water with you. There are no marked trails or helpful rangers at hand if you should get into trouble.

As you return to the highway and head north once more on N.M. 44, Huerfano Mountain looms on the right. To the Navajo, Huerfano Mountain and the land around it are sacred, the place where Changing Woman raised her sons, Monster Slayer and Born for Water. The boys rid the world of evil and made it safe for the Navajo people to emerge into this world from below the earth. Plans to develop an asbestos dump near Huerfano Mountain, known to the Navajo as *Dzilth-Na-O-Dith-Hle,* or "changing mountain," raised the ire of Indian leaders in 1992, who were unmoved by arguments that the area lacked historical significance. The fact that the land is the source of the Navajo creation story makes it holy to the Navajo Nation. In the distance Angel Peak's "wings" point to the sky, and to the west you can spot Shiprock's "sails."

before the region was again settled in the late 1800s.

At Bloomfield follow N.M. 544 to improbably named Aztec for the next stop. The town takes its name from the ruins within the city limits, ruins that are completely unrelated to the Aztecs of Mexico. When parts of the Jicarilla Reservation opened up to non-Indians in the 1870s, Anglo settlers, familiar with the exploits of the Aztecs, named the ruins after the ancient Mexican people.

As you enter Aztec on Main Street, you will notice the beautifully preserved Victorian buildings, pastel colored or red bricked, each retaining its individuality. Stop by the Aztec museum at 125 North Main for a copy of a walking tour of Aztec, and take time to wander through rooms that show off articles collected by Aztec families and businesses. Some rooms are furnished like a homestead. Some are arranged like old-fashioned businesses—a barber shop and post office, even a law office. Other rooms are chock-a-block with people's treasures—a fossil collection and dozens of salt and pepper shakers—and tools from the first oil boom. The museum has built a frontier village outside, which will delight youngsters who may be tired of being on their best museum behavior. Next door, the Gladys Payton Memorial Park has a playground and benches that encourage you to stretch and rest awhile before setting off on the walking tour. If you have a recreational vehicle, you can hook up here.

The walking tour takes you down Main Street past a replica of an old opera house, the general store, and the bank and other commercial buildings from the last century. Along the tree-lined streets paralleling Main Street, you can find good examples of turn-of-the-century houses: Queen or simplified Anne, Hipped style, and Gothic Revival. Lover's Lane has lost many of the tall trees that once provided shade and privacy for romantic encounters, but it is still pretty. An old ditch system built in 1878 runs across Lover's Lane, and it still works.

The next stop, Aztec Ruins National Monument, sits along the Animas River, a brilliant sight in the fall when the cottonwoods are golden. Outside the monument, a minor tourist industry has grown up. Inside, you can become acquainted with the history and culture of the area by viewing a videotape at the Visitor Center and browsing in the museum. Samples of the characteristic black-on-white pottery, jewelry, and textiles of the Chaco and Mesa Verde people, and artists' drawings of how the pueblo might have looked, will help you to understand the world of the Anasazi.

There are several ruins at Aztec. Only West Ruin and a smaller site to the north, the Hubbard site, have been excavated and are open to the public. Some work has been done on the East Ruin, enough to establish that Mesa Verdeans had probably done most of the building, but most of the rooms have been left unexcavated. Depending upon the level of interest (and attention span of younger members) of your party, you can spend a lot of time here, following the trail in and out of the West Ruin, once a huge apartment building, or you can concentrate your visit on the Great Kiva, the beautifully engineered meeting place for the community.

Like other ruins in the area, Aztec's buildings were constructed by people using designs and techniques from Chaco and were remodeled during a later occupation by Mesa Verdeans. You can discern different architectural features, the distinctive T-shaped doorways of the Mesa Verde builders for example, as you walk through the wide plaza and in and out of the living quarters and small *kiva.* You can look into the Hubbard site (but not explore it), notable for the three concentric walls that enclose a small *kiva* and living room. No one knows exactly why the Anasazi used this design, but the building was probably used for religious gatherings. The impressive Great Kiva, the only one of its type in the Southwest, is beautifully restored, with massive pillars to hold up the roof, natural light sifting through, and benches along the circular walls. This is an appropriate place to sit and reflect on the lives of the people who raised a three-storied pueblo beside the river and then left precipitously in the late 1200s, tired of fighting enemies or disease, most likely unwilling to wait out the devastating drought that occurred at the end of an already dry century.

Before leaving Aztec, you can rest in the tree-shaded park next to the ruins or stop at Riverside Park, which provides a soccer field, a dirt bike trail, and paths along the river for your enjoyment. To reach your next major destination—Mesa Verde National Park—you can either take U.S. 550 north to Durango or head west briefly on 550 before picking up N.M. 574. Our tour takes you on the latter route, heading north to Hesperus on N.M. 140, a beautiful two-lane road through badlands and ranching country, past tidy homes and cotton-woods, paralleling the sparkling La Plata River parkway and crossing the Southern Ute Indian Reservation between the Colorado border and Fort Lewis. At Hesperus, a tiny ski area, you join U.S. 160, more poetically known as the San Juan Skyway, one of the nationally designated scenic byways. Depending on the time of year, you can marvel at snowcapped mountains, golden aspen, or a riot of wildflowers in alpine meadows.

At the ranger station in Mancos, U.S. Forest Service personnel provide a wealth of information on the forest and all kinds of sports and adventures, from trekking with llamas to bike riding, whitewater rafting, and hunting. If the Museum of the Mesa Verde Cowboys is open, it is worth a visit. Housed in an old home, exhibiting collections from postcards to old glass, the museum follows in the tradition of small-town museums everywhere.

From Mancos the high mesas that hide the fabled ruins of Mesa Verde National Park loom to the left. At the entrance to the park, a well-maintained road (open all year, unless snows are particularly heavy) begins a steep climb up to the north rim. Morefield Village, the park's only campground, is situated not too far from the entrance. Even at the height of summer, there are usually campsites available, but it is best to reserve ahead if you would like to camp here. Stop next at Park Point lookout with its panoramic views of the San Juan Range, Sleeping Ute Mountain, Shiprock, and the mesas to the south. It is a short hike up to the lookout, where illustrative markers describe these points in detail. Only a few signs of civiliza-tion—the town of Cortez and smoke from distant generating plants—intrude on the vista. From Park Point it is only five miles to Far View Lodge and the visitor center, but the road is narrow and winding, and the temptation to stop at the pullouts for photo-ops may make the trip longer than you expect.

Mesa Verde can be "done" in a half-day if you restrict yourself to the museum and the two major ruins, Cliff Palace and Spruce Tree. Allow a long day for exploring the Far View and Mesa Top ruins or Wetherill Mesa as well, two days for all of the above and Balcony House. (Keep in mind that you can only visit Balcony House with a ranger, tours are limited to groups of fifty persons, and at the height of summer, waits may be up to two hours. It is a good idea to make Balcony House your first stop.) If you are traveling in the summer season, you can spend the night at the campground or the lodge; these facilities close in late October, although the park itself is open year-round. Cortez and Mancos both have motel accommodations and RV sites.

Far View Visitor Center shows off contemporary Indian arts and crafts, and you can sign up for guided tours of the ruins. Visitors with disabilities can ask for a guidebook to the ruins, also available at the museum. A short drive from the center, Far View Ruins is an example of the development that took place at Mesa Verde. You are invited to walk along the walls of the main ruins and peer in at the living rooms and *kivas*. Within a short walk are an excavated pit house (as the name implies, a home dug out of the ground) and what may have been a prehistoric reservoir. Should you arrive at Mesa Verde in the late afternoon, you can easily explore Far View ruin in an hour.

Just west of the visitor center is the road to Wetherill Mesa, open only in the summer months. Wetherill is named for the cowboy from Mancos who, with his brother, came across the Cliff Palace Ruins while searching for cattle in a snowstorm. He spent many years helping archaeologists as they uncovered the homes of the Anasazi. Wetherill is only twelve miles away, but again the road is narrow and winding, certain vehicles are restricted, and it can take up to an hour to get there. Because of its relative inaccessibility, far fewer tourists visit Wetherill, a couple of thousand versus the many thousands who crowd Chapin Mesa. Allow some time to ride the little train that takes you between ruins. You can take self-guided tours of the mesa-top Badger House community and the Step House cliff dwelling, and get a sense of the development of Mesa Verde while covering much less ground

than you would on Chapin Mesa.

For a chronological view of Chapin Mesa's history, you should start with a tour of the pit houses and pueblos along the Mesa Top Ruins Road. The Basket Makers who built the pit houses constructed them on the mesa and in caves along the cliffs between A.D. 500 and 750. Later they built their houses above ground, with walls of mud, in curving rows, like modern apartment or townhouse developments. By the year 1000, the Mesa Verdeans were constructing dwellings of stone, two or three stories high. Remains of all three types are found along the one-way road that loops atop the mesa and provides pullouts for views of a number of ruins across the narrow canyons. You may want to limit your number of stops, depending on the age and endurance of your group; younger members may not appreciate the subtle differences between the earliest and later ruins. Do stop at a few of the pullouts; try to find Square Tower, and let the kids walk among the ruins at the Sun Temple. On this loop you cross a corner of the Mountain Ute Reservation, which operates small gift and refreshment booths.

When you have finished the loop and absorbed as much history as you care to, follow the signs to Cliff Palace. Around 1200, the Anasazi began to move back into the caves along the cliffs where their ancestors had once lived. Cliff Palace is the best known of these dwellings; Spruce Tree House is a smaller but similar development. A visit to just one of these ruins may suffice for those on a tight schedule. At the viewpoint to Cliff Palace, signs recommend that if you are not in good physical condition, you should be content to gaze at the palace from this vantage point. A narrow—very narrow—path squeezes between the rocks and down a steep ladder before you come to Cliff Palace. This ruin is spacious enough for little ones to run around in, and signs encourage you to climb into some of the dwellings. The square towers and round *kivas* are good examples of the fine stone construction of the Mesa Verde people. The climb back up to the mesa via more ladders and stone stairways is crowded in the summer; factor in waiting time for your visit.

A short distance down the road from the Cliff palace, Balcony House is accessible by a thirty-two-foot ladder and is open only in the summer. Tours of Spruce Tree Dwelling, a little farther on, operate year-round, weather permitting. Built on a smaller scale than Cliff Palace, Spruce Tree is reached by a short and easy hike down into the canyon. (You may take longer hikes into the canyon as long as you register with a ranger.) At the Spruce Tree Museum, dioramas of Anasazi life and exhibits of pottery, baskets, and textiles flesh out what you have already learned about the Anasazi in your explorations. Close by, the Ranger Club changes exhibits periodically.

It is a short drive from Mesa Verde to Cortez, a town that prides itself on its proximity to Mesa Verde and other archaeological sites. The University of Colorado (CU) has collaborated with the city of Cortez in establishing the Cortez-CU Center on Market Street, whose museum displays finds from archaeological sites, as well as birds, insects, and plants of the area. You can take tours from the center to various digs and to the ruins at Hovenweep, Mesa Verde, and Ute Mountain Tribal Park.

From Cortez, U.S. 160/666 stretches almost straight south back into New Mexico. Sleeping Ute Mountain is now closer on your right. Be on the lookout for the Ute Mountain Pottery Plant fifteen miles south, where you can join a tour of Ute Mountain Tribal Park. You will be accompanied by a guide in your own vehicle. In the park you can take a day hike, camp at a primitive campground (no running water), or backpack into more remote areas of the park. The park covers an area much greater than Mesa Verde, some 125,000 acres, with equally astonishing though undeveloped ruins. The Utes regard this territory as sacred; only recently have portions of the park been opened to outsiders. Because there are so few visitors and the ruins have not been restored, the park has an untouched quality about it. When the federal government shut down for a day in 1990, tourists who couldn't get into Mesa Verde National Monument were pleasantly surprised to learn that they could still visit pueblo and cliff-dwelling sites at Ute Mountain Tribal Park.

When U.S. 160 branches off to the west of Highway 666, you can take a detour of about 18.5 miles to Four Corners Monument, the place where four states—Utah, Colorado, New Mexico, and Arizona—meet. Four Corners is a somewhat desolate spot, but this might be your only chance to be photographed spread across four states.

From the turnoff point to Four Corners, U.S. 666 crosses into New Mexico and heads for Shiprock. Founded in 1903 as an agency for the Navajo Reservation, Shiprock retains a turn-of-the-century air with its old Bureau of Indian Affairs housing and boarding-school buildings, while the presence of a new and bustling shopping center jerks you back to the present. Shiprock remains an important center for Navajo tribal business, trading, education, and health care. The town is crowded with visitors in October, when the Northern Navajo Fair attracts both Navajos and non-Indians to the rodeo, rides, and arts and crafts exhibits. Southwest of town, Shiprock Peak raises its imposing "sails" to the sky.

After leaving Shiprock, you will follow the San

Side Trip to Bisti Badlands

Nearer to Farmington, signs of commerce once more clutter the landscape, but there is one last detour that will take you back to a time before even the earliest civilizations you have seen on this trip existed. In Farmington turn south on Highway 371, also called the Vietnam Veterans Memorial Highway, to reach the Bisti Badlands. This is a beautiful road, and it is an easy drive to Bisti, twenty-seven miles south. Once past the Farmington city limits and the Dunes recreational area, criss-crossed by the trails of four-wheelers, you find yourself on the Navajo Reservation, its vastness broken only by some Navajo Agricultural Products Industry buildings, a radio tower, an occasional house or mobile home, unmarked dirt roads leading off to little settlements, and flocks of sheep and goats sometimes herded only by dogs. This is the country eloquently described by Tony Hillerman in his many mystery novels set on the reservation. Keep your eyes open for a small sign that indicates the turnoff to the Bisti Badlands. A

Juan River as it parallels U.S. 64 on the right, irrigating the valley and transforming the high desert. The town of Waterflow and the massive buildings at the San Juan Generating Station will be on your left. At the turnoff to Kirtland a sign points out the Four Corners Power Plant, a huge electricity generating plant whose smoke—it is said—was visible to the naked eye of astronauts on the moon. Guided tours of this facility and the San Juan station may be of interest to those who want to see up close how the huge plants operate. Reserve places at least two weeks ahead. Nearby coal mines, which deliver coal to the power plants, also allow individual tours. Morgan Lake, next to the Four Corners plant, attracts sailboarders and picnickers to its blue waters. A different experience awaits you at the trading posts along the way, at least one of which has been in existence almost since non-Indians were first allowed to settle in the area.

graveled road leads slightly southeast past the Gateway Mine to the small parking lot at the entrance to the Badlands.

A map of the 3,968-acre area illustrating the main trails is posted here, but it is wise to have your own detailed map along, as you are likely to be the only visitors, and there are no real trails and no park rangers about. You should also take lots of water and sturdy boots for the hike into the rocky area. This is not too difficult for young children, though they may be hot and bored and lag at the beginning of the hike before you reach the rock formations. Near the parking lot, arroyos carved from soft, black rock provide shelter for a quick picnic. (There are no prepared picnic sites or restrooms here, and camping is not allowed.) South of this area, a faint trail points you to the rest of the badlands, where the action of wind and sand have carved the shale and soft sandstone into weird gray and ocher shapes. The area is rich in petrified logs and fossils from the prehistoric animals that roamed the basin millions of years ago; look but don't touch, or at least don't remove.

Back in Farmington, residents and visitors enjoy special events throughout the year: a balloon festival and Riverfest in May and the Anasazi Pageant, performed all summer. Freedom Days over the Fourth of July celebrate the holiday with a multitude of activities: country-western dancing, a pow-wow, a triathlon, and the traditional parade and fireworks display. Baseball fans flock to the nationally known Connie Mack tournament in early August, when amateur baseball teams from all over the country and Puerto Rico vie for the World Series championship. The Labor Day Tohta Festival invites you to an arts and crafts show and Indian rug auction. Christmastime in Farmington, as in the rest of New Mexico, is celebrated with *farolito* displays.

TOUR THREE
RIO ARRIBA

3

Places:	Española, Abiquiu, Tierra Amarilla, Chama, Dulce, Tres Piedras, Ojo Caliente
Mileage:	Approximately 175 miles, excluding side trips
Suggested travel time:	A week or a weekend
Highways:	U.S. 84/285, U.S. 84, U.S. 64/285, U.S. 64, U.S. 285
Accommodations:	Española, Chama, Dulce, and Ojo Caliente
Camping:	Santa Clara Canyon, Abiquiu Lake, Echo Amphitheater, El Vado Lake, Heron Lake, near Chama, Jicarilla Reservation, and Carson National Forest

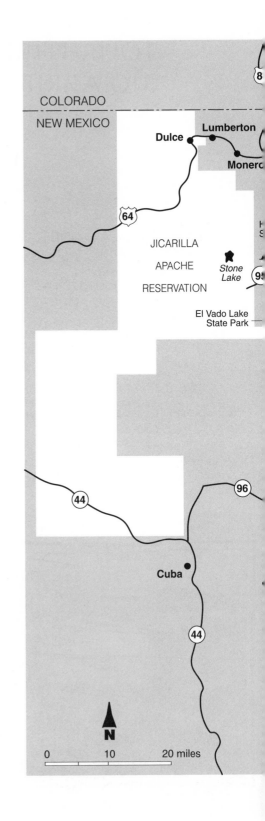

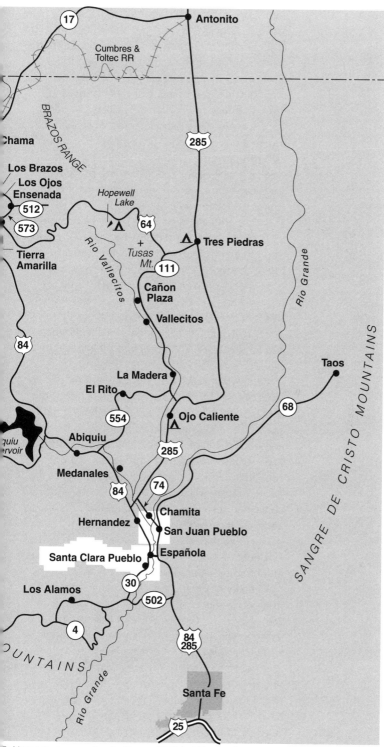

Antonito

Cumbres &
Toltec RR

17

285

BRAZOS RANGE

Chama

Los Brazos

Los Ojos
Ensenada

512

573

Tierra
Amarilla

Hopewell
Lake

Rio Vallecitos

64

+
Tusas
Mt.

Tres Piedras

111

Cañon
Plaza

Vallecitos

84

La Madera

El Rito

554

Ojo Caliente

Abiquiu

quiu
rvoir

285

68

Taos

SANGRE DE CRISTO MOUNTAINS

Rio Grande

Medanales

84

74

Hernandez

Chamita

San Juan Pueblo

Santa Clara Pueblo

Española

Los Alamos

30

502

4

OUNTAINS

Rio Grande

Santa Fe

84
285

25

E: Numerous campsites in Carson National Forest, Santa Fe National Forest and
la Apache Reservation

3

Tour Three explores Rio Arriba County, one of New Mexico's largest and most fascinating counties. The tour wanders through wide river valleys and narrow canyons, bisecting mountain ranges and the Continental Divide. It takes you into Hispanic mountain villages, across vast ranchlands, and through Indian reservations. Travelers can ride a pack horse into the national forest or take a train trip on a narrow-gauge railway, run the rapids of a wild river, camp beside a mountain lake, enjoy a meal in a well-appointed restaurant, purchase hand-carved furniture or newly spun yarn, or take a course in archaeology.

Before embarking on Tour Three, be prepared for driving on two-lane highways, dirt roads, and through lonely miles in mountainous terrain. The top of the tour—a high, spectacular stretch of Highway 64—is usually closed in the winter. Española and Chama have a range of gas stations, stores, restaurants, and small hotels, but those who prefer roadside picnics, modest inns and motels, and local cafés will find much to their liking during this journey.

Begin your journey on the southern outskirts of Española on U.S. 84/285, where small farms, tidy orchards, mobile homes, old adobe houses, and a scattering of businesses introduce you to the fertile and historic Española Valley. Unless you choose to explore beyond Española's predictable commercial zone, this economic and population center of Rio Arriba County will appear to be little more than a convenient place to stop for food, fuel, information, and perhaps a night's rest. However, there is more to Española than meets the eye, so drop in at the Española Chamber of Commerce to pick up maps and brochures that describe the city and region.

The city of Española is comparatively young, founded in the 1880s as a major stop on the Denver and Rio Grande Western Railroad, but the valley in which it is nestled has been inhabited for many centuries and reflects the longtime Hispanic and Indian heritage of the area. San Juan Pueblo and the site where Don Juan de Oñate established his headquarters at San Gabriel del Yunque in 1598 lie just to the north of Española, Santa Clara Pueblo hugs its southern boundaries, and dozens of old Hispanic neighborhoods and communities make up the small city and its environs. Those who live in and near Española own modest farms and ranches, are employed at Los Alamos National Laboratories, commute to Santa Fe, or work in local businesses. Vendors sell fresh green chile, red chile *ristras,* melons, apples, and other produce from the region; their pickups and little trailers dot the roadsides in and out of Española throughout the summer and early fall.

Española contains a wonderful mixture of new and old, important and trivial, spiritual and material enterprises. Northern New Mexico Community College, site of a tricultural festival held each October, attracts students from throughout northern New Mexico. Española supports a regional hospital, hosts the Rio Arriba County Fair each June, and points with pride to its new library and the venerable Bond House Museum. There is also a large ashram for the Sikh Dharma Community, an East Indian religious sect with many non-Indian followers, to the immediate southeast of town. Each year hundreds of Sikhs, their friends, and a smattering of state politicians gather at the ashram to discuss issues of international and personal significance. Española is also famous for its low-riders, automobiles both new and old that have been lovingly restored, customized, lowered, and painted with glittery colors in designs that often depict religious symbols. Weekend evenings and holidays will find Española's main street a slow-moving showplace for low-riders from throughout the valley.

Proceeding at a similar pace, perhaps, an important eighteenth-century expedition passed through the Española area, carving a route that roughly parallels some of this tour. In 1776, two Franciscan friars, Francisco Atanasio Dominguez and Sylvestre Velez de Escalante, were sent by their superiors in Mexico City to open a northern passage to California. Although the Dominguez-Escalante Expedition never fully achieved its purpose, it did lay the groundwork for the later Spanish Trail. And Fray Dominguez, in his reports about his pre-expedition visit to the missions of the region, provided historians with a graphic, detailed picture of life in late eighteenth-century New Mexico.

To visit Española's Bond House Museum, drive through the southern outskirts of Española and take the first U.S. 84/285 turnoff, marked by a left turn and stoplight about a mile down the hill that serves as Española's southern entrance. This leads across the Rio Grande. Signs guide you to the Bond House Museum, located just a few blocks north on U.S. 84/285 and then a block or so to the west. Franklin Bond, a Canadian who was a sheep rancher, wool broker, and owner of a vast mercantile empire in northern New Mexico, built Bond House in 1887. Over the years, the original two-

Side Trip to Santa Clara Pueblo

If you wish to explore Santa Clara Pueblo and its Puye Cliff Dwellings, turn left (south) on N.M. 30 immediately after crossing the Rio Grande on U.S. 84/285. You will soon enter the boundaries of this large Tewa-speaking pueblo where more than two thousand people live on the pueblo's forty thousand acres of high desert, mesas, mountains, and river valley. Some residents farm, many work in nearby Española or Los Alamos, and still others create the pueblo's famous red and black pottery.

Five generations of the Tafoya family of Santa Clara are famous for the pottery they make and sell here at the pueblo and at art galleries across the nation. The vessels made by the Tafoyas and other Santa Clara potters are noted for their precise carving, matte painting, and highly polished finish. Santa Clara also boasts another art form, tempera paintings that depict the daily and ceremonial life of the pueblo. Signs within the village announce shops and homes where you can purchase examples of Santa Clara art.

If you are lucky, you may arrive at Santa Clara during one of the feast days that the pueblo shares with visitors. For example, during the feast of Santa Clara, celebrated each August 12, the pueblo welcomes friends and neighbors to room structure gained many rooms and fancy decorations, soon becoming Española's Victorian showpiece. An interesting example of nineteenth-century adobe architecture, it sits on a hill and must have once enjoyed an uncluttered and commanding view of the rural valley below. Donated to the city in the late 1950s, Bond House was the Española City Hall for many years.

As U.S. 84/285 heads north out of Española, it passes the city's new clusters of handsome commu-

enjoy a variety of dances: the Harvest, the Corn, and either the Buffalo or the Reindeer. The tribe also sponsors modestly priced guided tours of the village, its craft shops, and its cliff dwellings throughout most of the year.

A few miles south of the Santa Clara village offices, a small road, Highway 5, leads seven miles west to the Puye cliff dwellings and beyond them to Santa Clara Canyon. The extensive Puye ruins include cave dwellings, simple houses, and some many-leveled stone structures. Ancestors of present tribal members once lived along the mesa tops of the Pajarito Plateau, a four-hundred-square-mile deposit of volcanic ash that extends downward a thousand feet in some places. Visitors can climb ladders and use footholds to explore this ancient pueblo, with its pictographs, *kivas,* and life-giving springs. Children will relish this chance to explore caves and run and play, as Santa Clara's children have for hundreds of years. Down the road, Santa Clara Canyon offers fishing ponds and streams, campsites and hiking trails. The cliff ruins are open all year, but the canyon area and its campground are usually closed from November through March. The Pueblo collects an entrance fee to the ruins and canyon, and charges separately for specific activities—fishing, camping, or guided raft tours, for example.

nity buildings, including the library, city hall, and police headquarters, followed shortly by the campus of Northern New Mexico Community College. Explore the curving paved and dirt roads that intersect along here and elsewhere in town to gain a sense of the diverse communities that surround and comprise Española.

A number of small settlements, including San José, Fairview, and Hernandez, have almost been swallowed up by the northern outskirts of Española, but their old churches, post offices, cemeteries, and schools can still be seen from the highway. Those who have a fine eye for landscape can try to pick out the view that photographer Ansel Adams captured when he took his famous photograph "Moonrise over Hernandez." A classic black-and-white study that preserves the mood and essence of this valley as it was many years ago, "Moonrise" has become one of the most famous photographs of this century. (Clue: The view Adams found is toward the east.) Here also begins the section of Rio Arriba County in which there are hundreds of excellent examples of an architectural style unique to northern New Mexico. In her book, *American Adobes: Rural Houses of Northern New Mexico,* Beverley Spears describes the style. Architecture buffs might want to look for examples in homes, churches, and outbuildings as they drive through the Española and Chama River valleys. The architectural characteristics include adobe construction, exterior walls stuccoed in pastel tints or white, outside woodwork in a contrasting color, pitched corrugated steel roofs, paneled doors, and buildings that were originally built in a series of one-story rectangular rooms. While some of the houses that display these features are abandoned, others have been proudly restored. Travelers can find small bed-and-breakfast inns in a few of the homes.

About five miles outside of Española, as the valley widens and settlements grow sparse, U.S. 285 leaves U.S. 84 and goes right (east) to Ojo Caliente and other villages, and then north into Colorado. But Tour Three continues its journey northwest on U.S. 84, with the Chama River meandering alongside or below the highway. Depending on the season, the river valley's cottonwood trees provide a soothing counter-point—brilliant green in the summer, shimmering gold in the autumn—to the stark cliffs and mesas that dominate the horizon. The gradual change in colors on the buttes and mesas signals the entrance to "Ghost Ranch Country," where Georgia O'Keeffe lived and painted for many years. A number of spiritual centers have developed here over the last decades, and visitors now also enjoy hikes, raft trips, visits to guest ranches, fishing, camping, and quiet seminars within this dramatic landscape.

The village of Abiquiu, once the site of a Tewa pueblo, sits to the left of the highway atop a bold mesa, providing a 180-degree view of the Chama River Valley. You climb up to Abiquiu by taking a sharp left-hand turn off U.S. 84, passing the post office that sits beneath the town. Abiquiu's history is as colorful as its surroundings. Originally located three miles to the west, the settlement endured Indian assaults and waves of sickness during the first part of the eighteenth century. After one particularly destructive raid in 1748, Abiquiu's settlers abandoned the site, returning to stay only after a protective plaza was constructed by Governor Cachupin, who also promised that soldiers would be stationed nearby. When the Dominguez-Escalante Expedition passed through here on its way to California in 1776, Abiquiu boasted a sizable population, including many *genízaros*. Two years later it was a stage-stop on the route to Los Angeles, and by the middle of the next century, traders, trappers, and the military considered Abiquiu an important settlement.

Visitors can walk through Abiquiu's big, irregu-larly shaped plaza, which is anchored by the mission church of Santo Tomas. Georgia O'Keeffe's large home, on the right as you exit the village, is not open to visitors. However, as you look out on the stark landscape that surrounds Abiquiu, you can almost imagine yourself standing within one of the artist's famous renderings of outsize cliffs, mountains, and mesas. Below the town are roadside conveniences—a gas station and general store, an inn, a restaurant, and an RV campground.

At least three religious centers—Muslim, Presbyterian, and Catholic—have chosen to locate near Abiquiu. You first observe the newest, a

Muslim mosque and the Institute for Islamic Studies, as a long, tan presence up against the cliffs across the valley from Abiquiu. To reach the mosque (there are no signs), drive west on U.S. 84 alongside the river, crossing it twice beyond Abiquiu. Less than one-half mile after crossing the second bridge, look to the right for a dirt road that heads across an arroyo toward the white cliffs in the distance. Take this road. After about a mile, you will pass a large two-story adobe house, the Institute for Islamic Studies. Then you will climb on toward the adobe mosque designed by Hassam Fathi, a prominent Egyptian architect. Because the road is comparatively primitive, it is wise not to travel to the mosque if it has rained or snowed recently.

Back down on the highway, you will soon climb steep, red cliffs and see the Chama Valley and the huge and gentle S formed by the river. The road to Abiquiu Dam, N.M. 96, appears about seven miles beyond Abiquiu. Turn left here to visit the bright blue lake formed where the Chama River has been dammed and where fishing, windsurfing, and

Jemez-Cuba Side Trip

If you wish to take a side trip into the heart of the Jemez Mountains, or drive to Albuquerque via the town of Cuba and N.M. 44, continue on N.M. 96 past the small Hispanic villages of Coyote and Youngsville into the Jemez Mountains. Hunters and campers alike prize the rugged and remote beauty of the mountains, canyons, and forests that make up this parcel of Rio Arriba and Sandoval counties. You will find campgrounds and small lakes in the San Pedro Parks Wilderness, hiking and jeep trails throughout the mountains, and a scattering of villages where people prize their privacy and isolation (so watch for and respect signs indicating private property). Communities like Lindrith and Regina usually offer gas and food. Cuba, the service center for northern Sandoval County and gateway to the western slopes of the Jemez and San Pedro mountains, sits astride N.M. 44 and provides travelers with food, fuel, supplies, and lodging. The side trip to Cuba is about forty miles one-way, but because it carries you through the mountains, it might take longer than expected.

hunting for dinosaur fossils (which you do not remove) are favorite sports.

As you wind and climb along U.S. 84, you will be hard put to keep your eyes on the road. Wheezing cattle trucks and overloaded alfalfa wagons plunge down and strain upward and across the dramatic panorama that U.S. 84 bisects. Brilliant colors describe the geologic formations—Triassic reds, Jurassic sandstones—in the flanking mesas and cliffs. In the midst of all this desert and mountains, you can look down and see faraway windsurfers whizzing across azure Abiquiu Reservoir.

The Rio Chama that tumbles through canyons between El Vado and Abiquiu reservoirs is an official Wild and Scenic River, so designated by Congress in the late 1980s. This means that this stretch of water is protected from development and saved for rafting, fishing, and hiking. Commercial rafting outfitters, most of them based along the Rio Grande in Española, Santa Fe, and Taos, will take parties down the Chama when spring runoffs and rainfall have been sufficient. Rafting season usually lasts from late spring through early summer, sometimes longer. Few roads lead from the highway down to the river, but the staff of the Rio Chama Information Center at Ghost Ranch Living Museum can answer your questions about routes to the river, water elevation and canyon conditions, permits, and how to contact an outfitter.

Ghost Ranch is located about six miles or so past the road to Abiquiu Reservoir and Dam. Its cluster of adobe buildings, workshops, and cabins sits a mile from the highway, hidden beneath spectacular cliffs, with access to cool canyons and hiking trails. Once a working ranch that dates back to 1766, Ghost Ranch is now a favorite place for weekend retreats and week-long seminars on a variety of topics sponsored by several institutions. Visitors can tour the ranch headquarters, its museum, solar energy projects, and archaeological displays. Ghost Ranch is owned by the Presbyterian church and has developed a respectful relationship with those who live in Rio Arriba County by encouraging local art and craft traditions, offering year-round recreational programs, sponsoring the High Desert Research Farm, and maintaining a seed bank to preserve a variety of staple crops not only from this region but from around the world. It is said that Ghost Ranch was named after the *brujos* who live in the nearby canyons. In 1947, paleontologists discovered the remains of a small, swift dinosaur within one of those canyons; named Coelophysis, it is now New Mexico's "official dinosaur."

At Ghost Ranch Living Museum, less than two miles north of Ghost Ranch on U.S. 84, you will find a welcome respite of shade and the opportunity to explore the ecology of northern New Mexico within a small, easily traversed exhibit area. Children might enjoy the displays of living plants and animals that emphasize the delicate balance within nature that must be achieved if living things are to exist in this environment. For example, an entire room is devoted to the beaver. Here reside several live beavers in a complicated and very real dam. Many of the animals that live at the museum were sick or wounded, rescued by the founders and the curators of the small facility. The U.S. Forest Service provides self-guided tours and information at the Visitor Center.

Just beyond the Living Museum, a dirt road on the left (impassable when it rains) will bounce you thirteen miles through high scrub and along the Chama River to a Benedictine monastery, Christ-in-the-Desert. The soaring adobe chapel is distinctly modern, but the priests and brothers who live here follow ancient monastic traditions. They may invite you to accompany them in daily garden, craft, and contemplative activities. Sometimes visitors stay in the guesthouse that is part of the adobe complex; others come only on Sundays for Mass. We suggest you make visiting arrangements ahead of time.

A short trip north from Ghost Ranch Living Museum leads to Echo Canyon Amphitheater, a good place for children to walk and run a bit. The amphitheater also demonstrates for them the effects of erosion and how echoes work. There are shaded camping and picnic areas in which you can hear children's laughter bouncing off the canyon's sandstone walls. During his 1967 battle with authorities, land grant leader Reies Lopez Tijerina claimed this canyon for heirs of the Tierra Amarilla Grant.

Twenty miles later, Tierra Amarilla is situated beneath the dramatic backdrop of the Brazos Cliffs, surrounded by wooded foothills and undulating grazing land. First settled as Las Nutrias in 1860, the town was part of a huge land grant that the Mexican government made in 1832 to Manuel Martinez, his heirs, and several of his neighbors. The fifty families who settled Las Nutrias, and also founded the villages of Los Ojos, La Puente, and Los Brazos, came from Abiquiu with Francisco Martinez, Manuel's son. All three villages and Tierra Amarilla have been designated historical districts because of their unique architectural and historical heritage. From 1872 to 1881, this was the site of the Ute and then the Jicarilla Indian Agency; it took the name of the grant, Tierra Amarilla, when the Rio Arriba county seat was moved here in 1880.

3

The question of ownership of the Tierra Amarilla Land Grant, which reaches up to the Colorado border, has led to many legal controversies and standoffs over the years. In the late 1960s, the *Alianza Federal de los Mercedes* (Federal Alliance for Land Grants), led by Reies Lopez Tijerina, appropriated the town's stately courthouse in a confrontation over land rights. Injuries occurred and a statewide manhunt resulted in Tijerina's arrest. More recently, armed local farmers staked ownership to nearby ranchland in a highly publicized case, which was eventually settled out of court. Those who hike, camp, or fish in this area should carry U.S. Forest Service maps with them to ensure that they do not encroach on grant property. However, little of this emotionally charged history is evident in the town of Tierra Amarilla, where pickup trucks outnumber cars and where great pride is taken in caring for the Santo Niño Catholic Church and nearby rectory, both of them built of sturdy adobes topped with elaborate tin roofs. There are gas stations, small grocery stores, and a nationally recognized community-based health clinic in Tierra Amarilla.

Tour Three will eventually bring you back to Tierra Amarilla, connecting with U.S. 64 to cross the Brazos Mountains; but first, you will continue north to visit Chama and Dulce, then return south to Heron and El Vado lakes and the nearby village of Los Ojos.

Chama, famed as a cattle and ranch center, is about sixteen miles up U.S. 84, which picked up U.S. 64 at Tierra Amarilla. You can find travel information, restrooms, and brochures about the surrounding area at the Chama welcome center located where U.S. 64/84 veers west from N.M. 17. A brochure describing a walking tour of Chama is also available at the center.

Chama blends cowboy, hunting, and Hispanic traditions in its architecture and ambiance. A fishing, hunting, and ranching center for the surrounding region, the town boasts several annual tourist events and reflects the importance of the lumber industry. Chama is also a winter sports mecca—especially for snowmobilers and cross-country skiers, who enjoy hundreds of miles of open, snow-covered terrain.

If you are visiting Chama between June and October, be sure to book tickets beforehand for a ride on the Cumbres and Toltec Scenic Railroad, the historic narrow-gauge train that chugs through the mountains. Leaving Chama each morning, the small, black, coal-driven engines haul passengers up and over Cumbres Pass to Osier, Colorado, where everyone pauses for lunch, either at the nearby restaurant or for a picnic in the meadow alongside the tracks. Another train also starts early in the morning from Antonito, Colorado. After meeting for lunch in Osier, the trains chug back down the mountains, across high trestles and bridges, past ghost towns to home. The Cumbres and Toltec is an unusual railroad in many ways. It has been jointly owned by New Mexico and Colorado since the 1970s. The two states purchased this portion of the tracks, engines, and cars from the Denver and Rio Grande Western Railway Company after it ceased passenger and freight operations between Antonito, Colorado, and Farmington, New Mexico. Railroad and history buffs were successful in their challenge to both states to save an important piece of their railroad heritage. Cumbres and Toltec fans will argue about the best time for the train ride. Is it in the summer, when meadows are filled with wildflowers, streams are running, and cattle are grazing? Or is it in the fall, when the hillsides are a stunning patchwork of golds and crimsons, and when you might catch a glimpse of cowboys on roundup?

If you would like to visit Dulce and the home of the Jicarilla Apache Tribe a half hour west of Chama, take U.S. 64/84 at the Y in the road near the entrance to Chama. The highway will lead you across high ranchland and the Continental Divide (7,766 feet), often following the abandoned roadbed of the old Denver and Rio Grande Western Railroad to Dulce.

This is wide-open country, with little to interrupt the drive. You will cross grazing land and the W. A. Humphries Wildlife Area, where hunters stalk deer, elk, and bear, and where colorful flowers blanket the hills after a rainy spring or wet summer. Two settlements, one of which is a ghost town, barely break the unpeopled landscape. Monero sits in a little hollow, its remnants of log buildings and abandoned mining shafts a reminder of its more active coal-mining days. Perching right on the edge of the Jicarilla Reservation, Lumberton's most arresting feature is its Catholic Church of St. Francis. Look to the left for a glimpse of bright white scallops, almost like an immense birthday cake against the sky. Drive down a small dirt road and visit this restored marvel of adobe construction and fanciful interpretation. The church is outlined in bright blue, its tin roof, belfry, and white coat sparkling in the sun. As you leave Lumberton, you will pass another artistic endeavor, a faded hunting mural painted across the facade of the old Mercure General Store.

Dulce is at the north end of the Jicarilla Apache Reservation, which contains almost three quarters of a million acres of mountains, small lakes, ranches, streams, and prime hunting country. The Jicarillas are Athapascans, kin to the Navajo and other Apaches. They once roamed throughout much of Colorado, Texas, Oklahoma, and New Mexico. As hunters and gatherers, they moved with the seasons, settling down in northeastern New Mexico in the seventeenth century, then moving closer to the Rio Grande by the 1850s. In 1887, the United States Government deeded them the reservation land on which they now live.

Jicarilla tribal enterprises include the ownership and management of the local award-winning motel; oil, gas, and forestry businesses; the care of the elderly (financed from proceeds of a flock of sheep known as the old people's herd); and oversight of hunting and other recreation activities on reservation land. The tribe also supports an independent school district, Head Start programs, and housing projects.

Dulce is the reservation's largest town, where most of the tribe's 2,500 members live. In Dulce, you can purchase the fine handwoven baskets from which the Jicarillas received their name. Woven from local grasses in intricate patterns that have changed little over the centuries, the baskets win ribbons at the New Mexico State Fair and are proudly displayed in the motel gift shop and at the Tribal Museum near the center of town. Jicarilla women also produce prizewinning beadwork earrings, belt buckles, and key rings. A visit to the museum, presided over by the artisans, will acquaint you with other tribal crafts and historic moments.

When you visit the Jicarilla Apache Reservation, venture beyond Dulce. Hunters come here from all over the world to take home wildlife trophies, especially mule deer and elk. The tribe recently opened Horse Lake Mesa Game Park, southeast of Dulce, where bull elk and bear are hunted with Jicarilla guides, sometimes in the snow, on horse-back, on foot, and in four-wheel-drive vehicles, at elevations that are usually above eight thousand feet. You can also camp, fish, and hike at one of the reservation's eight lakes.

The Jicarilla people invite visitors to share in two annual events. The tribe sponsors a roundup each summer, during which you can watch a rodeo, Indian dances, and other festivities. The Goiiya Feast Day in September blends ceremonial functions with public events as tribal members pitch tepees, engage in foot races between rival clans, participate in amateur rodeos and traditional dances, and enjoy campfires at their campground near the lake. Contact Jicarilla tribal offices in Dulce or consult with the staff at the motel so that you have proper permits and travel directions before you visit campgrounds or lakes on the reservation.

Now it is time to backtrack to two of New Mexico's favorite high-elevation lakes and then to begin the journey east across the Brazos Range to Tres Piedras. Drive eastward on U.S. 64/84, then skirt south past Chama, almost all the way back to Tierra Amarilla, a trip of less than an hour.

If you have been curious about the sheer Brazos Cliffs that appear ahead in the east, take a brief side trip and turn toward these quartzite marvels

3

on N.M. 512, driving through the village of Los Brazos (an Historical District) to Enseñada, where you can study them more closely. You are permitted to travel through this privately owned land toward the two-thousand-foot-deep Brazos Box Canyon. Look for a waterfall that runs only during springtimes and summers after sufficient snow has fallen in the mountains.

Just north of Tierra Amarilla, go west a few miles on N.M. 95 toward Heron Lake, and be prepared for vistas that seem incongruous in this dry, desert land. Spring runoffs from the western slopes of the Continental Divide are channeled through a tunnel to fill the reservoir that is Heron Lake. At the height of summer, sailboats, windsurfers, and fishing boats dot the lake's turquoise surface, and tents and trailers line its shores. Because it is a no-wake lake, Heron especially attracts sailors and fisherman, who troll in their boats down to the dam to catch Kokanee salmon and lake trout. Oddest of all, when you pitch a tent alongside Heron Lake, you fall asleep listening to waves lap against what was once a mountain and is now your campsite.

A five-mile hiking path and a narrow dirt road connect Heron and El Vado lakes, but you will probably choose to drive back on N.M. 95 to the U.S. 64/84 turnoff to Los Ojos, a small detour in the midst of your lake hopping. Not only is this a convenient route to El Vado Lake, it also provides you with the most stunning view of the Brazos Cliffs, gray and purple in the distance, like a child's drawing of the West.

Once the highway between Española and Chama curved through Los Ojos, a small village dominated by its church on the northern edge and

now known for its wool-growing cooperative, *Ganados del Valle* (Livestock Growers of the Valley). Reviving a two-hundred-year-old sheep-raising tradition that was in danger of being lost, community members organized themselves into an integrated sheepraising, wool-growing, weaving cooperative a number of years ago. Members of the cooperative raise several varieties of sheep, including the Churro, one of New Mexico's hardiest breeds, taking them to high pastures in the summer, then down to this valley in the autumn. You might be interested to note that finding adequate pasture has become a challenge to the Ganados enterprise. As land values in the Chama area have risen to meet recreational development demands, small farmers and ranchers have discovered that they cannot afford to lease or buy what their sheep and cattle require. In 1989, Ganados members, local ranchers, Chama businessmen, and the Governor of New Mexico met to talk about the issue of future grazing land and peaceful coexistence, eventually working out a compromise satisfactory to everyone. Members of the Ganados Cooperative spin, dye, and weave their wool into garments, rugs, and accessories, selling them in the wonderful old Burns Mercantile Building in the middle of Los Ojos. You can visit the store, Tierra Wools, and watch the weavers in action.

As you wind up and out of Los Ojos, watch for an inventively decorated religious shrine carved into the hillside on your left. After leaving Los Ojos, you will have barely returned to U.S. 64/84 before you turn right onto N.M. 112, a paved road that leads fifteen miles west to El Vado Lake and Dam. Crossing rolling grazing land, climbing toward pine trees, you will pass a few sparsely settled housing developments, an abandoned state forestry camp, and the turnoff to El Vado Lake State Park. About four miles of well-maintained dirt road bring you to the edge of El Vado Lake. Popular with water skiers and fishermen, El Vado boasts dozens of primitive and improved campsites and several boat ramps. Its steep banks are covered with pine trees, their scent reminding you that you are in the mountains at an elevation of almost seven thousand feet. Fishing is especially good both at the dam site and just below it on the Rio Chama. El Vado Lake covers the site of the small village of El Vado, a place where travelers once crossed the Rio Chama. All that is left of the community of El Vado is a cemetery along the lakeshore.

We have saved the most prized part of Tour Three for last. The highway splits at Tierra Amarilla, with U.S. 64 and this tour heading east to Tres

Piedras. It will take you more than an hour to drive from Tierra Amarilla to Tres Piedras over a well-maintained two-lane paved highway that many consider one of the prettiest in the state. We hope that you will take your time, picnic at one of the scenic overlooks, camp at Hopewell Lake, certainly pause once in a while to look down or up at what the volcanoes, glaciers, and upthrusts from the belly of the earth have created. If you are taking Tour Three during the winter months, you will have to forego the passage up and over the Brazos Mountains until next spring, because the highway department closes U.S. 64 once the snow becomes unmanageable.

Highway 64 crosses the entire northern tier of New Mexico, entering near Clayton on the eastern plains and leaving the state more than 400 miles later near Beklabito, on the Navajo Reservation. Tour Three will cross about a tenth of the splendid pathway. Shortly after leaving Tierra Amarilla, you feel yourself beginning to climb along this narrow gray ribbon that soon cuts through forests of ponderosa pine and Rocky Mountain juniper. You pass meadows and ranchland traversed in the winter by cross-country skiers and snowmobilers. In the autumn you might see the empty horse trailers of cowhands who are out riding in steep canyons and along piney ridges pursuing cattle during roundup. Occasionally a recalcitrant heifer will separate from its mother and lead everyone on a merry chase along the highway. As you reach the summit of the Brazos Range, scenic lookouts appear. Look down on the Chama Valley, find the volcanic cinder cones off to the northeast, and gaze all the way across to the Jemez Mountains. Do not miss the overlook that makes you think you could almost reach out and touch the Brazos Cliffs, which soar to an altitude of ten thousand feet and then drop down two thousand feet into the Brazos Box. Sheltered picnic tables at several of the overlooks provide the perfect excuse to pause awhile for a high-altitude snack. While it might seem that here you have reached the summit of this trip, you will wind and curve down, then up again to the summit of the lesser-known Tusas Range.

Although this journey is lovely during any

season (save winter, when it might be lovely, but is impassable and impossible), spring and autumn are favorite times to make the trip. Bright green aspen leaves quiver and dance during the winds of spring, and some of the mountain meadows are covered with tiny wild iris in early June. Late September finds each hillside splotched with deep green, then shimmering gold, then the startling oranges and reds of the scrub oaks. It is less likely that you will see wild animals—although bear, deer, and elk live here. However, you will frequently spy a hawk soaring across the empty sky. There are no towns from Tierra Amarilla to Tres Piedras, and only Hopewell Lake has campsites and fire pits. When you reach N.M. 111, at the curve that circumvents a meadow, you will have entered the Carson National Forest, and you will be less than ten miles from Tres Piedras and the trip south on U.S. 285. *(See Side Trip to Cañones Plaza and El Rito on page 92.)*

Tres Piedras signals the end of your passage on U.S. 64, which leaves you to traverse east across the Taos Plateau, crossing the Rio Grande Gorge Bridge north of Taos. Take U.S. 285 south to Ojo Caliente and San Juan Pueblo, roughly paralleling the route taken decades ago by the old Denver and Rio Grande Western Railroad. Tres Piedras is named for the granite rock, sometimes seen from the east as three distinct piles, on which it sits. A gas

Side Trip to Cañones Plaza and El Rito

Those adventurers who enjoy the challenge of driving across steep mountain terrain can take a side trip on N.M. 111, a one-lane dirt road that follows a series of streambeds ten miles to Cañones Plaza, picking up a paved road there that goes on to El Rito and Española. New Mexico 111 is somewhat dangerous in any weather; do not use this road if it has rained recently or looks like it may do so soon. Also, logging trucks consider the road their own, and we do not argue with logging trucks. However, for the fearless, the trip will prove exhilarating.

Thick forests of ponderosa pine cling to the mountain as you zigzag up and then down, pausing at three summits, each followed by an abrupt plunge. A skinny horse trail follows the streambed, sometimes veering off into meadows or favorite hunting spots. Forest Service signs announce rough passages back to Hopewell Lake or to Petaca, fourteen miles away. You will find many likely camping spots, although none is developed and none has water. Near the third summit, you will look down upon Cañones Plaza, a scattering of tin-roofed houses winking

station, a fancifully painted old schoolhouse, a few homes, a ranger station, some summer cabins, and a 180-degree view of the Taos Plateau and distant Sangre de Cristo Mountains—this is Tres Piedras.

As you drive down U.S. 285 toward Ojo Caliente and the terminus of Tour Three, you sweep across a high plateau that is flanked by mountains. Wheeler Peak, New Mexico's tallest mountain (13,161 feet), dominates the Taos and Truchas ranges of the Sangre de Cristos to the east. The foothills of the mountains that you just left, the Tusas and Brazos,

in a valley ringed by multiple mountain ranges.
Most of those who live here farm or log, or drive
out of the valley to work. There is a general store
with gas in Cañones Plaza.

New Mexico 111 becomes paved as it leaves
the mountains and heads south through the
valley to another, larger settlement, Vallecitos,
where the homes, most built in classic northern
New Mexico style, huddle next to each other
along the very narrow street that bisects the
village. The Rio Vallecitos, an active little stream
even in times of drought, accompanies you
through a series of narrow basins, across
meadows, to La Madera, where small farms and
neat vegetable gardens surround modest adobe
homes. Just beyond La Madera, turn left on
N.M. 554, leaving behind green valleys, entering
dry piñon forests, and passing through sandy
arroyos. In the distance, El Rito appears, a
comparatively large community, many of its
traditional homes restored and hidden behind
high adobe walls. Several small restaurants, a
store or two, a large Catholic church (San Juan
Nepomuceno), and the El Rito Branch of
Northern New Mexico Community College lend
El Rito an almost cosmopolitan air. New Mexico
554 leads you back to U.S. 84 and Española.

roll gently on the west. You are driving across
alluvial fans, perhaps over rocks similar to Precam-
brian samples that were found near here, some of
them more than 1,300 billion years old. You will
not be able to see the former roadbed of the
Denver and Rio Grande Western Railroad, but be
assured that its engines once chugged across this
countryside, stopping at a junction about twenty
miles south of Tres Piedras for passengers to
disembark. The travelers would then drive across
the plateau, wind down the steep banks of Rio

Grande Canyon, cross the Rio Grande, and head for Taos.

Stop in Ojo Caliente for any number of reasons. Perhaps for gas and a soda along the main highway. Or for a picnic beneath a cottonwood tree. Or take the small road in the center of the village across the Rio Vallecitos to Ojo Caliente Mineral Springs, a small resort built around a series of springs. From the most ancient times, those who traveled through this region stopped for a soothing bath. Ruins of pueblos on the surrounding mesas and Tewa Pueblo stories about their hero, Poseyemu, who sprang to life from these mineral-laden waters, attest to the importance of this site throughout history. Comanches, Utes, and Apaches also refreshed themselves in these waters. An ancient, often-argued theory claims that Cabeza de Baca, an early Spanish explorer, was especially entranced by the springs, "the greatest treasure that I have found these strange people to possess." A North American explorer, Zebulon Pike, was a prisoner of the Spanish who had arrested him for trespassing in 1807; he too remarked on the springs. Each spring at Ojo Caliente has a different mineral content. Soak in the pools that have small amounts of arsenic (water temperature 113°), or take a plunge in the "iron" pool where the water is 109°, or swim in the large outdoor pool. Those who operate the baths also invite you to quench your thirst with their spring water. If your body aches from driving, request a massage after your soak. You can also enjoy a meal, camp near the river, or stay at the hotel or bed-and-breakfast inn.

Refreshed by your bath, massage, and picnic, continue through the narrow, winding river valley to the intersection of U.S. 285 and N.M. 74. Turn right here and head back to Española. The journey—and what a journey it has been—is over.

TOUR FOUR
THE JEMEZ
MOUNTAINS

4

Places:	Albuquerque, Bernalillo, Zia, San Ysidro, Jemez, Bandelier National Monument, Los Alamos, San Ildefonso, Santa Fe, Albuquerque
Mileage:	Approximately two hundred miles, excluding side trips
Suggested travel time:	One or two days
Highways:	N.M. 448, N.M. 528, N.M. 44, N.M. 4, N.M. 502, I-25
Accommodations:	Albuquerque, Jemez Springs, La Cueva, Los Alamos, White Rock, Santa Fe, and Bernalillo
Camping:	Santa Fe National Forest campgrounds along N.M. 4, Fenton Lake, Santa Clara Canyon, Bandelier National Monument, and Bernalillo

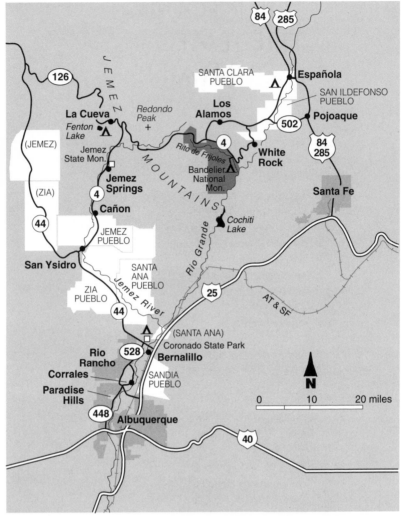

NOTE: Numerous campsites in Jemez Mountains (Santa Fe National Forest)

Short distances, plenty of amenities, never far from a city or an ancient habitation, a loop that can be done in a day—perhaps setting out from Albuquerque on a tour of Jemez Mountain treasures will appeal to you. Traveling between New Mexico's major population centers, you pass the ruins of long-vanished cities, trace ancient migration routes, and see living communities that have been in existence for over five hundred years.

The tour begins on the edge of the fertile Rio Grande Valley, crosses over to the smaller Jemez River, and ascends almost to its headwaters high in the old Jemez Mountains. You will see a cattle ranch in the middle of a spectacular volcanic crater, high tree-clad mountain passes, and the sharp tentacles of the Pajarito Plateau, and then steeply descend off the mesa back down to the Rio Grande. Magnificent ruins at Coronado and Bandelier await you, as do several Indian pueblos, the Jemez State Monument, and the city that gave birth to the nuclear age. Within a few miles you may pass carefully tended cornfields, centers of art and preservation, religious retreat houses, winter sports settings, or hunting and fishing sites that are an easy drive to—but still remote from—Albuquerque or Santa Fe.

The tour leaves Albuquerque via North Coors Boulevard (N.M. 448) on the booming West Side. Within a few miles north of the I-40 interchange, you will have passed the areas of major congestion. The black eyebrow of the West Mesa will be on your left for several miles now. Be sure to refer to the Albuquerque Tour (Tour Ten) to find out about the thousands of petroglyphs preserved here in the volcanic rock. Continue north until you reach the Corrales Shopping Center, at a large intersection where Corrales Bridge lies to the right and the new city of Rio Rancho is perched up on the hill to your left. Proceed straight here on into the old valley settlement of Corrales.

With its juxtaposition of the old and the new, of wealth and poverty, of the classic and the chic, of suburban and rural, Corrales remains typically New Mexican. Alfalfa fields, orchards, nurseries, and vineyards thrive amid elegant restaurants, inns, and crafts boutiques. Before long you will be able to spot a sampling of architectural varieties, from the basic L-shaped, flat-roofed adobes to Kansas-style farmhouses to modern high-peaked numbers that catch the eye and the sun, with an abundance of blue-trimmed Territorial-style windows throughout. The post office at the curve marks the present center of the village, and San Ysidro Church just beyond serves as a congregating point for religious and community functions.

Between the post office and the church, Los Colores is a textile museum specializing in rugs, blankets, and Mexican serapes. Open on weekend afternoons, it displays free to the public nearly two hundred of the colorful folk creations dating from 1750 to 1950.

A sign near the modern church directs you to the older San Ysidro Church, which is a short distance west on a gravel road. Across the ditch and around the bend, the well-preserved church, with classic cruciform design, tin roof, mud walls, and twin towers, awaits you. The comfortable old sanctuary has in recent years become a center for international folk music and dance, a community theater, as well as the site for an annual concert series under the auspices of the Corrales Cultural Arts Council. Venerable cottonwoods, irrigated

fields, and milk goats form the backdrop of the original church (now on the National Register of Historic Places), its newer community building next door, and the old cemetery across the road. San Isidro, patron saint of farmers, would be glad, we think, to see this building still a living part of the village.

The succession of old buildings, small farms, and pastures finally ends with a short climb west out of the valley. You will rejoin N.M. 528 at the River's Edge subdivision four miles south of the N.M. 44 intersection.

Coronado State Monument lies a mile east of the N.M. 528/44 junction. It is worth the short detour to visit this carefully preserved ruin, a city overlooking the Rio Grande dating from the 1400s, and temporary headquarters for Vasquez de Coronado during his pioneering explorations of the area in 1540–41. You can picnic and camp here, and enjoy listening to stories told by guides during summer evenings. At any time of the year, the self-guided tours and the reconstructions of agricultural, religious, and ceremonial life (including a *kiva* that contains one of the finest examples of prehistoric painting found in the United States) help give visitors an idea of the origins and early history of the people whose lands this tour encircles.

Head back west. A four-mile climb removes you completely from the long–settled valley of the Rio Grande. From certain spots near the top of the grade you can sight left and right along the line of ancient volcanoes that shaped the western side of this valley all the way downriver to Ladron Peak, seventy miles to the south.

As you angle in to the Jemez River, you will notice a sign for Santa Ana Pueblo, in existence at a location near here since 1693. Because of the danger of flooding, this site is closed to the public most of the year, and nearly all the pueblo residents live at Ranchitos along the Rio Grande and return here only for festivals. Your efforts to schedule a visit to the old pueblo can be rewarding. The calendar at the front of this book indicates the few times a year (including Christmas) when Santa Anans move back to the old village and welcome visitors.

Now the tour proceeds northwest up the Jemez drainage, characterized here by small cedars, clumps of *chamisa* and saltbush, walking-stick cactus, rocky arroyos, and the bunchgrass once dominant over all such shortgrass plains. Ahead are the green slopes, red cliffs, and the snowclad or cloud-covered peaks of the Jemez Mountains.

Suddenly, Zia Pueblo appears on the right, at the same time as you notice the newer houses along the highway. The old pueblo perches atop a lava hill with a church, water tower, and cluster of traditional stone houses overlooking the cornfields below. Zia has become famous for the boldly decorated pottery made here and for the sun symbol borrowed from an old pottery design that is now used as the official symbol for the state of New Mexico. Zia's traditions go back many centuries, its clans and religious life centered around the two *kivas* that work to maintain harmony within the community.

Fray Dominguez, official observer for the king of Spain, visited here in 1776 and reported a large, thick-walled, richly adorned church, the two small plazas open at their four corners, and the carefully constructed stone houses on the hill just as you see them today. Travelers one hundred years ago reported apples, peaches, plums, grapes, wheat, corn, chiles, and lots of watermelons—a greater variety of crops than the silty bottomland seems to support now. They recounted disputes with Navajos over livestock, troubles with other pueblos that go back to the time of the Pueblo Revolt, and Zia men who worked in nearby gypsum mines. Zia women still use powdered gypsum for the white ground on their pottery and distinguish their finely

4

crafted work with red sandstone and black volcanic inclusions—materials, as you will see on this tour, that are abundant. Because of Zia's relatively meager land holdings, both ceramics and painting continue as Important art forms. The pueblo's beautiful setting beneath the mountains, comfortably situated above the Jemez River, promotes a sense of well-being and peace in residents and visitors alike.

The old village, named for the farmers' patron saint, Ysidro, lies just a few miles north. Past the gypsum mine on the left, across the wide wash, San Ysidro maintains gas stations, stores, a school, and another "Corrales" of old and renovated houses, orchards, and farms. A winery and an attractive gift shop along N.M. 44 are evidence of the revival of local talent and enterprise. The town of Cuba, the turnoff to Chaco Canyon, and the cities of Aztec and Farmington lie ahead on N.M. 44. This tour of Jemez treasures turns right here, however, to follow N.M. 4 toward Redondo Peak, which has dominated the far northern skyline for the last several miles. Soon a post office and the small white San Ysidro Church appear on the right. As you cross the bridge, leaving the village behind, you will get a good look at the river that formed the little valley we are now entering.

The only surviving settlement from the original seven "pueblos de los Jemez" under Spanish authority, Jemez Pueblo thrives on both sides of the road. It is a town of many levels. Some of the houses occupy the higher ground on your right, but most of the population lives to the west, below the highway. A tour of the pueblo will take you up and down winding dirt roads, past fields, and old and new adobe houses. Near the western edge of town stands the old mission of San Diego de Jemez, freshly restuccoed, the locale of the San Diego Feast Day celebrated by the pueblo on November 12.

It seems natural that such a remarkable settlement, which has been on this site for over five hundred years and continues a way of life that has flourished here for nearly a millennium, should attract curious non-Indians. It is important to realize, however, how unlikely it is that a small pueblo can be a living museum for the world. Like all the surviving New Mexico pueblos, Jemez has artists, craftspeople, farmers and herders, builders, teachers, Ph.D.s, police, and religious leaders. Despite its enviable self-sufficiency, Jemez still must deal with most of the same challenges as the rest of late twentieth-century America—among them the preservation of fertile land and good water, the health of its people, and the education and safety of its children. Bear in mind that most pueblos are open to the general public on their feast days, and it is generally best to visit any pueblo when visitors are expected and welcomed.

Just north of Jemez Pueblo, N.M. 290 branches east toward camping and fishing sites in the mountains. The tour continues up the valley. Fields, gardens, old homesteads, bread and produce stands, huge cottonwoods, and red cliffs make this a memorable trip at any time of year. Jemez Pueblo's Red Rock park is the scene in summer of an arts and crafts fair. The pueblo has built ramadas for vendors to sell fry bread and frito pies to die for. It's almost a tradition to stop here for a snack on summer weekends. In autumn, however, tourists plan special excursions for the pleasure of seeing the cottonwoods, shady in sandy groves, turning golden under the October sky.

The Jemez Pueblo Reservation ends at the tiny settlement of Cañon. Trading posts at the edges of reservations have been a feature of the Southwest, for better or worse, since territorial days. At their best, trading posts have long provided a place for the Indian and the non-Indian worlds to meet and freely exchange goods and ideas. This seems especially true at the Jemez Cañon Trading Post, where the owners delight in sharing with visitors their admiration for their neighbors and introducing newcomers to the pottery and painting from Jemez Pueblo. They will tell you, too, about specific artists and their work, and about how to cross the river and climb the mesa to find the ruin of one of the old pueblos mentioned in early Spanish accounts.

The bridge across the Jemez River here invites you on a side trip of a different sort. A logging railroad that once carried timber down to sawmills in Albuquerque and El Paso crossed the river here, also, to wind its way up Guadalupe Canyon. Tunnels blasted by the railroad builders still attract sightseers up pretty N.M. 485 to campgrounds and trails for skiing and hiking.

Soon the valley begins to narrow and the grade to steepen. At several points along the river, there are paved picnic spots, access to fishing sites and at least one campground. Some are accessible to people with disabilities. By the time you reach Jemez Springs, the forest comes down the canyon sides to the river, opening occasionally into small fields and pastures. Jemez Springs, named for the hot mineral pools, now specializes in hospitality. A bed-and-breakfast, a deli, restaurants, antique shops, a bar, and a bathhouse featuring hot springwater containing twenty different minerals now adorn its main street, while three religious orders maintain retreats nearby.

The ancient village of Guisewa once thrived just upriver. Protected since 1970 as Jemez State Monument, the old Indian settlement and its Franciscan-style church give us some clues as to how life was in this valley before and after the arrival of the Spanish. Well-marked trails guide visitors around the pueblo, which has been preserved and restored as much as possible after years of abuse and neglect. Early photographs trace the destruction and more recent attempts at reconstruction at the site.

Fields, pastures, and exposed canyon walls have by now completely given way to the narrow forested valley and its boulder-strewn mountain stream. The agricultural yields to the recreational, the pastoral to hunting. Hot springs, high-country trails, fishing and hunting, and cross-country skiing lure visitors to the upper Jemez Valley year round. The Jemez Ranger Station has information on numerous hiking trails and can also provide tours to other hidden ruins in the area.

Centuries of mineral deposits—those same salts that flavor the hot springs—created the Soda Dam, a huge dike that appears to block the highway. This stopping place is usually crowded on weekends with people clambering over the rocks or dipping their toes in the mini-hotspring across the road. A popular picnic spot is Battleship Rock, whose prow dominates the narrow valley. From here, a not-too-strenuous hike leads up to Jemez Falls and to more hot springs and magnificent views.

A last steep highway ascent brings you out of the valley altogether and onto the rugged slopes of

Redondo Peak and the vicinity of Valle Grande. At La Cueva you can buy a fishing license and get information on Fenton Lake State Park, a short drive to the west. Here you might also inquire about road conditions along primitive N.M. 126 across to Seven Springs Fish Hatchery and to the San Pedro Parks Wilderness Area. Keep to the right on N.M. 4 here, which doubles back to the southeast. If you're not quite ready to leave the Jemez Valley yet, the Jemez Canyon Overlook and trail offer views back over the canyon you just left.

Along N.M. 4, several pullouts and forest trail and campground signs invite you to explore the Jemez backcountry. Jemez Falls campground has paths to an overlook of the falls. The hardy can climb down to the water and take a dip in the icy pools. The East Fork trail follows the ridge of a dramatic box canyon deep into the forest.

After several long ups and downs, you're at last over the brim of Valle Grande, the ancient caldera. Words seem inadequate to describe this landscape and the size of the caldera. It's a million years old, formed by a series of collapsed volcanos. It's beautiful in any season, meadow-like with the basin surrounded by rocky pine and aspen covered slopes. It's a privately owned ranch, grazing cattle helping to provide a sense of scale. The road makes a generous loop around the southern rim, giving you numerous views and perspectives. Beware of the lovely vistas as you negotiate the several tight curves that drop you down off the eastern rim.

Music Camp

New Mexico 502 heads north to Los Alamos proper at the edge of the national laboratory fence. For the trip into Frijoles Canyon, stay on N.M. 4 and follow the signs to Bandelier National Monument. A few miles down, across the scars of the 1980 Jemez fire, you arrive at the monument entrance, and then a short drive with sweeping panoramas of the Pajarito Plateau brings you to the monument headquarters. This huge archaeological site is so well documented and accessible that we will confine our guidebookish advice to a few superlatives. Whether you allow a few hours or several days, Bandelier can amaze, delight, and instruct people of all ages. Nearest at hand is the museum and slide show; then there is an hour-and-a-half trail among ceremonial *kivas* and cliff dwellings (hand over hand on sturdy ladders, if you wish). Farther afield, trails lead to the waterfalls down Frijoles Canyon, across mesas to the shrine of the Stone Lions and the Painted Cave, around to ruins of dozens of smaller villages, and past geologic as well as archaeological wonders. A developed campsite offers delightful surroundings and splendid views of the plateau.

The entire region around the national monument was once buried a thousand feet deep by ash from two immense volcanic eruptions. Compacted into easily workable and highly erodible rock, this material's porosity explains both the hand-carved cliff dwellings and the many deep gashes cut into the plateau by the forces of nature. The information brochures are not exaggerating when they tell you to take plenty of water and warn you that hikes over the highland areas of the monument will be interrupted repeatedly by dramatic descents into deep canyons followed soon after by long climbs back to the mesa top.

The spirit of pioneer anthropologist Adolf Francis Bandelier, who studied these ruins in the 1880s, pervades these canyons and mesas. The same questions that baffled him still interest thousands of yearly visitors to the monument: Where did the original residents come from, when, and why? How did they live, farm, get water, and hunt? When and why did they leave and who are their descendants still in New Mexico? Bandelier's hosts from nearby Cochiti Pueblo first brought him to Frijoles Canyon in the late fall of 1880. At that time anthropologists were just beginning to form a picture of the ancient city dwellers now called the Anasazi. Bandelier wrote extensive journals documenting his travels and hardships as, with his pueblo guides, he began to piece together their story in this remarkable land.

Leaving Bandelier you will have the choice of continuing northeast on N.M. 4 past White Rock and Tsankawi, a small, unexcavated ruin, and down off the mesa toward the Rio Grande, or of backtracking the short distance to follow the tour up to the City on the Hill, the Birthplace of the Nuclear Age, the brave new world of Los Alamos. The miles of chainlink fence with large, drab buildings behind will remind you about the origins of Los Alamos as you approach by climbing up wooded canyons with splendid views of the peaks beyond. New Mexico 502, the main street through Los Alamos, takes you into the commercial and cultural center of town, where there is a choice of restaurants, hotels, museums, and sports outfitters.

Everyone in Los Alamos knows Fuller Lodge, at 2132 Central Avenue, and that is an excellent place to begin your visit. The tourist center and nearby historical museum will orient you to the past and present, while the old lodge, with its grounds and pond, embodies the extensive lore of this newest of cities: the original Los Alamos Ranch School for boys begun here during the First World War; this very building, designed by John Gaw Meem, a dining and recreation hall for Ranch School boys which, with the stone addition, became part of the Manhattan Project in 1943 for the scientists working on the atomic bomb. Older residents of Los Alamos remember the hastily constructed barracks, the mud, the secrecy, the cold and starry nights, and the narrow bridge and security gate that admitted only those selected for the project. Some are familiar with the personalities—Einstein's letter to FDR which began it all, the conflicting egos of Edward Teller and Robert Oppenheimer, and the embittered Ranch School director, who was uprooted from the place he loved and watched his former students take jobs with the very defense establishment that had displaced him.

More recent lore recounts the waves of immigrants from all over the world who came to work at the well-financed lab; the relaxation of access; the opening of the road via the back gate up from the Jemez Valley; the basic government housing that evolved into comfortable, tastefully furnished homes; the new housing developments crawling out over the mesas and down to White Rock. Schools and churches appeared. So did an excellent public ski hill, a branch university, chamber of commerce, the Little Theater, and the Fuller Lodge Art Center. In the meantime, wartime pioneers including Niels Bohr, Stan Ulam, Kenneth Bainbridge, Enrico Fermi, and Sir James Chadwick gradually gave way to other figures—cold-war hardware technicians, researchers in exotic fields such as laser fusion, cosmology, and dynamical systems. A story from the 1970s has Mitchell Feigenbaum, one of the founders of the new science of "chaos," experimenting with a twenty-six-hour day. The rather disheveled form of Feigenbaum, a dynamicist who studied aperiodicity and turbulence, and who discovered constant patterns in very different natural phenomena, is remembered walking the pathways of Los Alamos, chain-smoking, on a sleeping, waking, and working schedule wildly out of phase with the sun and with the rhythm of the modern workaday world.

Of the thousands who have migrated to Los Alamos since the beginning of the Manhattan Project, many have followed their careers elsewhere and many have remained relatively unaffected by their strange new surroundings. Numerous others, however, have fallen in love with the high, thin air, the snowy winters, the slopes and peaks of the Jemez, the mesas, cliffs, and ancient ruins, and the neighboring pueblos and old Hispanic towns. These people have contributed to the life of New Mexico by means of the fine arts, through their involvement in historical, civic, and ecological activities, and by voicing their desire for harmony among nations.

A walking tour will take you in easy stages from the Historical Museum among all the original places just mentioned—including the Arts Center, Ashley Pond, ruins dating from the thirteenth century, and the more modern county and community buildings. At 15th and Central, a brand-new pride of Los Alamos, the Bradbury Science Museum, offers displays, demonstrations, rare early film footage of the wartime scientists, and hands-on activities for all ages. For outdoor enthusiasts, bicycling, skiing, rock climbing, golf, fishing, cross-country skiing, and white-water rafting opportunities lie close at hand. At this point, especially if you are traveling on a short winter day, you must decide whether to push on for Santa Fe or Albuquerque, or stay the night here, treat yourself to day or night views from Overlook Park in White Rock and leave more sightseeing for tomorrow.

When you are ready to leave Los Alamos, either Central Avenue or Trinity will take you past the old main gate and watchtower, and down the twisting hairpin curves off the mesa via N.M. 502. Pullouts midway along the descent give stunning views of the Rio Grande Valley below and the Sangre de Cristo Mountains opposite. Near the bottom, N.M. 4 from White Rock and Bandelier merges in from the south. A few miles farther along, N.M. 30 heads north towards Española. This is the road that provides access to the Puye Cliff Dwellings and to Santa Clara Pueblo, as well as to camping, fishing, and picnicking sanctuaries in Santa Clara Canyon, all described in the Rio Arriba Tour (Tour Three).

Continuing on N.M. 502, another short drive takes you to the famous Otowi Crossing of the Rio Grande. This is the site of extensive multistoried pueblo ruins that later became a freight stop for the Denver and Rio Grande Western Railroad (D&RGW); a one-lane highway bridge and gauging station for the Rio Grande's flow (still standing south of the present bridge); and a remarkable tearoom that has also become part of Los Alamos lore. Employed by the Ranch School, Edith Warner came to Otowi in 1928 and rented a house by the river from the family of San Ildefonso potter Maria Martinez. She befriended D&RGW railroad workers, San Ildefonso Indians, and scientists traveling to and from Los Alamos. The story of her wonderful hospitality has inspired several accounts; one of the most enduring is *The House at Otowi Bridge*, by Peggy Pond Church, the daughter of Ashley Pond, who founded the Los Alamos Ranch School.

Just across the river, but still under the spell of the Jemez Mountains, lies San Ildefonso Pueblo. The village perhaps migrated from the Otowi site west of the river during the 1400s. Its inhabitants certainly did retreat to the top of nearby Black

4

Pottery from Santa Clara & San Ildefonso

Mesa during times of conflict with the Spanish. But since the 1700s, the pueblo has shared the flat floodplain with cottonwoods, pastures, and cornfields. Most pueblos are small enough to take on the character of their settings and not dominate the landscape as most modern cities do: thus Zia's lava hill, Jemez' stair steps, San Felipe's narrow strip between river and mesa wall, and San Ildefonso's broad open bottomland.

A small tourist center, shop, and museum await you at the entrance to the pueblo. Here, amid old photographs and artifacts from the last century, you can learn something about the more recent history of the community (for example, why it has two plazas, each with its own *kiva*), about the ceremonial calendar, and events open to the public. You may marvel at that most famous of San Ildefonsans, Maria Martinez, whose style of hand-built matte-black design on polished blackware pottery commands worldwide respect. Small shops near the plaza sell the remarkable jewelry, paintings, and ceramics that this one small village produces. Whether you buy anything or stay for a ceremonial, San Ildefonso is a great place to relax for a moment and admire the people, the past, and the surroundings.

Back near the highway on the edge of the pueblo is the privately owned Cottonwood Trading Post. Carrying on a one-hundred-year-old tradition at the edge of the reservation, the store stocks staples, raw materials for craftspeople, and Indian arts and crafts.

The intersection of N.M. 502 with U.S. 285 here ends the tour of "The Jemez." You have circled an immense volcanic mountain, gazed upon some of New Mexico's best selections of landscape, and met people who represent the state's proud heritage of cultural diversity. We leave you now with choices to make. Please refer to Tour Five for travel to Taos and more of northern New Mexico's mountain villages. Consult Tour Twelve for Santa Fe's restaurants, shops, galleries, and museums. If you are returning to Albuquerque, keep in mind three choices of routes—I-25 down the Rio Grande alongside Cochiti, Santo Domingo, San Felipe, and Sandia pueblos; over the mountains through old mining towns via N.M. 14; or from Lamy across the high intermountain plain on U.S. 285 and N.M. 41.

TOUR FIVE
THE HIGH ROAD AND THE LOW ROAD

5

Places: Santa Fe, Chimayó, Peñasco,
Ranchos de Taos, Velarde,
Española, Santa Fe

Mileage: Approximately 150 miles,
excluding side trips

Suggested
travel time: One or two days, in addition to
time for Taos and Santa Fe

Highways: N.M. 590, U.S. 84/285, N.M. 503,
N.M. 76, N.M. 75, N.M. 518, N.M.
68, N.M. 389, N.M. 74, N.M. 68,
N.M. 76, N.M. 106, U.S. 84/285

Accommodations: Hotels and motels in Santa Fe,
Chimayó, Taos, Española; bed-and-
breakfast accommodations in Santa
Fe, Taos, Chimayó, Truchas, and
Dixon

Camping: Near Santa Fe, at Nambe Lake and
Santa Cruz Lake, in the Santa Fe
and Kit Carson National Forests,
and at Rio Grande Gorge State Park

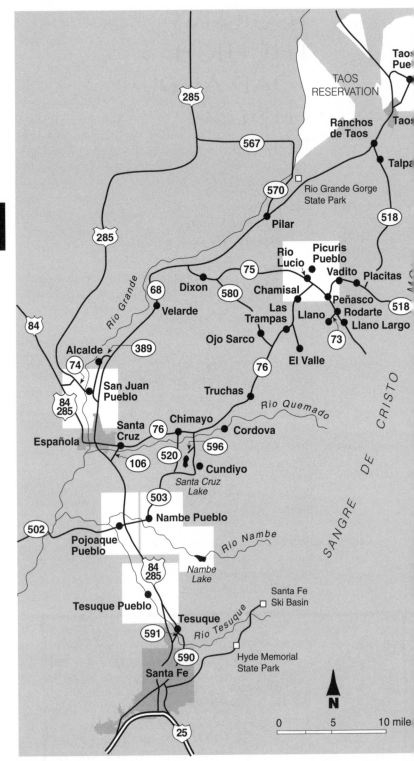

NOTE: Numerous campsites in Carson National Forest and Santa Fe National Forest

Whether on a breezy, hot summer day or on a stormy, cold day in winter, a drive from Santa Fe to Taos and back brings many rewards. The cool mountain villages along the High Road give relief from the summer's heat; snow-covered peaks loom large in the clear winter air; in between, the light green of aspen leaves in early spring or their brilliant yellow sheen in fall will charm you as you wander past places where life appears to have changed little over the centuries. That is just a fleeting observation, of course: The weavers who have held forth in Chimayó for eight generations attach their labels to their rugs with an electric heating gun; the tortilla factory in Peñasco is a clanking, automated affair; the wines of Dixon are pressed into polyolefin casks. Perhaps it is this mix of old and new that appeals so much—the microphone in the Iglesia de la Santa Cruz in front of the venerable polychromed *reredos* or the Kawasaki motorcycle outside the old adobe home close to the precipice in Truchas.

The High Road to Taos, the first half of your tour, was not entirely paved until the 1960s; the paving has accelerated changes that have occurred in the high, little villages. The Low Road, on which you will return from Taos, runs near the Rio Grande, through farming villages that also have changed with the passage of time, accepting an influx of artists and craftspeople to complement their agricultural production. This has been one of New Mexico's most popular tourist journeys for decades, but even when the crowds seem to press in upon you, as they may in Santa Fe or Taos, in the campgrounds in the Sangre de Cristo Mountains or the Santuario in Chimayó, a mountain trail or a back road a very short distance away will grant you solitude.

You will begin your escape at Santa Fe's bustling plaza. Head north on Washington Street, past the stylish boutiques and the screaming-pink Scottish Rite Temple. Shortly beyond all that pinkness is Hyde Park Road, leading to the Santa Fe Ski Basin. Seventeen convoluted but well-paved miles later, you can be twenty degrees cooler and four thousand feet higher—ski lifts will carry you to above eleven thousand feet. Trails lead in many directions from the well-appointed campground. From here you can spend an afternoon climbing Santa Fe

Baldy or a week exploring the magnificent Pecos Wilderness (information and the permit required for overnight hikes can be obtained at the Forest Service office in Santa Fe). Warmer and closer to the capital's attractions is the Hyde Memorial State Park campground five miles up the road.

Beyond the Scottish Rite Temple, the street name changes to Bishop's Lodge Road—this route was taken before you by Archbishop Jean Baptiste Lamy as he sought refuge from his labors in Santa Fe by traveling to his gardens near the village of Tesuque. The hills of northern Santa Fe were then uninhabited; now hundreds of tan adobe dwellings blend with the rocky soil, the piñons, and the junipers on the hillsides.

The village of Tesuque lies alongside a creek lined with more adobe homes and condominiums. Artists have long resided in this little community. Tesuque's unusual galleries include the extensive outdoor sculpture collection at the Shidoni Gallery and Foundry whose tours include dramatic pourings of molten bronze into intricately prepared molds.

The west bank of the same modest creek, now grown into the Rio Tesuque several miles down-stream, is the site for Tesuque Pueblo. A conservative band of less than seven hundred Tewas lives in blocks of adobe homes, some stuccoed, some mud-covered, and many two stories high, around a dusty plaza. The tall church of San Diego opens onto the plaza.

Many Tesuque dwellers are farmers; others are employed in nearby Santa Fe and Los Alamos. The tribe operates some businesses on its reservation: a campground and recreational vehicle park adjacent to the aptly-named Camel Rock alongside U.S. 84/ 285, and a bingo parlor not far away. Almost all traces of another tribal venture have now disappeared. In 1970, the tribe concluded a ninety-nine-year lease with a development company that put up sales offices and billboards on the highway, preparing to construct a large subdivision. Sixty tribe members were joined by environmental groups and Santa Fe city and county officials in opposing the development. Within three years, the gaudily painted sales booth was in ruins and the lease had been canceled.

The Tesuque you see now dates to 1694, when it was reestablished after the Spanish retook New Mexico. The tribe had figured prominently in the leadership of the Pueblo Revolt of 1680; the Spanish priest Juan Bautista Pío and another Spaniard were killed in the pueblo during the August night before the revolt began. Two Tesuque men coordinated the first strikes of the revolt, carrying news on foot from pueblo to pueblo.

Beyond Camel Rock, you will pass several other businesses before entering Pojoaque (pronounced po-hwakee) Pueblo land. You need not spend much time, as we did, searching for the pueblo. While you can drive through the tribal trailer park or the small shopping center, the Pojoaque tribe, now numbering fewer than five hundred members, has no plaza surrounded by homes, few tribal ceremonies, or traditional crafts. Like Tesuque, Pojoaque participated in the Pueblo Revolt in 1680. When the Spanish returned after twelve years of exile at Paso del Norte, they punished the people of Pojoaque, sending them scattering. Five families returned in 1706; the pueblo fluctuated in size and then disappeared in the early twentieth century. Since its resettlement in 1934, the pueblo has had more of a business than a cultural designation.

Just beyond the Pueblo Shopping Center, bear right, while N.M. 502 (and Tour Four) head east for Los Alamos and the Jemez Mountains. This curve takes you over the Rio Nambe bridge; follow the Rio Nambe east along N.M. 503. Not far up the road you will see the large, pleasingly simple, adobe Sacred Heart Church on top of a knoll. Turn right past the church, following the dirt roads east through the settlement of Nambe until you reach the pueblo. The tribal government occupies the most prominent buildings north of the small plaza. The Church of Saint Francis of Assisi is a modern jewel, a shell-shaped adobe with heavy, exposed, square beams. Several Nambe craftspeople construct pottery; some use the micaceous clay more typical of the pueblos to the north, such as Taos, while others adapt blackware designs more typical of neighboring San Ildefonso and Santa Clara pueblos. Farther up the valley, the tribe operates the Nambe Falls Campground, encouraging fishing in the three small lakes above the falls.

Head back toward Pojoaque and then turn right when you reach N.M. 503 again. You will climb past more sandstone structures reminiscent of Camel Rock as you go northeast into the foothills of the Sangre de Cristo Mountains. Perched on a cliff, squeezing the road on both sides, the hamlet of Cundiyó looks as if its old buildings might topple into the Rio Frijoles at any moment. Several miles beyond it, N.M. 596 will take you 1.5 steep miles to the shore of Santa Cruz Lake, a pristine reservoir set deep in a canyon among high tan walls. A small Bureau of Land Management campground and picnic area welcome you at the end of the road. Beyond Santa Cruz Lake, N.M. 503 descends again into a small settlement along the Rio Quemado, just east of Chimayó on N.M. 76. The narrow valley of the little river is carpeted with fruit trees; late in summer the fruit stands will open up, offering apples, peaches, and vegetables direct from orchards and gardens.

Chimayó is the center of the traditional handcraft business that continues to flourish in these mountains. Weaving shops in the little town contain several large wooden looms, operated by townspeople, but many of the rugs and woven vests on sale here come from the people of Chimayó and nearby towns, who have been producing blankets and rugs within their homes for generations. The old plaza of Chimayó lies south of the road, behind the weaving shops. It is surrounded still by very old adobe dwellings. Less than a mile farther south, along N.M. 520 in the tiny settlement of El Potrero, the Santuario de Chimayó reposes in a shady dell.

Santuario de Chimayó

The *santuario* has been famous for its sacred earth since before a church was built there. Legend has it that nearby Pueblo Indians relied on the healing powers of the dirt before the Spanish arrived in the late seventeenth century. In 1813, a leading Chimayó citizen, Bernardo Abeyta, asked permission to build a chapel on the site, naming it the Chapel of Our Lord of Esquipulas. Why Abeyta named the structure after a healing shrine in

Esquipulas, Guatemala, is a matter of conjecture. You can walk into the chapel, admire the lovely painted *reredos* and *bultos* on its walls, and then enter the small side room, where discarded crutches and braces outline a room enclosing the hole in the floor from which all can take the healing earth. Every year during Holy Week, thousands of pilgrims make their way to the *santuario,* some to pray for healing, some to fulfill a vow made to God for a favor granted.

Across a small plaza from the *santuario,* you may sometimes visit another privately built chapel, the shrine of the Santo Niño de Atocha. This sainted child from a town in Spain was venerated for years in the mountain villages. A settlement ten miles away, near Española, was founded with the name Santo Niño in 1864.

Back to the east again, on N.M. 76, you will have another chance to buy summertime fruit and vegetables or autumn's chile before heading up the long, steep, shadeless sandy hills to Truchas. About halfway up the slope, two small roads seem to fall off the right side of the highway into the town of Córdova in the valley of the Rio Quemado. Córdova is famous for woodcarving; among the striking wooden creations are small aspen birds, carts bearing Doña Sebastiana, the icon of death, and *nacimientos* depicting the birth of Christ. Descendants of the most famous carver of the area, José María López, and other villagers display inviting signs outside their homes. The reactions of the village elders to the profound changes that have occurred within their lifetimes have been preserved in words and pictures in psychologist Robert Coles's *The Old Ones of New Mexico.* Beyond Córdova, up a long road, is the Borrego Mesa Campground and the trail up the Rio Medio to the Truchas Peaks, which are easily visible from the entire area.

Truchas is an old town, dating back to 1752, and it sits on the edge of a cliff, its original two plazas unchanged centuries later. Aging adobe buildings, including a general store and a small café, look as if a strong push would send them cascading into the valley below. Above and to the north of the town are wide fields, beautifully green in spring, reaching right to the slopes of the Sangre de Cristos, with Truchas Peak, second highest in

New Mexico (13,102 feet) towering above the first ridge. Below the town, the Rio Grande Valley and the Jemez Mountains beyond complete the magnificent tableau. Robert Redford directed the 1980s filming in Truchas of John Nichols's classic comic tragedy, *The Milagro Beanfield War,* hiring many of the town's population as actors and extras.

Another farming village, Ojo Sarco, meanders along the Rio Sarco west of N.M. 76. In modern Spanish, *ojo* means "eye," while in the Spanish of the sixteenth and seventeenth centuries, it also denoted a spring. People of the Hispanic mountain villages, virtually isolated from the rest of the world for hundreds of years, maintained many archaic words and phrases in their language far into the twentieth century.

Similarly, Hispanics developed their own observances of Catholicism. In many villages you can see the *moradas* of the Penitente movement. *La Fraternidad Piadosa de Nuestro Padre Jesús Nazareno* (The Pious Fraternity of Our Father Jesus Nazarene), or *Los Hermanos Penitentes,* flourished in these mountain villages after the departure of the Franciscans from New Mexico in about 1780. The lay brotherhood maintained chapels, or *moradas,* in most of the northern villages (although Albuquerque and other larger towns also have *moradas*). Membership in the frequently maligned Penitente societies included many of the leading citizens of the towns in much the same way as community leaders might join a service club today (Bernardo Abeyta was the *hermano mayor* of the Chimayó *morada*). The *hermanos* were best known for their Holy Week activities. In some places, these culminated in the self-flagellation of the members during their march to the reenactment of the Crucifixion of Christ by one of the members. Bishop Lamy attempted to extinguish the practices of this group; only in 1947 did Archbishop Edward Byrne reverse the stand, honoring the Penitentes for their devotion and allowing them to carry out their ceremonies with the proviso that injury no longer occurred. The Penitente Brotherhood continues to draw followers, some of whom travel great distances to participate in seasonal ceremonies and affirm their devotion to their religion and traditions.

If you are truly adventurous and have a dry day and a high vehicle, drive west through Ojo Sarco, along the stream, the Cañada de Ojo Sarco. A beautiful, deserted dirt road will take you past streams and mesas and improbable rock formations down to the town of Dixon.

One valley to the north of Ojo Sarco, the village of Las Trampas displays its gem, the Church of San José de Gracia. San José parishioners and architects Nathaniel Owings, John Gaw Meem, and Alan McNown saved the historic church from destruction at the hands of the state highway department in 1966. They then rebuilt the church and its twin belfries, basing the reconstruction on an old photograph. Beautifully carved and painted vigas, thick adobe walls, and a legendary bell, María del Refugio, are features of the lovely building. As in many New Mexico villages, you may visit the church with the permission of the village's *mayordomo*. Inquire for the *mayordomo* in the little store across from the church.

As you leave Las Trampas, a glance to the right can reward you with a view of a small log flume carrying precious mountain water to the fields below. The importance of water to the villages' agricultural livelihood is obvious not only in Nichols's *Milagro Beanfield War* but also in his sequel, *The Magic Journey,* Frank Waters's earlier work, *People of the Valley,* and William de Buys and Alex Harris's recent account, *River of Traps.* Summer rains and winter snow in these mountain villages may seem plentiful to the inundated hiker or cross-country skier, but the fields prosper only by virtue of the irrigation water. Those who live here have become expert in using every drop.

Past another small town, Chamisal, N.M. 76 ends in a pastoral setting along the Rio Peñasco. Half a mile to the west on N.M. 75, you enter the pueblo of Picurís. From the hill above the pueblo, you will see three large buildings: the tribal governmental building, behind it the Church of San Lorenzo, and to the right the tribal museum, restaurant, and store. Visit the museum first—you must obtain escorted or self-guided tour permits here.

The history of Picurís parallels that of Nambe, Tesuque, and Pojoaque to the extent that this now-tiny pueblo was much larger until the Pueblo

5

Revolt. After the reconquest and an unsuccessful attempt to throw off Spanish rule again in 1696, the pueblo was abandoned; the population in 1706 when the last Picurís returned to their mountain fastness was only one-tenth that of the 1680 estimate.

Your tour will take you to several *kivas* up the hill from the museum, and to the impressive adobe walls of the Church of San Lorenzo, now being reconstructed by pueblo residents and outside volunteers after it collapsed in 1986. A small lake outside the picture windows of the restaurant beckons you to fish.

A few miles east up N.M. 75 you will come to the first buildings of Peñasco, a long, linear town made of several villages grown together. Abandoned movie theaters, mercantile establishments, and auto dealerships attest to Peñasco's past as a regional trading center. Several factors have led to the depopulation of these mountain villages and the loss of most of their businesses. The drafting of villagers into the armed services during World Wars I and II opened new vistas for many of them, while war industries increased job opportunities in Española, Los Alamos, Albuquerque, and Santa Fe. Improved roads and increased vehicle ownership took village dwellers into larger towns for shopping and entertainment. Although Peñasco is home to the only high school between Española and Taos, young people seldom stay in the mountains beyond graduation. On the other hand, many residents of Española, Santa Fe, and Albuquerque look to their mountain roots and return home for holidays and vacations.

Above Peñasco are three smaller villages, Rodarte (known for its woodcarving), Llano, and Llano Largo, arrayed along the Rio Santa Barbara, taking advantage of the river and the broad valley's farmland. At the end of the road past Llano Largo, you will reach the Forest Service's beautiful river-edge Santa Barbara Campground. The campground is a stepping-off point for splendid hikes (with a permit obtained at the ranger station just north of Peñasco) into the Truchas Peaks portion of the Pecos Wilderness.

Beyond two more small towns, Vadito and Placitas, N.M. 75 comes to an end at N.M. 518.

Turn left here and be prepared to climb sharply up U.S. Hill. Just below the crest on the far side, a turnout affords you a view of the mountains to the east. Mountain men trapping here in the nineteenth century sometimes boisterously disrupted the Taos trade fairs, and occasionally married into local families. One of these, the Frenchman Carlos Beaubien, married Taoseña Guadalupe Miranda in 1841. The two were granted title to what became known as the Maxwell Land Grant, a huge tract of land that extended beyond the northern and eastern horizons of all that you can see and was at its time the largest land grant in the Western Hemisphere.

You will now slowly descend the north slope of U.S. Hill through the National Forest. Large gateposts announce Fort Burgwin Research Center, an outpost of Dallas's Southern Methodist University. Looking like a fort from Davy Crockett's day, the reconstructed buildings of vertical, unpeeled poles have been rebuilt upon foundations left behind by the U.S. Army a century ago. Ruins of an abandoned pueblo are a major focus of students' activity, while visitors are invited to public lectures, concerts, and plays each summer. Fort Burgwin has entered into an agreement that will allow the Forest Service to build a visitor center on research center land along the highway.

From here, N.M. 518 descends gently along the course of the Rio Grande del Rancho to the towns of Talpa and Ranchos de Taos, just south of Taos itself. You will enjoy driving the dirt back roads of these small communities. Many artists and craftspeople live here, some displaying their works outside their studios and homes. The famous Church of Saint Francis of Assisi sits just south of the junction of N.M. 518 with N.M. 68, the "Low Road to Taos." This sculptural structure has inspired artists for decades. Most of the Taos school of painters and many photographers cut their New Mexico teeth on the church at Ranchos. Long and narrow, with small transeptal chapels, the interior of the church contains beautifully carved vigas and corbels and fine paintings of New Mexican and European origin. It is the exterior, however, that brings out the Instamatics and Hasselblads. Massive walls, four feet thick, are supported by huge adobe

Virgin of Guadalupe wood carving

buttresses. The whole is covered with the traditional mud adobe plaster, a work of love for the parishioners, as it must be frequently renewed. You may attend Sunday Mass here if you wish, becoming a part of the historic parish if only for a moment.

Those who plan to visit Taos should proceed north on N.M. 68. This small town and artists' colony, with its many boutiques, restaurants, and galleries, the Indian pueblo nearby, and Wheeler Peak (Tour Eight) draws crowds throughout the year. The excellent expert skiing at Taos Ski Valley and deep snow on the slopes of New Mexico's highest peak are major attractions during the long winter–spring ski season.

South from Ranchos de Taos, N.M. 68 can speed you back toward Española and Santa Fe if you cannot spend time exploring the beauties and detours surrounding you. Once reachable from north, south, or west, the Rio Grande Gorge State Park must now be approached from Pilar, twenty miles south of Ranchos de Taos, or from El Rito, west of the Rio Grande. From Pilar, take the dusty, graveled N.M. 570 along the east side of the river north to the campgrounds and the bridge. Fishermen occupy many campground sites, and rafters, in season, drift or hurtle by on their exciting trips down the river.

Pilar and Rinconada are the only settlements for twenty miles south of Ranchos de Taos. Just beyond a rural clinic, N.M. 75 angles off to the east along the Rio de Peñasco. The pretty little town of Dixon straddles the road just beyond the intersection. You will find it a pleasant, slow-paced place to stop. On a recent visit, we talked with a potter at a combined gallery and winery and watched a sculptor cutting stone in front of his atelier. The annual pre-Christmas open house, sponsored by thirty or so artists and craftspeople, offers the chance to visit studios, chat with their owners, and make holiday purchases. Local rock is used in many of Dixon's houses; two especially notable dwellings along the Rio Grande have been painstakingly assembled from small river-rounded stones.

Just below Dixon on N.M. 68, the Embudo Gauging Station measures the depth of the Rio Grande, again attesting to the continuing importance of water in New Mexico, especially in the Rio Grande. The river, which arises in Colorado and receives tributaries all along its course through New Mexico, nourishes a green stripe that cuts through the state from north to south. Paul Horgan's history, *Great River: The Rio Grande in North American History,* and Laura Gilpin's photographic essay, *The Rio Grande, River of Destiny,* tell in word and picture of New Mexico's dependence on the Rio Grande's sustaining flow.

Below the gauging station, a fine new bridge will attract you to the site of the old Embudo Train Station. The tracks are gone, but a water tower remains, still in good condition, along with several moldering and several restored buildings now used for a gallery and a restaurant. The Chili Line, as it was called, was a narrow-gauge railroad that hauled passengers, chiles, and farm products up and down the Rio Grande Valley. The narrow tracks of the Denver and Rio Grande Western Railroad and the standard-gauge spur of the Atchison, Topeka, and Santa Fe met at the little train station in Santa Fe (now a restaurant).

Driving along the Rio Grande, you will next arrive at Velarde, a farming town with many fruit stands offering opportunities to restock your supply of fruit, vegetables, and decorative *ristras* of chiles or dry corn. Most of the town and the orchards that supply fine apples lie to the west between the road and the river. Beyond Velarde, N.M. 68 is four lanes wide, straight, and well above the river. A more interesting route, N.M. 389, is none of the above, winding among the trees near the Rio Grande. Try one of many dirt roads that head west from the highway; we went down the one marked "Jemez House." Among the cottonwoods you will see many modest homes and several splendid mansions. Author Hamlin Garland's Swan Lake Ranch is one of the high-walled adobe castles; another, the hacienda of Los Luceros, is being restored by the American Studies Foundation.

New Mexico 389 becomes the main street of San Juan Pueblo. This is the largest of the Tewa pueblos. Over the centuries, the Tewas apparently moved slowly down the Rio Grande and the Rio Chama, forming villages and splitting apart into the present groupings, which also include San

5

Ildefonso, Santa Clara, Tesuque, Nambe, and Pojoaque. Obtain permission at the governor's office to walk among the low dwellings to the left of the main road. You will find two large plazas and two *kivas*. On the main road are the tribal administration building, the museum-like center for the Oke Oweenge crafts cooperative, and two large churches that are unlike those in any other pueblo. The main church is very tall and built of brick in a pseudo-Gothic style. Across the street is a smaller stone chapel, which must have made the French priests who served at San Juan Pueblo from 1868 to 1948 feel at home.

The Catholic church has played an important role in San Juan, although it was initially a confrontational role, as it was in most of the pueblos. In the early years of the seventeenth century, the colony's religious and secular leaders attempted to quash native religion. Leaders of the Pueblo religion were regularly punished for their activities. One of the forty-seven people flogged and imprisoned in 1676, a man from San Juan named Popé, was sufficiently aroused by his mistreatment to plan and lead the 1680 Pueblo Revolt, which successfully threw off the Spanish yoke for twelve years. The Spanish had learned some tolerance by the time they returned. Twentieth-century visitors to ceremonies in this and most other pueblos are often surprised to see costumed dancers emerge from a blessing in the Catholic church by the plaza to take their place in line for the ancient Indian religious ceremony. The French pastors Camilo Seux and Joseph Pajot, who together served in San Juan for eighty years beginning in 1868, were especially enlightened, encouraging Tewa tradition

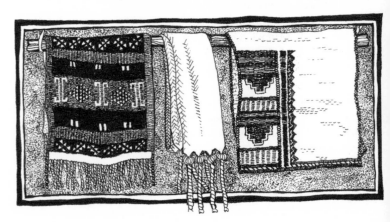

and Catholic beliefs alike to retain a strong hold on their parishioners.

If you enjoy Pueblo arts, you will find some of San Juan's characteristic light-colored, painted, or incised pottery for sale in the Oke Oweenge coop and in homes elsewhere in the pueblo. Beautifully loomed traditional Pueblo textiles and corn, seed, and bead jewelry are also San Juan specialties.

Take N.M. 74 out of San Juan back to the main highway, N.M. 68, which will take you immediately onto the long main commercial street of Española. Turn left at the traffic light on N.M. 76 for a quick trip to the "Villa Nueva de Santa Cruz de los Españoles Mexicanos del Rey Nuestro Señor Carlos Segundo." The villa called Santa Cruz was new in 1695, second only to Santa Fe among royally designated towns in New Mexico. It now exists as a section of the city of Española, where old adobe houses are grouped around a paved plaza in front of the huge 1733 Iglesia de la Santa Cruz. Warped high pine doors with white, quiltlike decorations will admit you to the interior and its remarkable collection of religious art and impressive architectural detail.

Spread out your maps in Santa Cruz plaza and plan the rest of your trip. If you have more time for touring, consider the Rio Arriba County tour (Tour Three), which leaves the center of Española on U.S. 84, or the Jemez Mountain tour that is still ahead of you when you return to the junction with N.M. 502 in Pojoaque. To return to Santa Fe, you can join the traffic on Española's main street or go slightly farther east on N.M. 76 and then return to the highway (U.S. 84/285) on N.M. 106 through more of the outskirts of the town.

The highway will lead you to Saint Francis Drive in Santa Fe, past the pueblos of Pojoaque and Tesuque, past Camel Rock, and past the Santa Fe Opera. The soaring, partially covered opera house is a fixture in the capital city now, bringing performers and patrons from around the world every summer. The season is short, and Santa Fe can be cold, so elegant opera wear is often hidden beneath down jackets and sleeping bags. But to see *The Magic Flute,* a modern premiere, or a Strauss tragedy with real lightning flashing is a galvanizing experience no matter how much rain trickles down your neck.

5

To get back to the plaza from Saint Francis Drive, turn left on Paseo de Peralta to Washington Street and the plaza. If you are not already late, take more time to look in the stores around the plaza for examples of the arts and crafts, modern and traditional, created in the mountain villages, pueblos, and settlements through which you have just traveled.

5

TOUR SIX
WHERE THE MOUNTAINS MEET THE PLAINS

Places:	Las Vegas, Fort Union, Wagon Mound, Roy, Clayton, Capulin, Raton, Cimarron, Eagle Nest, Angel Fire, Mora, Las Vegas
Mileage:	Approximately 500 miles, excluding side trips
Suggested travel time:	A long weekend or several days
Highways:	I-25, N.M. 161, N.M. 120, N.M. 39, U.S. 56, U.S. 64/87, N.M. 325, U.S. 64, N.M. 434, N.M. 518, I-25
Accommodations:	Las Vegas, Clayton, Raton, Cimarron, Eagle Nest, Angel Fire, and Mora
Camping:	Las Vegas, Chicosa Lake State Park, Clayton, Clayton Lake State Park, Capulin, Raton, Sugarite State Park, Cimarron, Cimarron Canyon State Park, Eagle Nest, Carson National Forest, Coyote Creek State Park, Storrie Lake State Park, and Santa Fe National Forest

6

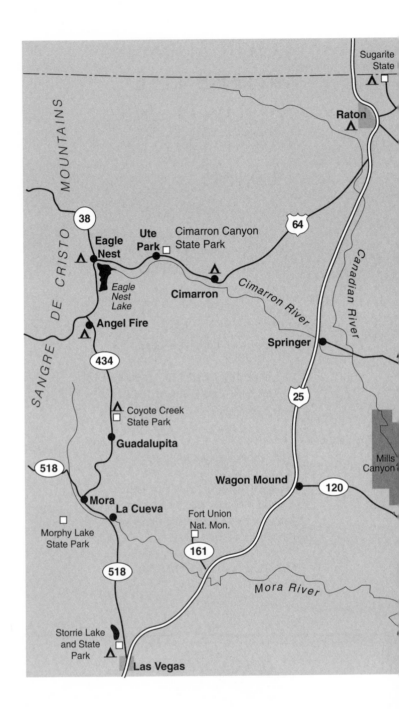

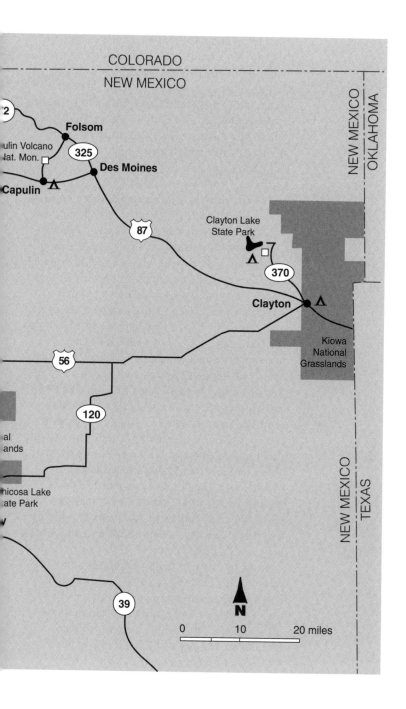

Many of us know the middle of New Mexico well—
its green Rio Grande Valley that winds a course
through the center of the state, its largest cities, its
string of Pueblo villages and historic Hispanic
communities that stretch from Colorado to Mexico.
But New Mexico is many other places. For those
with a taste for vast unpeopled distances, railroad
towns and crumbling villages, mountain streams
and pocket-size state parks, a trip to New Mexico's
northeast corner will be a treat.

This is a quiet journey. In some places, especially
if you travel outside the summer months, you will
seldom meet another vehicle and you can walk
historic paths almost alone. Give yourself a long
weekend or a short week, and prepare for some
narrow roads and long distances between amenities. Only rain and snow should deter you from
making this trip, so check the weather before you
leave. You will discover that almost every town you
visit has a gas station, but a wide selection of
restaurants, motels, and large grocery stores exists
only in Las Vegas, Clayton, and Raton. Communities like Wagon Mound, Roy, Cimarron, Eagle Nest,
and Mora invite exploration and promise all sorts of
surprises. You can wander through a nineteenth-
century frontier fort, track dinosaur footprints, and
descend into an extinct volcano. Several restored
hotels, unusual state parks, and a number of
historic districts offer places to eat, stay, picnic,
browse. As you drive from the mountains across the
plains and then back again, you will be delighted to
find that a land appearing so stark and unassuming
bears within it such richness.

It seems fitting to begin and end this tour in
New Mexico's Las Vegas. Las Vegas is a kind of
confused Victorian *grande dame* with one foot
planted solidly in the plains to the east and the
other in the foothills of the Sangre de Cristo
Mountains. This city of 15,000 is one of New
Mexico's best-kept architectural and historic
secrets. Long a Comanche hunting ground, settled
by Spanish farmers in 1835, a Santa Fe Trail staging
area for decades, and home to some of the Santa
Fe Railroad's largest enterprises, Las Vegas retains
the flavor of all those who have lived here over the
centuries. With nine historic districts and more than
nine hundred buildings on the National Register of

Historic Places, Las Vegas encourages visitors to wander its streets and poke into its past.

You can guide yourself through Las Vegas by using any one of a number of well-written and detailed walking or driving maps. Or you can make arrangements for your own personal guided tour. The Las Vegas/San Miguel County Chamber of Commerce will provide you with information and free brochures. The Roughriders Museum (many of Teddy Roosevelt's Rough Riders came from the Las Vegas area) is housed next door and offers a foretaste of Las Vegas within its dim and dusty display cases.

Public and private efforts have renovated many of the buildings and neighborhoods you will see in Las Vegas; others patiently await their face-lifts. Plan to spend a considerable amount of time in this interesting little city, beginning either on the west side of town at Old Town Plaza or at Carnegie Park, on the east side. By visiting both these public spaces and their surrounding neighborhoods, you will understand why Las Vegas was two very separate municipalities until 1970.

West Las Vegas came first, founded in 1835 by families from San Miguel, a Pecos River village to the west. The settlers developed their fields and built their homes around Old Town Plaza, and neighborhood streets still radiate outward from this tree-shaded center of community life. Walk a block or so in any direction from the plaza and you will discover adobe homes that date back to 1846 or earlier, their facades typically unadorned and fronting right on the street. If you were invited beyond the massive doors of some of these larger adobe homes, you might find interior courtyards reminiscent of colonial residences throughout Latin America. On the other hand, the buildings that face the plaza—a hotel, a former bank, and other mercantile establishments—exemplify the more elaborate Victorian and Italianate influences that arrived with the Santa Fe Railroad after 1879.

When you walk through the neighborhoods around Carnegie Park on the east side of town, you will be struck by the similarity of this part of Las Vegas to towns and cities in the American Midwest. The only surviving Carnegie Library in the state sitting smack in the middle of its green and leafy

6

park, handsome brick and stone homes of two and three stories dating from the 1880s, elm and maple trees, green lawns and screened porches—all stand in contrast to the Spanish-Mexican nature of Old Town Plaza. Other historic districts include the area around the railroad station (where bawdy saloons, hotels, and dance halls were balanced by more mundane mercantile businesses catering to the railway trade), the downtown portion of what was formerly East Las Vegas, and the Distrito de las Escuelas, a collection of adobe buildings south and west of the plaza.

As you pass between east Las Vegas and west Las Vegas, you come upon New Mexico Highlands University sprawling across the hills in the center of town. Founded in 1893 as New Mexico Normal University, Highlands is one of New Mexico's smaller state-supported colleges, with an enrollment of about two thousand. It prides itself on the diversity of its student population and its favorable student-teacher ratio. Highlands graduates include many of the state's leading educators, social workers, and business people who remember fondly their years spent on its tree-shaded campus.

Ilfeld Auditorium, a handsome sandstone building on University Avenue, is a good starting point for a campus tour. Built between 1914 and 1921, and named in honor of Adele Ilfeld, the wife of one of Las Vegas's most prominent merchants, this building is considered one of the state's best examples of Romanesque revival architecture. The auditorium is just one of many architectural styles evident on the Highlands campus. In fact, as you wander through quiet, leafy patios and across

broad plazas from one classroom building or dormitory to the next, you will come upon buildings that reflect New Mexico's Territorial period, or the Prairie style of Frank Lloyd Wright, or the ivy-covered walls of traditional eastern colleges. Somehow, the mix of genres seems to work, creating a comfortable and handsome campus. The university invites visitors to explore its campus, to chat with students and faculty, and to peruse areas of special interest, including the Arrott Gallery in Thomas C. Donnelly Library and the 1930s fresco inside Rodgers Hall.

Following Hot Springs Boulevard west from the Plaza, you will come upon Las Vegas's other large employer, Las Vegas Medical Center, the state's major mental health facility. A few miles beyond that, in Montezuma, you will find the Armand Hammer United World College of the American West, a two-year college preparatory school that brings together students from all over the world. You can visit the United World College, founded by the late philanthropist Armand Hammer and dedicated in 1982 by Hammer and England's Prince Charles. Perhaps your student guide will let you take a peek inside one of Las Vegas's architectural gems—Montezuma Castle, the huge fanciful building that looms over the school campus, and show you the nearby hot springs, and the community of Montezuma. The Santa Fe Railroad bought this property, which was originally the site of a U.S. military hospital, in 1879. Santa Fe officials constructed a spur line to Montezuma from Las Vegas, and built a series of hotels here, culminating in the structure you now see—343 rooms, with elaborate turrets, fussy balconies, and a guest list that included President Theodore Roosevelt, Kaiser Wilhelm, and Emperor Hirohito. No one stays in the abandoned Montezuma now. In fact, you could probably purchase it from the college if you were so inclined.

Because it sits at the foot of the Sangre de Cristo Range and the edge of the plains, Las Vegas is a regional health, education, and service center for the ranches and small towns around it. New Mexicans are also drawn to Las Vegas for outdoor recreation: fishing, swimming, and windsurfing at Storrie Lake north of town; ice skating on the pond

6

in Gallinas Canyon beyond Montezuma; hunting, llama-trekking, and camping in the surrounding mountains; bird watching at the Las Vegas National Wildlife Refuge. There are cultural, historic, and just plain fun events held in the Las Vegas area throughout the year. Las Vegas has a number of hotels and motels, a few bed-and-breakfasts, and many restaurants.

And now it is time to head out of town, to reach north and eastward almost as far as New Mexico goes. We suggest that you take I-25 north to Fort Union, crossing the long, rolling hills and pine-capped ridges, with the east face of the Sangre de Cristos a constant green or snow-covered companion. The Fort Union exit is about twenty miles north of Las Vegas. You then follow N.M. 161 for eight lonely miles to the ruins of the fort.

What a windy, silent place this is. In 1851, the United States Military Department built Fort Union on these barren plains for several reasons: to consolidate its Santa Fe Trail and settlement defenses against the nomadic tribes that still considered the region their home; to develop a fort that could become self-sufficient; and perhaps most important, to escape the "vice and extravagance" of its headquarters in Santa Fe. For more than twenty-five years, the fort served its purposes well and was for a time the largest fort west of the Mississippi. Fort Union protected travelers along the Santa Fe Trail, while also assuring them of a safe stopover before reaching Las Vegas. It provided Union troops to fight the Confederate invasion of New Mexico during the Civil War. A number of forts were constructed on this site over the years, the final version the one you now visit. Fort Union was a sprawling community of military and civilian personnel, with an ordnance depot, corrals, shops, a commissary, storehouses, a hospital, officers' quarters, even a sturdy stone jail that seems to have survived in the best shape of all.

An attractive Territorial-style visitor center welcomes you to Fort Union. Displays of military clothing and equipment, Indian artifacts, Santa Fe Trail information, maps of the region, and films complement the guidebooks and orientation that the center staff provide. You can purchase books and maps about the Santa Fe Trail, frontier life in

New Mexico, and the Southwest in general at the center's gift shop.

Fort Union is best understood by walking its quiet paths and standing next to its stone foundations and ghostly chimneys, all that remain of this once-thriving military outpost. Every once in a while, recorded music and cannon shots break the silence and ride the wind to nowhere. Youngsters will find it hard to believe that hundreds of people, including families with children, lived and worked here more than a century ago. But they will enjoy running along the paths between what were once buildings, discovering the ruts of the Santa Fe Trail, and pondering the fate of those once imprisoned in the jail. While camping at Fort Union is not allowed, you can picnic beneath its shady trees. The facilities in the visitor center are accessible to people with physical impairments, and some of its trails can be maneuvered in a wheelchair. You might want to avoid Fort Union on very hot summer days; otherwise, it is a choice spot any time of the year.

Drive back to I-25, where you have about twenty minutes to decide on a route east to Clayton, home of dinosaur tracks, prairie vistas, and a wonderful old hotel. You have two choices. If you wish to see the historic Dorsey Mansion, you will continue north about forty-five miles on I-25 to Springer and then head east on U.S. 56. If you would rather cross the Canadian River Gorge and see the state's smallest (sometimes almost disappearing) lake at Chicosa Lake State Park near Roy, you will turn east at Wagon Mound on N.M. 120. It is possible to accomplish all of the above by taking N.M. 120 to Roy, making a brief visit to Chicosa Lake, and then heading north on N.M. 39 to Mills and then Abbott, which sits on U.S. 56 just a few miles west of the Dorsey Mansion turnoff. Because we want you to see as much as possible, we will direct you to Wagon Mound and then to Roy.

The town of Wagon Mound sits beneath the rock formation that gave it its name in 1859. The small town was formerly Santa Clara, an important shipping point for fruit and other produce grown in the nearby Canadian River Valley. Wagon Mound was also the place where the two branches of the Santa Fe Trail joined together, providing Spanish-

6

speaking farmers and Apache, Ute, and Comanche people the perfect opportunity for joint attacks on Santa Fe Trail wagon trains during the 1847 Taos Rebellion against the American presence.

Wagon Mound is now a quiet community that pays respect to its railroad past. Its straight streets parallel and cluster around the Santa Fe Railroad tracks, although no passenger train stops here anymore. Take time to walk or drive through the town. You will find numerous examples of classic northern New Mexico adobe homes with pitched tin roofs, gabled dormer windows, and some fanciful porches and trim. Various efforts have been made to restore the old Santa Clara Hotel and other buildings on Wagon Mound's main street, Railroad Avenue, but success seems to have been minimal. Wagon Mound commemorates its past ties to dry land bean farming with an annual Bean Day celebration on Labor Day weekend. A parade, rodeo, dances, and a barbecue bring old-timers back to town to mingle with those who stayed and those who are visiting. You can find gas and food in Wagon Mound.

Look for N.M. 120 and drive east past Wagon Mound's school complex and the town cemetery, over a series of hills to enter the plains once again. Some might consider the next two hours spent driving across the New Mexico prairie to Clayton an exercise in boredom. But there are ways to enjoy the trip. For example, this road is so little-used that cattle look up from their grazing as a vehicle approaches. You might acknowledge their curiosity with a honk and a wave. Or just admire the scenery. The changing colors of the prairie grasses and the sky are sometimes subtle, often spectacular, always mesmerizing. After a summer of rain, the rangeland is a glorious and welcome green that seem to wave in the wind. In autumn, somber grays and browns in the immediate landscape contrast with pale blue and purple palettes in the distance. During a snowy winter, you just might want to avoid this road altogether: Fierce winds can cause blizzard conditions and snowdrifts in no time at all. And this is not just flat land. Up and down hills you will swoop, and then, about seventeen miles beyond Wagon Mound, you begin a remarkable and cautious descent into the Canadian River Canyon.

This is a six hundred-foot chasm carved over thousands of years by the predecessor of the little trickle of water you now cross, the Canadian River. While this river is usually quiet and tame, it can easily flood, and its currents are treacherous. In the late nineteenth century, an entrepreneur named Melvin Mills created a fruit and vegetable empire within a canyon of the river several miles upstream. The Mills Canyon enterprise was ten miles long and was crisscrossed by irrigation channels and cisterns that fed hundreds of acres of fruit orchards and vegetable gardens. Mills's produce supplied the Harvey Houses, the well-run hotels and restaurants built along the Santa Fe Railroad. A flood in 1904 wiped out the entire operation.

Now you enter Harding County, which has New Mexico's smallest population (987 people and declining in 1990). Harding County also retains the dubious distinction of having been born the day that President Warren Harding was inaugurated, March 4, 1921. This is beautiful country, home to hardy ranchers, rodeo queens, and some great high school football teams. The highway becomes narrow, bumpy, and curvy as it proceeds to the small town of Roy, the largest community in the county, although Mosquero is the county seat. In Roy you will find cafés, feed stores, gas stations, and a number of buildings that have corrugated tin on both their roofs and their sides. Roy once was a railroad town; the 146-mile Dawson Railway ran through it from Tucumcari to Raton.

If you are really in the mood for modest adventure (but not a swim), follow the signs on N.M. 120 for Chicosa Lake State Park, about seven miles away over paved and dirt roads. You can picnic or camp here and the children can play on the playground, but there might not be any water in the lake. If it has been a year of generous rainfall, though, this little puddle may swell into a modest pond. Backtrack to Roy and N.M. 39.

As you drive north on N.M. 39, a wide, well-paved highway, you cross the Kiowa National Grasslands, part of a national effort to preserve the tall prairie grasses that once were so prolific in this part of the country. Although there are no welcome signs to indicate your entrance into the grasslands, you will notice the native blue and side

6

oats grama grasses that form much of the rangeland. Stop to study the sturdy green bunches that
manage to survive drought, wind, herds of cattle,
and questionable soil. To your left you can sometimes spot the distant Sangre de Cristo Mountains
or the dark tracing of the Canadian River Canyon.
The town of Mills, about ten miles north of Roy,
was named after the enterprising Melvin Mills.
Trains once stopped in Mills to pick up grain and
drop off ranch supplies, but little remains of the
community. Between the buildings of what remains
of Mills, a dirt road heads west through the
grasslands, up and down several hills until it
reaches the edge of the canyon of the Canadian
River. The road turns rough and rocky, snaking
down the canyon wall, reaching Mills's beautiful
river-bottom land. You'll find the drive down
difficult but well worth the time. The river and the
canyon display a beautiful contrast in reds, blues,
and greens, with a few of the entrepreneur's grape
vines and fruit trees and the ruins of his stone
masonry home giving evidence of the long-ago
enterprise.

As you head for Abbott, you can sometimes see
the deer and the antelope play, and you will be
accompanied by bright sunflowers all along the
way in the summertime and early fall. If Abbott did
not constitute the intersection of N.M. 39 and U.S.
56, it would be easy to miss this former farm and
ranch community. Turn right on U.S. 56 and drive
to Clayton in a barely interrupted path across the
plains for the next hour. Should you wish to explore
one of New Mexico's most unusual structures, the
Dorsey Mansion, watch for a roadside rest area and
signs for the ranch about five miles east of Abbott
on U.S. 56. Because the mansion is now in private
hands, the best way to ensure a visit is to make
inquiries beforehand through the tourist information centers in Clayton or Raton. The mansion
caretakers offer guided tours if they have about one
day's notice; or you might chance upon a summer
weekend when a free open house occurs. Even if
you have not planned ahead, it still may be worth
the thirteen-mile trip north on an excellent dirt
road just to gaze at one man's folly.

Stephen Dorsey came to New Mexico in the
latter part of the nineteenth century. A former U.S.

Senator from Arkansas, he settled in the Clayton area, named the town after his son, helped to bring the railroad through the community, established a law practice, became involved in a post office scandal, and purchased the Triangle Dot Ranch, more than a million acres of land within Union and Colfax counties. There, in 1880, he built his mansion, first a comparatively  modest log cabin, which gradually grew into a many-chimneyed, thirty-six-room wood, adobe, and stone prairie palace with a dining room that could seat sixty and fireplaces made of Italian marble. As befits a country manor house, the mansion has columns, fountains, gables, gargoyles, and probably a ghost or two. It sits beneath a rocky hillside with hardly a tree to impede its view across hundreds of miles of grazing land to the distant mountains.

6

You will meet only a few pickups and cars as you drive east to Clayton on U.S. 56, a highway that seems to widen and narrow at whim. You might notice that many of the vehicles you pass are from Texas and Oklahoma because U.S. 56 is a favorite route for New Mexico's eastern neighbors who covet the state's mountains, streams, and vacation spots.

Rabbit Ear Mountain (named for Chief Orejas de Conejo, who is buried at its base) will guide you into Clayton, a quiet community of about three thousand. Clayton is the county seat for Union County and a service center for the many cattle ranches that dot this extreme corner of the state. Clayton is also headquarters for a weekly livestock auction that draws buyers from five states and for enterprises related to the nearby Bravo Dome, the world's largest reserve of carbon dioxide gas. More than one thousand wells will be sunk into the vast 1.2-million-acre dome in order to furnish carbon dioxide to oil fields in New Mexico and Texas.

In Clayton's distant past, dinosaurs roamed the area, leaving their footprints at Clayton Lake State Park. Clayton was the site of a major battle during the Spanish–Comanche War of 1717, an important stop on the Cimarron Cutoff of the Santa Fe Trail, but was not formally established until 1888. Thousands of cattle once trod a nearby branch of the historic Goodnight–Loving Trail, which transported livestock from West Texas to railheads and outposts further north. Among the region's seasonal attractions are the Union County Fair each September, an Arts and Crafts Festival in late October, and traditional Western dances during the end-of-the-year holiday season.

Clayton might be a good place to stop for the night, take a stroll, and have a meal. There are motels, restaurants, and campgrounds on the outskirts of town. In downtown Clayton, you can visit the Ecklund Hotel, built in 1892 by John C. Hill, but soon bought by Carl Ecklund, reportedly with the proceeds from a poker game. With its exterior opera balcony, four stories, and fancy public rooms, the Ecklund advertised itself as "the only first-class hotel between Trinidad and Fort Worth." Unlike many renovated hotels, the Ecklund remains true to its origins. The well-preserved and almost unchanged dining room features velvet booths. Hunting trophies adorn the walls of the wood-paneled, dimly-lit bar. Even the switchboard in the reception area reflects another era.

If your kids want to see real dinosaur tracks, you must take them to Clayton Lake State Park, an easy but curvy twelve-mile drive north of town on N.M. 370. You can also picnic, camp, fish, or swim here. The lake sits within protective hillsides, its blue waters sparkling in the sunshine. Signs lead you to a fairly rough half-mile-long path where dozens of dinosaur tracks have been preserved in the hard stone of the lake's spillway. Set down one hundred million years ago by eight different kinds of dinosaurs, the footprints were only discovered in 1982 and are still being studied. Best time for viewing: early morning or late afternoon when sun and shadows highlight them.

Once you have seen the dinosaur tracks, return to Clayton and then go west on U.S. 64/87 to Raton, visiting one of New Mexico's other prehistoric attractions, Capulin Volcano National Monument, along the way. As you travel across the plains, look for ruts of the Santa Fe Trail, the trade route used from 1822 to 1879 to connect the midwest to Santa Fe. The Cimarron Cutoff from this famous trail swings into New Mexico above Clayton and crosses U.S. 64/87 between the villages of Mount Dora (named after Stephen Dorsey's sister-in-law) and Grenville. Look for the cutoff marker on the north side of the highway near the Burlington Railroad tracks about five miles west of Mount Dora. Even before you come upon the marker, you can picture lonely wagon trains and straggling animals plodding across this empty landscape, moving slowly from water hole to water hole. Long shadows, silent buttes and mesas, the dark sliver of a distant train—this is a lonely journey even as the twenty-first century dawns. If you are taking this trip in the winter, pay attention to weather bulletins, because snow can sweep across the prairie and make driving hazardous.

As you near Capulin, you will become aware of numerous volcanic remnants, including black-topped mesas and deep craters scattered across the landscape. This lava-capped terrain not only contains many small mountains (volcanic vents from which lava flowed eons ago) but more ponds and other surface water than characterize most of New Mexico's upland plains. About ten miles before Capulin, you pass a space-age, solar-powered rest area and then the community of Des Moines, named after the larger city in Iowa (with the s in "Des" pronounced). Des Moines, which sits beneath Sierra Grande, one of New Mexico's largest volcanoes, serves the surrounding ranches, its school complex a center of activity for the area, the parking lots of its cafés filled with dusty pickups and horse trailers. Founded in 1907, Des Moines flourished in the mid-1930s when a dry ice industry developed here after the local discovery of carbon dioxide.

You can turn north on N.M. 325 at Des Moines to drive eight miles to Folsom, where a monument and small museum commemorate an important archaeological find. George McJunkin, a cowboy and one of many African-Americans featured prominently in New Mexico history, found several chipped stone darts among the bones of extinct animals as he wandered the grazing land of this area back in the 1920s. Archaeologists traced the tools to Folsom Man, part of a hunter-gatherer

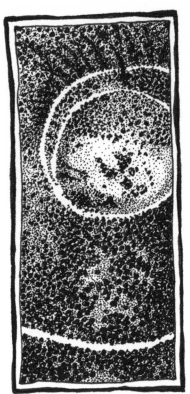

Capulin

culture that existed here twelve thousand years ago. The museum contains more stone implements and other reminders of ancient people, along with examples of area lore.

And then you see Capulin Mountain, an almost perfect version of every child's idea of a volcano. Turn right on N.M. 325 at the village of Capulin and proceed about three miles to the visitor center at Capulin Volcano National Monument. Here you can learn about this one-thousand-foot-high cinder cone that erupted only ten thousand years ago, not so very long ago in geologic terms. You can watch films about volcanoes, handle pieces of lava and other volcanic rocks, and ask questions of the center staff. There is a short trail near the visitor center that takes you past plants (including the chokecherry, *capulin* in Spanish) and other natural objects related to regional volcanoes. The visitor center, nearby picnic grounds, and nature trail are accessible to people in wheelchairs.

One of the ways to experience a volcano is to enter it. And this is your chance. Drive two miles up and around Capulin Mountain to its summit. Here you can look out over five states, find a series of other nearby volcanoes, and easily pick out the wagon ruts of the Santa Fe Trail. The Sangre de Cristo Range of the Rocky Mountains forms a magnificent backdrop to all you see. But you are here to descend into a volcano, and you do so by taking the steep but short (0.2 mile) path directly into the bottom of the crater. If you would rather observe this vent from afar, you can take a one-mile path, Crater Rim Trail, around the rim of the volcano. There are guideposts and explanatory signs along the way. Walk carefully; volcanic cinders can be slippery.

Refreshed by your brisk hike into the bowels of Capulin Mountain, you have only a short half-hour drive to Raton. To your left, rough cliffs, leftovers from a former lava plateau, accompany you across the Raton Basin to the outskirts of town. Cross I-25 and enter one of New Mexico's most important railroad and mining centers.

Raton is located at the bottom of Raton Pass, which has provided a pathway across this southern portion of the Rocky Mountains for centuries. Nomadic people came through the high canyon by foot. Much later, William Becknell and his packhorses crossed Raton Pass in 1821, the first of many supply trains that would carve the Santa Fe Trail. In the middle of the nineteenth century, Dick Wooten blasted a wagon road through the mountains and established a toll road for the Americans who now streamed into New Mexico. In 1878, the first locomotive crossed the mountains. Willow Springs, located eight miles south of Raton Pass, was the first stopover for wagon trains and others; over the years it grew into a small town. When the Santa Fe Railroad decided to locate its shops at Willow Springs, the town was officially founded and then renamed. It somehow became Raton ("mouse" in Spanish) and soon three thousand people were living there. When the many coalfields nearby were mined, its residents considered Raton the "Pittsburgh of the West."

Raton is still a transportation center. The first city in New Mexico for those entering the state from Colorado on I-25, it is full of modern motels, gas stations, restaurants, and other tourist facilities. Amtrak trains come through town twice a day, picking up and depositing local passengers and visitors who come to the nearby vacation areas. Raton also draws horse-race fans who come to La Mesa Park on weekends and holidays throughout the summer. During the Christmas season, Raton maintains its City of Bethlehem tradition with an elaborately lit display along the hillsides above town. People who camp, fish, and hike enjoy Sugarite Canyon, a state park located in the mountains about ten miles northeast of the city. It contains three lakes (one of which is shared with Colorado), an old coal-mining camp at the entrance to the park, and picnic and camping facilities. Two of Sugarite Canyon's camping and picnicking sites are accessible to people with

6

disabilities and there is a fishing pier on Lake Maloya specifically designed for those in wheelchairs.

Raton's original townsite, the area around First Street near the railroad station, offers you a glimpse into Raton's colorful past and its efforts to honor its unique and admittedly rowdy history. Stroll through the Raton Downtown Historic District to appreciate the more than seventy buildings that have been identified as worth preserving. During your walk, you may be especially interested in the structures that have been renovated or that are in the process of being restored. The Palace Hotel on First Street was recently an elegant restaurant featuring crystal chandeliers and somber Victorian portraits. Up on Second Street, the Shuler Theater, once an opera house and then a fire station, displays a community mural from WPA days and is gradually being restored. Other buildings, including the Santa Fe Railroad station and several antique stores on First Street, have changed over time but retain much of their original flavor. You can obtain maps, a guide for a walking tour of the downtown section, and other information about Raton and the surrounding area at the Raton Visitor Center, the Raton Museum on First Street, or at the public library.

Because your next stop is Cimarron, it is time to drive south out of Raton on I-25, exiting to the slower pace of U.S. 64 about five miles outside town. Soon you will come to a modern structure on your right. This is the National Rifle Association's (NRA) Whittington Center, a large shooting and training facility. More than 33,000 acres in the mountains and foothills provide turkey, elk, deer, and bear hunts, camping and RV grounds, and special training camps for NRA members. Nonmembers may also visit the center. You will then pass the Raton Industrial Park and the local airport. As you drive west, you slowly climb into a rougher countryside, with piñon trees scattered on the hillsides and snowcapped peaks up ahead.

About a half hour south of Raton, you will see a small dirt road leading west into the mountains. A sign indicates that this will take you to the Valle Vidal Unit of the Carson National Forest. If the weather is good, your vehicle sturdy, and time is no object, give in to your temptation and cross the Sangre de Cristo Mountains through this glorious valley. It will take you several hours and pavement will reappear only many hours and about eighty miles later, at Costilla on N.M. 522, near the Colorado border. But what a journey you will have experienced—mountain lakes, wandering elk and deer, snowy mountain summits, primitive campsites, and quiet

picnic places. Once part of the immense private Vermejo Park Ranch, the 100,000-acre Valle Vidal was deeded to the Forest Service in 1982 by the Pennzoil Company and now contains within its boundaries some of the premier hunting country in the state. It is a landscape worth every jolt and each dusty mile. Needless to say, there are no facilities within the Valle Vidal between here and Costilla. You should probably not venture into the Valle Vidal in the winter.

If the Valle Vidal did not beckon, then historic Cimarron does, and it is just down the road, snuggled up beneath the mountains on the other side of the Cimarron River. The mountain branch of the Santa Fe Trail crossed here, and coal and other mining enterprises filled the region, so Cimarron's tales are tall and traditions colorful, and include mountain men, gold seekers, trappers, miners, and traders. Now a thriving ranching and tourist center, Cimarron preserves its past carefully. While the highway through the small town is lined with restaurants and motels, its historic district is almost hidden off to the left of U.S. 64. Signs lead you to where Cimarron began in 1841. Here you find the St. James Hotel, built in 1880 as a stopover point for travelers on the Santa Fe Trail. The two-story brick structure, scene of twenty-six murders, was one of four hotels and sixteen saloons that Cimarron once boasted. Now the inn has been restored as a genteel reminder of wilder days. Just down the road from the St. James is the Old Mill Museum, constructed by Lucien Maxwell, one of New Mexico's famous entrepreneurs, gamblers, and businessmen, who inherited the seeds of his

vast holdings from his father-in-law, Charles Beaubien. When New Mexicans refer to the Maxwell Land Grant, they are talking about almost two million acres of land that spanned much of northern New Mexico, including the towns of Springer, Maxwell, Raton, and Ute Park, and part of southern Colorado. This was Lucien Maxwell's empire in the middle of the nineteenth century, and Cimarron was its headquarters.

Cimarron is a logical place to stay if you wish to explore the backroads and hiking trails that lead to old mining camps, ghost towns, mountain lakes, and trout streams. You can camp in Cimarron Canyon or Barker Wildlife Area, at RV campgrounds in town, or check into one of Cimarron's several motels.

Cimarron Canyon begins about five miles down the road and continues for the next fifteen or so miles. It is a dark, densely wooded area, with sheer palisades reaching skyward, often obliterating your view of the surrounding mountains. Fortunately, there are numerous pullouts so that you can appreciate the beauty of the canyon at a leisurely pace. Working ranches, summer camps, vacation homes, and the road to the headquarters of the immense Philmont Scout Ranch appear when the narrow canyon widens. Signs indicate the delineation between public and private land, including the Scout Ranch and the area around Ute Park, which was named after the Ute Indians, who roamed the eastern slope of Mount Baldy and were removed to reservations in Colorado and Utah only after much resistance. Ute Park was the termination point for a branch of the Santa Fe Railroad that once served the canyon, the Moreno Valley, and nearby ranches and mines. There are campgrounds along the river in Cimarron Canyon State Park, but you will discover that most of them are full of fishermen during the warm months of the year. In fact, if you wish to camp in the canyon, plan on an early arrival and have alternate sites in mind.

You swoop up and out of the narrow confines of Cimarron Canyon and suddenly you are on the top of a mountain that overlooks the Moreno Valley, with a spectacular view beyond it to New Mexico's premier summits, including Wheeler Peak, the state's highest point at 13,160 feet. Pull to the side of the road and study your surroundings. The Moreno Valley below you contains the small resort town of Eagle Nest, manmade Eagle Nest Lake, vestiges of numerous ranches, and a few ghost towns, including Klondike, Elizabethtown, and Virginia City.

The town of Eagle Nest, founded in 1920 as Therma, caters to hunters, fishermen, and winter sports enthusiasts. Here you will find bait shops and motels, cabins, and cafés. Drive through Eagle Nest on U.S. 64, skirting the condominiums and RV parks that have to a great extent replaced the farms and ranches that once filled the broad Moreno Valley.

Watch for signs to the DAV Vietnam Veterans National Memorial and follow its road up the hillside. Tour Eight provides details about Dr. Victor Westphall's moving and substantial tribute to his son and other Vietnam veterans.

About one mile beyond the DAV memorial, U.S. 64 intersects with N.M. 434. You will turn left (south) onto N.M. 434. This paved road takes you first to Angel Fire, a year-round resort with golf course, ski complex, hotels, condominiums, and accompanying tourist services. A comparatively new development that began as a ski area, Angel Fire has expanded south on N.M. 434 to include a country club, tennis courts, and small lakes. As you continue south, you will pass other resorts and vacation homes interspersed with a few working farms and ranches that seem to have survived the Moreno Valley's condo boom.

The blacktopped highway undergoes a radical narrowing a few miles after the Angel Fire com-

Mora

plex. Indeed, no vehicles wider than ten feet are allowed on this road, a fact you appreciate when another car meets you and you hug the shoulder and almost kiss a tree. Best advice for driving this skinny highway: go slowly and honk at curves. The wide, unspoiled valley near Black Lake is a welcome sight before you plunge back into yet another dark and shady canyon. Coyote Creek State Park, about seventeen miles beyond Angel Fire, has been carved out of the woods along the creek bed. One of the state's smallest parks, it includes all that most campers require, is presided over by friendly rangers, and promises quiet and solitude.

You are now close to Guadalupita, where the little river valley widens perceptibly. A peaceful, gentle valley of small farms and ranches, cattle and sheep, small orchards and Christmas tree farms, its old adobe homesteads face the highway or sit at the end of winding dirt roads. Grazing cows and upturned abandoned cars share fields outlined by rough wood fences and old corrals. You will see lonely cemeteries and stop for gas and soda pop at solitary general stores that have outlasted their villages. As you near Mora, the mountains of the Sangre de Cristo Range become more dramatic, fiercely protecting the villages that settled at their feet more than a century ago.

The outskirts of the small town of Mora appear as you pass beneath huge cottonwood trees lining the Mora River near the ruins of the old St. Vrain Mill. As soon as N.M. 434 meets N.M. 518, you are in downtown Mora, the county seat of Mora County (and the only unincorporated county seat in the state). These are the first curbs and sidewalks you've seen in a long time! Founded by Spanish-speaking settlers in 1835, originally designed as a buffer against American encroachment from the east, Mora has a heady history. Its citizens joined the Taos Rebellion in 1847, killing a number of Americans in the valley. In the 1860s, Mora's Church of Santa Gertrudis was the primary parish for a huge area of northern New Mexico and southern Colorado. One hundred years ago, Mora flourished, with flour mills, mercantile establishments, and fine homes lining its roads. In 1900, Mora County had the third largest number of homesteads registered in the New Mexico territory,

15,652. The Mora you see today is different—many of its adobe structures are boarded up or melting back into the earth, its young people have gone elsewhere to find work, and the county's largest employer is its small school system.

Mora is also one of New Mexico's prettiest places: a verdant, colorful valley that is surrounded by snow-capped mountains. Take time to drive west on N.M. 518 and explore this valley. You will find numerous examples of adobe architecture—pitched tin roofs, columned central porches, and intricate woodwork around doors, windows, and porches. The Cleveland Roller Mill Museum just up the road in Cleveland has been lovingly restored and features historical exhibits, guided tours, even a picnic table alongside the river. You can find food, gas, and lodging here in the Mora Valley.

In order to return to Las Vegas, drive east out of Mora on N.M. 518 toward La Cueva, site of another restored mill and home to New Mexico's burgeoning raspberry industry. Vicente Romero, founder of La Cueva Ranch, built La Cueva Mill in the 1870s to supply flour to nearby Fort Union. Now a National Historic District owned by the Salman family, the mill and the ranch form the intersection of N.M. 442 and N.M. 518. You can visit the mill, now one of the offices for La Cueva Ranch; an outlet for the raspberry operation sits across the street. In early autumn, caravans of cars arrive at the ranch as people from throughout the state come to buy their berries straight from the source. The raspberry crop also provides seasonal jobs for Mora County residents.

Proceed south on N.M. 518 the twenty-five miles to Las Vegas. To your right, like sentinels guiding you home at the end of your journey, the dark foothills of the Sangre de Cristos will stay with you until Las Vegas. Hidden within their canyons and valleys

6

Cleveland Mill

and accessible by a series of narrow roads are a number of small villages (Ledoux, Cañoncito, Manuelitas, Las Tusas), Morphy Lake State Park, and some vacation developments. To your left, edging onto the plains, a few old communities (Buena Vista and Golondrinas) share the landscape with cattle ranches and farms.

When you reach Storrie Lake, you are almost home. Soon you will be back where you started, in Las Vegas, where the mountains meet the plains.

6

TOUR SEVEN
ESCARPMENTS

Places:	Clovis, Portales, Fort Sumner, Santa Rosa, Las Vegas, Conchas Lake, Tucumcari, San Jon, Clovis
Mileage:	Approximately 380 miles
Suggested travel time:	Two or three days
Highways:	U.S. 70, N.M. 236, N.M. 267, U.S. 60, U.S. 84, I-40, N.M. 104, N.M. 469, N.M. 209
Accommodations:	Clovis, Portales, Fort Sumner, Santa Rosa, Las Vegas, Conchas Lake, Tucumcari, and San Jon
Camping:	Oasis State Park, Sumner Lake State Park, Santa Rosa Lake State Park, McAllister Lake Waterfowl Area, Conchas Lake State Park, and Running Water Draw State Park

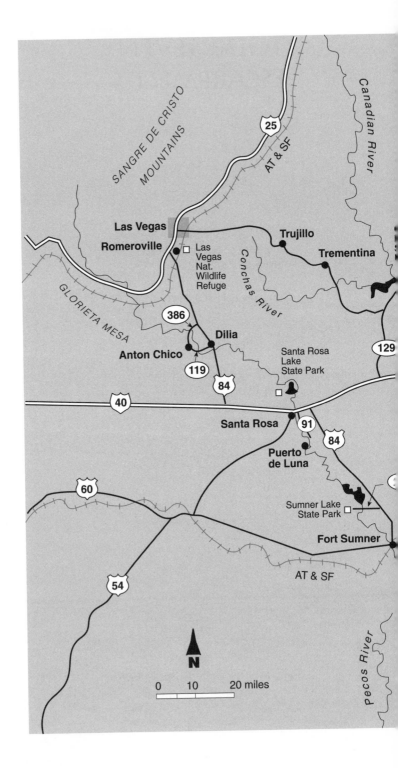

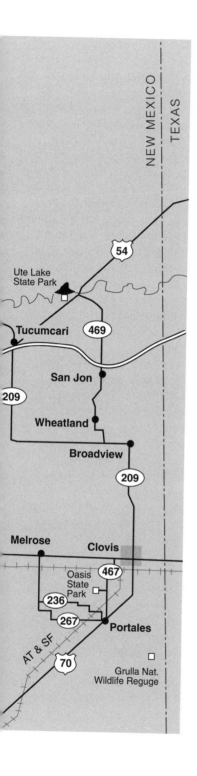

ESCARPMENTS   151

If you have a few days and a curiosity about places you never even knew existed, maybe this is time to venture east to Clovis, Portales, and Santa Rosa and give a seldom–visited land a chance to work its spell on you. This tour explores two rivers and their three levels. It begins on the High Plains, atop the Caprock, long safe from the erosion of major streams. Some of its principal attractions are the old settlements (and newer lakes) down along the Pecos, Conchas, and Canadian rivers. Most of the tour, however, occurs at midlevel, over the broad, grassy valleys of those same rivers. You will visit the venerable towns of Puerto de Luna and Anton Chico that have depended upon irrigation water from the Pecos River for their farms since the 1700s; the old Santa Fe Trail town of Las Vegas; the more recent irrigation districts of Fort Sumner and Tucumcari; the vast intervening expanses of plain and mesa devoted to grazing; and the rich farm-land on the High Plains.

It is a tour of escarpments, with abrupt and ragged changes of level from narrow canyon to wide valley to high caprock. Miles of jagged, layered rock walls define this entire region. By the time you are well into the tour, you can expect to be on intimate terms with the white, pink, or red bands within the rock layers, and you will have developed an appreciation for those twisted, fractured, endlessly looping natural boundaries. The coming of the railroads at the turn of the century imposed some order upon this chaos, creating most of the major towns that survive to the present. The six counties that the tour comprises still reveal the drama of their historical past—the huge cattle drives, trading with the Comanches, the Long Walk of the Navajo, the capture and death of Billy the Kid. They also offer the relatively recent attractions of wildlife refuges, dam site towns and lakes, fossil finds, and the growth and expansion of universities.

Most of the tourist and recreation sites in Clovis will be described at the end of this tour. We hope you will save time for it. Clovis began as the region's railroad center, and it has served as its agricultural and livestock center ever since. Maybe it is fitting that the tour follows U.S. 70 south from the middle of town, across the Santa Fe tracks,

Yucca

between the stockyards and the Curry County Fairgrounds.

Within a few miles, you will be out on the Caprock—that high, open "ocean"—locked in place by a forty-foot-thick layer of tough rock. In its youth, the Pecos River nibbled and crumbled its western edge. The same thing happened in Texas, most spectacularly at Palo Duro Canyon near Amarillo. In between, however, the Caprock remains intact, with thick, rich soils generally undisturbed by erosion from arroyos and rivers. Here is a place where the archetypal figures of geometry reign. The dome of the sky, the circle of the horizon, parallel and intersecting planes, converging lines—all these have been evident here since long before high school students had to study Euclid's postulates.

Nine miles south of Clovis, watch for the sign to Blackwater Draw Museum. Here in 1932 a highway crew uncovered mammoth remains in a huge gravel pit. Their discovery shed light on the Clovis people, one of the oldest Paleo-Indian cultures known in the New World. Some twelve thousand years ago they fashioned characteristic spearheads, the "Clovis Points," to bring down large Pleis-tocene mammals. The gravel pit was once a pond where Clovis people surprised and killed thousands of animals. Blackwater Draw Museum, located near the archaeological site, displays numerous remains of the six-ton Ice Age mammoths and the weapons used to subdue them. Although much of the archaeological evidence disappeared before the first formal excavation was undertaken in 1962, enough has been preserved to impress the ordinary person with the importance of these finds. When combined with the similar Folsom finds farther north, they provide important clues to the mystery of the earliest known life on the continent.

Oceans covered the surface here during the geological past, making the rough places smooth with deposits of abundant sea life. The layers later rose and began eroding. At one time the entire Caprock drained eastward, and Blackwater Draw was a river that ran east to empty into the present Brazos River in central Texas. Further uplift in the earth's crust, however, reversed the direction of drainage in this area, turning it west toward the

Pecos. The old riverbed here became a series of lakes, springs, and sand-filled sinks. The ancient valley, now called the Portales Valley, can be traced from Taiban (at the edge of the Caprock) east to the Texas line past La Tule and Tierra Blanca lakes, and the salt lakes that comprise the Grulla National Wildlife Refuge southeast of Portales. The state of New Mexico has opened one of the most fascinating remnants from the ancient river as Oasis State Park; it is six miles north of Portales, reached via N.M. 467.

In 1902, Will Taylor homesteaded on the natural artesian lake amid shifting sand dunes and began planting trees around it. Now huge cottonwoods, chinaberries, locusts, and cedars grace the two-hundred-acre park. Here, in addition to enjoying camping and picnicking facilities, the stocked pond, and a nature trail, you can savor the deep shade of those wonderful trees, listen to the wind rippling the grass on the surrounding plain, watch children enjoying the dunes and the sparkling water, appreciate the wealth of mastodon bones still unearthed, and, relaxing in this oasis, feel even more at one with the high, open *llano*.

Between Clovis and Portales, U.S. 70 has made a wide curve, following the tracks of the old Pecos Valley Railroad. This railway line came through in the early 1890s, promoting agricultural settlement and the promise of irrigation all the way from Pecos, Texas, to Portales. At one time, special Pullman cars transported tourists roundtrip from Clovis to Carlsbad Caverns. The railroad missed the original settlement at Portales Springs, a watering place that had been a stopover for bison hunters, cattle drivers, and Billy the Kid's gang. The springs, whose arched portals Spanish speakers called *portales,* thus gave way to the new Portales on the tracks, soon to become the county seat of Roosevelt County, home of Eastern New Mexico University (ENMU), and "peanut capital of the world."

Clovis and Portales are close enough to be rivals, but each has its own specialties. Since 1927 when the legislature authorized the teachers' college (which later became ENMU) for the eastern plains, Portales has been a college town, and much of the life of the city still revolves around the university.

Located in the southwestern quarter of town, the spacious and shady ENMU campus has adopted the pattern of its administration building—English Tudor style with multicolored brick walls and slate roofs. The university offers undergraduate and graduate programs in business, education, fine arts, liberal arts, and sciences, as well as selected vocational-technical specialties.

The campus is a great place for walking, relaxing, and watching the fountains. The bold new theater at the northwest corner of the campus proclaims the importance of music and drama to the life of the university. It sponsors music and drama programs and is home to a local symphony orchestra. The Roosevelt County Museum, at the edge of the campus on U.S. 70, exhibits household articles, tools, and antiques from the late nineteenth and early twentieth centuries. Science fiction enthusiasts and fans of local author Jack Williamson will appreciate the Jack Williamson Science Fiction collection in the Golden Library.

Irrigation has made agriculture the major industry of Roosevelt County. Peanuts, cotton, wheat, corn, milo, hay, and potatoes head the list, followed by livestock feeding and dairy farming. Portales and the university jointly celebrate the annual Peanut Valley Festival in October. This is a perfect opportunity to visit Eastern's campus, browse the arts and crafts booths, and sample the peanuts and the varied and delicious cuisine prepared by the international students at ENMU.

Heading west out of Portales, most of the traffic takes the "Floyd Highway" (N.M. 267). However, we recommend that you follow U.S. 70 back to the square and turn north on Main Avenue, which becomes the "Bethel Highway" (N.M. 236). This back road zigzags along section lines and reveals the ups and downs of agricultural settlement on the high plains. Prosperous farms alternate with abandoned homesites. When homesteaders arrived with the railroad, the law granted them 160 acres per person or as much as 640 acres per family. Most people came expecting irrigation water to be available, but few areas actually had reliable irrigation projects until the 1940s. Meanwhile, families tried dry farming and experimented with a diversified pattern of grain cultivation, dairying, and livestock production. Scores of homesteaders left before they could "prove up" (stay the required five years) and lost their farms.

Some folks managed to last until they did get water. Then they had to begin dealing with the added costs, the salinization, decreasing soil fertility, and increasing pest problems that go along with high-input agriculture. During the 1970s and 1980s farms continued to fail at an alarming rate. The controversy over the attempt by the U.S. Air Force to acquire yet more farm land to expand the Melrose Bombing Range just west of here highlighted the issue in the mid-1980s. As in many farming areas of the country, the trick here is in finding a balance between a stable economy and a healthy environment.

As you take the turns on N.M. 236 and notice the farm roads that appear every mile, faithful to the cardinal points of the compass, it is easy to remember the Homestead Act, which since 1862 has delineated the entire Great Plains region. Townships six miles on a side consist of thirty-six sections. The law allocated two sections per township to provide for "common schools." Sections (640 acres) are subdivided into halves, quarters, and lesser fractions creating landholdings of 320, 160, 80, and 40 acres. Normally, surveyors plotted roads every mile to give public access to each quarter section. The resulting grid pattern seems to fit here and to be taken for granted in much the same way that the rectangular street grid (which originated with the Italian Renaissance) has become the norm in cities throughout the world.

After negotiating the numerous right-angle turns on N.M. 236, you may be relieved to go straight north on N.M. 267 across lush grazing land to Melrose. A favorite gathering place for locals and tourists alike is the well-endowed fruit stand just east of town on U.S. 60. Potatoes, sweet potatoes, fruit in season, pumpkins, squashes, honey, peanuts—all attest to the richness of the area. Melrose got its start with the Santa Fe Railroad's "Belen Cutoff," built at the turn of the century to eliminate much of the mountain hauling that the earlier route via Raton required. At that time, railroad builders were awarded up to ten sections of land for every mile of track laid.

Companies like the Santa Fe then lured settlers to towns often platted to include schools, churches, parks, and a denominational college. In the days of steam locomotives, the railroads needed a water source every 20 miles and a repair center (like Melrose) every 90 to 110 miles. Diesel engines freed rail travel from both requirements. Saint Vrain, Tolar, La Lande, Yeso, Cardenas, Grier, Cantara—the mostly vanished cutoff towns along this stretch of U.S. 60, both east and west of Melrose—are a reminder of those early railroad needs, and unfortunately, of the transitory and vulnerable nature of settlement in this part of the world.

Some of the drama of life on the high plains has been preserved in Melrose in an excellent collection of work by WPA artists. You will find works by Sheldon Parsons, Gene Kloss, Helmuth Naumer, H. B. Schleeter, José Ray Toledo, and others two blocks north of the highway in the school superintendent's office.

A highway marker at Stinking Springs just east of Taiban tells of the capture here of Billy the Kid in December 1880. Nothing remains of the stone house where Sheriff Pat Garrett's posse trapped Billy and his gang; but you can cross the tracks and have a look at the salt cedars along Alamosa Creek and imagine a cold winter day and a bunch of freezing, hungry men trying to hold out against Garrett. Michael Henry McCarty, alias William Antrim, alias William H. Bonney, alias Billy the Kid, first appeared in the New Mexico Territory with his family in Santa Fe and Silver City, and later on his own near Roswell. He shot Sheriff Brady in Lincoln, took part in the various battles of the Lincoln County War, hid out at Portales Springs, surrendered to Garrett here at Taiban, was shipped to Old Mesilla to be tried, and was marched back to Lincoln to be hanged. After a spectacular escape from the Lincoln County Jail, he returned again to this area. Three months later Pat Garrett finally tracked him down and killed him at old Fort Sumner.

Although at first most New Mexicans were glad to forget Billy the Kid and the lawlessness he symbolized, after he became a legendary hero the places he had frequented began to boast about their roles in his life and death. At no place is this more evident than here. On two different occasions Billy returned to this area with a price on his head when he could easily have slipped off to "Old Mexico." What attracted him? Was it a girlfriend? The intriguing and romantic story of Billy's life is dramatized on summer nights at the Caprock Amphitheater (near the end of the tour). Meanwhile, the Billy the Kid Outlaw Gang—a good-natured band of history buffs, business people, and local promoters who realize that if blue skies,

Datura or
Jimson Weed

waving wheat, friendly towns, and attractive parks will not lure tourists to eastern New Mexico then the Billy the Kid legend will—maintains its corporate headquarters in Taiban. The Big Red Indian Trading Post here houses official memorabilia of the gang, as well as rooms of old and miscellaneous items and biological specimens.

At Taiban you are already partway off the high plains. Designers of the railroad and highway preferred to follow the gradual descent that the creek provides instead of the dramatic drop-offs often encountered at the edge of the Caprock. As you head west out of town, you will descend below the mesa tops, see the cliff wall stretching around to the north, and then behold the Pecos Valley below. The river, the cottonwood groves, the old fort, and the present town of Fort Sumner lie ahead.

Turn south after milepost 301 for Fort Sumner State Monument and the grave of Billy the Kid. The 3.5-mile drive will reward you with views of the site of the old fort (including Pete Maxwell's house, where Pat Garrett shot Billy), Billy's tombstone (twice stolen and returned in recent years), the private Old Fort Sumner Museum, and the Bosque Redondo bird refuge. Migratory waterfowl, including sandhill and whooping cranes and blue herons, still rest here on their travels up and down the Pecos.

The state monument museum recounts the history of this site, which began as a centuries-old stopping place at the cottonwood grove on the

7

Pecos, then saw the construction of the fort during the Civil War and the lavish twenty-room house of Maxwell Land Grant heirs, followed by the fort's destruction by flood and partial restoration in recent years. It also tells the gruesome tale of the "Long Walk" of the Navajos, the winter of 1862–63 when Colonel Christopher Carson destroyed their crops and homes and then marched the tribe here from the Fort Wingate area. After several years and the failure of that resettlement policy, the Navajos were allowed to return across the four hundred miles to their present reservation. Plans are now being considered that would create the Bosque Redondo Memorial Project, to help preserve the memory of that time for Navajos, for Mescalero Apaches (who were also imprisoned here for a while), and for the general public.

Since Portales, the tour has followed the Fort Sumner Trail, a portion of the path over which John Chisum, Charles Goodnight, and others drove cattle from West Texas north to military outposts and railheads in Colorado and Wyoming. Long before that, the expeditions of Antonio de Espejo (1582) and Gaspar Castaña de Sosa (1590) explored this part of the valley of the Pecos. The town of Fort Sumner began as a civilian settlement calling itself Sunnyside Springs. Its inhabitants raised food and furnished other amenities to the fort. After the army withdrew, Fort Sumner flourished as a cattle town, a stagecoach stop, then a division point for the railroad, and eventually as the center of the irrigation district created by the construction of Alamogordo Dam upriver on the Pecos, growing quantities of apples, melons, grapes, sweet potatoes, and alfalfa.

Fort Sumner celebrates a four-day "Old Fort Days" festival in mid-June. Beginning with a staged bank robbery on Thursday and highlighted by a melodrama in the high school gym on Saturday night, the fiesta includes a black powder shoot, a "cowbelle" beef cook-off, an old-time camp meeting, a dog show, a water polo contest, an old fiddlers' contest, a Western dance, a Billy the Kid marathon, and an enchilada dinner.

Downtown Fort Sumner features another Billy the Kid museum, some of the fine secondhand treasure stores so plentiful in eastern New Mexico, and the intersection of highways. Turn north here on U.S. 84. Ten miles up the road N.M. 203 takes you six miles west to Sumner Lake State Park, site of Alamogordo Dam and its lake. A little town of unpretentious houses and cabins, some dating to the 1940s, sits across the dam. It has long been a retreat for people from a wide area. Once you have enjoyed what the lake offers (a choice among camping, fishing, boating, and water-skiing), you must make a decision. Retrace your steps back to U.S. 84 and head into Santa Rosa, with the Pecos Escarpment at a distance on your right, views of mountains on your left, and grass, cattle, wind, and sky near at hand. Or, if you feel adventurous, take the twenty-nine mile back road to Puerto de Luna by following N.M. 203 west from the lake. After leaving the pavement and route markers behind, continue proceeding mostly west and avoid all temptations to turn onto ranch roads until you see signs for Santa Rosa.

This second bold option will return you to the pavement and to a Pecos Valley with steep, high walls just south of Puerto de Luna. A green ribbon of irrigated farms stretches up both sides of the river from this point. Follow the highway (N.M. 91) across the river to see the plaza and the century-old church of Our Lady of Refuge, and the remains of a business district that once featured Alexander Grzelachowski's Mercantile (frequented by both Pat Garrett and Billy the Kid) and the former Guadalupe County Courthouse. This old settlement also played a role in Rudolfo Anaya's novel *Bless Me, Ultima,* the story of a boy whose loyalties are divided between the hardworking farmers of his mother's family (here in Puerto de Luna) and the stockmen of the llano on his father's side. Toward the end of the novel, the young hero runs from Puerto de Luna back to Santa Rosa, the same path up the Pecos, twisting between the spectacular cliffs on either side, that N.M. 91 now follows into Santa Rosa.

However you choose to get here, Santa Rosa is a small marvel. Peculiar geologic formations created the series of springs and natural lakes for which the city is famous. Underground springs feed Hidden Lake east of town, a favorite spot for admirers of Indian pictographs. James Wallace Park and Power Dam, south of town, offers excellent fishing (license required). El Rito Creek flows right through town and fills Park Lake, "the world's largest free swimming pool." Just east of Park Lake, a rock-rimmed pool far deeper than it is wide lures swimmers and scuba divers to its icy, clear recesses. This is Blue Hole, an artesian spring long a home for brilliant goldfish. Divers report that they can look up through ninety feet of water and see the stars of the night sky. What an enviable natural wonder, right in the heart of town, where you can gaze (or plunge) into the blue depths! How fortunate for a Santa Rosa child to have grown up with such cool and enchanting oases nearby!

Nine miles north, Los Esteros Dam backs up Pecos River water into the eighteen-thousand-acre Santa Rosa Lake. The state park here includes land grazed by pronghorn antelope as well as a site, near the edge of the llano, believed to have been favored by *comancheros,* traders who bartered with nomadic Indians of the plains. From atop the dam, far-off mesas rim the northern horizon; and in the middle distance, you can see several arms of the lake and some of the many miles of shoreline, which feature a boat ramp; camping and picnicking sites; comfort stations; a disabled-access nature trail and fishing for bass, walleye, and catfish. Looking downriver, the twisting, rocky gorge of the Pecos lures youthful spirits back toward Santa Rosa's crystal pools.

Settlers came to Santa Rosa during the 1860s, part of the migration of Hispanic people out of the core area of the northern New Mexico mountains. In 1897, Don Celso Baca built a chapel here dedicated to Santa Rosa de Lima, the first canonized saint of the New World. The Santa Rosa church, built later, and the hacienda headquarters of the Baca family continue in use, off N.M. 91 as you come into town from the south. When the territorial legislature created Guadalupe County in 1891, it honored Our Lady of Guadalupe, the vision of Jesus' mother, Mary, who appeared with messages to Juan Diego at the Indian town of Tepeyac, near Mexico City, in 1531. Puerto de Luna served as the first county seat during the 1890s until the Rock Island Railroad decided to make Santa Rosa a division point on its new transcontinental rail link between Chicago, El Paso, and Los Angeles. In 1901 four thousand railroad workers arrived in Santa Rosa. The railroads brought a smallpox epidemic, a roundhouse, prosperity, the county seat, and later Route 66 and Interstate 40 to the new town. After the railroad shops left, Santa Rosa came to depend upon ranching and farming trade and, increasingly, upon tourist business from the highway. You can choose among numerous motels and restaurants that line old Route 66 east-west through town.

The tour now follows I-40 up the escarpment on the west flank of the Pecos River. Through layers of eroding rock, past jutting promontories and inviting meadows, the superhighway makes the six-hundred-foot climb that represents eons of geologic time within a distance of five miles. Once on top, this far side of the Pecos offers views ahead of Glorieta Mesa and (to the right) of the mesas that form the Canadian Escarpment. Take the exit for U.S. 84, and for several miles you will be alone with another patch of high plain. The stands of grass on both sides of the road make it easier to imagine how the wide llano felt to Rudolfo Anaya's characters when "the grass was as high and as green as the waves of the ocean." Within a few miles, banded, notched mesa walls again come into view with mountains behind.

Thirteen miles north of I-40 the road drops once more to cross the Pecos River. Now we visit a section of the river with a seventy-mile string of villages settled continuously since the 1600s, which reminds us of the importance of New Mexico's "second river" to the exploration, settlement, and lore of the state. First you will see the cottonwoods and small farms and reddish stone houses of Dilia. Sacred Heart Church occupies center stage just off the highway on N.M. 119. Like many other small town churches in the area, Dilia's remains open during daylight hours, or the *mayordomo* may live nearby and can let you in. The altar screen, the choir loft, the stations of the cross, as well as details of the construction and maintenance of these thick-walled sanctuaries—all represent fascinating subjects for study and contemplation.

Anton Chico lies on a twelve-mile detour that will loop back to U.S. 84. On the way you pass the water tank and great stone buildings of Upper Dilia. Continue west, cross the river again, and turn right into old Anton Chico. Two tall spires locate

San Jose Church, where in 1880 the weddings of both Pat Garrett and Sallie Chisum, daughter of the Chisum Trail founder, took place. Nearby, Abercrombie's Store dates from the 1870s, when the town was the seat of the one-million-acre Anton Chico Grant and a magnet for freighters, cattlemen (including Billy the Kid), sheepmen, and traders. From Anton Chico in December 1880, Pat Garrett set out with his posse in pursuit of Billy and his gang. Earlier, in 1841, the Texas–Santa Fe Expedition passed near here on its mission to take possession of the eastern drainage of the Rio Grande for the Republic of Texas. Before progressing very far from Anton Chico, this force was overpowered, disarmed, and marched home via El Paso. Actually two communities, a lower and an upper, the high rock walls and heavy carved

Anton Chico

doors of both parts recall their settlement as frontier fortresses.

To continue the Pecos River loop, return to the Y in the road at the edge of town, and go right—which looks like the wrong way because it proceeds south for a bit before looping around to the northwest. Then enjoy the farms, pastures, and shady old homes of the valley. This will be your last look at the Pecos. No road leads farther upriver from here toward Villanueva, Ribera, San Miguel, or Pecos Village, but Tour Nine does include those old places.

Back on U.S. 84 north, continue across the plain, but keep a lookout ahead for mountains. By the time you have reached the old settlement of Los Montoyas, the road has squeezed itself up against the steep, white-capped walls that border wooded uplands. As you twist and climb, you can set your compass to the northwest against two landmarks up beyond Las Vegas. These are Hermit Peak and the usually snow-covered Elk Mountain, links in the largest mountain chain in the state, the Sangre de Cristo Range. Soon the highway begins to share the right-of-way with the Santa Fe Railroad. Amtrak passenger trains still use these tracks between station stops at Lamy and Las Vegas. Get on I-25 at Romeroville and watch for signs for N.M. 104 to exit east opposite Las Vegas. Tour Six describes Las Vegas, named "the meadows" by Spanish speakers—the settlement that straddles the boundary between the mountains and the plains, the trees and the grass. A left-hand turn here would divert you at least momentarily from the present tour, but would take you into the old city that is the gateway to the historic sites and recreation areas of northeastern New Mexico, that was once a major stopover on the Santa Fe Trail, and now is home of Highlands University.

Highway markers a few miles east along N.M. 104 direct you south to the Las Vegas National Wildlife Refuge. The four miles in to Crane Lake bring you out upon a peninsula of prairie bordered by deep, timbered canyons, which has long been a natural sanctuary for many birds and mammals. A short walk leads to Fred Quintana Overlook. From this vantage point above Crane Lake, you might spot sandhill cranes, teals, the Canada geese that winter here, antelope, mule deer, or golden eagles. Lake McAllister Waterfowl Area, three miles farther south, offers fishing from March 1 through October 31, boats limited to trolling speed. The refuge contains numerous other marshes and ponds, as well as sizeable areas of cropland to grow feed for the birds. These lakes, sitting high atop the prairie instead of nestled in a valley, challenge a person's idea of what would appeal to migrating waterfowl. The ducks, cranes, and geese must like it, because they choose these shallow windswept pools with a few lonely trees instead of the narrow protected canyons below.

The seventy-five miles east of Las Vegas to Conchas Lake are some of the least frequented in this part of the state. No travel services exist, and even those at Conchas may be closed during the off-season, so check your gas gauge before leaving Las Vegas. Without distractions along this stretch of road, we remember how attentive New Mexicans have long been to the clouds and the weather. Share the driving, giving everyone a chance to look up. The sky is more than half the world here, deep blue and cloudless or filled with a bewildering variety and beauty of shapes, colors, and textures. Or look back upon the Sangre de Cristos stretching nearly across the horizon. About eighteen miles out, the road crosses the headwaters of Conchas River, the stream that fills Conchas Lake before emptying into the Canadian River. The tour will remain within a few miles of these rivers until we climb back up onto the Caprock near San Jon.

A stone church and old stucco schoolhouse mark Trujillo, the first settlement on this road. Some of the buildings made of *terrones* probably date from the early 1800s. Photographers who love old buildings will find many subjects here—ancient houses and barns, stone and mud walls, metal roofs. Just beyond Trujillo, you are in for one of the most spectacular descents in New Mexico. The road crawls down the left side of a deep wooded gorge. After a while the canyon opens up, and you can see another plain far below, surrounded by the same cliffs that now enclose you. At one point on the downgrade, the road passes through a reddish layer of rock, which continues at this level for miles in both directions, along the mesa sides and around the hills. Having finished the thousand-foot drop, you see it all from a new angle, encircled by an immense escarpment tied together by the red stripe, the impressive litter from its fractured layers scattered at different degrees of uneasy equilibrium down the steep slopes. Corazon Creek cut the gorge we came down, and Corazon Peak lies ahead. Corazon Hill is something a person knows by heart after only one trip.

Travelers with postal business may turn off the road at the sign for the Trementina Post Office; an old ranch house complete with cats, lilacs, and flowers awaits you. The friendly people there, who have herded livestock under the ever-present mesa all their lives, can tell of the history of the region and direct you to the ghost town of Old Trementina, several miles off the highway.

Turn right to stay on N.M. 104 just past the

Trementina Post Office sign. Settlers in the 1870s never could figure out the Conchas River and named their town Variadero because it kept changing. There is a good bridge now and a few families and fruit trees in the little valley. At the junction with N.M. 129, we turn left and join boaters, campers, and fishermen who may be going to Conchas Lake.

The dam separates Conchas Lake State Park into two sections, the north shore and the south shore. Both offer boat ramps, water-skiing, campgrounds, picnic areas, and some of the best walleye and crappie fishing in New Mexico. The south shore, however, offers more extensive tourist amenities, including a nine-hole golf course, a thirty-eight-room lodge with restaurant and meeting facilities, an airstrip, and marine service and repair.

The thirty-one-mile stretch into Tucumcari parallels the Canadian River and the Canadian Escarpment to the north. Red-washed hills and low ridges color and shape this valley. To the south, an irrigation canal carries water from Conchas Lake to the Tucumcari Irrigation District, passing through

Horned lizard

several tunnels and crossing under the road near the Quay County line. Along the rest of the way into Tucumcari you can expect to see irrigated alfalfa, milo, corn, or other crops in season. At about the same point where the farming begins, a state historical marker tells the story of old Fort Bascom, four miles north on the banks of the Canadian River. Only low adobe mounds now remain of the outpost that served the army in the 1860s and 1870s in its campaigns against the Comanches and Kiowas.

The tour slips into Tucumcari the back way on North Second Street, takes the overpass above the railroad tracks, and deposits you downtown near the old railroad station. From this point U.S. 54 (Center Street) follows the Rock Island line northeast toward Ute Lake State Park; Dalhart, Texas; and the Midwest. Continuing south on First Street, you will find the Tucumcari Historical Museum (on South Adams), which displays twelve-thousand-year-old artifacts left by the Paleo-Indian big-game hunters, articles from the early ranching and railroad days, gems, minerals, and barbed wire. Just east of town, the Ladd S. Gordon Wildlife Area hosts ducks and geese during the winter, as well as visiting eagles, and people who hike and fish. In times past, these lakes have watered most of the folks who left the things exhibited in the museum: the Pleistocene-era hunters, more recent Plains Indians, cowboys on the Goodnight and Loving Trails, Comancheros, and later settlers.

During the last full week in June, the Tucumcari Piñata Festival features a Queen's Pageant, races, music, food booths, and a parade. Quay County holds its fair the third week in August at fairgrounds on the west edge of town. Residents of Tucumcari also take pride in their city hall and library, both built in new New Mexico style, using the design motifs of Pueblo and Colonial builders. You will find most of the motels and restaurants of Route 66 fame along the I-40 business loop. Follow this street east when leaving town and get on the Interstate a few miles out. Tucumcari Mountain, visible since the old Fort Bascom marker, now appears close at hand and still resembles a 1930s car. The irrigated farms continue for several miles, and an escarpment (remember the one you left as you descended into Fort Sumner?) appears again on the south.

Turn south off the freeway at San Jon. The proprietors of the antique store that occupies an old church there have information on the Caprock Amphitheater and know the history of the little town. Its name at first looks like some kind of English-Spanish variation on Saint John, but it really is a proper Spanish word (pronounced san-hone), meaning a big ditch.

A short drive south on N.M. 469 takes you to the bottom of the escarpment. The Caprock waits six hundred feet above, while the highway twists back and forth in its ascent. Local people call these "the breaks," the fractious, jumbled, and alluring boundary between the simple elegance of the upper and lower plains. The way up is startling at any time, but at sunset, or in a lightning storm, it is breathtaking. The top affords views in all directions—down ragged canyons, across the valley below, and out over the llano. Turn left just at the summit for the Caprock Amphitheater. Since 1987, the New Mexico Outdoor Drama Association has performed Don McAlavy's "Billy the Kid," Thursday through Saturday nights, from late June through late August. Produced by and for families, the musical drama brings to life the folk hero who has fascinated generations of Americans.

The forty-nine miles into Clovis complete the tour and return us to where we began, on the solid high ground of the Caprock. There will be no more ups and downs, no eroded canyons or gullied arroyos, but straight roads, right-angle turns, pasture and crops up to the right-of-way. The highway does not seem like an intruder here. With no need for cut and fill, it came into being without the accompaniment of rock drills, blasting apparatus, or gigantic earth-moving equipment, and seems content to lie atop the bedrock and blend in with the earth and sky.

An old stone school building identifies Wheatland, and the winter wheat for which it was named abounds in all directions. Short and low in late fall and winter, greening in the spring, and by June tall and wavy and ripening, the crop invites you to pick your season to be charmed once more. Dancing with the wind, the rough heads and straight stalks ripple and change colors against the sky—it is the world's picture of beauty and abundance. The handsome school at Grady, as well as the spacious public park, swimming pool, and tennis courts, attest to the wealth that this land can generate. Another sharp curve brings you into Broadview. Since the early 1980s, several innovative farming and ranching families in this part of New Mexico have discovered old and new methods of raising food in healthful, sustainable, and profitable ways.

Whatever you might think of guidebook authors who encourage travel at night when there is little they can tell you about to stop and see, and despite the sights you might miss, driving into the night has a special magic, especially here on the llano. During the period before the vast horizon turns into an immense darkness, the sun disappears, leaving clouds afire and shafts of multicolored light. For a while the streaks change every minute—red, pink, and orange against the blue-green, blue-gray, blue-black sky. Pale white splotches linger in the west, holding light in the world long after the sun has set. By the time it is completely dark, the full panoply of the heavens embraces you, and the planets and constellations are visible in every direction and not, as in the nights of other places, just glimpsed through wedges between trees or mountains. If you are lucky enough to be traveling at the time of a full moon, the rarest of sights is in store—the huge moon rising in the east while across the world the crimson sun slips down in the west.

New Mexico 209 conveys you to the heart of Clovis. If your needs are for meals and overnight accommodations, you will probably find what suits you on Prince Street (which brings you into town), Main Street (a mile west), or on Seventh Street, the route of east-west U.S. highways 70, 60, and 84. If you are looking for rest and relaxation of an outdoor kind, Clovis people recommend the spacious and well-kept Hillcrest Park and Zoo, located on Sycamore Street, north off East Seventh.

Seven and one-half miles north of town, the city of Clovis operates Ned Houk Memorial Park, 3,320 acres of rolling land on both sides of Running Water Draw. Numerous picnic shelters, playground equipment, volleyball courts, softball diamonds, overnight camping facilities, and four hundred acres of shaded lawn help explain why this park is a favorite for family outings and group events.

A glance at the history of Clovis will give some perspective to the city's other attractions. It all began with the railroad. The new town got its name, in fact, because a railroad official's daughter had been studying French history and chose for it the name Clovis, the first Christian king of the Frankish Empire. By 1910, two railroads—the

"Belen Cutoff" from the Rio Grande through Amarillo, and the Pecos Valley line to the south—used Clovis as their regional center. The creation of Curry County soon followed with Clovis as county seat. Both grazing and dry-land farming had been important industries here, but the 1950s saw the beginning of deep-well irrigation, which turned the southeast third of the county into an agricultural cornucopia of corn, grain sorghum, potatoes, vegetable crops, and cotton. Curry County, one of the smallest in New Mexico, leads all other counties in the production of wheat, sorghum, and sugar beets. The city's weekly livestock auctions rank among the top twenty in the nation, and Clovis leads all other horse and mule markets in the United States. At about the same time as the irrigation boom, the location of a Tactical Air Command Base at Cannon Air Force Base eight miles west of town added another ingredient to the area's economy. Expansion of the base in the 1990s promises even more jobs and local benefits.

You will find the stockyards and livestock auction on the southwest edge of town—cattle sales Wednesdays through Fridays, horses and mules on Mondays. The Fairgrounds, five miles east, hosts the largest county fair in the state in late August and the Pioneer Days Rodeo around Memorial Day, in addition to maintaining year-round the "Oldest House in Clovis" Museum. Travelers with musical or artistic tastes are directed to the Old Lyceum Theater at 411 Main Street. This landmark, built in 1919, fell on hard times in the 1970s. A "Save the Lyceum" group purchased the theater in 1982 and restored it to its original splendor. Now conventions, live drama and musical productions, talent shows, and film festivals keep the old place in continual use.

Clovis residents are pleased with the educational opportunities available to them. Eastern New Mexico University began offering college-level courses here in 1961. The Clovis campus soon came to rival the parent institution, serving three thousand students in credit programs in various academic and vocational areas at its new setting on the east edge of town. In 1990, Clovis voters approved independent status for the institution, as Clovis Community College. Clovis public schools, widely feared for their football prowess, also consistently place at the top in state music competitions.

A fact known by rock-and-roll enthusiasts but unsuspected by the general public is that Buddy Holly, Buddy Knox, Charlie Phillips, Jimmy Gilmer, and Roy Orbison all recorded their hits here in Clovis. The Clovis Music Festival, held annually in mid-August, celebrates Norman Petty and all the performers who recorded in his studio. The event includes five days of appearances by rock and country stars, a parade, car shows, hot-air balloons, and a tour of the original studios on Seventh Street.

Whether you are planning your first trip to the places described in this tour or wanting to go back again for another look, we suggest consulting the calendar in the front of the tourbook to help make your journeys even more fulfilling. For example, taking this tour in late August would mean that you could catch the Billy the Kid drama at the Caprock Amphitheater, go to the Curry County Fair, and maybe also attend Tucumcari's Piñata Festival. On the other hand, an earlier trip in June would be the right time for the Fort Sumner celebrations. Traveling in October is best for golden cottonwoods in the valleys and the Portales Peanut Festival, April and November for migrating cranes, and early spring for watching the countryside coming to life. Winter can be a beautiful season in all parts of the tour, but visitors are forewarned of the hazards of sudden snowstorms that can afflict the entire area. Whichever time you pick, we are confident you will enjoy the trip.

TOUR EIGHT
THE
ENCHANTED
CIRCLE

Places:	Taos, Taos Pueblo, Questa, Red River, Eagle Nest, Angel Fire, Taos
Mileage:	Approximately seventy-five miles, excluding side trips
Suggested travel time:	Two days
Highways:	N.M. 68, N.M. 240, N.M. 522, N.M. 38, U.S. 64
Accommodations:	Taos, Questa, Red River, and Angel Fire
Camping:	Taos, Rio Grande River park, and along N.M. 38 and N.M. 64

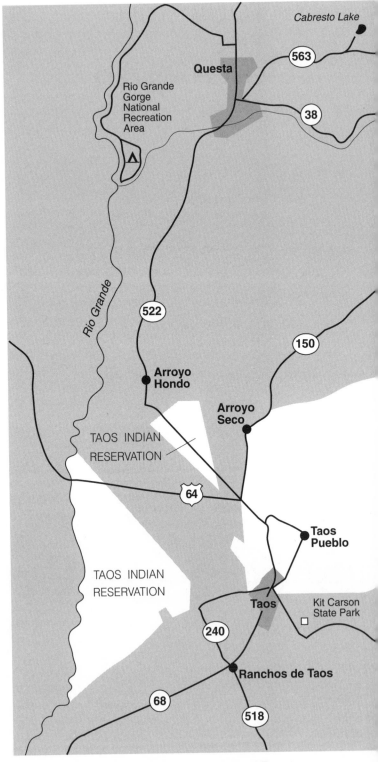

NOTE: Numerous campsites in Carson National Forest

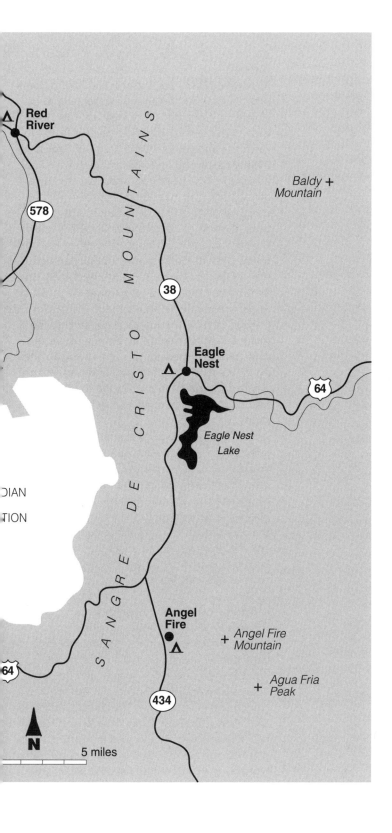

Taos, a town best known for its ancient three-storied pueblo, is the starting and end point for this compact tour. Taos is also famous for a history that intertwined Hispanics, Indians, and Anglos, sometimes in peaceful trade ventures, sometimes in violent confrontations. The area was "discovered" early in this century by writers such as D. H. Lawrence and painters beginning with Ernest Blumenschein and Bert Phillips. Skiers were later attracted to the nearby ski resort founded by a Swiss. Today the town center is packed with tourist shops, while Taos Pueblo fiercely guards its traditions. Outside of Taos the tour (popularly known as the Enchanted Circle) loops through several small towns with intriguing names and varying personalities—Hispanic Questa, Western-styled Red River, and tranquil Eagle Nest—bypassing the resort of Angel Fire to double back through the narrow Taos Canyon to Taos. The loop is about seventy-five miles; taking time out for a rest or a picnic and some rapid sightseeing, you can do it in an afternoon. We recommend longer. Taos warrants a full day to appreciate the pueblo, the galleries and historic buildings in town, and to browse in the shops.

For those travelers driving north to Taos, we recommend the approach to Taos on N.M. 68; as you climb out of the narrow Rio Grande Canyon onto the plateau, you see the Sangre de Cristo Mountains rising on the east and the north, and the plateau stretching out to the west, broken only by the dark slash of the Rio Grande gorge. The pueblo and the town are tucked under the shadow of Pueblo Peak and the Sangre de Cristos; little communities dot the mesa.

Ranchos de Taos may once have been a farming center for local Indians. Spanish settlers moved into the area in 1716, but frequent raids from nomadic Indians prevented permanent settlement until the latter part of the century, when most of the hostilities were over. The Spanish and the Taos Indians who resettled Ranchos de Taos fortified its church and plaza anyway. The church, named for Saint Francis of Assisi, looks like a fortress from the rear, its massive walls and solid form much photographed and painted. This is what you see from the highway as you drive into Ranchos. Be on your guard; the driver in front of you may suddenly recognize a view from a Georgia O'Keeffe painting or Ansel Adams photograph and screech to a stop without warning.

From the square in front, the church appears less massive, its twin bell towers and cross presenting a more traditional appearance. Inside, the church is shaped in a cross, dominated by the large *reredos* at the head framing old portraits of saints. Another *reredos* fills the north transept. Paintings and pieces of art from Europe and the Colonial period of New Mexico, tin candleholders, and wooden stations of the cross decorate the church. If you wish, you can view a portrait that is said to glow mysteriously in the dark. Whitewashed walls contrast with the dark wood of the pews and the enormous *vigas.* Although old, this is an active parish, whose members maintain the church by plastering the exterior walls with mud in the traditional fashion, and celebrate Mass regularly including at Christmas time, when they light bonfires, or *luminarias,* in a little cemetery in front of the church.

Ranchos de Taos was aptly named for the little farms that sprang up south of Taos. The village centers around the church and plaza, ringed by studios, souvenir shops, and a restaurant, but most of Ranchos spreads east and west of the highway. An exploration along the winding old dirt roads that lead out of the village will take you to crumbling adobe homes, rambling haciendas, brilliant flower gardens, irrigated fields, and splendid views of the mountains and mesas. The road west of Ranchos de Taos, Highway 240, leads into Taos past the Martinez hacienda, avoiding the sprawl of new buildings that have sprung up along the main road into town.

The hacienda lies just off the road, across a bridge straddling the Rio Pueblo. Simple but impressive, the hacienda was constructed during the Spanish colonial period (1804–27), when colonists lived a hardscrabble life. The Kit Carson Foundation has restored the hacienda; when you step into it today, you become part of the early nineteenth century. You may purchase a ticket here not only for the hacienda but also for the two other museums operated by the Foundation, the

Blumenschein and Kit Carson homes.

The hacienda belonged to Don Antonio Severino Martinez, a merchant who transported goods from Mexico up the Camino Real. He bought a small building for his family when he moved to the area in 1804 and over the years added to it, placing the new rooms around two courtyards, or *placitas.* The family's rooms and activities centered around the larger *placita;* servants' and utility rooms faced the smaller *placita.* For reasons of security—raids from Plains Indians were not uncommon—the thick adobe walls had no exterior windows. Two *zaguáns,* or gates, were the only entrances for the *carretas,* or carts, which brought in trade goods from Mexico for sale. The hacienda's thick walls are made of hand-smoothed adobe with rough wood supports; a few pieces of simple furniture rest on hard-packed mud floors. In the midst of such practicality, however, Don Antonio had his workmen make wooden planks for floors of the special rooms, for example, the *gran sala.* Don Antonio needed such a grand room; he was the *alcalde* of Taos for several years, and the family remained influential in the area. Don Juan, the youngest son, ran the hacienda after his father's death and later served in the legislature.

The eldest son also served in the legislature, although he was a priest; Father Antonio José Martinez was both the spiritual and political leader of northern New Mexico. His visibility brought him into conflict with Bishop Lamy, when the latter began his reform of New Mexico in the 1850s. Excommunicated by his bishop, Father Martinez led his own church until his death. Today he is remembered for his work in education and for his advocacy on behalf of his parishioners and constituents.

Because the rooms of the hacienda have been restored authentically—the kitchen with its utensils and herbs, the trade room with Mexican merchandise—you can participate vicariously in the activities of the hacienda. Sometimes a craftperson will be weaving a shawl or carving tiny birds from local woods in one of the display rooms. A short walk through the grounds of the hacienda leads you along the river, shaded by cottonwoods, with an unobstructed view of the mountains. In fall the Old Taos Trade Fair is reenacted here, when mountain men mingle with Indians from Taos and the Plains, and everyone enjoys native foods, crafts demonstrations, and entertainment. The fair recalls the trade fair held annually in Taos, when Indians came from all directions to trade with colonists. The hacienda is also open for weddings and other local functions, so it continues to bustle with life.

To reach the town of Taos proper (or San Fernando de Taos to distinguish it from the pueblo named for San Gerónimo), follow Highway 240/ Ranchitos Road into town and park near the plaza. (You could bypass Taos completely by taking Upper Ranchitos Road from its intersection with N.M. 240 to N.M. 522, the road to Questa and points north. This is a lovely section of Taos, the narrow road passing under shady trees and past old homes. This might be the route for those people wanting to make the circle tour before exploring the town and pueblo.)

If you take the direct route into Taos from Ranchos de Taos, you may be dismayed by the approach. Progress means new buildings. Although many of these are built in the requisite adobe style, they cannot escape what they are: gas stations, motels, fast-food joints, and modern shopping centers. But once in Taos, you find yourself in a small town whose narrow streets surround an old plaza and lead to homes that belonged to Kit Carson and Governor Bent, to artists' galleries and inns. A logical place to start exploring Taos is the plaza, where you may join a guided walking tour of the town or you can set out on your own.

The old Taos plaza has taken on a modern look since 1976; it is now multilevel and bricked over. Shade trees and iron benches invite the traveler to sit and watch the traffic and people go by. On weekends and holidays local residents cruise the plaza, sometimes in low-riders that have been lovingly worked on so that they perform amazing hydraulic feats. In the center of the plaza the American flag flies twenty-four hours a day. At one time this was a unique honor granted to Taos by Congress to thank Kit Carson and friends for protecting the flag from local Confederate sympathizers who tried to tear it down during the Civil War.

The bandstand was a gift from art patron Mabel Dodge Luhan, who arrived in Taos in 1917, and, fascinated by her surroundings, remained until her death, attracting many other artists and writers to the locale. The iron cross in the southeast corner is a memorial to New Mexicans who died in the Bataan Death March during the Second World War. To the north of the plaza the old Taos County Courthouse has been taken over by shops and galleries, as have most of the buildings that once served the townspeople in more traditional and practical ways. Around the plaza, shops display a mixture of serious art, tourist trinkets, and collections of T-shirts. On the south side, La Fonda hotel, famous for its D. H. Lawrence paintings, stands on the site of an old store, owned by men whose names are well known in Taos, Charles and William Bent and Cerán and Marcellin St. Vrain. The men were prominent businessmen of their time; Charles Bent became the first American governor of the Territory of New Mexico.

Put La Fonda on hold until later and continue on foot, leaving the plaza at the southwest corner and following the road to Ledoux Street, a narrow thoroughfare that takes you to art galleries, the old Blumenschein home, and the Harwood Foundation and public library. In summer, the hot sun can be uncomfortable, which makes the cool adobe interiors of these old buildings even more attractive. R. C. Gorman, the famous Navajo artist, has a gallery in an old adobe home on Ledoux. Here you find examples of his distinctive prints, paintings, sculptures, and ceramics.

Close by, the Blumenschein House is open to visitors. Ernest Blumenschein was one of the co-founders of the Taos Society of Artists. The story of how he came to New Mexico is famous: Blumenschein and his friend Bert Phillips were on their way to New Mexico in 1898 to paint the West. Their wagon lost a wheel near Questa, and the men repaired it in Taos. Phillips remained in Taos; Blumenschein visited over the years, settling permanently in 1919. Other artists joined them, producing romantic paintings of the West. The home Blumenschein lived in, with his wife and daughter, dates from the 1790s. Blumenschein bought four rooms in 1919, adding more rooms over the years. A mixture of European and Spanish colonial furnishings fill the rambling home, whose comfortable rooms, including the busy kitchen and the bedrooms, are kept as they were during the Blumenscheins' time. Ernest, his wife, Mary, and daughter, Helen, all painted. Their paintings cover the walls, along with works of other well-known Taos artists.

Next door to the Blumenschein House, the Harwood Foundation building is also a National Historic Site. The building was once the home of the Jaramillos, contemporaries of Kit Carson. After the University of New Mexico purchased the building in 1935, John Gaw Meem expanded it, keeping the Pueblo Revival style that Bert Simpson, the previous owner, had helped make famous in New Mexico. Taoseños are privileged to have their public library housed in these airy rooms with high ceilings, polished wooden floors, and old bookshelves. History buffs should ask about the extensive collection of Southwestern history books. Children enjoy their special reading room in the east wing, enhanced by toys and models. Works by many of the famous artists who lived in Taos hang on the walls throughout the building and in the gallery upstairs, where you can also view the Mabel Dodge Luhan Santo Collection.

If you are on a leisurely visit to Taos, you should explore some of the other streets north of Ledoux Street and west of the plaza, before heading back to the plaza. Stop in at La Fonda Hotel. Photographs of friends of the owner line the entrance to the lobby, which is hung with Indian rugs, bullfight memorabilia, portraits of famous citizens of Taos, and other paintings. You must pay a fee to view the D. H. Lawrence paintings, which are kept in a locked room. These paintings were once banned in Britain; modern voyeurs will wonder what the fuss was about.

Leave the plaza by the eastern entrance and head east on Kit Carson Street. Kit Carson's Home and Museum is another of those massive, walled homes built around a patio, so favored by early settlers. The famed scout bought this home as a gift for his bride, Josefa Jaramillo, when they married in 1843. The family lived there for twenty-five years, and Kit Carson became a respected member of the community. (Carson is not so revered in Navajo country, where he is better known for his forays against the Navajo in Canyon de Chelly and on the Long Walk.) Three of the museum's rooms are furnished as family rooms; the other nine rooms highlight the life and times of Carson and other Taos–area trappers with a collection of artifacts ranging from mundane household goods and chatty letters to genuine archaeological relics.

Back on the main street, walk north past shops featuring the latest in Southwestern chic and art to the historic Taos Inn, whose lobby dates from the 1800s, when it was the enclosed courtyard of a grand home. It is not far to the next stop, the Stables Art Gallery, run by the Taos Art Association. The Spanish colonial home now shows changing exhibits by local and other artists. After your visit to the gallery, it is time to return to your car. As you head for the parking lot, follow Bent Street to Governor Bent's house, where that unfortunate man was killed at the time of the American take-over of the territory. The Taoseños—Hispanics and Pueblo—did not welcome the change to American rule and revolted briefly in what is called the Taos Rebellion, killing not only the governor but several members of his family. South of Bent Street, the house of Long John Dunn, a famous gambler and stagecoach driver, has been divided into a series of shops selling everything from coffee to old maps to the ubiquitous T-shirts, all connected by a board-walk.

A pillar carved by Nicholas Fechin

As you drive north on Main Street, you pass Kit Carson Park, where the famous scout is buried, along with other important personages like Mabel Dodge Luhan. Leafy trees will provide welcome shade and a play area for active children. In October, the Wool Festival is held here, a celebration of sheep and other wool-bearing animals, with demonstrations of shearing and weaving and other entertainment. Next you come to the Fechin House and Studio, designated as both State and National Historic Sites. Nicholas Fechin, a Russian artist who lived in Taos in the 1920s and 1930s, built his home and studio in traditional Southwest style, then personally hand-carved not only the furniture but the doors, windows, gates, posts, a fireplace, and a staircase with traditional Russian designs. The result is a fascinating mixture of Southwest and Russian country styles, which form a backdrop to the exhibits of Eastern art that especially interested Fechin. When you leave Fechin House, keep north on Pueblo Road (or Paseo del Pueblo Norte) to get to the pueblo.

Taos Pueblo, set at the foot of the Sangre de Cristo Mountains and divided by the Rio Pueblo de Taos, or Pueblo Creek, has been settled since around A.D. 1350. About one thousand people live here, in buildings little changed since they were built centuries ago. The Taos Indians speak Tiwa, as do the pueblos of Sandia, Pícuris, and Isleta, but your guides and most of the people you will meet are English-speaking, for the lives of the Pueblo Indians have been intertwined (not always happily) with nearby Anglo and Hispanic settlers since they started wandering into the area. The pueblo is one of only two pueblos—the other is Acoma—that charges an admission fee (there are extra charges for photographing or sketching), but the price is well worth it. You can join a guided tour if you wish; in summer the pueblo is crowded with visitors, but in winter, you are more likely to be one of only a handful of people and may walk around the plaza on your own.

As the northernmost of the pueblos, Taos was isolated from the other pueblos and Spanish settlements. Although the Spaniards did build a mission here in 1617, there were few settlers in the area during the early colonizing efforts and up to the time of the Pueblo Revolt of 1680. This did not keep Taos from joining the revolt. Indeed, Popé, a San Juan Indian, planned the revolt with others from Taos after he was flogged by the Spanish for practicing witchcraft and had fled his own pueblo. Many years later, Indians joined local Hispanics in revolts against both an unpopular Mexican government in 1837 and the Americans fewer than ten years later. Despite such setbacks, the town of Taos has grown, and the pueblo has coexisted, sometimes uneasily, with its neighbors to the south. Men of the tribe have traditionally farmed their land, but as the population has grown while acreage remains constant, more members of the tribe have left the pueblo, either to work in town or out of the county, returning only for feast days.

8

Taos architecture remains the model for pueblo architecture, although in most pueblos only one-story homes remain. Taos has deliberately preserved the structures three or more stories high that provide homes, storehouses, and places of worship for pueblo residents. Conservative leaders have only recently allowed windows and doors on the lower floors. Originally, there were no entrances to the lower floors as a protection against marauders. Ladders—then and now—are the only means of entry to the top floors. The pueblo residents still use *kivas* and other sacred places for ceremonies. The public is not allowed access into these places, or indeed to most of the pueblo. Do not disregard the off-limits warning signs.

One building that is open, however, is the San Gerónimo church at the west end of the plaza, its whitewashed walls contrasting with the dominant adobe color of the other buildings ringing the plaza. The church is built on the site of the original mission built in Taos in 1617 and destroyed in the Revolt of 1680. Reconstructed in 1707, the mission was again destroyed in the uprising of 1847, when Indians, fearful of the power of the new foreign presence, tried to drive away officials of the American government. San Gerónimo is much smaller than some of the other mission churches, but it is striking, with Indian designs delicately traced on bright white walls. The church is named after San Gerónimo, or Saint Jerome, the patron saint of the pueblo. Mass is celebrated here on Sundays and on the many Catholic saint's days that Taos, like all the other pueblos, celebrates side by side with traditional feast days. One of the pueblo's most sacred days is set aside for rituals at Blue Lake, high above the pueblo in the Sangre de Cristo Mountains. Blue Lake's site had been included in lands appropriated by the federal government after the Americans took over New Mexico. Years of negotiations passed before the lake was returned to the tribe. No outsiders are allowed to witness these rituals.

Although Taos Pueblo keeps secret its religion and many of its traditions, its residents are happy to share several feast days with the public. One of the most popular honors San Gerónimo at the end of September, when thousands of visitors crowd the plaza to enjoy food, dancing, the antics of the *Koshare* (who pick on visitors and residents alike), the pole-climbs (where young men try to seize a dead sheep at the top), and foot races. The pueblo also invites outsiders to celebrate Christmas with them—to join in the procession of the Virgin on Christmas Eve and to watch the Deer Dance the next day. Festivities in early January commemorate New Year's and Three Kings Day with the Turtle and Buffalo or Deer dances; dancers perform the Corn Dance for the feasts of the Holy Cross, San Antonio (Saint Anthony), San Juan (Saint John), and Santiago (Saint James). Check with the pueblo before you plan to take a trip; you may be fortunate enough to join in these celebrations (leave your cameras at home, however; picture taking on feast days is not allowed).

Taos drums, carved from wood and topped with cowhide, are famous for their tones; you can purchase these and the typical Taos pottery made from micaceous, glittery clay at shops around the plaza or at the museum gift shop near the plaza. The modest museum displays artifacts from historical Taos. Although you may not go beyond the plaza to explore more of the pueblo, you can go horseback riding with a guide in the summer and sleigh riding in the winter. Inquire at the information center at the museum for directions to the horse ranch.

As you leave Taos headed north on N.M. 522, past the businesses strung along the side of the road, you will notice how houses are set haphazardly on the plain: old adobes, new condos, and the ubiquitous mobile homes. Taos is definitely not a planned community. At the intersection with N.M. 64, take a sharp left turn and follow the signs for the Millicent Rogers Museum. This gem of a museum is named for a Taos resident who collected Hispanic and Native American art. Ms. Rogers did not focus on only one aspect of Indian art; she collected it all—jewelry, textiles, baskets, pottery, and paintings. Her collection became the core of the museum's collection when it was founded in 1953. A number of pots by Maria, the famous potter from San Ildefonso, and her family, form one of the more important treasures of the museum. The collections are housed in a lovely

8

Southwestern building that enhances not only the Native American works but also examples of the Hispanic arts of New Mexico—santos, colcha embroidery, weavings, and other arts. You will also find more humble utensils and tools from the seventeenth and eighteenth centuries, along with works of modern New Mexican artists and craftspeople.

Leaving the Millicent Rogers Museum, you are not far from the Rio Grande Gorge. At the intersection with N.M. 64, turn left and follow the highway across what appears to be an endless plain but which is soon interrupted by the gorge. Park before the gorge and walk across the narrow bridge. Hundreds of dizzying feet below, the Rio Grande appears to be a trickle. During raft-running season, you can watch the rafters below preparing to navigate the famous Taos Box, where the river flows between the high cliffs. (If you are interested in a raft trip during your tour, make arrangements with one of the companies that arranges "floats" down the Rio Grande, starting south of Taos at Pilar or north of Taos for the Box run.)

To explore the famed Taos Ski Valley, take another side trip via N.M. 150. The road is paved and well maintained to accommodate the thousands of skiers who descend upon the valley in winter. It crosses the plain before skirting the *arroyo seco,* or dry ditch, from which the community of Arroyo Seco takes its name. Crowded around a curve in the road, restaurants and guesthouses cater to the skiing crowd. Outside Arroyo Seco, the highway looks down at Valdez before it winds through the valley, entering the Carson National Forest and paralleling the Rio Hondo as it heads up to the ski area. An old toll road built to take miners up to Amizette, a small town on the site of the present-day Ski Valley operation, once traveled this same route. Today the valley bustles with the activities of skiers in the winter and language and music institutes in the summer. Some practice sessions and performances of the Angel Fire and Taos Music Festivals are held at the ski lodge. Looking up at the ski lift, which takes skiers up the steep hillside, you can appreciate why Taos has the reputation of being one of the most challenging ski areas in North America. But beginners can ski here too; slopes are gentler once you get past that first ascent. In summer, you can hike up to Wheeler Peak, the highest point in New Mexico, via a well-marked Forest Service trail. The easy sixteen-mile roundtrip offers spectacular views. Another, shorter, route is via Williams Lake. Be sure to check on the exact route and weather conditions before you start, and carry water and warm clothing.

For the Enchanted Circle portion of your trip, return to N.M. 522 and head north. Soon you dip down into Arroyo Hondo, a small community blessed with wondrous views of the Sangre de Cristo Mountains and the western high plain. At one time, back in the 1850s, Arroyo Hondo was a center of religious folk art, and craftspeople turned out fine paintings and santos for their church, the *moradas* of the Penitentes, and private chapels. Little of this art remains in the village.

At milepost 10 a sign points to the D. H. Lawrence Ranch, site of the famous English writer's burial place, now used as a retreat for the University of New Mexico. If you take a short detour here, you find yourself on a gravel road for some five miles until the road splits again, with the right fork continuing up to the ranch. You may enjoy the short trip up to the ranch to view the peculiar, hand-built mausoleum that contains the writer's ashes. The Lawrences had visited Mabel Dodge Luhan at her ranch in Taos and were fascinated by the place. Mabel owned the land on the mountainside and gave it to Frieda Lawrence in exchange for Lawrence's manuscript for *Sons and Lovers*. D. H. Lawrence loved the ranch site; he and his wife lived there for two years.

At milepost 14, a road leading to Lama is on the right, one to Cebolla Mesa to the left. A prayer stick and flags in the Buddhist tradition announce the Lama Foundation's presence about 3.5 miles in, with a sign noting that the foundation is open to the public on selected dates throughout the year or for longer visits if you make arrangements with the foundation members on one of those days. The town of Lama is made up of scattered homesites along the road. A rough dirt road to the west loops around Cebolla Mesa, leading to the very edge of the Rio Grande Gorge, where the adventurous can follow a steep trail down to the river.

Farther on down N.M. 522, a road off to the left takes you to the Red River Fish Hatchery, a delightful field trip that teaches how fish are "grown" and released into streams and lakes in New Mexico. You can camp along the hatchery road. As the highway dips down into Questa, you may catch sight of Turquoise Lake to the left (this was actually a filter tank for the huge molybdenum mine nearby and a source of great anxiety for environmentalists). You will also see the tumbling waters of the Red River before it enters the Red River Canyon to the east. Questa's fortunes rise and fall with those of molybdenum, an element used in tempering steel, and much of the area has a temporary look, although the village history dates from 1821. By 1849 about one hundred families farmed the area; they called their settlement San Antonio del Rio Colorado (Saint Anthony of the Red River). The Church of St. Anthony, down a little hill off the road, is Questa's oldest building, dating from 1873. Later, with the building of a post office, the town became the more prosaic Questa, which in Spanish means slope. Farming and trading continued as the lifeblood of the area until the early part of this century, when molybdenum mining began. There is still ranching and farming, but when the mine was active, most of the work force in the area received its paycheck from Molycorp.

Three miles north of Questa on 522, the well-maintained N.M. 378 takes you through tiny Cerro down to the Rio Grande Gorge National Recreation Site. Here the Rio Grande meets the Red River, and a Wild Rivers Celebration is held in the late summer. You can camp on the canyon rim and hike down to the river for fishing or just communing with the river gods. Rangers lead guided hikes on weekends from Memorial Day through Labor Day, explaining the ecology and geology of the site. You can obtain information about the area on your own at the visitor center and the overlooks throughout the site, and take unguided walks along the paths at the bottom of the gorge. Naturalists, fishermen, and canoeists will all find something to do at the Wild River area; the less active can watch the clouds go by.

Backtrack to N.M. 38 and head east to Red River, past a funky antique store advertising the famous Questa honey and the Busy Bee honey farm. Just out of town a tiny, bright turquoise lake tempts you to stop and picnic, but there will be several such spots along the way. A ranger station here provides Forest Service maps of the Carson Forest, which extends over half of the Enchanted Circle, and detailed maps of the Wheeler Peak Wilderness Area. Farther in, steep canyon walls edge the road on the left; Red River parallels the road on the right. An entrance to the closed Molycorp Mine from the road intrudes on the wilderness. At Goat Hill a small campground with picnic tables, primitive restrooms, and easy river access for little ones invites you to stop for a rest. In the fall the aspen and cottonwood paint brilliant gold flashes against the deep green mountainsides, and wayside shrubs pick up the color in varying shades. Columbine Creek Campground provides more picnic places and many campsites for overnighting. Notice on the left the leftovers of Molycorp Mine spilling down the hillsides, and at milepost 6 the huge plant buildings and gray tailings held back by a brave line of pine trees.

Near milepost 10 are several more campgrounds—Fawn Lakes, Elephant Rock, and Junebug—and then, as the canyon widens, you are suddenly in Red River. Like many other Western towns, Red River began when prospectors settled in the attractive valley and named their town after the waters of the river, which ran red after a rain. The fortunes of the little town depended on the availability of metals, leading to a boom and bust economy. The Molycorp Mine helped boost the population, but Red River has never again equaled the population of four thousand or so that lived there in the late 1890s. Recently, the popularity of winter sports has made tourism the major industry and has caused an identity problem. Red River does not seem to know whether it wants to be a Western town or an alpine village—the new lodgings and stores reflect both. As you drive into Red River, to your right you will notice old cabins and the abandoned ski lift from the Powder Puff ski area, which has been replaced by new equipment and modern condos in Red River. In the summer, visitors enjoy the cool climate, jeep tours, hiking, and fishing. The West Fest in June, hosted by well-known Western singer Michael Martin Murphey, brings together the talents of cowboy poets, singers, and horsemen. Fall brings the Aspencade, and the winter season ushers in all kinds of snow sports.

While you are in Red River, you might take advantage of the relatively easy access to hike to Wheeler Peak, New Mexico's highest mountain (although till now you probably have not even noticed it among the many lofty peaks). Wheeler is popular because it is a relatively easy climb, with spectacular views from the top. This trip must be made in the summer, and even then the weather can vary; be prepared for cold winds and rain, and be on the alert for lightning. Just out of town, N.M. 578 follows the West Fork of the river and then up the Middle Fork (four-wheel-drive recommended), where a hiking trail leads past Middle Fork Lake and up to the summit of Mount Wheeler. Because of the easy access to Wheeler from Taos Ski Valley, you might prefer not to interrupt your loop tour at this juncture but to save the ascent for later. There are other enjoyable hikes out of Red River that vary in length and difficulty—some trails are reached by car, others from the ski lift. Be sure to check at the Ranger Station on N.M. 38 or in Red River on the exact location and difficulty of the trails before you set out.

Out of Red River the road signs direct you to Eagle Nest, the next town of any size. The road climbs along the side of the valley with views of Wheeler Peak on the right. You will pass an exit to Enchanted Forest on the right. In winter this is a Nordic ski area with trails for the inexperienced and experienced skier winding through the forest, leading to some breathtaking scenery. At its highest point, 9,820 feet, the road goes over Bobcat Pass before descending through meadows into the widening Moreno Valley, with views of rangeland, some old log cabins, and ruins of brick buildings to the right. Look for a sign to Elizabethtown, once a thriving wild west town but now little more than a crumbling cemetery.

Eagle Nest sits at the edge of Eagle Nest Lake, a bright blue body of water with Angel Fire Mountain and the Sangre de Cristos as a backdrop. The private lake, very popular with fishermen, resulted from the damming of Cimarron River in 1919. The little town was built soon after and named for the golden eagles that soared among the mountains. Motels, bait shops, restaurants, and a general store are strung along Main Street. Continue the loop by heading south on U.S. 64.

The DAV Vietnam Veterans National Memorial, the first memorial to Vietnam veterans, soars from the hillside just off the road near Angel Fire. There is room for parking and an easy path up to the chapel, even for visitors in wheelchairs. Victor Westphall and his family built the chapel in memory of Dr. Westphall's son, who was killed in Vietnam in 1968. The Westphalls wanted the memorial to take advantage of the natural beauty of the area, and they built a simple yet commanding chapel on the hillside. Outside, the building resembles a seagull; inside, the focus is on one tall, narrow window overlooking the Moreno Valley. There is little else to distract the visitor. A tiny exhibition area honoring Vietnam veterans was added after the Disabled American Veterans took over the maintenance of the memorial.

Looking out from the memorial, you can see the resort of Angel Fire off N.M. 434. Advertised as a full-season resort, Angel Fire attracts golfers, fishermen, and music lovers in the summer and skiers in the winter, especially since its snow-making machines free it from dependence on the weather. Balloon fiestas, seminars, and art shows keep visitors coming to Angel Fire year-round. Modern condos distinguish the little town from its neighbors (see Tour Six). As you return to U.S. 64, you climb up to Palo Flechado Pass before descending into the narrow Taos Canyon, where the road parallels the Rio Fernando de Taos. Fall, when the road is lined with varying shades of gold from river cottonwoods, aspen, chamisa and other colorful shrubs, is a particularly lovely time to take this drive. There are several camping spots along the way, and homes ranging from fancy to humble, all in their own way taking advantage of a beautiful setting. Highway 64 ends up in downtown Taos, but there is a bypass that brings you out near Ranchos de Taos, a shortcut for people heading directly to Santa Fe and points south.

Taos and the Enchanted Circle pack so many sights and activities into one short loop that it would be wearying to see and do everything on one trip. Keep this tour handy as you get to know the Taos area better. On your return you may want to visit the Taos Spring Arts Celebration in May and June and the Poetry Circus, also in June; or the Pueblo Pow-wow in July; to hear both classical and country music all summer; to experience the Wild Rivers Celebration; to visit the Trade Fair and Wool Festival in the fall; and to ski in winter.

TOUR NINE
OLD
HIGHWAYS
TO
EVERYWHERE

9

Places: Albuquerque, Clines Corners, Villanueva, Pecos National Historic Park, Pecos, Cowles, Lamy, Galisteo, Moriarty, Albuquerque

Mileage: Approximately 270 miles, excluding side trips

Suggested travel time: A weekend

Highways: I-40, N.M. 3, I-25, N.M. 63, N.M. 50, U.S. 285, N.M. 553, N.M. 41, I-40

Accommodations: Albuquerque, Moriarty, Pecos, and Galisteo

Camping: Albuquerque, Moriarty, Villanueva, Pecos, and Santa Fe National Forest

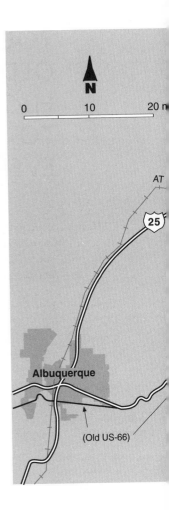

N

0   10   20 m

AT

25

Albuquerque

(Old US-66)

When the mountains beckon, the kids want out of the house, and you need to renew your spirit and sense of what New Mexico is all about, head east and north from Albuquerque for a few days on the road. You can manage this tour, which consists of old highway haunts, prehistoric ruins, and high mountain camping, even if your calendar seems too full and your wallet too flat. So fill up the gas tank, throw the sleeping bags into the car, give each child a fishing pole and a pocketful of change, and get set to meander back and forth through the

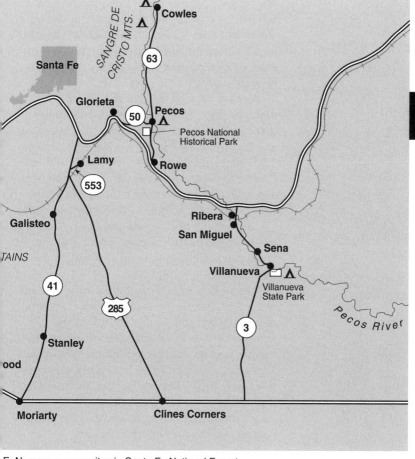

E: Numerous campsites in Santa Fe National Forest

centuries and along the trails that crisscross this
small piece of New Mexico.

Tour Nine will hustle you along two Interstates,
I-40 and I-25, that are filled with motorists and
truckers bent on making it to Los Angeles or Kansas
City or the Grand Canyon. You can also chug
across parts of old Route 66 and find sections of
the Santa Fe Trail. But most of the time you will
drive on narrow roads that snake up canyons or
across the plains. Feel free to spend your dollars on
cactus candy or a book about high desert wildflow-

ers. Let your children watch trout fingerlings at a fish hatchery, and then catch a grownup rainbow along the Pecos. Stay in a fashionable inn or make your own campsite in the high country. Savor roadside picnics, meals next to the campfire, or local specialties in little cafés.

We have planned this tour to begin at Albuquerque's "Big-I." Here I-40, which covers 2,461 miles between Wilmington, North Carolina, and Barstow, California, meets I-25, which travels 1,063 miles between Buffalo, Wyoming, and Las Cruces, New Mexico. Avoid the Big-I at rush hour, and head east on I-40 toward the Sandia Mountains when traffic is light. As Tijeras Canyon opens up, you and the truckers will gear down in order to sweep up the foothills and out onto the plains. You know that you are, indeed, on your way to somewhere!

When I-40 plunges through the canyon, you will notice that Albuquerque seems reluctant to give up its urbanity, and so its houses and trailers and minifarms spill eastward across the foothills of the Sandias, over the backside of the mountains, on to Edgewood, Zuzax, and even to Moriarty, almost forty miles away. Bypass Moriarty for now, and save it for the return trip, when everyone needs a break and a meal. Instead, keep driving toward that many-leveled horizon of plains and rimrock to the east.

While you drive, watch for the small two-lane highway that parallels much of the Interstate. This is one of the remaining stretches of Route 66. Often called The Mother Road, Route 66 was the main link between Chicago and Los Angeles for much of the twentieth century, its 2,400 miles inspiring songs, a television show, and travel memories for millions of Americans. Created in 1926 to speed up the trip across two-thirds of the country, Route 66 was fully paved by 1937, its path through Illinois, Missouri, Oklahoma, Texas, New Mexico, Arizona, and California quickly lined by everything the traveler might need, and then some. In 1928, businessmen and boosters joined together to form the National U.S. 66 Highway Association, promoting the highway in regional and national events, the most painful of which must have been a 3,422-mile footrace run in 1928 from Los Angeles to New York, the western portion of it along Route 66. For forty years, Americans drove Route 66 as truckers, tourists, and traveling salesmen, spending their nights in tourist cabins and small motels, eating chicken-fried steak and drinking coffee in local cafés, stopping at roadside attractions to buy desert waterbags or to see gigantic rattlesnakes, and changing tires along the asphalt ribbon that was either swallowed up or bypassed when the Interstate highways like I-40 were constructed.

New Mexico's share of Route 66 began at the eastern border near Glenrio and exited in the west at Manuelito, near Gallup, much as I-40 does now. However, the highway originally took its travelers in a big northern loop just past Santa Rosa, winding along and crossing the Pecos River, following old gold-seeker and trading trails north past Romeroville and Pecos, and west to Glorieta and Santa Fe. From the capital city, the first Route 66 bent south, then meandered through Pueblo land to Albuquerque. When a straighter path from Santa Rosa to Albuquerque was completed in 1937, those who drove 66 were spared at least a half-day of curvy, intense driving. You can visit New Mexico's remnants of the historic highway by stopping in towns along I-40; their main streets, sometimes named "Route 66," evoke memories of the old highway. On this tour, take any of the exits between Albuquerque and Clines Corners and drive the old highway, meeting up again with I-40 as you wish. Michael Wallis's book, *Route 66, The Mother Road,* details the Highway 66 saga.

To capture the spirit of Route 66 and to assure yourself that you are truly "on the road," stop at Clines Corners (about twenty miles east of Moriarty), where U.S. 285 heads north to Santa Fe and south to Roswell. Long a crossroads, Clines Corners was named for its originator, Ray Cline, who built a gas station here in 1934 and soon added a restaurant and souvenir store that typified many of the tourist stops along The Mother Road. You can still gas up at Clines Corners, fill your thermos with coffee, and let your kids loose in a wonderland that will soon part them from the quarters jingling in their pockets. A cigar-store Indian waits at the door outside, a larger-than-life one-armed bandit greets customers inside, and the aromas from the fudge factory ("Twenty Different Kinds of Fudge!!!") mingle with piñon incense and bayberry candles as tourists wander through aisles of sea-opal jewelry, coonskin caps, Indian dolls, bins of polished rocks and fool's gold, T-shirts, slingshots, coffee mugs, Ecuadorian ponchos, arrowhead key rings, maps, and chile jelly. Suspend tasteful judgment for the moment. Remember, people have been trading along this historic pathway since the Plains Indians brought beads, feathers, and buffalo skins west to the Pueblos. They were followed by traders like Josiah Gregg, who worked a trail along here from Fort Smith, Arkansas, to Santa Fe in the 1800s. Little has changed except the mode and speed of transportation, and perhaps the quality of merchandise. Clines Corners is also the place where travelers caught in snowstorms on I-40 can find refuge. Almost every winter, the managers of the restaurant and store shelter dozens of tourists and truckers who become stranded and spend the night sleeping on the floor between the beaded belts and the souvenir placemats.

Unless you are traveling I-40 in the winter, when storm clouds heavy with snow frequently menace from above, it is hard to imagine that blizzards could ever touch this part of New Mexico. But if you look around, you will see that the countryside is hilly, low juniper and piñon trees cover the ground, tall ponderosa pines survive on the ridges, and snow fences and piles of sand stand in readiness. The altitude is between 5,000 and 6,500 feet, and winds can be fierce. On the other hand, if you are touring in the late summer after a wet spring, all manner of wildflowers will greet you under a cloudless, benign blue sky. Black-eyed susans, rabbitbrush, globe mallow, sage, Indian paintbrush, and purple wild asters line the road and march up and down arroyos and hillsides.

At exit 230, about thirteen miles east of Clines Corners, take N.M. 3 and go twenty miles north, through more piñon and juniper, past green, flat rangeland broken up with a yucca here, a clump of sage there, with pale stone outcroppings on either side. There will be no towns or services between the Interstate exit and Villanueva, only a lonely signpost or two pointing the way to ranch headquarters that are far off the well-maintained highway. It is also unlikely that you will meet many cars along this quiet stretch, which keeps pulling you toward the distant Sangre de Cristos.

At the crest of a final hill, you will peer down into a narrow valley formed over the centuries by the Pecos River, which runs orange and heavy with silt in late summer or trickles in a shallow stream when snowmelt or rainfall has been skimpy. Across from you, on the hilltop, is Villanueva. Villagers farm the valley below in neat patches of alfalfa, hay, and corn. Old orchards are squeezed in between the fields. If you peer farther to your right, you will spy Villanueva State Park along the riverbank. A sign directs you down the steep hill and across the river to Villanueva and the main area of the park. So down you wind, pausing to gaze up at small adobe houses or long narrow trailers with hollyhocks and cosmos, morning glories and zinnias planted in their front yards. Stay on the paved road and aim for the red tin roof of the church.

Villanueva was founded at the beginning of the 1800s. You can see that the town was built with thought given to safety—its sturdy stone and adobe houses, stores, and community buildings are carefully placed in prominent positions on the highest points of its hills. In many ways, Villanueva still resembles a fortress, having survived more than the

nineteenth-century Apache and Comanche attacks that it was built to withstand. Unlike many of New Mexico's villages, Villanueva continues to support a regional elementary school, several small grocery stores, a community center, and its church, despite the exodus of many of its youth and high unemployment rates in surrounding San Miguel County. Walk around the village, buy soda at one of the stores, and admire the classic adobe architecture still evident in the doors, courtyards, and porches of Villanueva's homes.

One of Villanueva's proudest landmarks is its church, Our Lady of Guadalupe, built in 1818, and the centerpiece for the town. During the 1976 bicentennial year, the women of Villanueva unveiled a two-year project that chronicles the history of the village in a tapestry hung along the interior walls of the church. Thirty-six women sewed forty-one colorful panels to commemorate special community events through nearly two centuries of Villanueva life. There are depictions of May crownings of the Blessed Virgin, chicken pulls, death carts, weddings, laundry time down along the river, and the paving of the road. The archbishop presided over the dedication of the tapestry, assisted by the governor, the townspeople, and hundreds of friends, relatives, and former residents. Years later, the scenes along the church walls are just as crisp and fanciful as the day they were sewn, their bright colors complementing the dark *vigas* and corbels in the ceiling. A recent addition to the church, a fresco by Federico Vigil of Santa Fe, surrounds the statue of the Virgin of Guadalupe in the sanctuary and highlights the tapestry's hues. Villanueva encourages travelers to visit its church. The women who guide you request that tour groups call the rectory ahead of time to make arrangements. Otherwise, just stop in at the Villanueva General Store across from the church on N.M. 3 and ask for a guide.

Villanueva offers overnight accommodations only at Villanueva State Park. This quiet park also provides picnic facilities and a place to fish and hike. Follow N.M. 3 as it curves past the church and out to the stop sign at the end of the village. The park is to your right about 1.5 miles down the hill, and is situated on low bluffs right beside the river. Families sometimes spend a couple of days camping here, catching fish, taking bicycle trips to explore the surrounding countryside, and walking up the hill into Villanueva for groceries.

To continue the tour, go left on N.M. 3 at the stop sign in Villanueva and descend into the valley, which winds beneath dark mesas, the highway's direction determined by the river's wandering course. Cottonwood trees and old political campaign signs vie for space between the road and the *acequia* that babbles along, flowing into fields, vineyards, and orchards in the spring and summer. A series of villages, beginning with Sena and ending with Ribera, straddles the road, their adobe houses usually in pristine repair, but sometimes left to melt back into the red earth. The narrow Pecos River swings to the other side of the valley and then appears again as a generous swimming hole next to the highway, surrounded by tamarisks, willows, and Russian olives. You will pass old churches and schools, new mobile homes, and a restored farmhouse that is now a winery. Most of the settlements through which you drive have lost their families over the decades; household after household has left and moved to Santa Fe or Albuquerque or California. Those who live here must travel to Las Vegas or Santa Fe for work, and their older children endure long bus rides to schools in larger communities.

This quiet, rural stretch of the valley is historic. The path along the Pecos was explored by Coronado and Espejo, and was used by Plains Indians for their entrance into the Sangre de Cristo Mountains and to the pueblo communities along the Rio Grande. San Miguel del Vado, about ten miles north of Villanueva, was first settled in 1794 by *genízaros*. San Miguel's large, white, twin-towered church was built in 1805–06 and remains the most prominent building in the village, all of which has been declared a National Historic District. In the late nineteenth century, wagon trains from the Santa Fe Trail crossed the Pecos River in San Miguel; the river's depth and width made fording it easier here than in many other places either upstream or downstream. Ribera is the last village on N.M. 3 before you turn northwest on I-25, about thirteen miles after Villanueva. At Ribera, you cross the Pecos River yet again, then the Santa Fe Railroad tracks, soon passing beneath the Interstate to come out from under it on four lanes of smooth concrete, where the whizzing cars and fast pace are a marked contrast to the quiet ride you have just experienced.

In the same way that your trip on I-40 paralleled some of old Route 66, your journey along this portion of I-25 traces another historic path, the Santa Fe Trail. The Santa Fe Trail linked Independence, Missouri, with Santa Fe, New Mexico, and opened in 1821. It left Missouri, entered Kansas, and separated into two sections near Fort Dodge, Kansas. The northern, or Mountain Branch, followed the Arkansas River to La Junta, Colorado, where the trail then bent south toward Raton and Watrous, in New Mexico Territory. The Cimarron Cut-Off, the more southerly route, meanwhile had crossed the Arkansas River at Cimarron, Kansas, and then headed across the present-day Oklahoma Panhandle to rejoin the main trail at Wagon Mound, New Mexico. The combined trail passed through Las Vegas, crossed the Pecos River at San Miguel del Vado, and headed toward Glorieta and Santa Fe, as I-25 does. Many of the small villages now bypassed by the Interstate from Raton to Santa Fe were major stops along the Santa Fe Trail. San Miguel del Vado, for example, was one of New Mexico's most important towns in the heyday of the traders and the trail. It is easiest to trace the original ruts of the Santa Fe Trail from the air or after a light snow has fallen, but a sensitive eye can distinguish the old path in many places along the way. Historians, writers, and photographers guide visitors to Santa Fe Trail sites in their books: *Along the Santa Fe Trail,* by New Mexico's Marc Simmons and Joan Myers; *Images of the Santa Fe Trail* and *Maps of the Santa Fe Trail* by Gregory Franzwa. Children will enjoy a book called *A Tree on the Trail* by Holling C. Holling.

The Sangre de Cristo Mountains, dark green, heavy, and ever present, loom in the distance as you drive along I-25. Huddled in their foothills and almost invisible from the Interstate, Pecos National Historic Park is your next stop, at exit 307 at Rowe, about twelve miles west of Ribera.

Take N.M. 63 about five miles across Forked Lightning Ranch, once owned by Buddy Fogelson and his wife, Greer Garson, to the park entrance. For a long time, Forked Lightning's signature pink-and-blue gates and buildings provided an informal and unofficial entrance to the old Pecos Mission. A 1990 Act of Congress changed the nature of the relationship between the ranch and the park. The legislation expanded the boundaries of Pecos National Monument from 356 acres to 5,865 acres, including more than 5,000 acres from the ranch, which was donated to the Park Service. The legislation also changed the designation for Pecos Monument, making it a National Historic Park, so that now all the surrounding former ranchland, which includes parts of the Pecos River and the Santa Fe Trail, can be preserved, interpreted, and open to the public.

All this activity served one purpose: to protect the historic Pecos Mission. You will agree that the restored structures, the unexcavated ruins, and the site itself are well worth preserving. Signs on N.M. 63 direct you to the visitor center, a handsome building with one room devoted to the long history of this valley and its people. Colorful murals accompany displays of familiar artifacts like kitchen bowls, sandals, and crude but inventive weapons. There are brief narratives, line drawings, and some photographs to provide an historical context for your trip through the ruins.

As you leave the visitor center, you face huge unexcavated mounds, with a path climbing up to several rebuilt structures, including a *kiva,* and to other rooms and buildings that are partially excavated. Interpretive signs will guide you as you explore this timeless monument to an ancient people. Your children will enjoy climbing down into the *kiva,* racing along the trail, and imagining what it must have been like to live in this green and wide-open place.

It is likely that the Pueblo people lived in this area from about A.D. 1100, when they began to move eastward from their homes along the more western rivers. A few centuries later they had consolidated their dwellings into villages. They eventually built a multistory structure here similar to buildings you now see at Taos Pueblo. By 1450, there were more than six hundred rooms where the Towa-speaking people lived, going off to tend their corn, squash, and bean crops during the day, returning to their living quarters at night. At one point, about two thousand people lived here. In many ways, it was a small, self-contained town. Because of their location, the Indians also were traders, exchanging their agricultural goods for buffalo skins from the Plains people to the east and cotton from the pueblos to the west and south. When Coronado passed this way in the middle of the sixteenth century, he found a bustling, active village.

The people of Pecos were initially hospitable to the Spanish explorers, but bad experiences with some of Coronado's men and with members of the Espejo expedition in the 1500s led to hostility when later groups passed by. Franciscan missionaries came in the 1600s and built a large mission church and *convento,* introducing wheat, cattle, metal tools, and the adobe building block. During the Pueblo Revolt of 1680, the Pecos church was destroyed; a new church was built atop the foundation of the original mission after de Vargas's reconquest in 1692. One hundred years later, the pueblo was declining in both population and prosperity. By 1838, only about twenty people were left, and they trekked southwest to Jemez Pueblo, where Towa-speaking kin lived. Travelers on the Santa Fe Trail in the mid-1800s used the lonely walls of the Pecos Mission church as a landmark.

Now that you have steeped yourself in the history of this valley, maybe you would like to do some fishing or hiking in the mountains. Take a left on N.M. 63 as you leave Pecos National Historic Park. Stop in at the Santa Fe National Forest Ranger Station about a mile up the road and ask the rangers about available campsites, the fire danger rating, and fishing possibilities. If you plan to enter the Pecos Wilderness within the national forest, obtain a permit and inquire about high-country hiking and camping.

You are now in the community of Pecos, a good place to purchase some groceries and gas. New Mexico 63 curves through what you might consider the center of the village, but most of the town is east of the river, which explains why the large stone church, La Iglesia de San Antonio del Rio Pecos, St. Anthony's, seems to sit with its back to you. If the church is open, enter its cool interior. The church is home to an important Mexican baroque painting, *Our Lady of the Angels,* which hangs high above you. Juan Correa, an eighteenth-century Mexican artist, painted it for the Pecos Mission, where it hung for decades. When the Pecos survivors abandoned their pueblo in 1838 and went to Jemez, they took the painting to St. Anthony's for safe-keeping. The painting is returned in a procession to the Pecos Mission on the first Sunday of August for an annual feast-day Mass.

Founded in the 1700s, Pecos has always been an important service center for the people of the surrounding valley and mountains. It supports a school district, grocery and hardware stores, a few restaurants and gas stations, a motel or two, and sometimes an art or crafts gallery. At almost seven thousand feet, Pecos is the gateway to a recreation area that draws thousands of people annually.

As you head up N.M. 63 along the Pecos River, you will pass the Benedictine Monastery. This Catholic retreat center includes a church, dormitories, and gardens. Monastery Lake, a popular fishing spot open to the public, lies just beyond the last retreat house. Next you spy Lisboa Springs Trout Hatchery, New Mexico's first hatchery, built in 1921 and run by the state Department of Game and Fish. Your youngsters can see where the fish they might catch begin life. Nestled in a shady spot along the river, Lisboa Springs has self-guided tours that show you the process of trout rearing. Almost two million rainbow trout come from this hatchery each year for placement in the Pecos and its tributaries. You can move from pond to pond (called "raceways" in hatchery language), observing the ever-increasing size of the fish.

After Lisboa Springs, you climb and wind through the canyons of the Pecos about twenty miles toward Cowles and trailheads into the Pecos Wilderness. You will pass weekend cabins, summer camps, and a few resorts along the small portions of the canyon that are privately owned, but most of this mountain territory is part of the Santa Fe National Forest. Picnic grounds and day-use areas

9

line the narrow highway, which is paved as far as Terrero. (Efforts to widen and pave more of N.M. 63 were halted by a court order in 1990.) Those who like to fish can either pull off to the side of the road and walk down to the river, or wait for the easy-to-use fishing pond near Cowles.

Be on the lookout for places to camp. Three kinds of campgrounds are open to vehicle campers: you can find private campgrounds along the lower part of the river; the U.S. Forest Service maintains about six overnight camping areas, including several that are accessible to people with disabilities; and New Mexico's Game and Fish Department manages a few sites. Pick a spot right along the river, or pull into a site along the mountain slopes. Wherever you choose to camp, you will enjoy the quiet pines, the fast-moving clouds overhead, and the sound and scent of the wind as it sweeps through the trees.

Because so many people enjoy the Pecos, certain camping spots are periodically taken out of use so that vegetation can be restored. You will personally experience this heavy usage on summer weekends, when a steady stream of pickups and recreational vehicles plies this stretch of road. The narrow canyon only sustains a certain number of visitors in quiet and comfort.

If you plan to camp for a couple of days, make sure you also explore the nearby canyons and trails, whether on foot or by horseback. You can rent horses for trail rides or pack trips at a number of stables along the way. For a unique experience, try hiking with a llama! Inquire ahead of time—through local outfits—about these trips. Those who want to hike into the Pecos Wilderness to high-country lakes and mountain meadows begin their trek at one of the trailheads, most of them north of Cowles. You will find parking spots and directional signs at the trailheads. And remember to obtain a wilderness permit and leave word of your destination at the ranger station back in Pecos.

After your picnic, fishing expedition, or night under the stars, retrace your tracks back down to the village of Pecos, head out of town, and turn right (west) at the intersection of N.M. 63 and N.M. 50. Roadside attractions and many small businesses accompany you on this skinny, curvy road that leads to the site of the Glorieta Battle-field, about five miles from Pecos.

Confederate troops under General H. H. Sibley came north from El Paso and a victory at Valverde, New Mexico, to meet Union forces on a battlefield near here in March 1862. In what many consider the "Gettysburg of the West," Union troops burned Sibley's supplies, and the provisionless Confederate troops fled south. A highway marker describes and commemorates the battle. Civil War buffs recently obtained formal historic status for this battlefield. The recent discovery of Confederate graves and skeletons near here has added to its mystique. The private Glorieta Battlefield Museum is open to the public and displays battle memorabilia and Civil War artifacts.

New Mexico 50 will take you back to I-25. The steeple of the Glorieta Baptist Conference Center can be the beacon that guides you to the Inter-state. Once on I-25, you pass up, down, and through the foothills and canyons of the lower reaches of the Sangre de Cristos as you wind west about ten miles to exit 290, where U.S. 285 to Lamy and Galisteo heads south. Santa Fe is a few miles ahead, but you will go south, passing some of the capital city's suburbia, including El Dorado. This is a quiet housing development best known since the 1980s as the place where Edward Howard, an American who spied for Russia, used disguise and escape tricks learned during his CIA days to give FBI agents the slip, fleeing to the Soviet Union from under their very noses.

The turnoff to Lamy is a few miles down U.S. 285. Take N.M. 553 to Lamy (about a mile) if it is picnic time or if you want to visit the Legal Tender, a restaurant that is on the National Registry of Historic Places. You might find it hard to believe, but this tiny settlement has been the train stop for the city of Santa Fe ever since the Santa Fe Rail-road, following the Santa Fe Trail from Kansas City, headed for the Pacific. Somewhere along the line, engineers decided that the south rim of the Santa Fe Basin was too steep for long trains, so the main line deposits passengers here, sporadically shuttling freight to Santa Fe via an auxiliary track. Amtrak trains still load and unload passengers at the station in Lamy in the afternoons. A small private

9

railroad also uses these tracks to carry visitors back and forth between Santa Fe and Lamy during the tourist season. A brick platform, shady trees, and soft green lawns might tempt you to spread out a picnic lunch. Across the way, the Legal Tender Saloon and Eating House, in a restored Victorian building, provides lunches and dinners with a view of the comings and goings of the trains. Lamy is a quiet place, home to some artists; it hosts an annual kite-flying contest in April.

You will come back to U.S. 285 briefly, cross above the Santa Fe tracks, then turn right (southwest) on N.M. 41 almost immediately. You are now in the Galisteo Basin, which for a while runs beside Glorieta Mesa, one of the southern remnants of the Sangre de Cristo range. This vast, grassy area right on the edge of the plains was home to several pueblos, including San Cristóbal Pueblo, which was even larger than Pecos Pueblo. It was always subject to attack, and the Tano people who settled and farmed here over the centuries fled west and settled along the Rio Grande in the 1600s and 1700s; none of their sites is open to the public.

Centuries before, Indians of the Basket Maker periods left sophisticated abstract designs on the cliffs and rocks of the basin, and some of them are preserved to this day.

Soon you will come to Galisteo, a green and leafy aberration in this land of tawny range grasses and rugged arroyos. Galisteo is near the site of a pueblo that was abandoned in the 1780s. The village was recolonized by Spanish settlers during the period of Mexican rule in the next century. Several of New Mexico's old Hispanic families can trace their roots back to Galisteo, where proud homesteads and large farms once thrived. Now Galisteo, a twenty-minute drive from the capital city, is almost a fashionable suburb of Santa Fe, its rambling adobe houses hidden behind high walls and under immense cottonwood trees, its fields eroded and abandoned. Picturesque dirt roads connect historic homes and modest dwellings. Few signs indicate where anything is, but if you poke around, you can find a bed-and-breakfast or a small inn. There is a little grocery store across from the Catholic church.

Once out of Galisteo, you again feel part of that inland sea of wavy blue grasses, the Galisteo Basin. You are surrounded by distant mountains. Behind you is the Sangre de Cristo range, to the west the Jemez and the Ortiz, to the southwest the Sandias and the Manzanos. Get out of your car to pause, turning in a silent circle to observe the mountains and to listen to the wind. This might also be a good picnic spot; only curious (and fenced) cattle can disturb you. As you drive straight south thirty miles to Moriarty, you pass a few ranches, and then you come to Stanley. Once upon a time, Stanley boasted a couple of hotels, a train depot, and some stores. Now it is populated almost solely by members of one of New Mexico's largest ranching families, the Kings, and their King Ranch Headquarters. Bruce and Alice King, whose extensive family has cattle holdings in Santa Fe and Sandoval counties, have been a popular governor and first lady of New Mexico several times.

Let us assume it is a late afternoon in the summer. Promise your family a restaurant dinner in one of the large or small cafés in Moriarty. But first, after easing onto the main street (old Route 66) from N.M. 41, travel east a bit to Buford Station, across from Crossley Park. This is the location of New Mexico's first gas station. It featured public restrooms and predated even Route 66. Then stop in at the Moriarty Historical Museum, housed in the old stone fire department building on the south side of Route 66. Here you will find extensive arrowhead and pressed glass collections, a variety of military uniforms and war memorabilia, photo albums of community events, stereoptic pictures, and early farm implements and kitchen appliances. Show your kids what a lawnmower used to look like, and ask your daughter if she would like to wear a dress like that to the junior prom. A volunteer guide will gladly add personal histories to many of the found treasures that sit in crowded cases.

Once you have wandered through Moriarty looking for a place to eat, you will know that the old center of town, named after Michael Moriarty, who homesteaded in the area in 1887, lies to the

south of the Interstate. It was established in 1903 with the coming of the New Mexico Central Railroad. Moriarty hosts a Pinto Bean Fiesta every summer to commemorate the Estancia Valley's prized crop, the pinto bean. For more than thirty years, until the droughts of the mid-1940s, hundreds of dry-land farms produced tons of pinto beans. Moriarty also honors the evil Professor Moriarty of Sherlock Holmes fame with a "Brothers Three Society" meeting at the Frontier Bar each November.

After dinner, perhaps you will be blessed with a New Mexico sunset as you head back east on I-40. If it is a late fall afternoon or an early evening in the summer, high storm clouds might wash against the sky. And then, like magic, every color of the rainbow, plus some you may never before have seen, will pulse before you. It is a sunset by the painter Wilson Hurley set above the black bulk of the Sandias. What a wonderful way to end your trip.

TOUR TEN
ALBUQUERQUE

Suggested travel time:	At least two days
Route:	City streets
Accommodations:	Hotels, motels, bed-and-breakfasts throughout town
Camping:	At east and west ends, and in the Manzano Mountains east of town

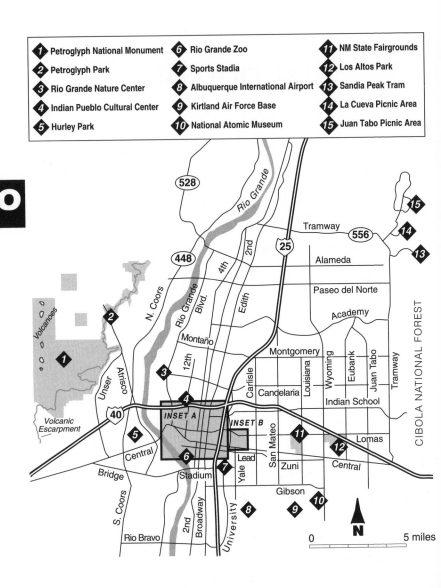

1 Petroglyph National Monument	**6** Rio Grande Zoo	**11** NM State Fairgrounds
2 Petroglyph Park	**7** Sports Stadia	**12** Los Altos Park
3 Rio Grande Nature Center	**8** Albuquerque International Airport	**13** Sandia Peak Tram
4 Indian Pueblo Cultural Center	**9** Kirtland Air Force Base	**14** La Cueva Picnic Area
5 Hurley Park	**10** National Atomic Museum	**15** Juan Tabo Picnic Area

Albuquerque is the biggest city in the state but seems to abdicate its role as "big city." The spread of businesses and homes from the mountains on the east to the river, mesas, and volcanoes on the west is confined on the north and south by the open land belonging to Pueblo tribes. Albuquerque is an urban space with wild edges. Albuquerque's people tend to be friendly and genuine, which emphasizes the small-town aura of this metropolis. It is difficult to find any areas of concrete jungle, although Albuquerque has many of the trappings of big cities—interlocking freeways, railroads,

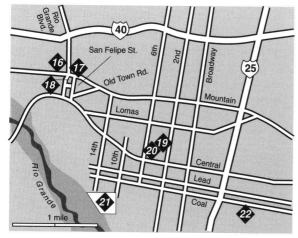

16 NM Museum of Natural History

17 Albuquerque Museum

18 Old Town Plaza

19 Civic Plaza

20 Albuquerque Public Library

21 Rio Grande Zoo

22 Roosevelt Park

23 UNM Law School

24 Medical Center

25 Maxwell Museum of Anthropology

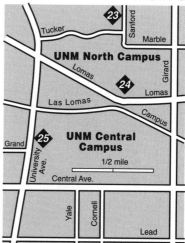

airports, shopping malls, banks, homelessness, crime, schools, hospitals, theaters, restaurants, and hotels.

Albuquerque also has quiet places, beautiful places, places to buy a good book or listen to a good concert, watch a minor league baseball team, and enjoy a huge annual State Fair. Albuquerque is the home of the state's largest university, several fine museums, scenic parks, and tree-shaded neighborhoods, all within a lovely natural setting. The Sandia Mountains are its eastern boundary and a row of extinct volcanoes form its western edge, with the Rio Grande cutting a green swath down the middle. Though it gets very little rain (eight inches or less per year), Albuquerque has an adequate water supply, so it boasts colorful gardens and venerable cottonwood trees. It frequently bears the heat of the desert on summer days, but the city of almost half a million people benefits from the cool nights resulting from the high altitude (five thousand feet).

Albuquerque is a transportation hub and has been almost since its inception. At its founding in 1706, Albuquerque lay at the crossroads of the Camino Real between Mexico and Santa Fe and a major east-west route through the mountains. Interstate freeways have replaced El Camino Real and the trail through the pass. Albuquerque became a railroad center when the Atchison, Topeka, and Santa Fe Railroad built a route past Albuquerque in 1880. The railroad's roundhouse and shops employed thousands of Albuquerqueans and greatly stimulated growth of the town, creating a "new town" in the process. In the 1930s, Transcontinental Airways chose Albuquerque as a stop on its pioneering cross-country flights. The town continues to play a major role in air travel. Its fine new airport (see the Airport Entrada section at the front of the book) is the state's only site for many major airlines.

Near the junction of the two freeways, north-south Interstate 25 and east-west Interstate 40, huge all-night truck stops accommodate many long-haul customers. Interstate 40 replaced portions of Route 66, the Chicago-to-Los Angeles highway described in the television series "Route 66." In John Steinbeck's *The Grapes of Wrath,* Highway 66 was also the escape route over which refugees from the Midwest Dust Bowl fled to California in the 1930s.

As Albuquerque reaches toward and beyond its natural and logical boundaries, "in-fill" also takes place. Land in the Rio Grande valley on the north and south that has been traditionally devoted to truck gardens and alfalfa fields is now more profitably given over to homes and the ubiquitous shopping centers that dot the landscape. Some business people encourage this growth, while many residents worry about the shrinking green space and increasing congestion.

Size was also of concern to Albuquerque's first settlers, but it was the settlement's small size that was initially troubling. When a group of Bernalillo residents broke away from their town and established the Villa de San Francisco de Alburquerque in 1706, they prevaricated a little, overstating the number of residents, and named the town after the Viceroy of New Spain, the Duke of Alburquerque (the first r was later dropped), in order to convince him to grant the town a patent. The thirty families established their homes around a plaza near the Rio Grande, built a church—the predecessor of Old Town Plaza's current San Felipe de Neri Church—and raised their crops and animals on fields that had been used in centuries past by Tiwa Indians.

Slowly the small town grew, changing little after becoming part of newly independent Mexico in 1821 and then coming under American control in 1846. For a few days in 1863, a Confederate garrison was established in Albuquerque after Union forces retreated to Santa Fe. These momentous events came and went without leaving much visible sign of change on the quiet town. The coming of the railroad, however, altered Albuquerque dramatically.

The railroad shifted the center of Albuquerque about two miles east of the old plaza to a new downtown area along the tracks. Saloons, shops, railroad repair facilities, hotels, brothels—all were located in "New Town," which eventually was connected with Old Town by a horse-drawn trolley. Like other boom towns, the new Albuquerque was a rough and active place, given to hard work and hard play. On the other hand, an act of the territorial legislature led to the establishment of the University of New Mexico in 1889, although secondary and even elementary schools were then in short supply throughout the territory.

Its founders built the University of New Mexico on a bluff well to the east of the town in 1889. After World War II small homes and businesses surrounded it, and now it is encircled by a city that has spread as far east beyond it as the mountains will allow (farther, if you count the burgeoning settlements east of Tijeras Canyon). Albuquerque has also spread to the northwest. Until the 1980s, there were only a few houses scattered across the barren "West Mesa," as the land west of the river is

10

called. Tens of thousands of people have moved into developments on the western escarpment in recent years, creating heavy traffic and crowded conditions at the area's schools.

Albuquerque's population tripled soon after the railroad came. In the early years of the twentieth century further growth was based in part on the health industry as Albuquerque became home to many Easterners escaping to a climate where they hoped to recover from the "white plague," tuberculosis. The town experienced another growth spurt with the coming of World War II, when the defense establishment became a major player on the Albuquerque scene. Kirtland Air Force Base and Sandia Army Base (later to be absorbed into the air force base) were built during the war, as was a major munitions maker, Sandia National Laboratories.

Sandia Labs, located on the air force base, the base itself, and other defense-related industries remain significant employers of Albuquerqueans. Electronics firms built several large plants in Albuquerque in the 1980s, and high-tech industry continued to expand during the 1990s, but the city has virtually no heavy industry. Instead the state's largest city supplies government, banking, law, retail trade, and educational and medical services to the smaller communities surrounding it.

Even before the coming of the interstate freeways in 1956, Albuquerque's center had begun a tentative move eastward beyond the university, with the establishment in 1947 of one of the country's first shopping centers, Nob Hill. A much bigger shopping center, Winrock, was opened in 1961, along the edge of the new freeway. With Winrock's major mall competitor, Coronado, less than a mile away, this new "uptown" area has drawn away much of the congestion and the life of "downtown" by the tracks.

Like most western cities, Albuquerque sprawls, but it is also a place of small, interdependent neighborhoods, traditionally grown up around schools, irrigation ditches, builders' developments, and church parishes. Some areas, like Atrisco and Los Griegos, were independent towns or land grants that became engulfed by the growing city. Some of the neighborhoods have created organiza-tions to improve their appearance and safety.

everal neighborhoods have long-standing
community celebrations, such as the Christmas
Posadas procession in Barelas and the annual Fiesta
in Old Town. A few of the neighborhoods have a
predominant racial or ethnic group, such as
Duranes, which is largely Hispanic, and the mostly
African-American community in the Eugene Field
neighborhood. Chinese, Armenian, Greek, Italian,
and other settlers who came to Albuquerque at the
beginning of the twentieth century are now
dispersed throughout the city.

Albuquerque does not lend
itself well to a circle tour—the
city is just too big. Can you see it
all in one day? Maybe you can, if
you are willing to forego museums and stay out of intriguing
boutiques and galleries. We will
describe a tour of Albuquerque
that you could take in a day, but
you will probably want to break it
into bite-sized pieces that are
easier and more pleasant to
digest.

Visitors tend to gravitate to six
sections within and immediately
around the city: the mountains,
uptown shopping centers and the
university in the Heights, Old
Town and Downtown in the
Valley, and the new Petroglyph
National Monument on the West
Mesa. Most of these areas lend
themselves best to parking your
car and walking, although
Albuquerque's limited public
transportation makes a car helpful in getting from
one section of town to another.

Start your tour in the far northeast part of
Albuquerque, where Tramway Boulevard meets
Tramway Road, accessible from exits on Interstate
40 east and Interstate 25 north, respectively. At this
"corner"—actually only a street sign indicates
where the north-south boulevard curves into the
east-west road—you will be right below the steep
western slope of the Sandia Mountains. Just below
you, off Tramway Road, Forest Road 333 will take
you up and up all the way to two lovely picnic

10

grounds overlooking the city, Juan Tabo and La Cueva. The picnic tables cluster about the trailheads of a number of popular paths into the mountains. Trails within the Sandias are deceptive; they offer magnificent vistas, fauna, and flora, but the 3,700-foot climb to the Crest presents the usual dangers associated with high altitudes and rapidly changing weather. Be prepared.

Modern-day Albuquerque nestles right up against the Sandias, occupying land where sheep and cattle grazed until after World War II. Expensive, many-windowed houses reflect the late afternoon sun from their perches in the Sandia foothills. The west side of the Sandias is a designated federal Wilderness Area, a remarkable feature so close to a major city. Hikers and picnickers can enjoy the beauties of the mountain within a few minutes of any part of town.

The adventurous person who may not be ready for that long climb to the Sandia Crest can ride the majestic Sandia Tram instead. From the point where the two Tramway streets meet, go a few blocks south, then head up N.M. 556 to the base station of the tram, where you can leave your car. The tram boasts two large cabins, supported by widely spaced towers that take you up the Sandia Crest. Along the way we have seen eagles, bears, and mountain sheep from its windows. Once at the crest, you can hike, ski, or ride the skylift over wildflowers or snow, depending on the season. You can have a meal at the restaurant or just stand on the ridge to see the breathtaking vista that extends in all directions.

Proceeding southward from the entrance to the tram, you can enjoy both sedentary and strenuous pleasures at the Elena Gallegos Picnic Area—shaded tables, trails for hikers or mountain bikes, and a recently developed trail to the crest. Once part of the huge Elena Gallegos Land Grant that reached from the Rio Grande to the crest, this tract remains unsullied by houses as a result of public-spirited, patient work undertaken by several organizations, including the city, the Forest Service, and the Albuquerque Academy.

Between the Elena Gallegos Picnic Area and Interstate 40, a number of smaller trails lead into the Sandia foothills, some of them going all the way to the crest. One of our favorites is a short trail from a parking area just south of the east end of Candelaria Road, which leads up a streambed to a huge granite spillway and a terrific view of Albuquerque. Shortly before the Sandias meet I-40 and Tijeras Canyon, a fallen piece of mountain granite, Supper Rock, sits grandly within its own city park, a favorite spot for an evening picnic.

Leaving Supper Rock, go back to Tramway Boulevard and south, then turn on I-40 west. Though this may not seem to be the most scenic strip of highway, a whole village of prairie dogs will vouch for it. On the south side of I-40, a bike trail parallels the highway west between the Tramway and Eubank exits. The sandy soil on both sides of the bike trail is home to a huge prairie dog colony. While you bike the stretch, or by parking your car at either end and walking toward the mid-point at Juan Tabo, you can see the little rodents sunning themselves, whistling to one another, and darting into their numerous holes. At Eubank, exit heading south, and then turn right on Copper. You will pass one of Albuquerque's largest parks, Los Altos, on your way down to Wyoming. You can play almost any sport you want at Los Altos: baseball, golf, swimming, horseshoes, even bocce. The park straddles the freeway, with a pedestrian overpass taking you from the golf course south of I-40 to the other fields and courts, as well as to the Albuquerque Garden Center, on the north. Turn south again on Wyoming to the Kirtland Air Force Base.

Employer of almost twenty thousand Albuquerqueans (if one includes Sandia National Labs), Kirtland forms the southeast border of the city. Most of the base is off limits to visitors, but two interesting sites are accessible with a pass you can obtain easily at the gate on Wyoming. A huge B-52B bomber that will draw your kids' oohs and aahs is parked about a mile south of the entrance gate and announces the National Atomic Museum. This is the plane that dropped the last United States atomic bomb tested in the atmosphere. Exhibits in the museum tell the story of atomic weapons—from the initial theory to the wartime Los Alamos Manhattan Project, from refinement of the weapons and their delivery systems to the H-bomb. Other exhibits tell a more peaceful story of energy development. The Solar Power Tower, an awesome collection of sun-reflecting mirrors focused on a collection point, sufficient in power to melt through an inch-thick aluminum plate, is one such development. It sits on the plains ten miles southeast of the museum. The building alongside the Power Tower houses displays about research efforts going on at the facility. Helpful employees provide guided tours.

One of New Mexicans' favorite destinations will be your next stop, especially if you come at State Fair time in September. Head back out of the base on Wyoming, turning left on Central Avenue. The State Fairgrounds is bounded by Central, Louisiana, Lomas, and San Pedro. Life in the rest of New Mexico almost stops during the two-week run of the fair, as everyone piles into the family pickup along with the prize pigs, pies, and pumpkins for the ride to Albuquerque. Tall elms along Main Street provide shade from the sun; while out on the midway, the heat, noise, and the fun are almost palpable. Exhibits of the best in Indian and Hispanic art, prize livestock, bales of wool, flowers, model railroads, vegetable peelers, and almost everything else found in New Mexico compete with the Ferris wheel, the horse races, the night-time rodeos, and popular singers for visitors' attention. During the rest of the year, the Fairgrounds are less raucous, but seldom empty: Horse shows, art and craft exhibitions, parties, political events, and flower displays bring thousands to the area during the "off season." A huge open-air flea market takes place on the grounds every weekend except during the Fair.

Having seen Albuquerque from the top of the Ferris wheel or after buying a knick-knack at the

State Fair wool winner

flea market, continue down Central to Nob Hill, which begins at a sparkling white neon-lit and tiled archway about two miles west of the Fairgrounds. This strip of Central Avenue east of the university has enjoyed a renaissance since the late 1980s, establishing itself as a center for upscale boutiques, vintage clothing stores, art galleries, bookstores, antique stores, and sidewalk cafés and restaurants that cater to young adults and families.

A mile west of Nob Hill on Central is the largest and oldest of the state's universities. The University of New Mexico was founded in 1889. It greatly increased in size when returning GIs began to flood the campus after World War II. Not a Rio Grande re-creation of the ivy-covered walls and lawns of Eastern campuses, the university has proudly reflected its Southwestern roots since President Tight in 1906 ordered the previously Victorian Hodgin Hall to be converted into a Spanish Pueblo–style building. Later buildings have followed suit, some more imaginatively than others, resulting in a campus that retains a uniquely cohesive and Southwestern look.

There are two outdoor focal points on the campus: the large, L-shaped plaza area between Zimmerman Library and Johnson Gym, and the duck pond, a tranquil little lake west of the library. The peaceful nature of the plaza belies the hectic pace of a university that is home to more than twenty-five thousand students. Weekends are especially quiet, the plaza given over only to the occasional skateboarder or bicyclist or a student hurrying to the library. Parking nearby is easy on weekends and when school is not in session. At other times, when parking is more difficult, stop at the Campus Parking Office at Buena Vista and Las Lomas for information, a permit for parking in the always crowded lots, and a campus map.

Make up your own tour of the university, using the campus map. Consider including the several Spanish Pueblo–style buildings designed by the late John Gaw Meem, especially the lovely high-ceilinged west wing of Zimmerman Library, recently restored, and the Spanish Mission–style University Chapel. Zimmerman Library is a fine place to find out about New Mexico and the states surrounding it; its special collections include current books about this area in the handsome, comfortable Anderson Room. Archives of historic materials, largely about the Southwest, are usually found in the Coronado Room. If it is maps you are looking for, locate MAGIC: The Map and Geo-graphic Information Center in the impressive underground Centennial Science and Engineering Library has maps for planning your next adventure, whether in New Mexico, the Himalayas, or Zimba-bwe.

There are several small, manageable museums on campus. The Maxwell Museum on the west edge of the grounds has a permanent exhibit relating the history of the human presence in the Southwest. Its changing shows might display Guatemalan textiles or the pottery of New Mexico's own Mimbres Indians. The university's anthropology department boasts an international reputation not only for its explorations into Southwestern ruins, but also for forays into paleolithic and prehistoric sites around the world. The University Art Museum in the Fine Arts Center and the biology and geology museums in their departments' buildings can fill up a morning most enjoyably.

So far, you have seen only part of the main campus. To the north lie the schools of medicine, law, pharmacy, and nursing, each on its own plaza. UNM's South Campus is devoted to sports: soccer and baseball fields; tennis courts; a track; a football stadium; and the well-known "Pit" (the University Arena), a largely underground basketball arena, which is filled during winter games by the raucous cheers of more than fifteen thousand New Mexico Lobo supporters.

If it is lunchtime when you finish touring the university, you can find any type of food on Central where it passes UNM, or pick up something to eat and take it to the cool dales of Roosevelt Park at Coal and Spruce, a few blocks south and west. This pretty park was sculpted by bulldozers under Mayor Clyde Tingley's personal direction during the Depression. The mayor's friend and benefactor, Franklin D. Roosevelt, continues to be honored by this, a favorite Albuquerque city park.

Continue westward down the slope into the valley via Central Avenue. As you pass under the tracks of the Santa Fe Railroad, you will enter downtown, or New Town, as it was known when the railroad first came to the area. Still the legal, financial, and governmental center of Albuquerque, downtown is no longer its commercial center. As in many other cities, downtown in Albuquerque tends to be quiet at night and on weekends, although good jazz, rock, and New Age music are beginning to emerge from clubs, bars, and theaters along Central Avenue. It is always difficult to buy a suit, a loaf of bread, or a piece of fabric in downtown Albuquerque. On the other hand, you can attend a concert or a play, enjoy a meal in a variety of restaurants, or purchase an African necklace, a Panama hat, or a turquoise bracelet in one of the many specialty shops. With the completion of an addition to the city's convention center and the building of a large hotel (the smaller of the two large pink skyscrapers dominating the skyline), downtown boosters hope to bring more business to this area by the tracks, which once bustled with abundant activity.

To take a walking tour of downtown, start from Civic Plaza at Third and Marquette. The plaza sports a splashing, multileveled fountain, with cascading water that cools the feet on summer days. The multicultural Summerfest on summer evenings and other events at noon during the week enliven the plaza for Albuquerqueans and visitors alike. Three large hotels are within one block: the Hyatt, the Doubletree, and the stately La Posada Hotel, Conrad Hilton's first major hostelry. Courthouses and government buildings wall the west side of the plaza. In the 1980s, the city closed off two blocks of Fourth Street south of the plaza to create a pedestrian mall; people now sun themselves on benches set along a brick-lined walkway that replaced a street. Two blocks from the plaza, Albuquerque's handsome city library, at Fifth and Copper, offers a fine book collection and excellent information services. Another block away, at Fifth and Central, the old KiMo Theater slumbers during the daytime but rocks at night with stage shows, plays, dance, opera, experimental and classic films. Especially during the holiday season, the KiMo fills up for performances by La Compañia, Albuquerque's fine bilingual theater company. A masterpiece

of Southwest Art Deco, the KiMo is decorated with cow skulls, Indian motifs, and murals of Indian Pueblos.

The KiMo treats theatergoers at intermission and passers-by at other times with its own art gallery. In fact, Albuquerque, both in the downtown area and elsewhere, has a great many art galleries, some specializing in Indian art, some in Southwestern themes, others showing more cosmopolitan samplings of arts or crafts. Monthly "Artscrawls," begun in 1990, encourage Albuquerqueans to spend an evening in a selected group of galleries greeting friends, artists, and gallery owners; viewing the surprising variety of art; and sampling refreshments.

Two other privately owned and renovated former movie theaters on Central are part of the downtown entertainment scene. The Sunshine Music Theater at Second Street offers jazz or chamber music. The El Rey, near Sixth Street, has concerts that feature dancing and a wide array of musical styles.

You can head west on Central from downtown, just as horse-drawn trolleys did when the area was new and raw and separated from Old Town by a couple of empty miles. But first take a detour, especially if there are any children with you, to the Rio Grande Zoo, a few blocks south of Central on Tenth Street.

African wildebeests, Asian elephants, North American seals, a pair of roadrunners and an entire village of pert prairie dogs will greet you at the Rio Grande Zoological Park, near the Rio Grande on Tenth Street at Atlantic. Once a tawdry exhibition of animals in small wire cages, the zoo has emerged as an excellent collection of animals housed in naturalistic settings. Humans can also enjoy the zoo's setting. Its cool grassy lawns beneath tall cottonwoods offer plenty of lunch spots. A band shell by a large fish pond makes the zoo a site for concerts, as well as picnics and family outings.

To get to Old Town from the zoo, return to Central and head west; you will see signs for Old Town and the plaza. Compact Old Town is definitely a place to park your car and walk, although the old, uneven sidewalks are not easily accessible to people with disabilities. Alleyways and small courtyards, side streets and covered sidewalks make up the labyrinth that is Old Town. Old Town encircles a plaza, which is the geographic, historic, and cultural center of the area. The plaza's bandstand provides a platform for political rallies, wedding photos, fiesta dancers, and band concerts. The wrought-iron benches around the plaza provide a good spot to ponder Albuquerque's rich and varied past and present life. San Felipe de Neri Church, on the north side of the plaza, is the neighborhood parish church and was established in 1706. Old Town neighbors often claim the adobe benches in front of the church for a chance to talk or to absorb the sun on a cool winter day. The present church structure was begun in 1793 and has been frequently altered in small ways. On Christmas Eve its twin gothic towers and the church's surrounding walls and walkways are illuminated by thousands of *farolitos.*

The buildings east of the plaza were once farm buildings, part of a defensive construction pattern ordered by the government of New Spain at the end of the eighteenth century. Now you can barely see the buildings for the visitors. Crammed into most corners of the plaza's old buildings are art galleries, small boutiques, and numerous Indian art stores, offering goods ranging from Asia-made tomahawks to the most exquisite Acoma Pueblo pottery or Two Grey Hills Navajo rugs. Jewelry and pottery vendors ply their wares under the portals east of the plaza.

Children play on the cannon in the plaza, a replica of those used during the Civil War. In 1862, when Albuquerque was very briefly part of the

10

Confederacy, a skirmish occurred near the plaza before the Confederate retreat. The presence of a military garrison between 1846 and 1867 was a boost to the local economy and afforded some protection to the settlers.

Ropes of drying chiles often obscure the facades of the shops on the south side of the square. Chiles are brilliant red at harvest time and then dry to a deep burgundy. Ground chile pods make a hot sauce that smothers burritos, enchiladas, and *sopaipillas* in Albuquerque homes and restaurants. Until the 1930s, chiles were grown on truck farms a few blocks north of the plaza. Now most of the chile pods are grown in other parts of the state, but pockets of farmland still exist within the network of irrigation ditches in the valley around Old Town.

On the west side of the plaza, tourists may find horse-drawn carriages for hire. The corral for the nineteenth-century military garrison, south and west of the plaza, is still a parking lot. Local actors often stage gun battles along the plaza's western edge. Although there was once a jail one block south of here and hangings were carried out on Old Town portals, gunfights were never common occurrences in this quiet agricultural and artistic community.

The Albuquerque Museum, just east of Old Town, should be your next stop. This fine small museum, on Nineteenth Street at Mountain, concentrates on history and art. Visitors to Albuquerque will especially appreciate the well-mounted permanent exhibit detailing the history of Albuquerque and New Mexico, with maps and artifacts from all of Albuquerque's many ages. A replica of an early twentieth-century cinema features a historical film about Albuquerque, including the role 1930s Mayor Clyde Tingley took in developing and promoting his beloved adopted home. Rotating exhibits from the museum's collection and visiting exhibits such as the block-buster Maya collection fill the other galleries.

The Albuquerque Museum conducts excellent walking tours of the area. Guides emphasize local history and architecture, spicing the talks with tales of ghosts and hidden gold in the buildings of Old Town. Many surprising discoveries await you in the surrounding maze of shops, galleries, chapels, and courtyards. A new children's museum is located in the hotel just north of Mountain Road, and for those who are not squeamish, a rattlesnake museum coils in the southeast corner of the plaza.

Just east of the Albuquerque Museum, a new Albuquerque favorite fronts the north side of Tiguex Park: the New Mexico Museum of Natural History. A soaring roof line and two almost-life-sized bronze dinosaurs at the entrance, "Spike" and "Alberta," invite you to enter. There, you can walk into a simulated volcano, feeling the heat and hearing the sounds. You can marvel at skeletons of the ancient beasts that so captivate young children, ride the Evolator into past ages, and see a spec-tacular movie at the museum's Dynamax Theater. Recent visiting exhibits have included the dinosaurs of China (their first trip outside their native land) and the nature photography of Eliot Porter.

There are several hotels, bed-and-breakfasts, and motels near Old Town, ranging from a modern skyscraper north of Old Town to several older Route 66 "tourist courts" on Central Avenue. You might spend the night here before setting off on another day's exploration of Albuquerque—a day in the old neighborhoods of the valley and the ancient petroglyphs of the West Side, intermingled with Albuquerque's most recent and fastest-growing developments surrounding the West Side's volcanic escarpment.

North of Interstate 40, high bluffs reach up from the west edge of the Rio Grande; south of the freeway, the climb is more gradual. These palisades divide the North Valley from the West Mesa, while the South Valley extends to the western boundary of the metropolitan area. Neighborhoods in the valley seem to be much less uniform than those in the Heights. Modest dwellings ringed with chile plants and cornfields often sit cheek by jowl with expensive adobe homes or colonial mansions. Cocks crow, low-riders cruise, men and women jog, and nature-lovers hike. Once these neighbor-hoods were separate villages, strung out along the Camino Real from Los Padillas not far from Isleta Pueblo on the south to Alameda on the north.

Much of the joy of visiting the valley neighbor-hoods comes from slowly driving through them or walking the irrigation ditches that both divide and unify neighbors. Drive along Guadalupe Trail or Rio Grande Boulevard in the North Valley; or Twelfth Street, Sawmill, or the west end of Mountain Road near Old Town; or Atrisco, Sunset, Los Padillas, or La Vega in the South Valley, or locate irrigation ditches on a map for a prolonged ramble.

Start at the north end of the valley. Balloon Fiesta Park, not far west of Interstate 25 off Alameda Boulevard, bustles with activity early each October during the Balloon Fiesta. The event is said to account for more photographic film sales than any other event in the country. Over six hundred huge, shining, fancifully colored nylon envelopes are inflated here to the delight of their owners and thousands of spectators. The balloons then float over the city in directions dictated by wind and the skills of their pilots. Performances by sky divers, stunt pilots, musicians, and cooks please the shivering crowd in the chill of early morning at the park. Mass ascensions and competitions are complemented by the Special Shapes Rodeo (the inflation of enormous cow, polar bear, tennis shoe, and Santa Claus balloons among others) and the balloon glow (nighttime transformation of the balloons into giant Chinese lanterns).

In much of the North Valley, farming and ranching have gradually yielded to housing. Drive past horse ranches and chile fields, head south to the west end of Candelaria Road, where the Rio Grande Nature Center was built in the 1980s for young and old to learn about the natural resources of the Rio Grande Valley. An outwardly unobtrusive, almost underground structure designed by Albuquerque architect Antoine Predock, the center gives visitors details of the ecological setting surrounding them under the cottonwoods. You may gaze through the large windows in the center's library or through peepholes in the fence of the lake filled with frogs, muskrats, turtles, ducks, and geese. The lake creates a lively foreground for the view of the Sandia Mountains. Trails into the *bosque* reach to the river's edge. The Nature Center is a part of the Rio Grande State Park, which is being developed along the Bosque's course through Albuquerque. When finished, the park will offer the city's residents and visitors several points of access to the river. The new Rio

Looking into a hot air balloon

Grande Botanical Gardens on Central just east of the river will be an important central point of the state park.

Head back a mile or so east on Candelaria to Twelfth Street, and then go one mile south. Here, just north of Interstate 40, is the museum and showpiece of the All-Indian Pueblo Council, the Indian Pueblo Cultural Center. A restaurant, a small museum relating to Pueblo history, a large Indian crafts sales area, and a courtyard filled on weekends with Indian dancers are all within the impressive semicircular building that reflects one of Chaco Canyon's large ruins.

Then drive south through the Sawmill area surrounding Twelfth Street. Turn left on Central and then right again on Eighth Street, where you will enter Barelas. Each December, the families of Barelas re-create one of the longest-running, most popular celebrations of *Las Posadas*, a community reenactment of Mary and Joseph's attempt to find lodging in Bethlehem. Cross the Rio Grande on Bridge Street and turn left immediately after the river onto La Vega. Follow its twisting path south to see something of South Valley life—fields of corn and chile, do-it-yourself homes, chapels, and murals. Then head west on Blake to the South Valley's main street, Isleta Boulevard. Farms, shopping centers, adobe houses, and mobile homes are all mixed up on Isleta all the way south to Los Padillas (just north of Interstate 25), where you turn right to go through the southernmost village in the string. Notice one of New Mexico's many "Black Mesas" to your left above what was once a separate small village. Turn right again when you get to the end of Los Padillas at Coors Road. This high-speed highway will take you north again, to the section of town known as the West Mesa.

In contrast to the venerable South Valley, the West Mesa is raw and new, the most rapidly growing part of Albuquerque, with houses sprouting up weekly. Many of these homes command superb views of the Rio Grande, the Sandias, the volcanoes they are beginning to surround, and the volcanic escarpment studded with Indian petroglyphs. Past St. Pius High School on a bluff above the river, turn left on Montaño, then right again on Atrisco to visit a new national monument.

The Petroglyph National Monument preserves the artwork of ancient people who apparently camped above the Rio Grande and carved or pecked their designs into the volcanic rock about them. Just off Atrisco, and northwest of Montano, there is a large concentration of these drawings— animals, people, and objects—in the lava on the hillside. No one knows the precise significance these drawings had for the first Albuquerqueans, the Indians who left them. Some may have been religious symbols, some may have been left as messages, and some may simply have been the equivalent of modern-day doodles. Many of them give hints about a long-ago civilization's art forms, clothing, and relations with animals. The national monument, with a visitor center, trails, and interpretive programs, will protect them and make them more accessible to visitors.

Beyond Petroglyph National Monument, Atrisco Drive rises sharply between dark volcanic rocks to a gently sloping plain and Albuquerque's band of five small volcanic cones, arrayed neatly along a fault line. Park at La Boca Negra Park's horse facility or the model airplane flying pad. From there it is less than a mile's rough walk to the nearest volcanoes. The short climb up the slopes provides a commanding perspective of Albuquerque below and of Mount Taylor to the west. This is a good place to take stock of what you have seen. Is Albuquerque New Mexico's one "big city" or is it really just a grown-up series of small towns?

TOUR
ELEVEN
SANTA FE

Suggested
travel time: One day or many days

Highways: Interstate 25, U.S. 84/285

Accommodations: Many hotels, motels, and bed-and-breakfasts. It is difficult to find space during the summer opera season, ski season, and when the legislature is in session.

Camping: Campgrounds along N.M. 475 and private campgrounds

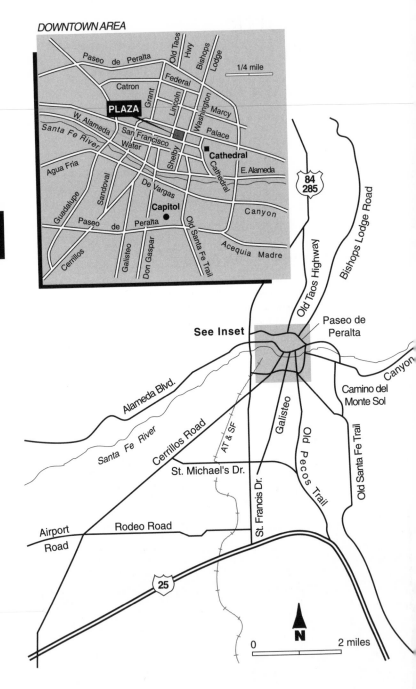

DOWNTOWN AREA

Santa Fe is a place to walk and to browse. After spending hours in a car, bus, or plane looking out of windows onto vast panoramas of mountains, mesas, and sky, you can now move at a slower pace, wander, and look closely at details. Here you can savor a variety of cuisines, the textures and designs of adobe walls and coyote fences, the millwork or hand-hewn wooden details in doorways, window frames, and gates. You can admire pressed-tin or *viga*-and-*latilla* ceilings, geraniums on windowsills, icicles hanging from corrugated tin roofs, shrines to saints or departed loved ones, or the neon decorations on a chile boutique. Details of all kinds are part of the enduring charm of Santa Fe.

Santa Fe has experienced many changes over the centuries, not all of them welcomed by its inhabitants. Throughout all the changes in ethnic composition, political dominance, economic base, architectural style, fashion, and lifestyle, the city of Santa Fe has retained its appeal for visitors and citizens alike. Much of the past is preserved, and the predominantly earth-colored buildings of the small state capital still cluster beneath the blue-green Sangre de Cristo Mountains as they have for hundreds of years.

Remains of a fourteenth-century Pueblo village lie underneath parts of Santa Fe, but Pueblo people were no longer living in this region when Don Pedro de Peralta established the capital of "The Kingdom of New Mexico" here in 1609 or 1610. The Spanish colonists were driven out by the Pueblo Revolt in 1680 and returned in 1692 under the leadership of Don Diego de Vargas. New Mexico, as part of Mexico, became independent from Spain in 1821. Americans began trading along the new Santa Fe trail in 1822 and took control twenty-four years later. Confederates governed the city for two weeks in 1862.

Santa Fe's first settlers were farmers. Later, trade overshadowed agriculture, and today tourism and art are the major industries. The business of governing the state is evidenced in the proliferation of government buildings. Architectural changes have not been as dramatic, since the materials used, earth and wood, remain the basic vocabulary of builders within Santa Fe's historic district.

However, along the commercial entrances to the city, there are myriad curious architectural combinations of steel, glass, and adobe (such as a pueblo-style McDonalds) that mimic the traditions of downtown Santa Fe. Over the years, residents have been tolerant of influxes of counter-culture seekers, politicians, retirees, refugees, hippies, yuppies, and others.

Many people are surprised at the size of the City of Santa Fe—only 60,000 people. You can park your car in one of the many parking lots near the plaza and walk to most of the important sites. The heart of the city is the plaza, the place to sit and note the mixture of people or to start your pedestrian wanderings. With the plaza as hub, you can travel around the hub and then along the spokes of the Santa Fe wheel to see the city. First stroll through the plaza, where you may encounter art shows, musicians, archaeologists examining the ancient trash dump beneath the plaza, other strollers from around the world, and clusters of adolescents. The plaza was once larger than it is now, when it was the oblong rectangle prescribed by the Spanish government and included the block of businesses now on the eastern edge of the plaza.

Spanish Market

Take a moment to savor this historic place, which has witnessed so much change. Tall cottonwoods and elms shade the white metal benches and the controversial obelisk that stands in the center of the plaza. The benches are a good place to feast on a sumptuous pastry or scorching burrito and watch other visitors. During the Mexican era, a pyramid with an eagle on top stood on the plaza. The dirt plaza later became a bullring, but was soon replaced with market stalls for produce sold by farmers from surrounding villages and pueblos. Later, Americans placed a white picket fence around the square and used the space for unloading wagons at the end of their trade journey along the Santa Fe Trail and for public punishment of criminals. The obelisk went up after the Civil War, with an offensive reference to local "savages." Now the white stone is corrected. A bandstand took center stage on the plaza for a while, and now booths for the grand Indian market and the intriguing Spanish market are hoisted up and disassembled every summer. *Portales* were added around the square in 1967. The clock on the northwest corner is the third on the plaza. Push-carts offering hot food have recently been rolling onto the plaza. Watch for pet parades, political rallies, religious processions, and fashion shows, planned or extemporaneous.

To walk off that burrito or napoleon pastry, cross over to the Palace of the Governors on the north side of the plaza. Vendors from nearby Pueblos sell shining silver and handsome turquoise wares beneath the portal. Once you are inside the Palace of the Governors, we recommend that you buy membership or multiple–admission tickets, since you will probably want to visit other museums in the state museum system. Away from the noisy plaza, you can choose to examine the ancient carriages and old horse carts in the patio that symbolize the end of the Santa Fe trail, or cross the patio into the palace print shop and bindery. There, amid old presses and stacks of paper, inks and rollers, linen thread and binder's glue, you can see fine books and marbleized papers. Here you can learn printing techniques and the importance of presses to the territory and state of New Mexico.

From the patio you may also enter either the museum's fine gift shop or the history exhibits that fill the galleries. The building itself is the most important exhibit. This adobe structure, now reduced in size, has stood here since the winter of 1609–10. It was once the most imposing component of the royal *presidio,* the fortress built by the followers of Don Pedro de Peralta. During the Pueblo Revolt of 1680, nearly one thousand colonists and six thousand head of livestock found shelter within the palace. The colonists were besieged here for five days. When their water supply was diverted by the Indians, Governor Otermin led the surviving colonists out of the city and three hundred miles south to safety. The victorious Pueblo people used the building for many years, ridding it of some of the European trappings, until Governor de Vargas took the palace again in 1692. Mexican provincial governors were headquartered in it from 1821 to 1846, and then American territorial governors, with a two-week Confederate hiatus, occupied the palace until 1907. Additions and restorations in 1911 resulted in the current exterior.

Adjacent to the palace's northeast corner, you will find the museum's new history library, manuscript and map collections, and photo archives. A tiled mural commemorates special people and events, with names and dates interspersed with the ceramic art of José Cisneros. The new public library is across Washington Street. From the palace, visit the many and varied shops that cluster along East Palace Avenue and within Sena Plaza. The adobe buildings here are laid out in the Spanish colonial town pattern (*trazo*), in which small buildings with interior courtyards and common walls form a continuous facade. One of the *placitas* was built in 1831 by José Sena for his bride. The Senas had twenty-three children, so they regularly added rooms until the building reached its present size. The fountains, swings, and summer flowers in the courtyard make this a peaceful place. The area's ancient brick and flagstone walkways, interrupted by pillars and posts, make maneuvering difficult along this block. The new Museum of Contemporary Native American Art is easily accessible across the street. It offers a variety of interpretive exhibits, stunning modern shows, and a showplace for the Institute of American Indian Art.

For a broad panorama of Santa Fe, head north on Otero Street and then jog left and up the spiral ramp to the Cross of the Martyrs. The cross memorializes twenty-seven Franciscan missionaries slain in the Pueblo Revolt in 1680. The view makes the climb worthwhile.

Or, you can turn south at the end of the Sena Plaza block and walk across the shady little park toward the sandstone Cathedral of St. Francis. The bronze figure in front of the twin towers represents Bishop Jean Baptiste Lamy, the real person behind the fictional Bishop Latour in Willa Cather's locally controversial book, *Death Comes for the Archbishop.*

Lamy, a newcomer to the area, was not always sensitive to the local leaders or traditions. He oversaw the construction of the cathedral, laying the cornerstone in 1869 on the site of two previous churches that had been built about 1622 and 1714. Inside, to the left of the altar, in the Sacred Heart Chapel, is the statue of Mary which, it is said, inspired the reconquest by the Spanish and accompanied de Vargas to New Mexico. Known for years as "La Conquistadora," the statue was recently renamed "Our Lady of Peace." You will not find the statue there in September because parishioners carry her in procession to Rosario Chapel in commemoration of her journey with de Vargas.

As you leave the cathedral, you come upon another imposing brown building, La Fonda. An inn or hotel has occupied this corner at the end of the Santa Fe Trail since 1846. The present hotel was a Harvey House in the early twentieth century and has always been a popular tourist center. Step inside, let your eyes become accustomed to the dim light, and enjoy the handsome paintings by Gerald Cassidy, the garden patio restaurant, the window displays from various Santa Fe shops, and the eclectic traffic in the lobby.

Wander through La Fonda and then out the side or back, south, toward the Loretto Chapel on Old Santa Fe Trail near Water Street. Archbishop Lamy missed his home chapel in Paris, the Sainte Chapelle, and so had this chapel built in the same Gothic style. A small admission fee entitles you to study the design of the chapel, complete with a description of the mysterious— reputedly miraculous—construction of the graceful spiral staircase that leads to the choir loft. Chamber music performances here are well suited to the delicacy of the surroundings.

The Inn at Loretto embraces the small chapel and is an example of contemporary use of Pueblo-style architecture. The inn forms an ideal setting for the thousands of *farolitos* that glow along its rooftop edges on Christmas Eve. *Farolitos* are traditionally made with a candle set in a bed of sand within a plain paper bag. They light the way for the coming of the Christ Child and bring blessings to the homes where they are lit. *Farolitos* were preceded by the use of small bonfires, called *luminarias,* instead of paper bags;

bonfires continue to complement the *farolito* bags in some parts of Santa Fe on a cold Christmas Eve.

Old Santa Fe Trail continues south across the Santa Fe River. Because it is now only a trickle here, it is hard to believe the river was once used to support commercial river traffic. The land adjacent to the river was also used for the transport of goods, and was built up with stables, carriage shops, and warehouses. This riverfront stretch is a good place for a picnic. One block farther south on Old Santa Fe Trail is the ancient San Miguel Church. A church was built on this site in 1636 for use by Indian slaves. Its destruction during the Pueblo Revolt left only the foundations, which were used in its reconstruction. Walk behind the church on its left side to see the "oldest house," and then turn around to walk along De Vargas Street past small adobe houses that are several hundred years old and were once home to Mexican Indian slaves.

You can meander back to the plaza to browse in the shops and galleries that now specialize in international fabrics, Indian art, or pottery. Until quite recently the plaza was Santa Fe's mercantile heart and was surrounded by hardware stores, shoe stores, and simple restaurants. Consider the plaza your launching site for other tours on foot or by car or the new bus system. To the southwest and beyond, you can explore the state government buildings and the Guadalupe/Agua Fria sections of town. To the north you will find the Museum of Fine Arts, myriad galleries, and the Rosario Chapel. You may drive out to the Santa Fe Opera, a flea market, areas for hiking and skiing, Bishop's Lodge, and the Shidoni Sculpture Gallery. To the far southeast on foot (if you are wearing good hiking shoes and have lots of energy) or by car, four more museums, a nature center, a lovely church, and a host of art galleries and artists' studios beckon. Let us begin by heading south.

The large, round building across the river on Paseo de Peralta between Old Santa Fe Trail and Don Gaspar Avenue is the site of the state legislature—the Capitol, or Roundhouse. You can take a tour of this building, shaped like New Mexico's Zia sun symbol, or wander by yourself to look at the historic displays, listen to the clicking of heels on the marble floor of the rotunda with its inlaid seal of New Mexico, go upstairs into the legislative galleries, or take the elevator to the fourth floor to the governor's office, where you will discover the changing art exhibits in the Governor's Gallery. The Roundhouse is furnished throughout with work by some of New Mexico's finest craftspeople. The vast collections in the State Library Building, northwest of the Roundhouse on Don Gaspar Avenue, are open to the public. Some advanced skateboarders ply the steps and sidewalks when they think the coast is clear.

To the west, on Guadalupe Street, the Santuario de Guadalupe sits on a bluff at the river's edge. Rebuilt and remodeled several times since its construction in the late eighteenth century, this simple and handsome structure is now used for choral and chamber music concerts, exhibits of Spanish colonial art, religious artifacts, and contemporary art shows. Enjoy the flavor of old agricultural and residential Santa Fe with a walk along Agua Fria Street. The adobe homes here were once part of prosperous farms. The close-knit community's San Isidro Church is farther along Agua Fria Road. Make your return stroll down Guadalupe Street, where restaurants and boutiques will pique your interest and appetite.

The northwestern spoke from the plaza takes you into the Museum of Fine Arts. It would be easy to pass many hours in this building, sitting in front of the massive fireplace on a winter's day, listening to the fountain amid the hollyhocks in the courtyard in the summer, admiring the sculpture gardens, purchasing posters and postcards in the gift shop, or listening to chamber music performed in St. Francis Auditorium. The sound seems somehow richer under the dark *vigas* of the ceiling, surrounded by the murals depicting the life of Saint Francis of Assisi. The Santa Fe Chamber Music Festival is held here each summer. There are also art exhibits that feature the museum's outstanding collection of work by native artists and those artists who were drawn to New Mexico by the quality of its light and the community of fellow artists. The Fine Arts Museum also hosts traveling exhibits and juried shows in the lofty galleries.

There is much more art to be seen in the trend-setting galleries surrounding the museum, some

11

specializing in representational landscapes and portraits, others with extraordinary crafts or collections of Native American work. Antique, traditional, and contemporary art is shown in galleries around the city, but many are concentrated near the plaza and along Canyon Road.

The northeastern spoke of the wheel with the plaza as hub takes you on Washington Street past the U.S. Courthouse on the Federal Oval. The oval roadway hints of its past as a mule racetrack. Within the oval, the stone block-building houses the court and some fine murals by William Penhallow Henderson.

Washington Street becomes Bishop's Lodge Road at the spot where you are confronted with the huge pink Scottish Rite Temple. Continue north along the right side of the temple and you soon encounter the turnoff to Hyde Park Road and the enticing possibilities of skiing and wilderness travel in the mountains. Here the fall contrast of yellow aspen against evergreen forest is spectacular. Bishop's Lodge Road takes you to Bishop Lamy's chapel at Bishop's Lodge and to Tesuque, where you will find artists' studios and the foundry, gallery, and sculpture garden of Shidoni. An annual summer show fills the seven-acre lawn with delightful, poignant, dramatic, and some touchable sculptures, as well as picnic tables.

You will need a car or bicycle to go out of Santa Fe proper. Beyond Tesuque is the Santa Fe Opera and the adjacent flea market. The opera is a spectacle not to be missed even if you "don't like opera." Order tickets in advance or take your chances on standing room the night of the performance. The opera season extends from early July to the end of August and usually includes five different operas, lavishly and elegantly staged. Tailgate parties are de rigueur and often feature candlelight and champagne. Wear your warmest waterproof jeans or satin cape when you go to a performance. You may tour the opera facilities during the day. Contact the Santa Fe Opera office for details.

Canyon Road is the southeastern spoke of the wheel from the plaza hub. It begins off the eastern stretch of the Paseo de Peralta loop on the south side of the Santa Fe River. Canyon Road is narrow, parking is difficult, and access for travelers with special needs is a problem, but the galleries, studios, restaurants, antique stores, crafts shops, and boutiques are worth the effort. When you think that you have reached the end of Canyon Road, keep going to find Cristo Rey Church where Canyon Road and Camino DeLoria intersect. Although Cristo Rey Church is relatively new, designed by John Gaw Meem and built in 1940, the priceless thirty-two-foot-high stone *reredos* within are ancient, given to the Catholic church in 1760 by Governor Don Antonio del Valle. The central figure in the altarpiece is Our Lady of Light, who is surrounded by New World cherubim in feathered headdresses and by a congregation of saints. The stone came from nearby Jacona, New Mexico, to be carved in Santa Fe by Mexican workmen. The *reredos* were made for a military chapel on the plaza and were moved several times before finding a home at Cristo Rey Church.

Still farther along Canyon Road, where it follows its footpath origins, you will find art and nature combined at the Randall Davey Nature Center, a project of the Audubon Society, which is open to the public. You can tour the late painter's house and surrounding sanctuary with a nature hike or bird walk.

Back on Canyon Road there is a turnoff south onto Camino del Monte Sol that will usher you along past the hand-built adobe homes of the artists' colony that thrived here in the 1920s and up to the rich cluster of museums on the hill. A turnoff to the left at Camino Cruz Blanca will take you to the handsome campus of St. John's College, an unusual institution with a curriculum based on the reading of the Great Books. Clever murals grace the buildings of this small college. A shorter turn to the left off of Camino Monte Sol on Mt. Carmel Road will present you with a view of the dramatic murals at the monastery. At the end of Camino Monte Sol, you can tour the massive National Park Service Regional Headquarters. There are several small exhibits, but the building itself is the primary feature. More delights for the eye are found a five-minute walk to the west from the park headquarters in the remarkable collection of museums.

The strength of the Museum of Indian Arts and Culture lies in the frequent demonstrations and events involving Indian artists. The handsome displays give you an overview of Indian cultures

Zozobra

and artists' expressions through the ages.

The usually broad view of Indian Arts and Culture is complemented by the sharper focus given by exhibits in the Wheelwright Museum, a short, rough walk away behind the Museum of International Folk Art. Inside the central chamber of the hogan-style museum, there is an exhibit of the work of a particular artist or genre. Downstairs the squeaky wood floor lends authenticity and the atmosphere of a reservation trading post to the Case Trading Post and its rich collection of Native American art.

The cultural wealth of another segment of the New Mexican population is well represented in the Museum of International Folk Art Hispanic Wing. The intriguing displays convey a sense of history and family values, and invite the visitor to learn more through the use of computers and tapes in the exhibits. The Alexander Girard Collection of folk art within the Museum celebrates both the skills and creativity of anonymous artists of the world and the whimsy of the collector. You can walk through the collection quickly for color, pattern, and smiles, or take more time to study each grouping of trains, robots, dolls, or stitchery. This eclectic museum also stages exciting temporary exhibits and frequent events that relate to or create folk art.

Another southern spoke from the plaza, Old Pecos Trail, takes you to the Center for Contemporary Art and the Children's Museum. These two centers afford a glimpse of Santa Fe's artistic present and future. While the Center for Contemporary Art showcases contemporary dance, photographic, literary and visual styles, the artistry of Santa Fe's children is fostered next door. In a city that seeks to please the palates and palettes of adults, the Santa Fe Children's Museum is a refreshing surprise. A miniature blue door opens the way to a collection of activities and exhibits that encourage creativity, curiosity, and delight. Live insects and reptiles, costumes to try on, building materials, a climbing wall, and a climbing maze allow children to make their own discoveries. Adults, too, will enjoy the changing exhibits and the challenges of the permanent features in the museum.

To complete your journey around the wheel, take the southwestern spoke, Cerillos Road, which is studded with franchise food spots, car dealerships, retail businesses, and a few cultural gems that serve students and contribute to the cultural life of Santa Fe. The spacious New Mexico School for the Deaf serves the entire state, and the Institute of American Indian Art is a prestigious art school for Native Americans from around the country. The unusual Paolo Soleri Amphitheater on campus is the site of reggae, folk, classical, and rock concerts. The College of Santa Fe offers outstanding drama and printmaking in addition to its normal curriculum.

The character of Santa Fe is presented not just in its spaces but also in its events and its people. Santa Fe continues to change; some of those changes are reflected in its community calendar. Fiestas, markets, and folk plays have centuries of tradition here and are slightly different in each presentation. Brochures available around town will give you specific information about the music and drama series, summer storytelling at the Wheelwright, museum activities for children, horse racing and the rodeos that have become mainstays of the Santa Fe scene. Read the bulletin boards in restaurants, cafés, and hotels that present a colorful patchwork of notices of events relating to art, health, sports, food, and philosophy that show passing fancies and the infancy of new traditions.

A glance in the Santa Fe phone book will show you that this city is unlike any other in the country. There is a long list of Sanchez, Martinez, Garcia, and Lujan families; Brown, Smith, and Jones families have columns; and the remainder of the book is seasoned with simple or tongue-twisting names that bespeak origins from every distant continent and from ancient times on this continent. As you wander around Santa Fe, listen for the languages—Keresan, Spanish, French, Navajo, Japanese, and many others. Santa Fe is an ever-changing combination of sights, events, and people.

11

TOUR TWELVE
AROUND
THE
SANDIAS

Places: Albuquerque, Bernalillo, San Felipe,
Cochiti, La Cienega,
Santa Fe, Madrid, Tijeras,
Albuquerque

Highways: N.M. 313, I–25, N.M. 22, N.M. 16,
N.M. 587, N.M. 284, N.M. 14,
N.M. 536, I–40

Mileage: Approximately 150 miles,
excluding side trips

Suggested
travel time: One long day or an easy weekend

Accommodations: Albuquerque and Santa Fe

Camping: Albuquerque, Bernalillo and close
to Santa Fe

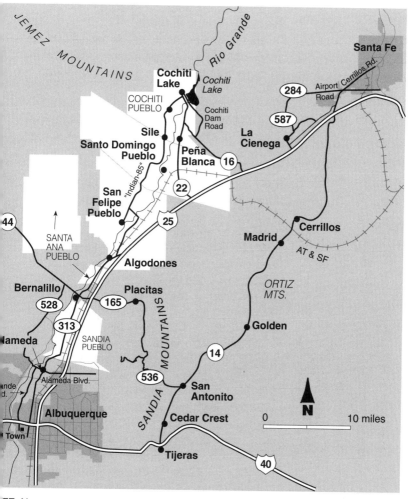

CAMPSITE: Numerous campsites in Jemez Mountains (Santa Fe National Forest)

Like most visitors to the state, many Albuquerqueans clog Interstate 25 on weekends, heading for Santa Fe as fast as their wheels will carry them. The Interstate travels a pretty route, bending around the northwest corner of the Sandia Mountains, across foothills and arroyos, and up La Bajada Hill. But in its speed and convenience, the Interstate bypasses many interesting sites in the middle Rio Grande Valley. This tour avoids much of the Interstate highway, but takes you through Indian pueblos, small towns—living, dead, fading, and reviving—along the banks of the Rio Grande, and through the Ortiz Mountains. You may want to stop in Santa Fe, but surely getting there (and back) can be most of the fun.

Start from Albuquerque's Old Town Plaza. The plaza is quiet early in the morning, chiles hanging in *ristras* from the adobes, tourists and vendors not yet arrived. Head north on San Felipe Street, then west on Mountain Road and north again on Rio Grande Boulevard. Shun Interstate 40 as you pass under it. Leaving the city's northern limit, you will begin to see some large, distinguished homes on both sides of the Rio Grande: the Dietz Farmhouse, La Quinta, and Los Poblanos between three and four miles from Old Town. Others seem more distinguished for their size than their style. Horses have played an important role in this part of the valley for centuries. White board fences along the road enclose horse pastures near the long, low adobes favored in the North Valley. Los Ranchos village center on the east side of the road includes a small museum to visit between tennis or racquet-ball matches.

A bitter fight over new bridges to cross the Rio Grande pitted North Valley residents against proponents of the burgeoning developments on the west side of the river in the 1970s, 1980s, and 1990s. Evidence that the valley lost at least one of the battles comes where Rio Grande Boulevard crosses over the Paseo del Norte, a six-lane bridge and highway connecting the West Side with Interstate 25, a boon to those who live on the West Side and commute into Albuquerque, a bane to those who cherish their quiet North Valley life style.

Where Rio Grande Boulevard comes to an end, turn east on Alameda Boulevard. Turn north again on Fourth Street—old U.S. 85—at Alameda's twin-spired Church of the Nativity of the Blessed Virgin Mary. Leaving the environs of Albuquerque, Fourth Street crosses a bridge over the North Diversion Channel. This concrete-lined arroyo looks peaceful for most of the year, but when a large thunderstorm drops water on the Sandia Mountains or their foothills, torrents of water stream down the paved arroyos through Albuquerque's populous Northeast Heights, providing instant flash floods. The North Diversion Channel is intended to collect water from the entire Northeast Heights and dump it safely into the Rio Grande just west of this crossing.

Immediately after the Diversion Channel, keep left to remain on what was U.S. 85—the former designation for the Pan-American Highway—now N.M. 313. Shortly afterward, on your left, you will pass Shady Lakes, a privately operated haven for fishermen, with no license required. The series of shaded ponds in the Bosque teem with trout, bass, and catfish—"thirty cents an inch" and display a Monetesque collection of water lilies. Two miles farther, east of the road, you reach Sandia Pueblo, the first of the six Sandoval County Indian pueblos. All of the Sandoval County pueblos—Sandia, Jemez, Zia, San Felipe, Cochiti, and Santo Domingo—are described as *Tanoan,* referring to a common set of religious and organizational practices.

The village of Sandia occupies twenty-six acres in the middle of the tribe's twenty-four-thousand-acre reservation, stretching from the Rio Grande to the ridge of majestic mountains that are also named Sandia. A small Catholic church, four *kivas* near the plaza, and a cluster of old adobe homes surrounded by modern single-family homes make up the village of about 250 people on the sandy plains between the river and the mountains.

Language, geography, and quirks of history have isolated Sandia from its neighbors. The metropolis of Albuquerque lies between Sandia and Isleta, the only other tribe that speaks the southern Tiwa language. The present pueblo site has been intermittently occupied since the 1300s. During the 1680 Pueblo Revolt, the three-thousand-member tribe abandoned the village. Some of the tribe probably went to neighboring pueblos, and others may have moved to Hopi, where they built the Pueblo Payupki on Second Mesa. Mistrust is said to have existed between the Hopi and Sandians because of the differences in their religious priorities; the Sandians called on river gods for a good harvest, and the Hopi called on rain gods. The Sandians returned to the present site in 1748 and apparently formed two communities, one made up of the Hopi refugees. Other Tanoan Rio Grande pueblos then distrusted the Sandia tribe because of the Hopi influences on the Sandians' religious rites.

The Sandia tribe mines sand and gravel pits, operates an enormous bingo parlor, and recently opened a fishing enterprise on the reservation. Tribal members also graze sheep and cattle on the foothills, and have pioneered a grazing method to improve rangelands and watersheds by using domestic livestock to imitate the large, compact herds of antelope and elk that once thrived here. Hay and alfalfa grown along the bottom land near the river complement natural forage.

Much of Sandia culture remains intact. The complementary Catholic and traditional religions of Sandia prosper, and feast days and dances are important to the village. A *cacique* chooses the governor and other tribal officers, and most tribal problems are settled internally. The community supports a well-respected tribal government, a good Head Start program, a library, and the preservation of open space. It is probably only the presence of Sandia and the other pueblos along the route from Albuquerque to Santa Fe that keeps the area from becoming one continuous suburb.

New Mexico 313 next enters the small town of Bernalillo. This site alongside the Rio Grande has been inhabited for at least seven hundred years. It is still possible, when digging in the town of Bernalillo, to come across pottery sherds and other evidence of departed civilizations. The Coronado State Park and Monument, across the river, preserves the remains of one such pueblo, once called Kuaua. Here, in the pueblo's complex of more than 1,200 rooms and kivas, Francisco de Coronado and his troops stayed during the winter of 1540–41, as they paused during their misbegotten search for the elusive, gold-filled city dubbed Quivira. Bernalillo itself was probably founded by Don Diego de Vargas or one of his captains shortly after the Pueblo Revolt of 1680 had been put down, although Spanish haciendas had existed in this part

Coyote fence

of the Rio Grande Valley many years before the revolt sent the Spanish scurrying for El Paso del Norte. De Vargas and his men stopped in the area of Bernalillo on their way back north from El Paso. Returning there during one of his campaigns against Apache raiders, de Vargas died in this little town in 1704, either from wounds suffered in battle or from the relative ignominy of having eaten spoiled eggs.

In the days when the seventeen miles between Bernalillo and Albuquerque meant a day's journey, Bernalillo was an important trade center. Ranchers, lumbermen, and miners from the northern part of Bernalillo County (Sandoval County, of which this small town became county seat, split off from Bernalillo County in 1903) made Bernalillo their supply source for decades. Competing supply houses fronted the main street; their successors maintain smaller versions of the same stores facing one another across N.M. 313 to this day. TaGrMo Hardware and Lumber near the south end of town is the descendant of Bernalillo Mercantile, the hub of a commercial enterprise that reached north into the mountains. The "Merc" served as grocery and hardware store, grist mill, purveyor of supplies for Indian jewelers, hotel, and gathering place.

Local landowner Don José Leandro Perea, who once denied shelter to the American territorial governor, William Carr Lane, during a rainstorm, perhaps also denied his town the distinction and employment opportunities of becoming the regional center for the shops and roundhouses of what was to become the Santa Fe Railroad. The new railroad claimed it did not like the price Perea was asking for land in Bernalillo and took its business farther south to the environs of Albuquerque instead. This effectively sealed Bernalillo's fate to be a small, pleasant town. Perea's prices may not have been the determining factor; the railroad bypassed dozens of old Hispanic towns throughout the territory, preferring to create new cities and towns along its tracks.

As a small town, Bernalillo has retained its Hispanic flavor much more than Albuquerque, which attracted the Anglo-Americans who flooded the New Town by the tracks. Bernalillo's quiet has attracted artists and writers to live along its shady streets. The town also boasts an excellent library, a

12

A Matachines
dancer

haven for those interested in the literature of the Southwest.

The Hispanic roots of Bernalillo are never more evident than during the Fiesta of San Lorenzo, celebrated the week surrounding August 10, the feast day of the town's patron saint. A performance of the ancient dance drama, *Los Matachines,* is the most venerable and visible part of the town's fiesta. *Los Matachines,* an ancient morality play featuring Malinche, a young girl in a lacy white frock, goes on for several days. Meanwhile, a carnival atmosphere reigns in the streets and houses of the town. Another large fiesta of more recent vintage is the Wine Festival over Labor Day weekend.

Most of what you will see on the main street, El Camino del Pueblo, is of recent construction—the county courthouse, the municipal building including the library, and a number of commercial establishments. The more stately buildings of the eighteenth and nineteenth centuries are almost entirely gone. Toward the north end of El Camino, however, some of the adobe structures built by Bernalillo native mason and designer, Abenicio Salazar, have been preserved in the national historic district named after him, owned by Bernalillo resident Terry Lamm, who fought for their preservation. Three generations of Salazar's descendants have participated in the renovation of one of the best of those buildings, Our Lady of Sorrows High School, whose heavy adobe walls and stamped tin ceilings now enclose offices and small shops instead of rows of schoolchildren. You can walk through the old building. Spend some time looking at the old photographs of schoolchildren and town luminaries: The doughty Perea and the hardworking Salazar are both there. Over the past few years, Bernalillo residents have tried to restore Our Lady of Sorrows Church, across the main street, but its future is now almost as fragile as its powdery walls and listing steeples.

At the far north end of Bernalillo, at the intersection of N.M. 313 and N.M. 44, turn west on N.M 44 to the peaceful picnic grounds, crumbling walls, and restored *kiva* of Coronado State Park and Monument on the west bank of the nearby Rio Grande. New Mexico 44 continues to San Ysidro, Cuba, Jemez Springs, and Farmington; to the right, N.M. 165 proceeds east to Placitas. If you stay on

N.M. 313, passing the huge, controversial wallboard plant just east of the road, you will come upon Santa Ana Pueblo #2, as the sign painted on the water tank states.

The older Santa Ana pueblo, several miles northwest on N.M. 44 on the banks of the Jemez River, remains the traditional ceremonial center of this small tribe, but is occupied by few people except on its busy feast days in December and January. Santa Ana #2, or Ranchitos, as the tribe refers to it, is the tribe's home the rest of the time. A turn west off the highway into Santa Ana is a passage into what seems a quieter time. The Ranchitos land was purchased from Spanish settlers for farming early in the eighteenth century. Santa Ana's small, twentieth-century Catholic church is set in a cornfield on the north side of the village. Corn has been the mainstay of Santa Ana farming since before the arrival of the Spanish and is considered to be the tribe's mother and nurturer, a sacred plant. The recent popularity of blue corn coincides with Santa Ana's efforts to reestablish its agricultural tradition with large crops of the dark ears of corn. A mill located at Ranchitos prepares blue corn for its roles in tortillas, tamales, and other local specialties in homes and restaurants. The Corn Dance is held at Old Santa Ana on the feast day, July 26.

Santa Ana is proud of its artistic heritage, although there are few practicing artisans remaining in the pueblo. Some of the women stitch red-and-green patterns on the kilts and *mantas* they wear in ceremonial dances in Santa Ana and other pueblos. A traditional craft that has recently been revived is the intricate appliqué of straw mosaics on pitch-covered wooden crosses or boxes representing the transformation of the cottonwood trees and oat fields that you see around you into small art treasures. Santa Ana also operates a golf course overlooking the Rio Grande and the Sandia Mountains and a native plant nursery, preserver of "endangered seeds" and provider of seeds and plants to neighboring growers.

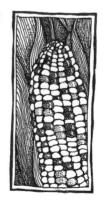

A few miles north on N.M. 313 lies Algodones, a small Hispanic settlement of modest homes and neat vegetable gardens. *Algodón* falls in spring from the village's many cottonwood trees over the roads and fields in lazy flurries, stirred by the wind. The fields of Algodones, squeezed in between the Rio Grande and Interstate 25, are largely planted with alfalfa, though small truck farm gardens harken back to earlier times, their fields and orchards yielding many types of produce, including the colorful chiles basic to New Mexico cuisine. If you are fortunate enough to arrive in Algodones during fiestas, you will see almost everyone taking part. A parade, Mass, and a grand dance usually take place on June 19 to honor the village's patron Saint Joseph. A school Christmas pageant is frequently presented each December. In years past, the pageants were held in the Archibeque Bar—the only hall in Algodones then large enough to provide seating room for all the villagers. The Archibeque bar setting was also appropriate because the Archibeques, along with the de Bacas, Baldonados, Vigils, and Garcias, probably form a majority of the town's population.

Beyond the little town, stay on N.M. 313 as it passes a power station and then open fields on its way to San Felipe Pueblo. Turn left before the modern San Felipe Elementary School. You will soon reach an intersection punctuated with four stop signs. The pueblo is less than a mile from here, across the Rio Grande and a short distance south. Visitors should ask permission at the governor's office before walking through the pueblo. Tribal offices are just south of the church.

The adobe-colored village of San Felipe fills the narrow ledge between the 650-foot-high Santa Ana Mesa and the Rio Grande, placing the pueblo in a closer relationship with the river than many of the other Rio Grande pueblos. When its people first separated from their Keresan-speaking kin of Cochiti, San Felipe was situated on top of the volcanic mesa; afterward the tribe settled on the site by the river, which has great importance in the lives and ceremonies of San Felipe's people.

You have crossed over the river on a concrete span, perhaps when the summer sun has dried cracked mud patterns into the riverbed, and children are playing in quiet swimming holes, or perhaps in the winter when pools are frozen over, or in the spring, when the brown water may be surging close to the village, almost overflowing its banks. This concrete bridge was preceded by a series of woven-branch cribs set on wood pilings and filled with rocks, supporting log planks. The San Felipe people also managed to cross the river in rafts and canoes guided by a rope ferrying system, before the cribs were built in the 1870s.

The natural moat formed by the Rio Grande did not prevent the Spanish from sacking the village in the 1680s, nor other pueblos from attacking when San Felipe became reconciled with the Spanish in the 1690s. However, the physical isolation of the village may have contributed to San Felipe's conservative nature in matters of religion and tribal organization. Collective social and religious responsibilities supersede individual interests at San Felipe, and modern religious and secular events are woven into the tribe's ancient traditions and practices.

San Felipe residents participate in the celebration of feast days by preparing food or ceremonial dress, by dancing, by chanting and drumming, by participating in the Mass, or by getting ready for guests. A Christmas Eve Mass in the old church celebrates the birth of the Christ Child with a rich fabric of interwoven Catholic ritual and traditional dance and music. More dances occur on Christmas Day, and festivities continue into the next week, culminating near the first of the year, when the tribe installs new tribal officials in ceremonies on the plaza. Feasting and dancing occur again on May 1 to celebrate San Felipe's patron saint and the time for the Green Corn Dance; the young corn thrives on the cold rain that so often accompanies the end of the dances.

Our plan originally had been to take you on Tribal Route 85, a dirt and gravel road, north from San Felipe through the tiny, isolated hamlet of Silé to Cochiti Pueblo. The road, which heads north immediately west of the bridge at San Felipe, is beautiful and parallels the river, which allows magnificent views of the mountains beyond the cornfields of the pueblo. But the sandy arroyos along the way have no bridges—they may be easy for a vehicle with four-wheel drive, but the rest of us get stuck. Therefore, after visiting San Felipe, head east from the four-way stop on a fully-paved road along the edge of the Arroyo del Tuerto, to Interstate 25, which you must follow north for about seven miles to the exit for Santo Domingo pueblo on N.M. 22.

Head west on N.M. 22 to a bridge over the Santa Fe Railroad tracks. The Santo Domingo pueblo lies about 1.5 miles south of this point. If you wish to walk through the village or go into the church, you should first ask permission at the governor's office in the community center near the entrance to the village. Not all ceremonies at Santo Domingo are open to outsiders; often tribal officials place guards at the entrance to the village during the private celebrations. Many dances are public, and Santo Domingo is accustomed to having visitors, as early Indian trading paths, colonial Spanish roads, American highways, and the Interstate have passed nearby.

Most pueblos are built in clusters around a plaza or a church. Santo Domingo, however, is made up of a series of connected homes along east-west corridors across the irrigation ditch from the church. The corridors are each named for a Rio Grande Pueblo—Cochiti Row, Santo Domingo Row, Zia Row, Jemez Row, Santa Ana Row, and San Felipe Row. The widest of these spaces is the plaza, a long, shallow hollow worn down by years of ceremonies and dances. The Turquoise Clan *kiva* fills the near end of the plaza, and the Squash Clan *kiva* is midway down the dusty strip in front of the *Koshare*, or clown, society house.

On any of the feast days, especially the Green Corn Dance in early August, the usual quiet plaza scene changes dramatically. The empty lot south of the church overflows with carnival rides and corridors of food booths that sell tamales and cotton candy, chile stew and snow cones, tacos and egg rolls. Interspersed among the food booths are vendors selling exotic feathers for ceremonial attire or ceramic Acoma pots or hand-stitched clothing. From across the ditch comes the sound of the drums. Moving from one row to another as you proceed to the plaza, you may be rewarded by intriguing glimpses of male dancers wearing woolen kilts and fox skins, and female dancers in black wool *mantas,* and laden with silver necklaces. Or you may see old women scurrying between one house and another with steaming baskets of food, their fringed shawls serving both as a protection from the weather and as hot pads. You may find the drummers of each clan emerging from the practice rooms and awaiting their turn to move down the plaza as they follow the pole bearer and lead hundreds of dancers of all ages. The two clan dance groups, Turquoise and Squash, alternate on the plaza, their intricate step rhythms punctuated by the antics of the *Koshare*. These clowns, their bodies painted in light and dark stripes, warn the Pueblo that attackers are on the way. The *Koshare* fight the battle in pantomime, defeating the invaders. Later the ugly mimes may dance alongside a child, make fun of another dancer's tennis shoes, or pretend to be Anglo tourists, to the delight of the crowd. The feast day is a culmination of the dancer's long practice, the *cacique*'s extended fasting and meditation, and all the families' preparation of a bountiful feast of chile, posole, salads, pies, and breads.

Visitors flock to Santo Domingo for arts and crafts fairs because members of the tribe are renowned for the making of exquisite jewelry. Santo Domingos work with silver and gold but are best known for their work with stone turquoise, coral, jet, and shell. *Heishi* necklaces, bracelets, and earrings range in size from turquoise beads the size of caramels to beads as fine as sand. The strands of metal beads are known as liquid silver, and the *heishi,* liquid stone. Many of the vendors under the plaza *portales* of Albuquerque and Santa Fe are Santo Domingos. Although the pueblo location has allowed frequent contact with other peoples, Santo Domingo has remained among the strongest and most conservative of the pueblos and serves as a cultural role model.

North of Santo Domingo, at Domingo Junction, an old trading post featured in the 1960s movie "Flap" advertises itself as the "most interesting spot in the West." The rusting Frazer automobile in front is authentic, as are samples of Santo Domingo jewelry inside, but Mexican Indians have made the imitation Navajo rugs, and the tomahawks may come from Taiwan.

Returning to N.M. 22, turn west and continue to the town of Peña Blanca. Peña Blanca is in many ways only a shadow of its former self. Once it was the county seat for Santa Fe County and an important political center. Now it is a small, quiet bend in the road with few reminders of its former activity. The rebuilding of the church that recently collapsed is nearing completion. Vines nearly obscure the roadside sign that advertises "Probably the best hamburgers in town."

Head west toward Cochiti Dam, where a large assembly of fishermen toss their lures into the spillway of the dam on the Rio Grande. Less than a mile later is the left turn that takes you about one mile to the pueblo of Cochiti and on farther south to Sile.

As you enter Cochiti Pueblo, you will see a neighborhood of new homes sitting atop high scrub land overlooking the Rio Grande and the irrigated pueblo fields below. Less than half of the tribe's irrigable land is now tilled. When the waters behind Cochiti Dam first covered some of the sacred tribal sites, Cochiti religious leaders buried ceremonial items as a symbol of mourning for the loss of the religious life of the tribe. Even before this dramatic event, an earlier dam, built in the 1930s, had caused a radical change in the pattern of Cochiti agriculture. Ancient religious rituals that had often reflected the flooding of natural arroyos had little relevance to irrigation ditches opened, cleaned, and closed by man and machine.

Cochiti has been inhabited for more than four hundred years, being well established by the time of Don Juan de Oñate's visit in 1598. Not long after Oñate's visit, a Franciscan priest, Juan de Rosas, established the first mission in the village, naming it San Buenaventura. The Cochitis continue to celebrate San Buenaventura Day, July 14, with feasting and dancing. The Church of San Buenaventura is large and beautiful, restored to its condition of three hundred years ago. Cochiti paintings; great, carved *vigas;* and statues of European and Mexican origin complete the rich, eclectic look of the interior. Dancers in tribal ceremonials often begin inside the church and then move out onto the large plaza nearby.

The Cochiti tribe banded together with the Apaches in a futile attempt to throw off Spanish rule in 1651. The next attempt, in 1680, in concert with most of the other Pueblos, was successful. The Pueblo Revolt threw off the Spanish domination of Cochiti for some fourteen years, until the returned Spanish under Don Diego de Vargas drove the Cochitis and allies from Santa Ana and San Felipe off their refuge atop the massive nearby Potrero Viejo. Peace has prevailed in the subsequent three hundred years.

Members of the Cochiti tribe were traditionally farmers and craftspeople, and they still excel in those fields as well as in engineering, education, and numerous other areas. Enormous water tanks at the edge of town have been painted to look like the drums for which Cochiti craftsmen are renowned. The drum-makers hollow out cottonwood logs and fit their ends with taut hide. The resonant sound and handsome appearance of the drums appeal to other tribes for ceremonial use and to interior decorators seeking to emulate "Santa Fe style."

Cochiti is famous for pottery, especially for ceramic figures, as well as drums. Like the women in most other pueblos, Cochiti women have made pottery vases for centuries. One Cochiti artist, Helen Cordero, joked that her pots "were never much good," so she sought another outlet for her talent. Her grandfather, a storyteller who charmed the children of the village with his traditional tales, became the model for her clay figures dressed in red and black with closed eyes as the story is being told to the hordes of children clinging to every part of the figure. Mrs. Cordero's appealing storytellers quickly became prominent among collectors and became very difficult to obtain. Other Cochiti women took up the genre, followed by potters from other pueblo tribes. Cochiti is now known throughout the world for its clay drummers and praying figures, as well as for its storytellers. Both pottery and drums are available for sale in the pueblo; directions to craftspeople's homes and showrooms may be obtained at the governor's office.

Returning to N.M. 22 just below the black, rock-covered dam embankment, continue to the left up the grade. Northwest of the dam, developers built the town of Cochiti Lake on land leased for ninety-nine years from a then bitterly divided Cochiti pueblo. The town is primarily a retirement and vacation community, built around a challenging golf course.

Beyond Cochiti, on a bumpy dirt road marked in fall by signs bearing a red and a green apple, lie Cochiti Canyon and the apple farm planted by Jim Young in the 1930s. Young, a New York advertising executive, moved first to Santa Fe and then to this remote and beautiful spot. He and his family planted an apple farm, which is now operated by the Dixon family. Each fall, New Mexicans load their families into cars or pickups and head for Cochiti Canyon to see the harvest under the beautiful blue sky and to purchase jugs of cider, and bags, boxes, and bushels of apples from the Dixons' hillside orchards. Several roads, including the road to Dixon's, head into the Jemez Mountains from Cochiti Lake. These roads may be only barely passable in good weather and worse in rain or snow. However, the views are wonderful. The road into Cochiti Canyon north of Dixon's fords the stream a number of times on its way to a dead end near the Tent Rocks, fantastic structures of aggregate standing like a silent army to the left of the dirt road.

Just north of the sign announcing entry into the town of Cochiti Lake, turn east and immediately south, onto the road that will take you across the dam's impressive earthworks. The U.S. Army Corps of Engineers maintains a small visitor center at the beginning of the road across the dam. Photos of the course of the river from Colorado to Texas are juxtaposed to a fascinating enlargement of a satellite view of the entire course of the Rio Grande in Colorado and New Mexico.

Crossing Cochiti Dam, billed during its construction as one of the world's largest earth-filled dams, you can see New Mexicans enjoying one of the desert's scarce commodities, water. You will also have a splendid view of mountains and plains in a grand circle. Cochiti Lake is at its highest in spring, as it fills with runoff from melting mountain snows. Spring's awakening means greater water use for agriculture in the irrigation ditches of the Middle Rio Grande Conservancy District to the South and more water is released from the dam. Cochiti is a "no-wake" lake filled with sailboats of all sizes in the summer. The state park on the west side of the lake offers camping sites and picnic tables. As you drive over the dam, impressive rock-covered earthworks seem randomly placed against some future battle here in dry country, but in actuality they are intended to receive floodwaters from the Santa Fe River, which empties its usually meager flow into the Rio Grande at this juncture.

Turn left on N.M. 16, which was built to provide access to Interstate 25 for residents of Cochiti Pueblo and Cochiti Lake. Two and one-half miles after the turn onto N.M. 16, highway signs announce a turnoff to Tetilla Peak recreation area, a picnic ground on the east shore of Cochiti Lake, and to La Bajada Village, a crumbling, largely deserted adobe settlement at the base of the cliff. This cliff, also named La Bajada (the descent), marks the separation of the Santa Fe plateau from the downfaulted Rio Grande rift. Black lava forms the top of the mesa and the jumble of red rock is the part of the Galisteo formation that was deposited here around seventy million years ago. Some cars complain when climbing the eight-hundred-foot grade from the bottom to the top.

New Mexico 16 reaches Interstate 25 halfway up La Bajada; turn northeast here for another seven-mile segment on the Interstate. Just before the summit of the long climb, you can search in vain for any sign of human habitation at the exit marked "Waldo." Waldo once housed a small colony of railroad workers. More recently, in the 1970s, its absence inspired an elaborate spoof carried out by the New Mexico Undevelopment Commission. This group, formed by New Mexicans anxious to slow the growth spurred by the state's Development Commission, took out advertisements in Eastern newspapers, purportedly offering land in New Mexico, mentioning the state's high crime rate, its lack of public services, and other alleged flaws. The development at Waldo remains empty, though development in other parts of New Mexico seems little affected by the now-defunct "Commission's" efforts. Where is Waldo, anyway?

After cresting La Bajada, you will have a fine view of Santa Fe, nestled beneath the foothills of the Sangre de Cristo Mountains. Turn west off the Interstate at N.M. 587 into La Cienega. The village of La Cienega straddles the narrow valley of the Santa Fe River. Homes and small farms perch along the road or nestle into the rough hillsides. Signs at the studios of potters, glassblowers, painters, and other artists indicate their hours of business. Most artisans welcome visitors and have artwork for sale on their premises. A festive open house in La Cienega each year just before Christmas brings shoppers and browsers to these studios.

As the dusty road dips and weaves back and forth across the little river, signs point the way to El Rancho de las Golondrinas, which is about two miles from the highway turn-off. The historic ranch was the first stop south of Santa Fe along the Camino Real for travelers from Santa Fe in the eighteenth and nineteenth centuries. As the road ran then, it was fifteen miles south of the capital city, just a day's journey by horse. For early travelers coming up from the south, the large hacienda was their last stop en route, a place to spend the night before reaching Santa Fe. The ranch, owned by the Baca family for two hundred years, prospered as a hacienda and a *paraje* for much of that time. Today El Rancho de las Golondrinas is leased by its present owners, the Paloheimo family, to the Colonial New Mexico Historical Foundation. Volunteer members of the foundation run spring and fall open houses that celebrate hacienda life as it was lived there two hundred years ago.

The Paloheimos restored the original ranch buildings, and assembled a variety of buildings, tools, and housewares to re-create a New Mexican colonial village. At the spring and harvest festivals, the village is briefly populated with knowledgeable craftspersons, musicians, farmers, and actors willing to explain the old ways as the barns, gardens, and workshop come to life. The open-air museum at Las Golondrinas is pleasant to visit at any time of the year.

After viewing Las Golondrinas, return to the dirt road on which you came, and continue northeast along the plain west of the horse track, Santa Fe Downs. The road twists and turns among newly built adobes scattered south of the capital. A small sign at a dirt road to the left indicates the playing field for one of New Mexico's less common sports, the Santa Fe Polo Grounds.

Shortly after passing the polo grounds, the road meets Santa Fe's Airport Road, just north of the small airport. (Santa Fe is the only state capital without regular air service; this one serves only general aviation.) Moments later, on the edge of a mobile home park that assures you that you have not entered Kathmandu or Lhasa, a white Tibetan Buddhist stupa (place of worship) rises above the trailers and small adobes within a walled garden. Kagyo Shenpen Kunchab Buddhist Center was built by Santa Fe disciples of Kalu Rinpoche. The construction of the stupa is faithful to the religion's tradition, with thirteen rings on the steepled top, a watchful eye looking out at its parishioners, and four steps of white stucco representing the stages of enlightenment. Friendly adherents to Buddhism will show you the inside of the shrine, a small ceremonial room with Tibetan drums and horns and highly ornate Buddhist murals on the walls.

Airport Road soon meets Cerrillos Road, one of Santa Fe's busiest and most commercial streets. If you intend to break from the tour to see a little of the capital city, it is more pleasant (and safer) to turn northeast off Airport Road onto Agua Fria Road not far beyond the stupa.

Continuing on (or returning to) the tour, head south on Cerrillos Road, quickly leaving the clutter behind, passing under Interstate 25 southward on N.M. 14 and passing the State Penitentiary, the site for both bizarre and ugly incidents. The girlfriend of one inmate, perhaps following the script of an old movie, hired a helicopter pilot to land inside the prison yard and carry her boyfriend to freedom. The convict was captured in Belen, seventy miles to the south, within the day, after a long chase by helicopters and planes in the skies above Albuquerque. New Mexico residents also remember the grisly prison riot of 1980, in which prisoners took guards and other prisoners hostage, and inmates settled long-festering scores with one another. The riot ended with thirty-two prisoners dead.

A small landmark sign seven miles south of the prison indicates the Garden of the Gods. The "garden"—vertical sandstone slabs and monoliths in hues of cream, salmon, and crimson, interspersed with junipers and piñons—makes a pleasant stop. To the east, you can see a large part of the drainage of Galisteo Creek, arid land now used for little but low-density cattle production. Until 1680, however, the Galisteo Basin was home to a number of Tano pueblos, among them Galisteo, San Lazaro, and San Marco. Inhabitants of these pueblos were active in the Pueblo Revolt of 1680. After the capture of Santa Fe from the Spanish, the Galisteo Basin pueblos moved en masse to Santa Fe and the Santa Cruz River. The towns where the Tanos lived were difficult to

12

defend from the raids of Utes and Comanches, and they were abandoned. When he reconquered Santa Fe in 1692, De Vargas evicted the Tanos from the Palace of the Governors and from the lands they had settled through the 1680s. The Tanos were then absorbed by the Tewa tribes along the Rio Grande. An attempt to repopulate Galisteo Pueblo in 1697 quickly failed. Once again in 1706, eighteen Tano families who had been living at Tesuque Pueblo reestablished themselves at Galisteo, but repeated Comanche raids finally ended the pueblo's existence between 1782 and 1794, when the remaining Tanos moved to Santo Domingo Pueblo.

Cerrillos, just west of N.M. 14, was at one time an important stop on the railroad, its depot the point from which much lead, coal, silver, and turquoise was shipped. By the middle of this century, however, the mines played out and a small town was left with its boardwalks and boarded-up false-front stores and hotels. Several of the stores have reopened as antique shops, and artists and other seekers of quiet have restored some of the town's old homes. A huge modern adobe house, built overlooking Galisteo Creek at the west end of town, offers a petting zoo (turkeys, ducks, goats, and sheep at last census), jewelry sales, and a small museum of local mementos.

The once resplendent Oscar Huber Memorial Ballpark sits along N.M. 14 at the north end of the town of Madrid. The ballpark's grandstand is covered now—you cannot see the dusty ball field from the stands any more, but you can enjoy a jazz or chamber music concert here on a number of summer weekends.

Madrid, like Cerrillos, was a mining town. From 1869 until the mine closed and the town withered away in 1954, tons of coal were taken from under the hills surrounding the town, and shipped up the railroad spur that led to Cerrillos, to other states, and later to the war-time efforts in Los Alamos. The same trains brought in the only safe drinking water available to the miners' families. The Old Coal Mine Museum at the mine's mouth near the east end of Madrid displays the town's original claim to fame. Though you cannot enter the mine itself, several mine buildings and pieces of rusty mining machinery are scattered about the museum's grounds for your perusal.

Houses in the former company town, some boarded up, some restored, crowd the narrow main street. On summer weekends and during the annual Madrid Crafts Festival weekend in late fall, and at the December open house, there is a fiesta atmosphere in the street, as visitors from more populous cities to the north and south invade for a melodrama behind the bar, a concert in the ballpark, or just to wander among the old houses. You will find a sizable community of artists and craftspeople in their galleries and shops, along with others who have escaped the noise and congestion of Albuquerque, Santa Fe, and other cities beyond New Mexico.

Madrid (pronounced to rhyme with "sad kid") was named after a captain in Don Diego de Vargas's army of reconquest, rather than after the somewhat larger city in Spain. New Mexicans knew Madrid best for its coal and for its annual Christmas decorations. The lighted displays were so famous, in fact, that Trans-Continental Airlines (one of the first companies to provide air transportation from one coast to the other and a predecessor to present-day TWA) detoured its night flights over the town each December so that passengers could view the spectacular exhibits.

A long climb takes you out of Madrid and into the Ortiz Mountains. There is little sign of habitation among the brown and green hills between Madrid and the small, optimistically named town of Golden. Miners using Spanish pans or 1930s Depression-idled power shovels have had limited success finding gold here, despite several centuries of attempts. Nevertheless, it is said that local residents have found free gold in arroyos after cloudbursts. Nearby are several ruined pueblos that were abandoned during the early Spanish period. Homes in Golden include one fancifully decorated with thousands of multicolored glass bottles, creating sparkling glass gardens in the dusty foothills. Information about Golden's pretty, small adobe church, and the keys for entering it, may be obtained from the priest at La Iglesia de San José in Cerrillos.

Shortly beyond Golden, N.M. 344 heads east over "Heartbreak Hill" (the heartbreak is for cyclists attempting the steep but exhilarating road) to the

12

mining town of San Pedro, of which no trace remains, and on to Edgewood. After descending from Golden to a bridge over San Pedro Creek, the highway rises continuously until it reaches San Antonito, the most northerly of the rapidly growing East Mountain suburbs of Albuquerque. At night, lights in the houses of the largely hidden town sparkle forth from their cover among the scrubby trees to your left.

At "The Triangle," just north of San Antonito, you can take N.M. 536 to the right fourteen miles to the crest of the Sandia Mountains. Less than a mile from the Triangle, you can visit one man's whimsical collection of memorabilia, Tinkertown, in a small museum open to visitors between April and October. A maze of moving mechanical dioramas are surrounded by collections of old signs, glass transformers, and welded sculptures, created or gathered by the museum's curator during his spare time.

New Mexico 536 is well maintained and plowed in winter, in part because it provides access to the Sandia Mountain ski area about midway up the mountain road. You can also reach the ski area and the crest from the west, though not by car, by walking up one of several hiking trails from the foothills below or riding the spectacular Sandia Tram.

The main attraction of N.M. 536 is the beautiful east slope of the Sandias, which provides a fine example of life zones stacked one on top of another, starting from the predominant piñons and junipers at the base of the road. The piñon has important parts to play in the traditions of New Mexico. Its wood warms the hearths of many homes during the winter, the smoke making the pleasant, pungent incense–like aroma that instantly reminds the traveling New Mexican of home. Its nuts are gathered by families in the fall, either for their own pleasure or for sale to purveyors of nouvelle Southwest cuisine.

From this upper Sonoran Zone, you then move into the ponderosa pines of the Transition Zone. These tall trees dominate the environment from about 6,500 to 8,500 feet, providing homes for squirrels and numerous birds. From there to near the top, the Canadian Zone includes the mountain area's colorful aspen. In summer, the light green of the mobile aspen leaves contrasts with the darker color of surrounding stands of conifers. In fall, the aspens turn brilliant yellow, joining the red of the scrub oak in a brief riot of color. Finally, near the 10,678-foot summit, spruces and firs predominate. A few fortunate visitors will see Rocky Mountain bighorn sheep near the crest; the large, heavily horned animals were described by Coronado but nearly eliminated by hunting and disease. Recently the picturesque animals have been reintroduced into the Sandias, the Jemez, and the Sangre de Cristos.

From the east side of the Sandias, you may not have any idea of the reason for the name Sandias, which means "watermelons" in Spanish. Although there is some controversy as to the source of the name, we prefer the story that early Hispanic settlers living to the west enjoyed the rosy glow off the peaks at sunset much as Albuquerqueans do now. As the sun sets, the pink contrasts with the dark "seeds" of shadowed irregularities on the west slope, appearing very much like the *sandias* that grow in the valley. From the crest you'll see Mount Taylor to the west, Albuquerque below, and a line of extinct volcanoes straight ahead on the city's far side. To the north the Jemez Mountains are in the distance, and a forest of steel—the TV and radio towers of Albuquerque stations in the foreground. South are Ladron Peak and the Manzano and Gallinas mountains; to the northeast, Santa Fe and the Sangre de Cristos; to the east, the San Pedro mountains and the plains of eastern New Mexico.

Albuquerque residents consider the Sandias their playground, a place to relax and cool off. The picnic grounds scattered up the road are filled on summer weekends, as Albuquerqueans and visitors occupy the tables and the woods near the Doc Long, Dry Camp, La Cienega, and Seven Mile picnic areas and use the trails on both sides of the mountain. In winter, snow sports bring out the crowds: downhill skiing at the ski area, cross-country skiing on one of the many trails on the east face of the mountain, or sliding down the slopes on sleds or inner tubes. The U.S. Forest Service established a snow play area for safe sledding or tubing about a mile above the ski area.

Seven miles up from the Triangle, a dirt road plunges down the northeast slope of the Sandias, following Las Huertas Creek down the mountain to the village of Placitas. Several miles above Placitas,

15

a walkway leads to Sandia Man Cave, site of what was at first thought to be a highly important archaeological find. In 1936, a University of New Mexico anthropology student, Kenneth Davis, found remnants of a prehistoric civilization deep in this cave. Taking a small box of his findings back to the university, he and his professor, Frank Hibben, astonished the scientific world with the news that the artifacts dated back about fifteen thousand years earlier than any previous dates in the New World. Later dating established that articles in the rubble pile Davis had uncovered had been used about ten to twelve thousand years ago, placing the pile in the same epoch as the findings of Folsom Man in northeastern New Mexico. No archaeological materials remain in the sealed-off cave, but the site, alongside little Las Huertas Creek, is peaceful and pretty, allowing you to consider the pleasures of living in this place and to wonder where the remains of Sandia Man are. As with Folsom Man, no human skeletal parts of the same age have ever been found here or elsewhere.

Back down along N.M. 14, you will pass through the community of Cedar Crest on the way to Interstate 40, which you reach just before the cement plant in Tijeras. The 1980s have seen a tremendous boom in building in Cedar Crest, Tijeras, and the surrounding area. New Mexico 14, perhaps inevitably, has become home to the businesses of the suburbs: shopping centers, small shops, and franchise restaurants.

With the Sandia Mountains on your right and the Manzano Mountains beyond Tijeras Creek on your left, a long downhill ride on the Interstate takes you into Albuquerque. Passing town houses and motels built since World War II on lands previously used only for grazing, continue west to the Rio Grande Boulevard exit, which will return you to Old Town Plaza.

TOUR
THIRTEEN
THE
MANZANO
MOUNTAINS

Places: Albuquerque, Tijeras, Chilili,
Mountainair, Gran Quivira,
Albuquerque

Mileage: Approximately 185 miles, excluding
side trips

Suggested
travel time: One long day or a weekend

Highways: I-40, N.M. 337, N.M. 55, U.S. 60,
N.M. 47, N.M. 309, N.M. 314

Accommodations: Albuquerque and Mountainair

Camping: Albuquerque, in the mountains near
Cedro, Tajique, Manzano, and Belen

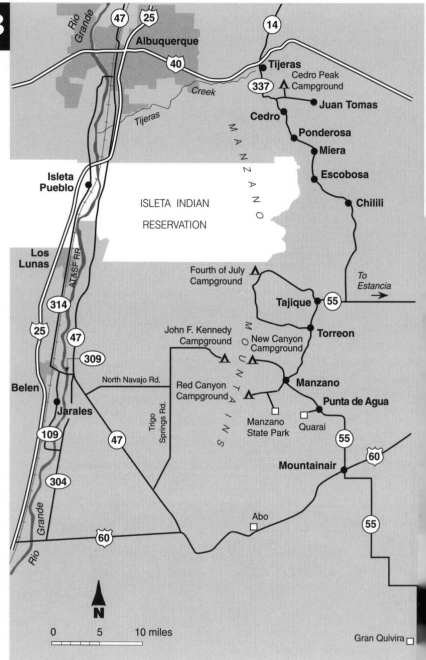

Albuquerqueans often escape to the nearby mountains when it is hot in the city or when snow provides opportunities to play up high. Most people tend to head north and east to the Sandia Mountains, but a few avail themselves of the lovely drive, uncrowded campgrounds, crumbling Hispanic villages, and fascinating ancient pueblos to the south, in and around the Manzano Mountains. Join the latter group one weekend on this short tour.

Head east out of the city on Interstate 40 or on the older parallel route, N.M. 333, a segment of old Route 66. A cool headwind blows down Tijeras Canyon in the morning as you ascend along Tijeras Creek. Almost nothing is left of the ancient pueblos that you pass along the way. Nor is there much trace of the Hispanic village of Carnuel, which was established in 1763, abandoned in 1771 due to Apache raids, and then reestablished in 1819 by a group of homesteaders from the small town of Albuquerque. The pass between the Watermelons and the Apples (the Sandia and Manzano mountains) is today a welcome connection between the high plains east of the mountains and the Albuquerque river valley and other towns to the west, just as it was a favorite route for Apache hunters and raiders coming off the plains, traders heading west, and farmers' families fleeing the Dust Bowl.

The town of Tijeras acts as a funnel for travelers from the east, north, and south heading west to Albuquerque and beyond. A general store, schools, and churches for the East Mountain area, and the Cibola National Forest ranger station lie at the center of the town, overshadowed by the dusty Ideal Cement plant on the hill south of town. Exit from the freeway at Tijeras, and head south on N.M. 337. The ranger station on your left houses a miniature museum where you learn about the mysterious mounds behind the ranger station and across the footbridge: the ruins of Tijeras Pueblo beneath the earth. The road climbs and twists through piñons and junipers, past the small towns of Cedro, Ponderosa, and Miera. Many people seeking quiet and solitude from their jobs in Albuquerque have moved into these little towns, supplanting the subsistence farmers. About six miles south of Tijeras, a small dirt road leads east to another small town, Juan Tomas. Along the way, you come to one of the public campgrounds closest to Albuquerque, Cedro Peak, which lies on the side of a small, conical mountain of that name. The wooded area around the peak boasts a network of trails and dirt roads perfect for mountain biking; maps are available at the ranger station in Tijeras. (Note: As in most wilderness areas, those within the Sandia and Manzano mountains to the north and west are closed to all vehicles, including mountain bikes.)

Between Ponderosa and Escabosa, on the west side of the road, the Sanchez family has a goat farm and cheese factory, popular with Albuquerque schoolchildren and other visitors as a friendly place to pet the goats and watch the goat cheeses being made. Mrs. Sanchez will offer you sample tastes of the cheese, stories of her life among the goats, and picnic tables for enjoying your lunch.

Just a mile beyond the town of Escabosa, the highway enters the Chilili Land Grant, a huge expanse that stretches about ten miles east from the crest of the Sandias to the grassy plains, and almost as far from north to south. Cattle have replaced the bean farms that were prevalent here at the beginning and middle of the twentieth century. Chilili's land grant dates from Mexican times in 1841 and was confirmed by President Theodore Roosevelt in 1909. The grant has been the focus of bitter fighting among some of the grantees' descendants since the 1930s, when a portion of the land was lost for failure to pay taxes on it. The shooting is over, but signs still indicate "This land is NOT for sale." Like all of the mountain towns between here and Mountainair, closure of the Chilili schools and improved access to Albuquerque shopping have led to fewer local services offered.

Adobe mud

Beyond Chilili, N.M. 337 continues to wind up and down the rolling, grassy hills, with the tree-covered Manzano Mountains far to the west. The crest of the Manzanos is divided four ways. To the north and south, it is part of the Cibola National Forest. The west side of the Manzanos in the north is part of Kirtland Air Force Base, and just beyond that, the Isleta Indian Reservation meets the Chilili Land Grant at the crest of the long ridge. Of these four owners, only the National Forest welcomes visitors, but the facilities offered there are particularly pleasant.

From Tajique, south of here, a seven-mile graveled road leads gently up through the foothills to Fourth of July campground. The campground is very popular for at least three reasons: It is a pleasant camping spot, close to the city, but away from its bustle and heat; it is a jumping-off place for a trail that connects to the twenty-two-mile Manzano Crest Trail, with magnificent views of the plains and tree-covered slopes to the east, and the moonlike, desolate landscape and Ladron Peak to the west; and in fall the rare (in New Mexico) maples and scrub oaks create a magnificent palette of red hues that light up the clear autumn skies. It is this display of color that led to the naming of the canyon and campground. The Manzano Crest Trail continues south from its intersection with Fourth of July Canyon. (It also heads north, but soon ends abruptly at the Isleta Reservation boundary.) Meadows full of wildflowers in the spring and summer alternate with wooded sections. Midway along the trail, hikers can visit the Forest Service's Capilla Peak fire lookout. Only at this point does a road reach the crest, and the campground of the same name lies here just below the ridgeline. Other trails branch off to the right and left before the Crest Trail reaches South Peak and then descends to the old pueblo of Abo. All the Forest Service campgrounds on both sides of the Manzanos— John F. Kennedy Campground on the west side, and New Canyon, Capilla Peak, and Red Canyon on the east side—are connected to the Crest Trail.

New Mexico 337 comes to a sudden dead end among the grassy rangelands of central Torrance County. New Mexico 55 heads east to the county seat, Estancia, a sleepy town once famous for its bean cooperative, which shipped hundreds of tons of pinto beans out along the now-defunct New Mexico Central Railroad. To stay along the edge of the Manzanos, turn right on N.M. 55; three miles later you will arrive at Tajique, named for a nearby pueblo, abandoned in 1675. As at the other Salinas Pueblos, life in *Taskike* became unbearable, at least in part due to the raids of the nomadic Apaches. Torreon lies a little farther ahead; it also was built on the site of an abandoned pueblo. Its name

Adobe bricks

comes from *torreones,* the defensive towers built by the Spanish to guard against invaders.

Manzano, the next town in line, gives the impression of having seen more prosperous days. Its senior citizen center and large Catholic church are the only remaining prominent buildings, its present belying its boisterous past. Manzano was the center of passionate battles in the late nineteenth century between sheep ranchers and cattle ranchers and between the long-time Hispanic inhabitants and the crusading journalist, Charles G. Kusz, who was assassinated as he worked at his press in Manzano in 1884. Even the title of his newspaper, *The Gringo and the Greaser,* implied confrontation. From Manzano, graveled roads give you a choice of campgrounds: the relatively primitive Forest Service campgrounds (pit toilets, no water) at Red Canyon, New Canyon, and Capillo Peak, and the lower, more developed Manzano State Park.

At the tiny hamlet of Punta de Agua, seven miles southeast of Manzano, the first of the three pueblo ruins that make up Salinas National Monument lies just a mile off N.M. 55. Once a large town of red-rock, grouped dwellings, Quarai is now memorable for the ruins of its impressive church, which had walls five feet thick. These ruins, situated on the side of a grassy hill far from any large town and facing eastward toward the edge of a great plain, foster peaceful contemplation. Peacefulness also comes with a quiet lunch among the cottonwoods in the picnic ground at the side of the ruins. (There is no camping at Salinas National Monument.)

From Punta de Agua, N.M. 55 bends around section lines to the railroad town of Mountainair. Created in 1901 when the Atchison, Topeka, and Santa Fe established the "Belen Cutoff" for freight trains heading east or west, Mountainair achieved a measure of renown in the ensuing years as a shipping point for beans, a site for summer lecture programs on the Chautauqua model, and then a place where Albuquerqueans could buy cars inexpensively. Just south of Main Street (U.S. 60), the Hotel Shaffer, whimsically decorated by its owner, "Pop" Shaffer, still caters to visitors. It has recently been reopened as a bed-and-breakfast inn and restaurant. The car dealerships, lecture tents, and bean warehouses are all gone now. In partial replacement, the National Park Service operates a visitor center around the corner from the Hotel Shaffer, offering exhibits and video programs about Salinas National Monument.

Gran Quivira is the second of the Saline pueblos that you will visit. Driving alternately south and east from Mountainair on N.M. 55, you will find this impressive pueblo twenty-five lonely miles away. The miles are punctuated by deserted ranch houses and school buildings, although a few ranchers still live along the road. Pop Shaffer lived in one of the ranches closest to Mountainair. His penchant for whimsy is well preserved in the fancifully carved and painted decorations at his Rancho Bonito. Information on visiting Rancho Bonito is available at the National Park Service visitor center in Mountainair.

Gran Quivira sits astride a mesa above the quiet plains, peppered with piñons and junipers. The Jumanos Indians who once lived here were among what the Spanish called the "Saline Pueblos," named for the large salt lakes a short distance to the east. Salt was one of the Spanish colony's most important exports to New Spain. It was exchanged for tools, candles, articles required for religious observances, and livestock needed by the colonists.

Living on the edge of the plains, the Jumanos took on some of the characteristics of their no-madic neighbors, although they were Tompiro Pueblo Indians like others nearby. The name *Jumano,* for example, was given them because of the stripes they painted on their bodies in emulation of Plains Indians with whom they traded. But like their other Pueblo neighbors, the Jumanos were forced to abandon their pueblo in the late seventeenth century, when the delicate balance between the Pueblos and the Plains Indians and their environment was upset. The demands made by the colonizing Spaniards transformed former trading partners into enemies.

Before they deserted Gran Quivira, however, the Jumanos built two churches under the direction of missionary priests. The ruins of both, including the massive Church of San Buenaventura, have been fully uncovered. Enter beneath the huge lintel at the east end of San Buenaventura and imagine the Jumanos sitting in the choir loft above, candles sputtering in the nave ahead as the priest intones his Mass. The church, roofless now under the blue New Mexico sky, plays host to rabbits, lizards, the circling hawk, and the curious visitor. The small visitor center shows video programs, including an excellent account of the excavation of Mound Seven, a warren of small rooms open for your examination between the two churches. As you climb on the walls of this set of buildings, you will come to a place where you can see one room on top of another. The lower one has arcs for two sides, suggesting the concentric circles of the older pueblo; the upper one has the rectangular configuration of the more recent pueblo. Many other mounds on the mesa top, still unexcavated, convey the size of this long-ago community.

Returning to Mountainair, head west on U.S. 60. Not long after leaving the little town, you come to Abo Junction, where a short spur takes you north to the pueblo of Abo. Like Quarai and Gran Quivira, Abo was once a large pueblo, and like them, its most salient feature is the large, high-walled red-stone Pueblo church. A pleasant self-guided trail takes you through the church buildings and then out among the cholla-covered hills, which show hints of the still-buried pueblo. Unlike Quarai and Gran Quivira with their vast vistas, Abo feels more confined, and the intrusion of a chainlink fence against vandals restricts the ambiance of the place.

Head west from Abo Junction on U.S. 60, turning northwest on N.M. 47. You'll pass the turnoff to John F. Kennedy Campground, the only camping spot in the national forest on the west side of the Manzanos or Sandias, and trailhead for a beautiful, sometimes steep trail entering into the Manzanos' trail system up the Cañon del Trigo. N.M. 47 crosses the train tracks of the "Belen Cut-off" and passes through Rio Communities on its way to the Rio Grande, which it skirts on the east side from Belen to Albuquerque. A left turn on N.M. 309 will take you across the river into the "Hub City."

Belen's cool riverside parks will warm your heart after a long drive. Its large train yard will be of interest to the children in your car; long strings of freight cars are switched from track to track at this "hub" of railroad activity where the north–south line meets the Belen Cut-off from the east, sending both freight trains and Amtrak trains northwest

Collared lizard

toward Gallup and Los Angeles. Close to the large railroad yard, you'll find the Harvey House Museum, which displays mementos and memorabilia from the Harvey Houses that served railroad travelers throughout the Southwest. Turn south on the road to Jarales, a small community on the east side of the tracks, for the P&M Museum that displays farming equipment and farm furniture and furnishings. In Jarales, you'll also find the Valencia Flour Mill, one of only two functioning mills in the state. If you're lucky, you'll be able to tour the mill, seeing machinery from another time still functioning at the end of the twentieth century.

Belen and Los Lunas, its neighbor to the north, are growing rapidly, largely as bedroom communities for Albuquerque. Both towns have maintained the western atmosphere that has characterized them for a long time; cowboy boots, pearl-buttoned shirts, boot jeans, and ten-gallon hats are the dress of choice, horses are often seen on the streets of both towns, and the horse and cattle auction on the north side of Belen is an excellent place to buy a horse, a steer, or a sheep—or just to watch and listen to the skilled auctioneer.

N.M. 314, once U.S.85, and before that *El Camino Real,* passes beyond the auction yard, the village of Los Chaves and two prisons into the center of Los Lunas. Just to the left of the town's traffic light , the stately Luna Mansion presides over a busy intersection. Long in decay, the last twenty years have seen the impressive home of the Luna family renovated, refurbished, and converted into a modern restaurant.

Continuing north on N.M. 314, you will soon have the opportunity to enter Isleta Pueblo. Isleta is a large pueblo—more than 3,000 Isletans now live there. The community almost certainly represents the weaving together of several threads after the Pueblo Revolt. Many of Isleta's pre-Revolt inhabitants fled south with the Spanish in 1680, where they established a new pueblo, now called Ysleta del Sur, on the Rio Grande southeast of present-day El Paso. Other Isletans went west, establishing a home with the Hopis and Sandias on Second Mesa. Some of both groups returned to fertile lands on the middle Rio Grande in the 1690s; their numbers were augmented by other southern Tiwas from surrounding villages, now no longer in existence, and by Piros and Tompiros from as far south as the present site of Socorro. A final thread was woven into the fabric by the arrival of a group of Lagunas in 1881 following a great religious schism in that pueblo.

Isletans farm and ranch the river-bottom lands of the pueblo and the foothills of the Manzano Mountains—pueblo lands reach in a narrow swath from the Rio Puerco in the west to the crest of the Manzanos. The tribe, guided by the first female tribal chairman of a New Mexico Pueblo, took steps in the 1980s and 1990s to assure that Albuquerque maintained the quality of the Rio Grande's water leaving the city bound for Isleta.

Many pueblo inhabitants commute to jobs in Albuquerque; a few are engaged in a revival of Isleta pottery and other traditional arts, which can be seen and purchased in several small shops fronting Isleta's large, dusty plaza. You'll enjoy another purchase to be made in these small shops, the fruit pies and oven bread made in adobe *hornos* scattered throughout the pueblo. The massive, white-painted mission church, named for Isleta's patron saint, San Agustin, dominates the north side of the plaza. High ceilings and white-washed walls, paintings and relics, and brightly-colored banners welcome Isletans and visitors.

Head north out of Isleta on N.M. 314. If in a hurry, you can rejoin Interstate 25 just north of the pueblo before the freeway crosses the Rio Grande to parallel its east bank. If you have more time, continue north on N.M. 314, appropriately named Isleta Blvd., which curves gently through farming land in the old communities of Los Padillas, Pajarito, Armijo, and Atrisco (now together know as the South Valley) before reaching its own river crossing on Bridge St., bringing you back to Albuquerque after a day or two of exploring mountain and high desert scenery, modern and ancient Indian, Hispanic, and Anglo settlements.

TOUR
FOURTEEN
SOUTHWEST
CIRCLE

Places:	Las Cruces, Deming, Columbus, Kingston, Hillsboro, Hatch, Las Cruces
Mileage:	Approximately 316 miles, excluding side trips
Suggested travel time:	A long weekend
Highways:	U.S. 70, U.S. 80, U.S. 180, I–10, U.S. 180, N.M. 152, N.M. 187, I–25
Accommodations:	Las Cruces, Deming, Kingston, Hillsboro, and Hatch
Camping:	Las Cruces, Deming, Rockhound State Park, Columbus, City of Rocks State Park, and Leasburg Dam State Park

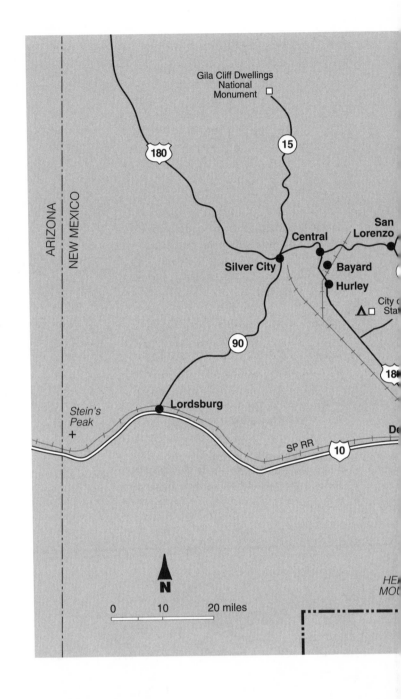

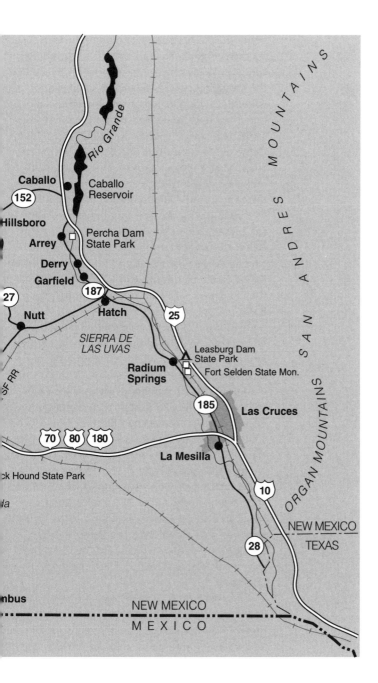

Caballo

152

Caballo
Reservoir

Rio Grande

Hillsboro

Arrey

Percha Dam
State Park

Derry

Garfield

187

27

Nutt

Hatch

25

SIERRA DE
LAS UVAS

Radium
Springs

Leasburg Dam
State Park

Fort Selden State Mon.

SF RR

185

Las Cruces

70 80 180

La Mesilla

ck Hound State Park

la

10

NEW MEXICO

28

TEXAS

mbus

NEW MEXICO

M E X I C O

SAN   ANDRES   MOUNTAINS

ORGAN MOUNTAINS

14

4

Many people have come and gone through the southwest quadrant of the state, which is now centered in Las Cruces: ancient desert dwellers of the Mogollon culture, Spaniards seeking gold, colonists looking for a place to live, miners digging for riches, and passengers on the Overland Stage route. Nowadays people come to stay; Las Cruces is one of the fastest-growing cities in New Mexico. Situated at the crossroads of several important highways, the city also attracts visitors, drawn by the easy access to desert and mountains, historic forts, and old plazas. This tour begins and ends in Las Cruces, and in between it loops west into desert country to Deming, turns north toward Silver City, and then heads east through the Black Range to briefly link up with I-25 before paralleling the Rio Grande on country roads through the fertile valley back to Las Cruces.

This tour is short on miles but long on experiences. You can stroll through New Mexico's second largest university and Old Mesilla's historic buildings, drive through the Chihuahua Desert, picnic among weird and wonderful rocks, climb over spectacular Emory Pass, and recall tumultuous mining days in now sleepy Hillsboro. As you head south toward Las Cruces at the end of town, follow the river as it winds by the chile capital of the world, share garrison life at Fort Selden, and then make Las Cruces your headquarters for other side trips: hiking in the Organ Mountains, shopping for Mexican crafts in Juárez, picnicking at White Sands. Set aside a day for visiting Las Cruces and Old Mesilla and another two days for the loop. The shorter Las Cruces–Deming–Nutt–Hatch trip fills an afternoon.

Lying west of the jagged Organ Mountains and east of the Rio Grande, Las Cruces spreads over the green Mesilla Valley. The older part of town is situated near the river, while newer areas are growing up on the high ground across I-25. Residents extol the good weather of Las Cruces, which makes it an important agricultural center, as evidenced by the miles of chile and cotton fields and pecan groves that surround the town. Sunny days also promote recreation; Cruceños golf and swim year-round in several parks, including Burns Lake.

Because Las Cruces has built outward instead of up, it may be difficult for the visitor to locate the downtown area or old Las Cruces. But Las Cruces has a rich history, with indications that an agricultural people lived in the valley by 1225 B.C. Farming peoples also lived here from A.D. 300, disappearing in the fifteenth century for reasons archaeologists cannot explain. Soon after, Spanish explorers making their way up the Camino Real (the royal road or King's Highway, which still exists in Las Cruces as County Road 75) from Mexico to Santa Fe passed through the Mesilla Valley. Don Juan de Oñate led a band of colonists through here in 1598; his journey is depicted prominently on a water tower on the west side of I-25. Other caravans of people and livestock followed Oñate's trail, turning off north of modern-day Las Cruces to cross the inhospitable desert via the Jornada del Muerto (the journey of the dead), as the river trail was too difficult for caravans. In 1830 travelers heading south from Taos were surprised by Apaches and killed near here. Those who found the bodies commemorated their death with wooden crosses; travelers passing the site named it La Placita de las Cruces (the place of the crosses), later shortened to Las Cruces.

In response to a request from the villagers of Doña Ana, a lieutenant from the U.S. Army garrisoned in the village surveyed a townsite near this location, laying out farm sites near the river and platting house lots on the low hillsides. The town took the name Las Cruces. The presence of Fort Fillmore a few miles downriver gave settlers a feeling of security, encouraging them to open businesses to serve the fort. Freight and passenger routes brought more people and goods; mining operations in the area also encouraged growth.

The original townsite is preserved in the Mesquite Historical District, east of the Downtown Mall. Pick up the walking tour of the historic area at the Chamber of Commerce office on Picacho Street; then drive, or walk, the short distance to the historic district. The district, bounded by Campo and Tornillo streets and Texas and Grant avenues (streets run north and south in Las Cruces, avenues east and west), is centered on Klein Park, which has been used by residents for recreation ever since settlers first started building their homes in the area. The residences still standing date from the 1870s and are constructed in the flat-roofed

Territorial and Spanish colonial revival style, with patios inside and thick walls facing the street. These homes have not been restored; they are not important because of their innate beauty, but because they date from another era.

The Atchison, Topeka, and Santa Fe Railroad located a station in Las Cruces in 1881, leading, as in Albuquerque, to the development of a new town near the tracks, the site of the Alameda-Depot Historical District. This district stretches between Chestnut and Amador avenues, with the northern section clustered between Reymond and Main streets and the southern section from the railroad tracks to Alameda Boulevard. Alameda, located conveniently close to the new railroad and watered by irrigation ditches, was the fashionable area to live in at the beginning of the century. Lovely old homes in Gothic, Queen Anne, Pueblo, and Spanish colonial styles remind you of more gracious times. Another important route, Las Cruces Avenue, was the first paved street in the city, blacktopped to give arriving travelers a good first impression of the city. Early in the development of the area, the Women's Improvement Association purchased land for a park. Pioneer Park, stretching over a city block, is still the setting for many community celebrations like the Fourth of July picnic.

To return to the downtown area, take Amador Avenue east to Main Street, where the distinguished courthouse sits solidly on its block and the Amador Hotel is now part of the county manager's complex. In the old days the Amador welcomed Benito Juarez, president of Mexico, and the less distinguished but no less famous Pat Garrett and Billy the Kid. For years the Amador family ran the hotel; memories of those days are preserved in several rooms, a mini–museum of the Southwest. One block south at Water and Lohman, a grinding wheel from El Molino, an old flour mill, commemorates the work of pioneers in the area. Look for the reproduction of Michelangelo's *Pietà,* dedicated to the Sisters of Loretto, who established the Loretto Academy in 1875 and brought schooling to the children of the area. The academy has been replaced by a shopping center named for the good sisters.

The Armijo-Gallagher house, one of the oldest

buildings in Las Cruces, is located on the grounds of the shopping center. Now the home of a savings and loan, the house has been restored. Visitors are invited to view the original furnishings in rooms on the second floor. One block north of Lohman, Main Street splits into Water (one-way going north) and Church (one-way south) streets, which encircle the Downtown Mall, built with the hope of revitalizing the city center. As in many towns, shops have still moved to malls on the outskirts. At the north end of the mall, Main Street becomes itself again. Here the Bicentennial log cabin, surrounded by modern buildings and almost swallowed up by them, invites you to poke around if you are visiting during the summer months. The cabin, one hundred years old, was moved from its setting in the Black Range to celebrate the two-hundredth anniversary of the founding of the United States. It contains authentic furnishings and artifacts used by the pioneers of the region. Also at the north end of the mall, the Branigan Cultural Center exhibits the works of local artists, features historical exhibits and paintings, and sponsors musical events and other happenings. The posters on the wall and the many brochures describing events held there attest to the vitality of the center. With its thick adobe walls and its cool tile floors, the center is an especially pleasant place in which to escape the summer sun. The Convention and Visitor Office is another source for brochures on what to do in Las Cruces, including an especially good handbook for visitors with disabilities.

Leaving the downtown area, head for New Mexico State University (NMSU), where the visitor center at O'Loughlin House provides information about NMSU. On this site, Las Cruces College was founded in 1888. The next year the college became the state's land grant institution, an agricultural and mechanical arts college known as the home of the Aggies; older New Mexicans still refer to the university as the A&M. NMSU published a campus walking tour to commemorate its centennial. If you cannot find a copy at the visitor center, pick up a campus map and make up your own tour, starting at the Horseshoe. In the center of the horseshoe, next to the flagpole, is the cornerstone of McFie Hall, the original campus building, which burned down in 1910. At the top of the shoe are the administration buildings, various science halls, and the new gym. At the northeast corner, you may join students as they head over to Memorial Tower, built to commemorate Aggies who died in the armed services; it is now a trendy cafeteria. North of the tower the Williams Art Gallery shows student and faculty work, and east of the gallery the University Museum highlights exhibits from its collections as well as traveling shows. Both of these buildings deserve your attention, whether you are a tourist or parent of an Aggie.

Heading south again, you find yourself in the International Mall, where students and the Las Cruces Symphony perform in the Fine Arts/Music Building. The Hershel Zohn Theater invites town and gown to the performances of the American Southwest Theater Company. Mark Medoff, Tony Award–winning playwright and faculty member, staged the premieres of many of his plays here, including *Children of a Lesser God* and *When You Coming Home, Red Ryder?* Those of you who enjoy walking and have aspiring Aggies in tow can loop back to the new Student Union Building for souvenirs, many featuring Pistol Pete, the mascot that represents Frank Eaton, writer and lover of the culture of the West. The murals on the outer walls of the Student Union Building were painted by art students from New Mexico's pueblos and the Navajo nation. The Pan American Center, scene of rock concerts and Aggie basketball games, is to the east of the Student Union Building, and in the distance is Tortugas Mountain with its whitewashed A (for Aggies). Before leaving the campus, drive south of Espina for a glimpse of dairy barns and fields, reminders of NMSU's original agricultural mission. The university emphasizes onsite research and development in agricultural science, as well as cooperation with agricultural agents throughout the state. Projects focus on issues that particularly affect the Southwest, for example, plant genetic engineering to develop crops that do not require much water and fertilizer, and solutions to water problems.

It is an easy drive from the university to historic La Mesilla; just take University Avenue due west. Fields surround the little town, whose main attraction is the old plaza at Calle de Santiago and Calle Albino. The Spanish names remind you that La Mesilla began its life as a Mexican town. The Gadsden Purchase of 1854, which was ratified in La Mesilla's plaza, transferred ownership of a piece of Mexican land to the United States, and La Mesilla became an American town and important trade center. La Mesilla also attracted its share of outlaws. Billy the Kid was held in the local jail and was sentenced to hang in 1881. He escaped that date with death only to be shot later at Fort Sumner by Sheriff Pat Garrett. Garrett was later killed by an unknown assailant and buried in Las Cruces' Masonic Cemetery. Unfortunately (or fortunately) for La Mesilla, the railroad bypassed it in 1881 in favor of Las Cruces. As often happened, this ended the importance of the town as an economic center.

Preserved much as it was one hundred years ago, La Mesilla is now a major attraction for visitors to Las Cruces. There are scores of tiny shops along its narrow streets, and La Mesilla also invites you to visit San Albino church, established by the Mexican government in 1851 and rebuilt in 1906; the Gadsden Museum, keeper of mementos of the Fountain family, which featured prominently in the life of the valley; the Fountain Theater; and the old Butterfield Stage building, now a popular restaurant that still caters to tourists much like the stage company did for its passengers in the 1800s. Off the plaza are galleries, restaurants, stores, and old homes with cactus gardens and inviting patios. Surrounding the entire historic settlement are fields irrigated by a network of ancient *acequias*. At Christmas time the plaza is lit up by thousands of *luminarias;* Cinco de Mayo is celebrated with as much verve and color as it is in Mexico, as is 16 de septiembre, the anniversary of Mexico's *grito,* declaring its independence from Spain.

Side Trip in the Mesilla Valley

South of Mesilla you can drive for miles through pecan orchards. Impressive at any time of the year—covered with spring blossoms or standing starkly in winter—the orchards are worth a side trip. You can reach Stahmann Farms on N.M. 28, stop and buy pecans along the way, and catch a glimpse of the cotton and chile operations that also indicate the area's agricultural importance. Farther south you cross the Rio Grande on the way to the little towns of San Miguel and La Mesa. Keep going on this road for a slow and pretty route to El Paso.

For your circle trip out of Las Cruces, you can take Picacho Avenue past swimming holes and across the river where the route becomes U.S. 180/80/170. Keep driving west here, enjoying Picacho Peak, which rises startlingly from the valley, until the road intersects with I-10. You can also reach the interstate from Calle del Paseo, dipping into a fertile strip of land kept green by the "Great River," before you climb onto the edge of the great Chihuahua Desert. Passing the Southern New Mexico Correctional Institute, note the signs warning you not to pick up hitchhikers. All around are sweeping views of the high desert, with the flat tops of the Sierra de las Uvas ("mountains of the grapes"—perhaps named for their deep purple color) conspicuous to the north; to the south, giant pylons carrying electricity march across the plain. Past the fairgrounds, Bowlins Old West Trading Post encourages you to break up your trip almost before you get started. For several miles, Akela Flats announces its presence, borrowing the Burma Shave philosophy of attracting attention with multiple signs, a parade of yellow-and-red billboards that advertise Indian-style gewgaws sold from Western shops.

Deming, the first major stop on the highway, is a pleasant town with wide streets and Victorian buildings, a fine museum, an unusual state park, and celebrations scheduled throughout the year. The first exit, Motel Drive, takes you to the visitor center at the intersection of Pine and Spruce streets. The Chamber of Commerce has dressed up the old railroad station, complete with a vintage train. It is fitting to start your visit here, because Deming was founded when the Southern Pacific reached this point in 1881 and constructed a roundhouse and repair shops. When the Santa Fe line joined the Southern Pacific from the northwest, Deming became an important transportation center.

Today Deming is noted for its pure water, good weather, and 355 sunny days a year, which have attracted not only snowbirds but wine growers from France. The world-famous Great American Duck Race takes place in August at the Deming Duck Downs. Ducks named Sir Francis Drake, Easy Quacker, and Rubber Ducky compete for a rich purse in the race and for the title of best-costumed duck, while their owners take part in the tortilla toss and outhouse race, vie for the Queen title, and feast on delicacies like green chile ice cream. You may also find rockhounds from all over the country coming together for the annual Rockhound Roundup in March, fiddlers competing in May, and everyone celebrating Butterfield Trail Days in July.

Take advantage of Deming's sunny weather and a walking tour plotted by the historical society to stretch your legs along the flat, wide streets named for metals (Silver, Gold, Platinum) and trees (Cedar, Pine, Spruce). You will pass old brick and stone buildings like the Baker Hotel, the old opera house, and Nordhaus Dry Goods. The Deming-Luna-Mimbres museum at Silver and Hemlock used to be the old armory; troops slept here on their way to defend the border with Mexico. Old rifles and military weapons are still housed here, as well as a collection of over six hundred dolls, many Indian relics, a transportation exhibit ranging from horse-drawn carriages to fire engines, and a "Way It Was" room. The museum is accessible by wheelchair.

Across the street, the Customs House is now part of the museum, and down at the corner of Pine and Gold the new Center for the Arts features changing exhibits and musical and recreational programs. Murals painted by high school students decorate the corners of Pine, Gold, and Silver. At the end of Silver Street sits the Luna County Courthouse, an imposing structure fronted by a leafy park and surrounded by tree-lined residential streets.

Rockhound State Park, south of town off N.M. 11, is one of those rare places where visitors are encouraged to pick up treasures—semiprecious stones left behind by centuries of erosion of the volcanic rock. Kids will delight in being let off the reins to gather samples of quartz, jasper, and chalcedony, which they may take home, and to walk—or run—among plants typical of the region—such as desert spoon, yucca, and prickly pear—while imagining themselves Folsom Age hunters in search of game. There are no trees or babbling brooks here, but the camping and picnic spots are sheltered by the Little Florida Mountains, and there is a splendid panoramic view of mountain ranges and peaks in all direction. Two miles south of the park headquarters, Spring Canyon State Park offers day-use hiking trails and similar desert views and the possibility of wildlife sightings. Although Rockhound is open year-round, Spring Canyon is

Side Trip to Columbus

A longer side trip takes you farther south on N.M. 11, past tiny Sunshine to Columbus (see Entradas), made famous by Pancho Villa's daring raid in 1916, when Columbus was home to Camp Furlong, one of a number of American camps along the Mexican border. Several hundred of Villa's followers attacked Columbus, killing eighteen Americans, but losing many more of their own. Determined to punish Pancho Villa, President Wilson sent General "Black Jack" Pershing's troops into Mexico, where they pursued Villa in vain. However, the chase did allow Pershing to experiment with the world's first mechanized army of trucks and jeeps, as well as a fledgling air force.

Ironically named after Pancho Villa, the park offers visitors camping and picnic sites, a small closed on weekdays during the winter months.

Those on a shortened schedule will follow N.M. 26 to Nutt and Hatch. Some maps highlight this route in green, promising a "scenic route"; expect pleasant rather than spectacular views. The road is good and climbs slowly through the rolling countryside. On the right in the distance are the Florida Mountains, to the left the Pony Hills and Cooke's Peak, named after Phillip St. George Cooke, who with his Mormon Battalion attempted to find the best route to California. Cooke's name is also attached to the springs at the foot of the mountain, although many thirsty groups before him had been grateful for the waters. The Butterfield Stage made the springs a regular stop, attracting Apaches, who wanted to put a stop to settlement, and bandits, who ambushed the travelers from the nearby canyon. The army erected Fort Cummings nearby to protect travelers and settlers, but all that remains of the fort are some crumbling walls. Similarly, little trace is left of the mining town called Cooke's Peak, which was abandoned when the lead ore played out.

museum (open on request), and markers showing the layout of the old camp among ruins of some of the original buildings. Notable is the garden, which has hundreds of varieties of cactus, easily viewed from a maze of pathways. The cacti bloom in April, the best time to view the creamy yucca, purple cholla, and other bright flowers. Winter is also a good season to travel here, but summers can be too hot. Climb up Villa Hill for an unobstructed view of the desert and the pyramid-shaped Tres Hermanas (three sisters) Mountains. In Columbus, the railway depot has been turned into a museum, which is open most of the year and exhibits local memorabilia. Spend some time learning Columbus history before you head north again to Deming, where you must decide whether to take the shortcut back to Las Cruces or a longer journey via the City of Rocks.

This route is a popular shortcut from I-25 to I-10, bypassing Las Cruces, so beware of heavy traffic. As you near Nutt, the Sierra de las Uvas appear on your right. From this view, the Uvas do not look flat-topped, as they do from the south. A corral and a cluster of cattle around a watering hole remind you that you are in ranching country. Farmers also grow onions on these high plains, and sometimes the pungent smell of onions fills the air. Suddenly you arrive in Nutt, the turnoff to Lake Valley and Hillsboro, with Nutt Mountain to the northeast. Continue your trip into Las Uvas Valley, past more herds of cattle and fields of hay, before you arrive in Hatch, where you have the choice of picking up I-25 or following the river along N.M. 187 into Las Cruces.

The longer drive from Deming via Silver City or City of Rocks takes you northwest on U.S. 180, a route drawn straight through miles of unbroken scenery. High desert vegetation, yucca and sage, grow among abandoned cars. Cattle gather around a lonely windmill. A few rough roads head off into the high country to the east, and to the west the

City of Rocks

Santa Fe Railroad tracks carry trains to Hurley and Bayard.

To reach the City of Rocks, turn right at the intersection of N.M. 61. You soon come to Faywood Hot Springs, once a popular spa but now apparently abandoned by its current owners, who warn prospective bathers of polluted water. A little farther on, a sign guides you a short distance to the City of Rocks, rising out of the high plain like a Southwestern Stonehenge. The rocks, formed from volcanic tuff, resemble all manner of creatures, real and mythical. Wind and water eroded the rock, creating the bizarre shapes. This is a wonderful area both for children and the not-so-young to run and climb and stretch their legs. The trails among the rocks could be maneuvered by someone in a sporty wheelchair, and the toilet facilities are wheelchair accessible. Tables and primitive campsites invite you to unpack a picnic basket and stay awhile, perhaps to climb to the observation point (five thousand feet high), wander through the botanical cactus garden (especially when it flowers in the spring), or inspect an Indian mill and grinding stone. Besides the cultivated garden, naturally growing cactus, desert plants, and flowers brighten the landscape.

To bypass Silver City, turn left as you leave the City of Rocks and follow N.M. 61 along the Mimbres River to San Lorenzo. This is a beautiful little valley any time of year, sparsely inhabited by ranching families. The Mimbres Indians lived here until the twelfth century, leaving as their gift to civilization the black on white pottery with distinctive designs that these days grace objects from T-shirts to placemats. Today no sign of these talented people remains. Only a few settlements and ranches and the general store and church in Faywood intrude on the pastoral scene. Watch for cattle, however, who use the road in a proprietary fashion.

If you are continuing on to Silver City from City of Rocks head back to U.S. 180, passing through the industrial corridor of Hurley, with its huge smokestacks and tailings (you can drive off the highway here to view the ultramodern smelter, one of your few opportunities to see industrial America at work in New Mexico), and the smaller copper mining and smelting towns of North Hurley, Bayard, and Central. The livelihoods of the citizens in these towns have long depended on copper taken from the huge Santa Rita open-pit mine. More recent history has focused on the struggle between union workers and management. A movie, *Salt of the Earth,* was based on incidents that occurred during a bitter strike by the mine workers in the 1950s, when the wives of the workers walked the picket lines in their place. Tourists with an interest in mines can obtain a detailed tour of the many mining sites in the area from the Grant County Chamber of Commerce in Silver City.

After your stay in Silver City (see Tour Fifteen), you will backtrack to Central, perhaps stopping along the way at the old army outpost of Fort Bayard, whose classic homes and barracks are now used as a nursing home. From Central take N.M. 152 to San Lorenzo, passing along the way the huge Santa Rita copper mine. Apache Indians used the copper from this area for their weapons.

The Spaniards who explored the region in the 1800s recognized the importance of the metal and soon opened a copper mine here, naming it and the small town that grew up here Santa Rita del Cobre. Apache warriors forced the Spanish to abandon their mine. At the end of the century, Americans bought the property and worked it sporadically until in 1909 the Chino Copper Company began operations. Later, in the 1930s, Kennecott Copper Corporation took over the mine and built it up into a huge operation. Santa Rita became the largest open-pit mine in the world, the nearby towns the sites of smelters and refineries. The old town of Santa Rita was soon literally swallowed up. An overlook allows you to peer down into the vast hole and watch trucks toiling up the sides of the pit with their loads of ore. Six miles east of the overlook, stop for a view of the Kneeling Nun, a thin tower of rock standing in front of a larger rock. Legend recounts that a nun fell in love with a soldier she was nursing and ran away with him. For this disobedient act, she was condemned to be on her knees for all time.

Across the Mimbres River sits San Lorenzo, a small agricultural village beneath the cottonwoods. From here N.M. 152 climbs out of the valley, passing through a landscape that varies from the scrub of high desert foothills to the dense, dark pine that blankets the Black Range. This band of mountains stretches sixty-five miles north to south, and some of its peaks reach an altitude of ten thousand feet. With more than two hundred miles of hiking trails and several streams and rivers, the somewhat isolated Black Range attracts explorers and those seeking solitude.

Highway 152 is not for the fainthearted; it winds tortuously along hillsides and through narrow gray canyons. Cattle and deer wander across it, day or night. Along the way are several vista points and campgrounds with picnic areas (Iron Creek, Railroad, Wright's Cabin). At Emory Pass (8,228 feet) take the left turnoff, which leads to the Forest Service lookout, a very short detour that you will not regret. Here you have a wide-angle view of the surrounding countryside, including the town of Kingston, which appears deceptively close.

Several curvy miles down, you reach Kingston,

once a populous silver-mining center, now home to just a few residents. Still attached to its exciting past, Kingston displays a sign outside town proclaiming that the Spit and Whittle Club, which began meeting in the nineteenth century, gets together here. One of the Spit and Whittle's charter members, Sheba Hurst, featured in Mark Twain's *Roughing It,* is buried in the town cemetery. Most of Kingston's buildings—an abandoned bank, a bed-and-breakfast, the old schoolhouse, the general store—lie off the highway along the main street to the left and up a gentle hill. If you detour onto it, you will find a few reminders of the days when there were more than twenty-seven mines in the surrounding mountains, miners exploded into town on Saturday nights, and Kingston's primary church was built with funds raised by ladies of the night.

Your next stop is Hillsboro, nine miles away. Another old mining town, little Hillsboro is now more famed for its Labor Day Apple Festival, a bakery named for angels, and its faithful and creatively restored buildings than for its rowdy past. This is a genuine former ghost town, its tree-shaded streets filled with two working saloons, restaurants, an old drugstore, a couple of bed-and-breakfast inns, a motel, church, post office, and an historic café. Hillsboro was once the county seat for Sierra County, relinquishing that status to Hot Springs/Truth or Consequences only in 1937. Recently Hillsboro has been the setting of Hollywood movies. Stop in at the Black Range Museum for a glimpse of this picturesque community's colorful past, including mementos of Sadie Orchard, the infamous madam turned respectable hotel owner.

Once you leave Hillsboro, you spend twenty-five miles or so descending from the foothills and crossing treeless plains. The Caballo Mountains fill the eastern horizon, with Caballo Lake almost a mirage at their feet.

Cross I-25 and take N.M. 187 past the residences of the Caballo Lake dwellers, under the interstate again, heading toward Arrey, where you find yourself in agricultural country, miles of fields planted with chiles, onions, alfalfa, and other crops. The road soon takes you by Percha Dam

State Park. Percha provides little more than restrooms, picnic tables, and fishing from the little dam. No swimming is allowed because of the swift-running water; a sign warns of the need for quick evacuation in the event of water releases.

Follow the two-lane blacktop road through tiny Arrey, where during harvest time drying red chiles spill out of the big sheds. At any time of year Price's Dairy invites visitors to stop and view its champion Holsteins. In winter the surrounding fields sit neatly plowed, waiting for planting, and in summer they sprout lush green produce. The road crosses the Rio Grande, which is rather narrow here, and runs through Derry. Again signs advertising chile companies remind you that chile is king here, while fruit trees, cattle, and a cotton co-op tell of other agricultural industries. From this area to south of Las Cruces, agriculture plays a vital role in the economy, and farmers grow not only familiar crops like wheat, cabbage, and pecans, but experiment with unfamiliar crops as well.

Garfield, one of the bigger towns in the area, is named after the president. It shows its age in its established neighborhoods, solidly built shops, and churches. Ahead and to the east, the Organ Mountains form the backdrop to Las Cruces. Tiny Salem is the last stop before Hatch, the most "urban" center in the Hatch and Rincon Valleys.

Sacks of chile

Founded as Santa Barbara, the settlement failed when Apache attacks grew too threatening in the 1850s. Like many towns in the territory, Santa Barbara's fortunes depended on nearby Fort Thorne's existence, waxing and waning as the soldiers came and went. When the last soldiers left in 1859, so did the settlers, returning in 1875 as life grew more predictable. The town was later renamed for Edward Hatch, the commander of the military district. Hatch boasts that it is the chile capital of the world; in New Mexico "fresh Hatch" stands for newly picked green chile, and in late summer New Mexicans line up to buy sacks of the hot stuff for roasting, freezing, and eating with everything from scrambled eggs to hamburgers. Hatch hosts a Chile Festival over Labor Day with lots of "red" and "green" (as in chile), a queen, arts and crafts, and fun and games. Look for the renovated Santa Fe Railway depot, which now houses a library and museum.

From Hatch the road twists through the narrowing river valley. Several homeowners have built houses right over the waterfront, banking on the fact that the river rarely floods, and beekeepers have placed colorful hives along the roadside. An old traders' trail, called the Salt Cedar Trail after the trees that grow along the river, followed the same route you are taking.

Soon after passing through tiny Radium Springs (named for the mineral hot springs in the area, not for any sinister nuclear association), look for the signs to Leasburg and Fort Selden. Fort Selden's adobe walls had almost dissolved by the time the state decided that the fort was too valuable an historic asset to be allowed to melt away and took action to stabilize the walls. You must use your imagination to see the officers and enlisted men's quarters, the soldiers marching on the parade ground, the stables and other areas of the fort that are now only marked by signs. Douglas MacArthur lived here as a little boy, when his father was commander of the fort, many years before he would become commander of a whole army in the Pacific. Like his father's, General MacArthur's career intertwined with New Mexico. Hundreds of New Mexicans were under his command during the unsuccessful defense of the Philippines during World War II, and many soldiers lost their lives during the disastrous retreat down the Bataan Peninsula. A small museum exhibits artifacts, including Indian pottery, and tells the story of Fort Selden's importance to the area. The fort protected settlers from Apaches and gunslingers until peace on the frontier made it an anachronism and it was abandoned in 1891.

Next to the fort, Leasburg State Park provides campsites, RV hookups, and other facilities for overnight use, with choice sites fronting the river. From the bluffs, you can look down at the river and imagine soldiers from the nearby fort swinging across the river on a rope.

As you near Las Cruces, pecan orchards crowd the Rio Grande. Some farmers use geese to keep the weeds down between the trees; later on, the unfortunate birds end up stuffed with dressing made of the very pecans they protected. Light industry and modern suburbs signal that you have arrived in Las Cruces.

Using the city as a base, you can explore the Organ and Franklin mountains to the east. This rugged area gets little rainfall, so be sure to take water with you on hikes or picnics. One popular spot is believed to have been the home of a hermit who was found murdered in his cave. To reach La Cueva, take University Avenue out to the base of the Organ Mountains. Past the highway, the road—at this point called Dripping Springs—is graveled; decide whether or not your vehicle can make it. There is a visitor center and picnic area at this site. Farther out on U.S. 70, over the San Agustin Pass and past the little town of Organ, you can get to Aguirre Spring campground on Aguirre Spring Road, a paved road that goes up the mountain. Hiking trails from these two areas and at other sites in the mountains are popular with residents, who also use the Organs for rock climbing. The Bureau of Land Management (BLM) takes care of the recreation areas. Pick up a pamphlet from the BLM or from the visitor center downtown for details of the trails.

Ending your trip where it began, in the Las Cruces area, keep in mind the events regularly scheduled in the city, like the Fourth of July celebration, the Southern New Mexico State Fair and Rodeo in September, the Whole Enchilada Fiesta in October (where you can partake of the world's largest enchilada), the Renaissance Fair in November. In December celebrate the feast of Our Lady of Guadalupe in special fashion in the village of Tortugas just south of Las Cruces. Residents and visitors climb up Mount Tortugas after a three-day fiesta commemorating the three appearances of Our Lady of Guadalupe to Juan Diego outside Mexico City. And Christmas in Old Mesilla, with the plaza alight with *luminarias,* is a favorite of local residents and tourists alike.

TOUR
FIFTEEN
MOUNTAINS
AND MYTHS

Places:	Socorro, Magdalena, Datil, Reserve, Glenwood, Silver City, Hillsboro, Truth or Consequences, Socorro
Mileage:	Approximately 480 miles, excluding side trips
Suggested travel time:	Four days minimum
Highways:	U.S. 60, N.M. 12, U.S. 180, N.M. 15, N.M. 35, N.M. 152, I-25, N.M. 1
Accommodations:	Socorro, Glenwood, Silver City, Pinos Altos, Hillsboro, and Truth or Consequences
Camping:	Socorro, Cibola National Forest, Datil, Gila National Forest, Apache National Forest, Silver City, Truth or Consequences, and Elephant Butte Lake State Park

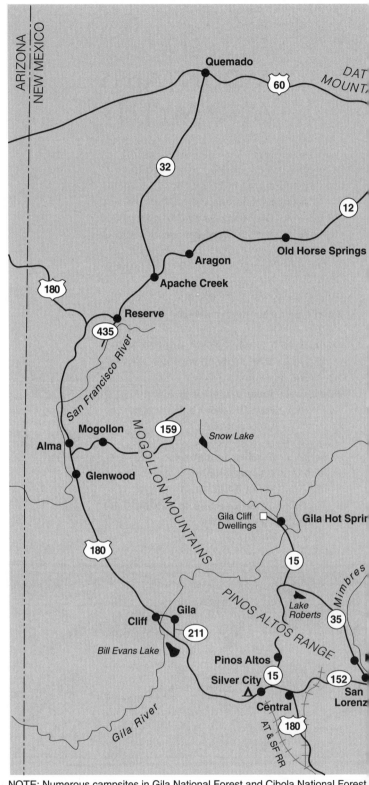

NOTE: Numerous campsites in Gila National Forest and Cibola National Forest

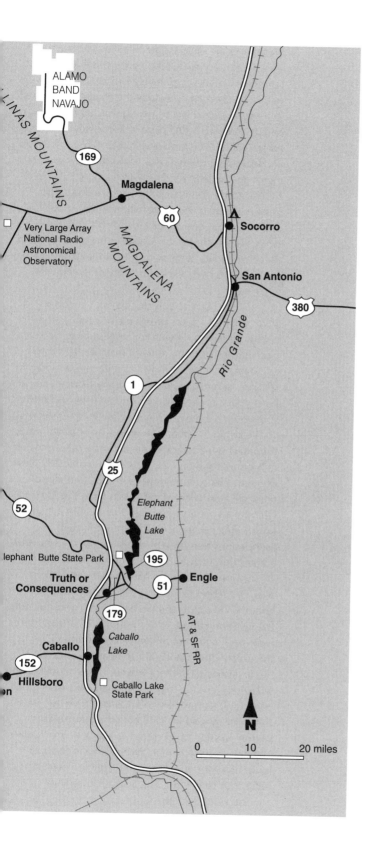

15

If your eyes are often bigger than your stomach and your dreams usually exceed reality, this is the perfect tour for you. You will probably look at the map of this ambitious circle and conclude that it can be traversed in a weekend. You will be wrong. For this trip, which begins and ends at the plaza in Socorro, is sometimes hair-raising, full of diversions that feed Western myths and legends, and very long. Along the way, you might encounter remnants of the ancient cultures of the Mogollon and Apache people, scientists who listen to the stars, more than three million acres of national forest, ghost towns, windmills and stock tanks, French champagne made in the desert, a town that changed its name to a radio program, and picnic spots next to rivers either bone-dry or raging with white water.

Anchored by the college towns of Socorro and Silver City, your journey will include many small communities, some with minimal services, others boasting a surprising array of restaurants, motels, and campgrounds. You will also encounter long sections of highway with few if any services, so have your car checked before you leave and make sure you have plenty of gas between major towns.

We begin in Socorro, a small city of about nine thousand people located seventy-five miles south of Albuquerque on I-25. Socorro is a uniquely New Mexican place, with neighborhoods that climb terracelike up Socorro Mountain from the Rio Grande, a college campus hidden within a championship golf course, a Catholic church built upon foundations that date back hundreds of years, and a plaza that is truly the center of town.

Socorro's population has gone up and down over the centuries. During the Archaic period (from about 6000 B.C. to the birth of Christ) and through the Riverine period, in the 1300s and 1400s, there were pre-Pueblo and Pueblo communities along the central Rio Grande Valley near Socorro. When the first Spanish settlers arrived in the middle of the sixteenth century, they established a series of small communities, converted the Piro Indians to Catholicism, and in 1628 constructed the San Miguel Mission on or near the site of a Piro Pueblo. The first Spanish settlers did not live in Socorro long, however. After the 1680 Pueblo Revolt, they fled south to El Paso. The Spanish colony of Socorro remained abandoned for more than a century. Although the Socorro Grant of 1816 brought a few Spanish settlers back to the area, it was not until Fort Craig was built twenty miles south of Socorro in the 1850s that the town became a permanent trading and social center.

A few decades later, in the 1880s and early 1890s, mining in the nearby mountains boomed, cattle ranching took hold, the Santa Fe Railroad came to town, and Socorro enjoyed its heyday. It was the largest city in the territory; cattle, silver, wine, and hides were shipped from it by rail all over the country. Eugene Manlove Rhodes describes the Socorro of those days in his book *Hit the Hard Line.* Although he changes Socorro to the fictitious Saragossa, Rhodes captures the physical and human energy of this frontier town as few historical descriptions can. Conrad Richter's *Sea of Grass* also describes the Socorro region. While the early years of the twentieth century were not kind to Socorro, the small city has recently grown into a stable and important scientific, ranching, and service center for central New Mexico.

Socorro's many old buildings reflect its changing populations and economic conditions in a comfortable blend of architectural styles including homemade adobe, nineteenth-century Victorian, California Mission, and Southwestern interstate. To visit some of Socorro's neighborhoods, start at Socorro's plaza, situated just west of California Street, the main north-south route through town. In the 1880s a local dentist planted trees and shrubs and established this plaza, now called Kittrel Park, in his honor. Both Dr. Kittrel and a fragment of Jumbo, the container that held one of the original atomic bombs detonated at nearby White Sands Missile Range are buried in the plaza.

You will discover a wealth of local history and architectural gems as you walk the narrow streets of downtown Socorro. The citizens of Socorro have fixed up a number of old homes and commercial establishments and have organized historic districts to preserve the composition and character of Socorro. While some of the old buildings have been restored—the Mission church and the Garcia Opera House, for example—others continue to deteriorate as only an unmaintained adobe structure can, the dirt of the adobe bricks melting with each rain until the walls crumble, door and window openings sag, and the roof falls in.

We suggest that you pick up a map at the

Socorro County Chamber of Commerce and take yourself on a walking tour to discover some of Socorro's historic and architectural highlights up close. For example, to the immediate north of the plaza, on Fischer Street, are two of Socorro's largest and most notable adobe structures—the Juan Nepomoceno Garcia House and the Garcia Opera House (a State and National Historic Site)—both built by the same family in the 1880s. Walk north past the Juan José Baca House, a large, rambling building whose disintegrating additions reflect a number of architectural periods. Soon you will come upon the San Miguel Mission Church, constructed in 1821, probably on the site of the original San Miguel Mission, which was abandoned during the 1680 Pueblo Revolt. You can enter the mission, stepping into the soft white interior; even on the hottest summer day, its thick adobe walls keep it cool. Stand in the middle of the church and notice the large *vigas* and corbels in the ceiling, the carved wood of the choir loft at the back of the church, and the deep-set windows. Outside the Mission, look back to the south and imagine what many historians conjecture— that Socorro's main plaza once stretched from the San Miguel Mission Church all the way to the present plaza.

As you walk south and west of the plaza, you will find a number of significant Victorian homes, one with a widow's walk, another implanted with horizontal reinforcement rods to protect its inhabitants against the mild earthquakes that sometimes occur here, another topped with the region's only copper roof. East of California Street, down near the Santa Fe tracks, a few buildings from the railroad era have been restored. The California Mission–style Val Verde Hotel once provided rooms to railroad travelers; now it houses a restaurant and shops and seems to come alive at night when old-fashioned lamps are lit at its entrance. North of the Val Verde, near the entrance to town, the three-story Hammel Brewery has become the Socorro County Historical Society Museum. The third brewery built in New Mexico, the Hammel Brewery is a wonderful rock and stone structure that began as one adobe room and then was added onto as the beer business grew during the late nineteenth and early twentieth centuries.

Up the hill, New Mexico Institute of Mining and

Technology, better known as New Mexico Tech, lies beneath "M" Mountain, its green and leafy campus filling the northwestern quadrant of Socorro. Founded in 1889, Tech has 1,200 graduate and undergraduate students from all over the United States and the world who specialize in subjects that range from petroleum recovery and research to explosives technology. Tech may not have an intercollegiate football team, but it boasts a spectacular eighteen-hole golf course, where the public can play year-round for a modest fee and around which the institute's California Mission—style buildings assume an almost supporting role. In the middle of the campus, perched beside a pond, Macey Center brings musical events, theatrical productions, art shows, and conferences to Socorro. At the New Mexico Bureau of Mines and Mineral Resources Building on the Tech campus, you can purchase New Mexico and regional maps and books or visit the Bureau's Mineral Museum, which contains over twelve thousand mineral specimens, both foreign and domestic. Members of the museum staff specialize in identifying unusual and unknown rocks that visitors bring to them.

Socorro is the base for a number of scientific projects that attract international attention and examination. At the Joint Observatory for Cometary Research and the Langmuir Laboratory, both located in the Magdalena Mountains west of Socorro, scholars study thunderclouds, lightning, and comets. The National Science Foundation sponsors the Sevilleta Long Term Ecological Research Project at a site along the Rio Grande just north of Socorro. And many who work at the Very Large Array project on the Plains of Agustin, fifty-four miles west of here, live in Socorro and commute to work. With farmers and ranchers coming to town for supplies, interstate travelers stopping for the night or for food and gas, and scientists lending their presence to the small city, Socorro's population seems to be waxing more than waning these days.

Now that you have spent some time in Socorro, head west. If you are on California Street, drive south through most of Socorro and watch for signs indicating U.S. 60 and Magdalena. If you have just finished your plaza-centered walk, stay on the west side of the plaza and drive south a few blocks on

Park Street to the intersection with U.S. 60 (Spring Street). Turn right and follow U.S. 60 across the railroad tracks, past the high school and hospital.

Soon you are climbing up and out of the Rio Grande Valley toward the Magdalena Mountains. Your trip from Socorro to Magdalena parallels the old roadbed of a railroad line known as the elevator, because it climbed two thousand feet in sixteen miles. Its trains carried cattle, lead, zinc, silver, and other ores down from Magdalena to Socorro and the Santa Fe Railroad's main line. About seven or eight miles outside of Socorro, as the terrain shifts from gentle ridges and slopes to the rougher foothills, stop and look back at the pale layers of mountains and mesas that frame the valley you just left.

In the twenty-five miles or so between Socorro and Magdalena, as you pull away from the valley below, you enter a region that is sparsely populated, where towns are hours apart, and where a faded signpost is the only indication that a ranch sits ten or fifteen miles away down a one-track dirt path. You have left the basin of the Rio Grande and now enter volcanic highlands, in which most of the rocks are composed of lava and tuff. You will observe ancient domes and depressions from volcanic cauldrons. And you will cross back and forth across the Continental Divide many times throughout this circle of canyons and tablelands, basins and valleys.

About fifteen minutes west of Socorro, signs point first to Mount Baldy (10,783 feet) crowning the Magdalena Mountains, and then to Water Canyon Campground, almost five miles away inside Cibola National Forest. Farther into the mountains, New Mexico Tech's Langmuir Laboratory is open to the public and accessible in the summer months by four-wheel-drive vehicle. Wide-open grazing country, herds of antelope, a campground or two, some forest trails, and ranch roads appear now and again as you near Magdalena.

You can tell that Magdalena is now only a shadow of her former self. Look at how large many of the old frontier town's buildings are. Brick or adobe, restored or crumbling, they symbolize the heady dreams of quickly rich miners and hard-working cattle barons. The presence of the railroad station (now City Hall) just off the highway in the center of town also hints at the bustling activity that once took place here. When the railroad first arrived, in 1884, miners from nearby Kelly established the town of Magdalena, naming it after the Magdalena Mountains. Mary Magdalene was the biblical figure who led a rowdy existence and then converted to a lifetime of penance, so it seems appropriate that this once-wild community bears her name. Depending on the placement of shadows and sunlight, you can sometimes make out the veiled figure of Mary Magdalene in the mountains above town.

Thousands of head of cattle and herds of sheep once plodded 132 miles along an historic cattle trail, the Magdalena Livestock Driveway, between Springerville, Arizona, and Magdalena, where they were shipped by rail down to Socorro and then east to stockyards and dinner plates. Some say that Magdalena was once the largest livestock shipping point west of Chicago. This spur of the Atchison, Topeka, and Santa Fe line also carried millions of dollars' worth of precious ore, wool, and timber out of the mountains. Stretch your legs awhile in Magdalena. Stop in at one of the local rock shops, pick up supplies at a general store, or pause to chat with those who have chosen to live here. You might plan your visit to Magdalena during one of the local celebrations held around here in the summer and fall. Whether your visit coincides with the Kelly Fiesta, the Riley Fiesta, or the Old-timers' Reunion and Celebration over the Fourth of July, you can join the fun at rodeos, parades, contests, and dances.

Before camping or hiking in the mountains, check in at the Cibola National Forest Ranger Station in Magdalena. The rangers can help you locate a trail, give you a permit to cut firewood, or discuss fire conditions. You can crisscross through the Magdalena and San Mateo mountains on two dirt roads, N.M. 107 and N.M. 168, which lead into the Cibola National Forest and eventually to two wilderness areas, Withington and Apache Kid, and a ghost town or two. Talk with the rangers about the roads, because mountain rains, invisible to you this far away, can make them dangerous.

This is also a good opportunity to visit the ghost of one mining town, Kelly, by driving two miles south of Magdalena on the dirt road just beyond the ranger station. Founded in 1870, Kelly was home to three thousand people, many of them miners who sent out rail cars filled with lead, zinc, and silver. The community remained populated by many enterprises until the 1930s, by which time the mines, the Pittsburgh Paint Company, and other businesses had departed. All you find here now are remnants of what were once a hotel, a school, and a general store, with a small, white Catholic church standing watch over it all. Another empty town, Riley, is not quite a ghost yet. It sits on the banks of the Rio Salado about twenty miles north of Magdalena. You can drive on a dirt road (not well-marked) as far as the river. From there, depending on the condition of the road, the river, and your car, you may have to walk across to see the church, small homes, and cemetery at this old sheep-raising and farming community. Former residents of Riley return here each spring for the Riley Fiesta, a combined homecoming and celebration of the town's past.

There is a small Navajo community, Alamo, about twenty-nine miles northwest of Magdalena on N.M. 169—a recently paved but narrow road. The Alamo Band of two thousand people lives isolated from the rest of the Navajo Nation on this distant reservation. Most members of the band are sheepherders, although a few artisans practice traditional crafts that are sometimes for sale at the Alamo Trading Post. A health clinic and school serve the community.

As you drive west from Magdalena on U.S. 60, the highway either curves through squiggly patches of piñon and juniper where you cannot see beyond the next bend, or it narrows down into a perfect V, its path straight and sure and visible all the way to the horizon. That wide, flat land just below the horizon is called the Plains of San Agustin and was once a Pleistocene lake bed forty-five miles long and fifteen miles wide. Today it is a huge basin of grass surrounded by the mountains of western Socorro and eastern Catron counties. This is where cowboys used to drive their cattle east from Catron County along the Magdalena Livestock Driveway to the railroad in Magdalena. Two former ranchers who lived in this area at the end of the nineteenth century, Montague Stevens and Agnes Morley Cleaveland, have each written of their adventures in crossing the Plains of San Agustin on horseback, by wagon, or in Stevens's two-wheeled cart pulled by a horse, when the journey between Datil and Magdalena took the better part of a day. Now you can zip across these treeless plains in less than an hour.

But first you should stop and visit a twenty-first–century phenomenon plunked down here like a vision from outer space. As you drive west and exit the wooded foothills just above the Plains of San Agustin, you may wonder about the tall, white dishes that march in distant rows. You are looking at the Very Large Array (VLA) operated by the National Radio Astronomy Observatory. Twenty-seven antennas make up the array and collect weak radio waves from celestial sources. Railroad cars carry the huge (235 ton) antennas along specially constructed double tracks to a series of placement pods. The antennas are then placed in various configurations, depending on the research goal. Scientists can also focus each antenna dish individually. Computers process radio signals that come to the antennas from outer space and relay them to scientists at the VLA who then study quasars, pulsars, black holes, and supernovas. The VLA observatory runs twenty-four hours a day, with teams of scientists from around the world conducting about fifty experiments per month.

You can reach the VLA by turning south on N.M. 52, about twenty-three miles west of Magdalena. Follow the signs along the dusty road (actually leading to a town called Dusty) to the VLA visitor center. Inside the building, which is usually unattended but has self-guided tours, exhibits include explanations of observatory operations, photographs from space, and duplicates of the hardware used in VLA research. Pictures, charts, maps, and videos enable even the most unscientific mind to comprehend the basic thrust of VLA activities. You can purchase booklets and other VLA mementos in the visitor center. A brief walking tour (not recommended on very hot summer days) takes you to the Whisper Gallery, where two people, children if you have them, can use smaller versions of the VLA antenna to demonstrate in a very effective way how the VLA "hears" signals from outer space. The walking tour can be extended to include visits to the control building and an antenna. You may also drive to the antenna

15

VLA antenna

assembly building. Much of the VLA observatory, including the visitor center, is accessible to people with disabilities.

After you have exercised your brain at the VLA observatory, switch gears and settle in for the rest of your trip across the Plains of San Agustin and up into the mountains to Datil. You leave Socorro County, once the largest county in the United States, and enter Catron County, lopped off its parent, Socorro, in 1921. Catron County is also huge, the biggest county in New Mexico in fact, with 6,929 square miles of lots of landscape and few inhabitants: 2,563 people lived in Catron County in 1990.

Datil sits in the mountains along a little stream, its cottonwood trees a source of shade and a contrast to the dark pines on the hillsides. The U.S. Army built a fort here in 1888 to protect settlers from Apache raids, and from it this small community grew. In Datil you will find a gas station, a grocery store, a motel, and a bustling, homey café at the intersection of U.S. 60 and N.M. 12. If you want to camp, there is a pleasant BLM campground, Datil Well, about a mile down either N.M. 12 or U.S. 60. The campground is the site of one of the water wells drilled along the route of the Magdalena Cattle Driveway so that cattle and sheep could be refreshed. Datil Well Campground includes hiking trails, simple shelters, and free firewood for campers.

Bear south on N.M. 12 toward Reserve, about seventy-five miles away. Skirting the western edge of the Plains of San Agustin, the highway climbs into mountains, passes through the Apache National Forest, curves past lonely windmills, crosses the Continental Divide, and dips in and out of green valleys where small settlements like Old Horse Springs and Aragon are reminders that communities in New Mexico begin where there is water. The Tularosa River, a modest stream, has brought people to these little valleys for hundreds of years. From 400 B.C. to A.D. 1100, Tularosa Cave, just east of Aragon, was a community of pit houses and masonry rooms. In 1693, a Spanish family named Aragon settled in the area and gave it a name. About two hundred years later, in 1874, the U.S. government moved a group of Apaches here and then built Fort Tularosa. Old Horse Springs got its name when soldiers traveling to Fort Tularosa (now Aragon) lost a horse, rediscovered it at the springs just west of here, and decided that this miraculous event deserved a place name. In Aragon you will now find a scattering of old homes (each with a steeply pitched tin roof because of the heavy snows), a tiny church, and a cemetery where soldiers from the surrounding territory were buried long ago.

Settlements like Aragon reflect how populations have changed over the centuries in southwestern New Mexico. For hundreds of years, the Apache Indians considered this entire region of the state their home, sharing it upon occasion with pre-Pueblo Indians, who tended to live in settled agricultural communities along rivers and streams. The two groups were frequently at odds with each other, the more nomadic Apaches sometimes raiding the farms and storehouses of their more sedentary Pueblo neighbors. When the Spanish arrived in the Southwest in the sixteenth century, the competition for land among those native to the region and those just entering it was intense. By the beginning of the eighteenth century, the Apaches had staked out for themselves all the territory to the south and west of present-day Albuquerque. Although Governor Juan Bautista de Anza was able to negotiate a peace treaty with the Comanches in the north, his efforts to do the same with the Apaches in this southwestern corner of New Mexico were unsuccessful. This was Apache land, its mountains and valleys their home, its antelope and other game their food source. When Spanish settlers and later American homesteaders and ranchers intruded on Apache territory, they did so at their own risk.

Foremost among the many Apache leaders was Geronimo, born in about 1829 near the headwaters of the Gila River here in Catron County. Geronimo's long and tragic life was centered around retaining or reclaiming what had belonged to his people. Back and forth between Old Mexico and New Mexico, up and down the steep cliffs and mountain passes he roamed, his very presence taunting the U.S. Cavalry units brought in to subdue the Apaches. The Apaches and the U.S. government frequently signed treaties, but just as frequently they both broke them. After years and years of warfare, Geronimo finally surrendered, satisfied by promises from the army that he and his people would receive adequate and nearby reservation land. But Geronimo was mistaken. Geronimo and his band boarded a train, convinced that they were headed for a reservation in Texas. Instead, Geronimo, his scouts, even women and children, were sent to forts in Florida, where many of them died in the heat and humidity. Geronimo later lived in Oklahoma, but was never permitted to return to his land of mountains and canyons. He died at Fort Sill, Oklahoma, in 1909. Some of his descendants are Chiricahua Apaches living in Arizona; others joined the Mescaleros and live in southern New Mexico.

As you drive through this vast and sparsely populated landscape, you will chance upon immense car cemeteries piled high with disintegrating automobiles and trucks of every vintage and description. It seems logical to wonder how all those hundreds of vehicles got here, and where all the people who once drove them went. We do not know. Speaking of driving, you may be tempted to drive fast along straight stretches of road that appear empty. We caution you that New Mexico levies heavy fines for speeding, and that state troopers cruise these highways.

At Apache Creek, continue south on N.M. 12 into yet another valley where modest adobe homes, shaded by cottonwood trees, wind along the creek bed. The landscape here is perhaps at its most glorious in the autumn, when the golds of stately cottonwoods contrast with the surrounding meadows and dark, wandering streams. At the crest of a hill, you peer down into Reserve, a cluster of tin roofs sparkling in the sunshine.

Once you reach Reserve, the seat of Catron County, you realize that the community is at once larger than it appeared from that hilltop and smaller than its political dominance of the county might indicate. Here in Reserve are the school system that serves much of Catron County, the services (gas stations, bars, general stores, churches, cafés) important to ranchers and loggers who live nearby, a ranger station for the Gila National Forest, the Catron County Courthouse, and rows of small homes that parallel the San Francisco River. The river winds its way south along N.M. 435 past three old settlements,

Upper, Middle, and Lower San Francisco, to the end of the valley, where the lumber mill sits. Reserve, founded in the 1860s by Mormon cattlemen, is now where Upper San Francisco was. It looks like a typical cattle town, the streets wide and lined with cafés, bars, and pickup trucks. There is a rodeo arena next to the Catron County Fairgrounds on the outskirts of town, followed by the windswept Reserve Airport. Leaving Reserve, stay on N.M. 12 and follow the signs to Glenwood, thirty-nine miles away.

Reserve is perched in the middle of the prehistoric riches of the Mogollon culture, which endured from about 300 B.C. to A.D. 1250. Food gatherers and hunters, the Mogollon people roved the mountains of the area, built pit houses (circular log dwellings partially dug out of the earth), perfected an agriculture for this semi-arid environment, and created prized and sophisticated pottery. Mimbres (or Mimbreño) painted pottery, found throughout this southwestern corner of New Mexico, is usually black on white, depicting stylized life-forms or complex repetitive geometric designs. Thousands of pieces of Mimbres pottery were produced during the tenth to twelfth centuries and now reside in private and museum collections. The Mogollon people were later influenced, it is believed, by the Anasazi, who came south into the region sometime after A.D. 900, eventually causing overcrowding and dispersal of the two groups. A number of Mogollon and Anasazi sites have been identified or excavated in this region.

A few miles southwest of Reserve, N.M. 12 ends and you continue your journey to Glenwood and Silver City on U.S. 180, which has joined in from the north. You drive up and down for miles, through tall pine trees, winding past campgrounds, over Saliz Pass, and suddenly begin a descent into the San Francisco River Valley, where horses graze and farmers experiment with vineyards. The flora has changed with the altitude—after forests of ponderosa pine and Douglas fir, hills of piñon and juniper, and riverside stands of cottonwood and apple trees, you now see stark yucca plants and Russian olive trees. Twenty-five miles south of Reserve, the community of Alma nowadays offers gas and groceries to the traveler. Once it was a large supply center for all the ranches and mines in the area, thriving in that role until about 1913 when things slowed down here, and so did Alma.

Side Trip to Mogollon

This is an adventure for those who enjoy hairpin curves and hair-raising vistas. The old mining community of Mogollon is nine miles up, down, and around on N.M. 159, a trip that you should not take at night, during a heavy rain, in a snowstorm, or if there are storm clouds to the east. But if it is a sunny day and you and your vehicle (which should not be pulling a trailer or anything else that is long) like narrow mountain roads, Mogollon and the trip there and back are worth the time and concentration you will need. That said, it should also be noted that you will probably pass senior citizens in old pickup trucks on their way to Snow Lake (which has a fishing pier for the people with disabilities) or bicyclists out for an uphill Sunday jaunt.

You begin to climb up N.M. 159 almost from the start, the road cutting along the edge of the mountain, growing progressively cramped, it seems, the higher you ascend. Like a corkscrew, you go up and up and then circle downward. The driver will have to save sightseeing for the way down, but note that you will be passing in and out of private and national forest land and that you can sight old mining equipment, including rusting buildings and old wooden mine shafts, built on the hillside across the way.

Mogollon sits within a very confined valley, the old miners' cabins, hotel, general store, and other wooden and rock buildings that line the narrow street cast in dark shadow the minute the sun passes from overhead. Mogollon is a lively place during the summer, with families and artists moving into restored cabins, little food stands opening up to sell tacos and soft drinks, and residents putting on weekend events, including art fairs and melodramas. The rest of the year, when "For Sale" signs seem especially poignant in front of deserted houses, when there is not a vehicle to be seen on the muddy street, Mogollon is quiet, almost abandoned. But this is what an old mining town looks like—and the ghosts of the past seem not so long gone. In fact, Italian film makers have found Mogollon a perfect setting for the "spaghetti westerns" so popular with Italian audiences.

Mogollon was founded after a soldier stationed at Fort Bayard (near present-day Silver City) discovered a rock with gold in it in 1870; he quietly filed a claim, and was soon followed by other miners. Mogollon was a wild place between 1870 and 1913, the year in which 40 percent of New Mexico's silver and gold production came from these mines. Its wooden buildings burned down several times, but the town always sprang back to life.

New Mexico 159, which is paved until about five miles beyond Mogollon, leads to several campgrounds (Bursum, Ben Lilly, Willow Creek, and Gilita), fishing streams, and trails into the Gila Wilderness. You can also follow a number of primitive dirt roads across the Mogollon Mountains into the heart of the Gila National Forest, cross the Black Range, and reach the ghost towns of Winston and Chloride, or go north across the San Mateos toward Magdalena. Check with forest rangers about road and fire conditions before you begin such journeys.

Like all trips, the drive back down to Alma from Mogollon seems shorter than when you came up. Now you can take some time to enjoy the scenery. A 180-degree view of plains, valleys, and row upon row of mountains confronts you, bathed in sunlight that either picks up each nuance of every distant canyon and pine tree or washes the entire panorama in a filtered glow. You probably can see all the way to Arizona, but the uncluttered horizon almost teases you into believing that you can gaze beyond Arizona clear to California. Do keep your eyes on the road, however, as you wind your way down to U.S. 180.

15

15

Back on the highway, you do not have too far to go before you come to Glenwood and another little side jaunt, this one short and on level ground, to Whitewater Canyon and the Catwalk. Glenwood's residents welcome travelers and campers and are trying to establish the small community as a gateway not only to the Gila National Forest and Wilderness Area, but also to other regional attractions. You will find a few gas stations, small resorts, motels, art galleries, restaurants, and RV facilities in the community. This is a good spot to enter the Gila, where 3.3 million acres of land are there for you to hike and explore, 790,000 of them declared wilderness, closed to motorized vehicles but open to anyone willing and able to walk or ride horseback. The ranger station at Glenwood is just south of town; the rangers can give you permits and maps, answer your questions, and advise you about the conditions of trails and campgrounds.

But first, look for the Catwalk signs as you enter Glenwood. Turn left (east) at a resort with cozy-looking stone cabins, wind past the state fish hatchery, and skirt what must be one of the smallest Catholic churches in New Mexico. You crisscross a riverbed and soon arrive at Whitewater Canyon. Here a shady picnic area and gentle stream will soothe you and your children just as it did the Apache leaders Geronimo and Nana, who often came here to rest during the Apache wars. The people of Glenwood are proud of the picnic area and the Catwalk trail, working as a community to improve both. Although you may not camp overnight here at Whitewater Canyon, stop and picnic, wade in the stream, and snooze beneath the trees.

The Catwalk lies just beyond the picnic area. It dates to the time when Whitewater Canyon was part of the mining boom started by James Cooney up near Mogollon. Miners built a mine and a town, Graham, here at the mouth of the canyon, but had to build a pipeline three miles back into the canyon to ensure a year-round water source. The first pipeline extended along the west side of the canyon. Soon more water was needed, so a second pipeline, named the Catwalk, was built to hang directly over the creek. Although the Graham mill closed in 1913, much of the pipeline survived, stabilized by the Civilian Conservation Corps in the 1930s, and then upgraded to a steel catwalk by the Forest Service in 1961. Now you can enjoy this 2.5-mile walk, part of it on a steel pathway that hugs the side of the canyon. Railings protect you as you progress up the gorge. Children can go at their own pace, peering down into the creek bed, picking their way along the rocks of the narrow canyon, enjoying the thrill of this unusual trek. Remember that the catwalk was constructed of steel to withstand frequent flash floods, so be aware of weather conditions as you enter the canyon.

The trip from Glenwood to Cliff and then on to Silver City is long (about ninety miles) but pleasant, especially if you pause at some of the interesting spots along the way. If you are hot and tired and enjoy mineral springs, you may want to detour to San Francisco Hot Springs, about 1.5 miles south of Pleasanton, where the San Francisco River finally leaves you after having accompanied you sporadically since Reserve. A small sign guides you off U.S. 180 onto a dirt road and then to the river, where a nearby spring and two pools await your plunge. Once the site of a hotel and spa, there are now no facilities here. Fellow bathers may or may not wear swimsuits. About nine or ten miles beyond Glenwood, watch for signs for the Leopold Vista picnic area at the crest of one of the many hills you will climb. This is a good place to picnic, stretch your legs, and listen to the silence of the immense panorama surrounding you. It was Aldo Leopold who conceived the idea of preserving large undeveloped areas of the country for future generations. His efforts led to the designation of the dark mountains and forests that lie before you as the Gila Wilderness, a part of the Gila National Forest. Leopold's *Sand County Almanac* contains sections about the Gila.

Few settlements interrupt your journey now. There are just the rolling hills, the grazing land, which is green after a rain or tawny during the winter dry times, a ranch or two, and always the mountains over your shoulder. You may want to stop at Cliff, a small town that serves the cattle ranchers and travelers who pass this way. Cliff stretches east of the highway and down toward the Gila River, which meanders through a wide bosque.

Cliff is the "Home of the Cowgirls and Cowboys," says the sign on the high school gym, and a well-used rodeo ring nearby proves it.

The village of Gila perches on the east bank of the Gila River, across from Cliff. It was once the headquarters for an immense cattle operation, the Lyons-Campbell Ranch, that was said to be sixty miles long and forty miles wide. A few buildings in Gila are left from those days. You might enjoy the detour N.M. 211 makes as it goes down into the leafy bosque, past grazing cattle, crosses the river, and then winds through the town of Gila and south back to U.S. 180. If you plan to hike into the Gila National Forest, this is another convenient entry point. Check at the little store in the middle of Gila, or make your plans first at the Glenwood Ranger Station.

Silver City is not too far now, about twenty-five miles. Along the way, the wide Gila River Valley changes back and forth from soft, rounded hills to stern, dry desert. Just past Cliff, signs point to Bill Evans Lake, a small reservoir created by the Phelps Dodge Company, where you can fish and picnic. Sometimes the flat land before you is broken by plants of the lower Sonoran Zone (below 4,500 feet)—spiky and spectacular yucca, dark and bushy creosote, and mesquite. But then you ascend once again into the upper Sonoran Zone (4,000 to 7,500 feet) and you are back among familiar piñon and juniper. As you near Silver City, you will notice that large ranches have given way to smaller "ranchettes," where families raise children and the children raise a few cattle or sheep for 4-H projects, where couples have retired to quiet vistas, and where everyone can get into Silver City easily for jobs or recreation.

Silver City is an old mining town, university community, Victorian treasure-house, and regional service center. The character of your descent into town will vary, depending on the time of your arrival. If it is night, lights will twinkle in crazy patterns beneath you, and you will wonder how to negotiate a straight path to your night's lodging. If you enter Silver City during the day, you will pause at the top of the hill near the new football stadium to plan your visit. It will be easy to pick out the green campus of Western New Mexico University below and to the right, then look beyond the

Some kinds of barbed wire

university to Silver City's old-fashioned downtown, a National Historic District, noting the newer parts of the city scattered over and among the hillsides and mountains where the silver that gave the town its name was mined.

Like all mining towns, Silver City straddles a series of hills and valleys, experiencing ups and downs in its economy that mirror its rocky setting. Situated at a pleasant altitude, about six thousand feet, it enjoys a climate that is seldom harsh. With adequate and somewhat predictable rainfall, the Silver City area has been home to humans since before A.D. 900. About ten thousand people live in Silver City today.

Archaeologists have discovered Mogollon ruins all over the region and within the borders of Silver City itself. The Mogollon people probably lived here because water was so plentiful in the marshy site they chose. The Mogollons lived first in pit houses dug into the earth, then built taller, multistory structures, the remains of which have been found within city limits. Some pottery discovered in the Silver City area, thin-walled, with graceful black-on-white designs, indicates that a branch of the Mogollon culture, the Mimbres, also lived here at some point. But all the Mogollon were gone from this region by A.D. 1300, for reasons that still remain unclear.

Next to dwell here were a more nomadic people, the Athapascans, who hunted, mined turquoise and copper, and had a tendency to raid their neighbors. In fact, some neighbors to the north, the Zuni, named them Apache, the Zuni word for enemy. Spain did not bother to colonize this southwestern corner of New Mexico for several centuries, initiating exploratory and mapping trips here only in the latter part of the 1700s. La Cienega de San Vicente, a small eighteenth-century Spanish or Mexican settlement, probably predated the founding of Silver City. After the discovery of copper in the region at the dawn of the nineteenth century, a community grew up around nearby Santa Rita. From the east came hunters and trappers, then miners, and then entrepreneurs, followed by soldiers sent to protect American interests. By the time silver was discovered to the south near Ralston (now Shakespeare) in 1870, Silver City's destiny was clear, and the town got its

15

name and had a town center of sturdy brick "eastern looking" buildings within the year.

Silver City still looks like a mining town, not just because it is set amid mountains and along hillsides, but because most of its structures reflect the unique atmosphere and energy that characterized Western boom towns of the late nineteenth century. In 1880, a city ordinance decreed that all buildings within the city limits be built of masonry construction, thus limiting the possibility of fire, the scourge of most mining towns. This ensured that future generations would be able to enjoy a townscape not too different now than what it was one hundred years ago.

Begin your visit to Silver City with a stop at the Silver City Museum on West Broadway, just down the hill from the Grant County Courthouse. Inside the old brick Ailman house, built in 1881 in an impressive Italianate style, museum volunteers and staff will show you around the multistory structure that has also been a firehouse, city hall, and boardinghouse. Now it is home to extensive exhibits tracing the history of Silver City through the people—Mogollon, Apache, Spanish, miners, ranchers, loggers, trappers, merchants, and others—who lived here. The museum recently added an attractive new wing, with a gallery for traveling exhibits and space for offices and workrooms. Browse through the museum gift shop, perhaps purchase the handy walking tour of downtown Silver City, and ask museum personnel for tips on getting to know Silver City and its environs.

Historic downtown Silver City is a great place to walk. Wander over to the Big Ditch, once Silver City's Main Street. After several big floods destroyed the brick pavement, ripped structures from along its sides, and lowered it to its present bedrock level, the town chose to recognize this gaping wound as an asset and rebuilt it as a park, a green and leafy oasis in the middle of town. Walk up and down Bullard Street, enjoying the sight of so many old buildings, including the Warren office complex, complete with hitching post in front. Turn up Broadway, where a number of building styles and materials reflect construction that took place here from the 1880s into the 1920s. Look up the hill at the three-story Grant County Courthouse, built in the 1930s as a WPA project and featuring murals by Theodore Van Soelen, terrazzo floors, Art Deco light fixtures, and marble wainscoting. You can have a bite to eat in downtown Silver City, walk through an art gallery, shop for travel items, or just enjoy its idiosyncrasies—high sidewalks, brick storefronts with cast-iron details, cowboys mingling with loggers, senior citizens sharing a café table with college students.

Silver City has several other historic districts. The Chihuahua Hill Historic District, south of downtown, preserves many adobe homes and other buildings that climb up the hillsides in informal ways, as they have since their first owners built them, adobe brick by adobe brick, decades ago. Two other historic neighborhoods, Black's Addition to the west and the North Addition, beyond College Avenue, preserve modest cottages and bungalows of historical and architectural interest. Your youngsters might like to know that the most naughty of kids, Billy, lived as a boy in Silver City, that he sneaked out of jail here, and that Billy the Kid's long-suffering mother lies buried in the town cemetery.

Western New Mexico University at the top of College Avenue is a small state university that offers courses to about 1,200 students. Fleming Hall, the college's first gymnasium, is now Western New Mexico University Museum. Inside the museum you will see not only reminders of the gymnasium's initial purpose—wooden "gym" floors, a high ceiling suitable for basketball games, and a mezzanine for spectators—you will also discover one of the largest collections in the United States of artifacts from the Mimbres people. The heart of the collection includes more than three hundred ceramic vessels with complex geometric designs, their centers punched out when they were buried with the dead. If you make arrangements ahead of time, the museum staff will accompany you to the locked storage room where dozens of Mimbres and Hohokam artifacts are kept. As the official Gila Gateway Station, the museum can also give you information about the nearby Gila National Forest.

Take a moment and wander the rest of the Western campus to enjoy its comfortable setting and to understand its role in the larger community. You will probably find students, older Silver City residents, and school-age youngsters with disabilities swimming in the large pool at the athletic complex. Piano students might be practicing in the practice rooms next to the fine arts hall, where traveling theater companies, the New Mexico Symphony Orchestra, and other artists play to Silver City audiences. Western makes a special effort to attract minority students and adults returning to school, sponsoring a number of campus programs to assist them.

Consider Silver City your jumping-off point for jaunts to humankind's distant past, for a camping weekend, for an introduction to rock hunting or bird watching, or for visits to enormous surface mines or old army forts. The headquarters of the immense Gila National Forest and Wilderness and the Gila Cliff Dwellings are to the north about forty-five miles. To the south and east of town are two operating copper mines, Santa Rita and Tyrone. Travel east on U.S. 180 to Fort Bayard, an army fort during the Apache wars and once the home of the black Buffalo Soldiers. Now a state-run, long-term-care hospital, the grounds of Fort Bayard are open to the public and include a three-story brick officers' quarters, traditional parade grounds, and the site from which heliograph signals were once relayed across the mountains to Fort Stanton. Nearby is a state elk refuge and nature trail accessible to people with disabilities.

Beyond Fort Bayard, past Central, you soon arrive at the fabled Santa Rita open-pit copper mine, owned by the Kennecott Copper/Mitsubishi Corporation. Visitors can view mining operations from an observation tower and look more than one thousand feet down into the multicolored mine, where terraces encircle a mile-wide cavity. Trucks drive along the terraces, removing ore and waste. Centuries ago, local Indians also mined copper here, as did the Spanish. Don Francisco Elguea of Chihuahua, Mexico, took over the mines in the nineteenth century, built a town, Santa Rita del Cobre, and also a fort, and used Apache slaves and Spanish convict labor to mine the copper. Because copper was difficult to extract, and because frequent Apache raids interrupted mining activity, the copper mine was worked only intermittently. In the late nineteenth century, a young mining engineer, John Sully, advised open-pit mining with steam shovels. As the shovels dug around the town, Santa Rita became isolated on an island in the middle of the pit. Finally, the town was abandoned and eaten up.

No trip to this part of New Mexico would be complete without a journey into the heart of one of the nation's largest and most rugged national forests, the Gila. Even if you just drive to the cliff dwellings for the day, the trip will convince you to return to camp, hike, maybe even raft the Gila or rent a horse, the better to penetrate the interior of these 3.3 million acres. While the road to the national forest, about forty-five miles away from the center of Silver City, is paved, it is narrow and winding, so the going will be slow.

Leave Silver City for the Gila on N.M. 90/U.S. 180, turning off onto N.M. 15 as you travel east through a commercial strip of shopping centers and motels. New Mexico 15 is well marked and leads you up and out of the valley, past attractive homes that perch on their hills as if ready to take flight. Follow the signs to Pinos Altos, an old gold-mining town, just six miles above Silver City.

The folks of Pinos Altos have arranged an effortless driving tour of the high spots of their little town, with signposts that guide you along its narrow dirt streets, past log cabins and miners' small-framed houses. However, you stand a much better chance of capturing the flavor of this survivor of the Wild West if you get out and walk. Some buildings are authentically old— the Hearst Church on Gold Avenue, for example—while others like the Opera House just look and act old. Wander past the McDonald Cabin, said to be one of the first cabins built in the county. Or pause at the place where Judge Roy Bean might have been a storekeeper. Stop in at the Buckhorn Saloon to enjoy a cold drink and the Wild West atmosphere. Pinos Altos also offers places to spend the night beneath tall pine trees, whether in an RV park or cabins.

But the Gila beckons. Get back on N.M. 15 and begin the slow ascent into more high pines, past little brooks, alongside sheer cliffs, and around mountainous bends and curves for the next two hours or so. There will be several scenic lookouts, so be ready to pry your fingers from the steering wheel, park, and stand up to breathe in the high-altitude, pine-scented air. Enjoy panoramas that

15

encompass more than fifty thousand square miles of mountain and forest extending into Mexico. After about thirty miles, pause at Copperas Vista to see all three forks of the Gila River. Stay on N.M. 15 throughout the trip, which has almost reached its destination as you pass through the town of Gila Hot Springs, where there are camping and RV services, hot springs, and several trail outfitters. Soon you are in a valley, crossing the Gila River, with the visitor center not far beyond.

A stop at the visitor center orients you to the Gila National Forest, the Gila Wilderness, and the Gila Cliff Dwellings National Monument. Displays of artifacts from the Mimbres and Apache people, graphic descriptions of the topography and wildlife of the region, and a shop that sells helpful books and maps give you a headstart for your Gila adventure. The Gila Cliff Dwellings are a short drive down the road from the visitor center. But they are more than a step back in time. Over the centuries, those who traveled and settled in the Gila River area frequently came across pottery fragments and ruins. The archaeologist Adolph Bandelier wrote about his discovery of the Gila dwellings in 1884. A little more than twenty years later, President Theodore Roosevelt designated the dwellings a national monument.

The cliff dwellings provide you with an opportunity to walk the very paths that the Mogollon people did seven centuries ago. You will begin the one-hour, one-mile loop hike at the ranger station, where you can pick up a leaflet that describes the self-guided tour. The hike is not a strenuous one, but it does require strength and balance, to say nothing of sturdy walking shoes, not flip-flops or high heels. As children walk these narrow paths, they should be careful, but they will enjoy this chance to climb and play in a kind of outdoor museum that is small and comprehensible. The cliff dwellings are open year-round. Because willows and cottonwoods shade the cliff dwellings, they are cool even in the middle of the summer, and the paths can remain icy long into spring.

Within the cave dwellings, you will see seven caves, six of which have prehistoric ruins. You can climb into some of these caves, noting the small size of the doorways, the ever-present fire pits, the wisdom with which rooms were sited, the care taken as walls were built. Although each cave is different and some are more complete than others, you will observe construction similarities in all the Gila cliff dwellings. The people who lived here were also superb farmers, tending their crops and their water sources carefully, and storing their precious food with equal caution. The Mogollon walked from these cliff houses to their fields, along the valley of the Gila River or up on top of the mesa.

Pitch a tent here in the valley or along the riverbed, or hike and camp along some of the 1,490 miles of trails within the forest. The only way to enter the Gila Wilderness is by foot or horseback. You can also take day hikes to explore the banks of the Gila River or to visit one of the nearby hot springs. If you decide to enter the forest, do so only if you are familiar with mountainous terrain and trails. Rangers can give you permits and information about fire and trail conditions. And you certainly should carry plenty of water and warm clothing. Days are sunny and nights are cold in this high country at any time of the year.

After leaving the cliff dwellings and the quiet river bottom, you will backtrack about eighteen miles on N.M. 15, again passing through the town of Gila Hot Springs. At the intersection of N.M. 35 and N.M. 15, you must make a decision. The shortest route back to Silver City is to duplicate your journey and remain on N.M. 15. If instead you turn left on N.M. 35, you will drive along Sapillo Creek past Lake Roberts and through the Mimbres Valley, ending up near the town of San Lorenzo, about twenty miles east of Silver City on N.M. 152. Those who continue this tour will take the latter route, turning east on N.M. 152 and

crossing the Black Range to Hillsboro and I-25. Because this leg of the journey is almost entirely mountainous, set aside several hours, in daylight if possible, to enjoy your trip.

A few miles down the road from the N.M. 15/N.M. 35 junction, you spy Lake Roberts, a sparkling blue man-made lake that looks perfectly natural in this mountain setting. Residents of the Silver City area enjoy day trips to this high-altitude lake, where they can fish, canoe, or drive their motorboats. There are also picnic and camping areas. Continue through the mountains, in and out of valleys, with frequent campsites and trailheads indicating that you are still in or near the national forest. Where the valley widens, ranches and cabins appear. The Mimbres Ranger Station near the town of Mimbres will be your last formal contact with the Gila National Forest.

And then you are most definitely in the Mimbres Valley: Yucca plants replace pine trees, and farm roads replace hiking trails. This valley was the home of the Mimbres branch of the Mogollon people from the third to the twelfth century A.D., when they left their valley. The Mimbres hunted in the surrounding hills, tended crops in fields along the river, and built pit houses, many of which remain as unexcavated ruins. (The Mimbres are best known for their elegant black-and-white pottery.) You will not find Mimbres artifacts on display in this valley, but the Silver City museums offer excellent Mimbres exhibits.

After you have left Mimbres, which is less a defined town and more a pleasant valley of scattered homes, orchards, and meadows, remain on N.M. 35 until you reach the junction with N.M. 152. To complete this circle, head east to Kingston on N.M. 152, crossing the Black Range to Hillsboro, a curving mountainous trip of about seventy-five miles that is described in Tour Fourteen. You will then drive on I-25 to Truth or Consequences. We suggest that you not make this leg of the journey at night, when wandering deer and cattle might intervene and when you would miss spectacular scenery. From Mimbres, you can also double back to Silver City on N.M. 152.

Read about the Black Range and the revived mining towns within it in Tour Fourteen. Stop at one of the many vista points you will encounter on

N.M. 152, enjoy a picnic beneath the Black Range's piney cliffs, browse through the little shops of Hillsboro, or spend the night at a bed-and-breakfast inn in Kingston or Hillsboro. Once you leave Hillsboro, you spend twenty-five miles or so descending from foothills and crossing treeless plains. The Caballo Mountains fill the eastern horizon, with Caballo Lake almost a mirage at their feet. Turn north on I-25, exiting for Truth or Consequences about fifteen minutes later at Williamsburg.

Why is it called Truth or Consequences? In 1950, the residents of Hot Springs, New Mexico, made a fateful decision. They accepted the offer of a radio and television game show, "Truth or Consequences," to change the name of the town to that of the program. In return, the town, soon known as T or C, received free national publicity and an annual spring fiesta. Ralph Edwards, emcee of the now defunct TV show, comes to T or C each year to host the celebration, bringing with him a few Hollywood celebrities for a parade, golf tournament, and other events. Although a number of citizens objected to the name change and sought to reverse the decision through elections, they always lost. The only major institution in town that retained its original name was the high school, still called Hot Springs High.

Truth or Consequences, the county seat for Sierra County, traces its inception to the many natural hot springs that travelers and residents of the region have enjoyed for centuries. The Apaches and other nomadic Indians found the springs around here a source of rest and healing, a neutral place where they could forget their rivalries for a moment. Farther south, the Garcia and Tafoya families founded the town of Palomas Ojo Caliente (now under Caballo Lake) around a hot spring in 1860. Cowboys built an adobe bathhouse at a spring near what is now the Elephant Butte Dam and another town, Palomas Springs, grew up around it. That town changed its name to Hot Springs, now T or C.

In the 1930s, the presence of the hot springs also drew Carrie Tingley, wife of New Mexico Governor Clyde Tingley, to encourage the construction of a hospital for crippled children on a hilltop south of town, where children with polio could be treated in the soothing waters. For decades, the white-columned Carrie Tingley Hospital was one of the few sources of orthopedic care for young children in New Mexico, and thousands of children came from all over the state to spend extensive periods at the hospital. A New Mexico writer, Rudolfo Anaya, wrote of a rehabilitative experience at Carrie Tingley in his novel *Tortuga.* The Carrie Tingley facility was moved to Albuquerque in the 1980s to provide better access to medical specialists. The lovely white building and its grounds are now the New Mexico Veterans' Center.

The Sierra County Historical Society commemorates the county's unique history as only a small-town museum can, with the Geronimo Springs Museum right in the heart of downtown T or C, on Main Street across from the post office. Built over the years by members of the community—civic groups, plumbers, electricians, mayors, and local fund-raisers—the museum now encompasses a number of old and new buildings. You ramble along through a series of rooms, which contain hundreds of pieces of Indian pottery, large, small, intact, broken; thousands of arrowheads displayed in amazing and intricate designs; stuffed animals— birds, snakes, and exotic reptiles; barbed wire of all sizes and kinds; farm and ranch implements, from mallets for felling buffalo to scythes; military uniforms from every war we ever fought; untold numbers of private collections, including masses of buttons and an entire early twentieth-century doctor's office. This eclectic assemblage is topped

off by the Ralph Edwards Wing, a roomful of photographs and mementos that pay homage to the man, the radio show, and the T or C Fiesta. This might be one museum that children will enjoy, for it overflows with a jumble of historic and fanciful items just like grandmother's attic.

About seven thousand people, many of

them retired, live in T or C. They come here for the sunny climate (the sun shines 318 days a year, they say), the moderate cost of living, the many mineral baths, and a pace that caters to people who like to fish and play golf and visit with each other. Because of its relatively mild climate, T or C also attracts "snowbirds" who start to arrive in November. They come pulling trailers that they hook up in one of the town's many RV parks, they enjoy a Southwest winter, and then they head back to North Dakota or Michigan once spring comes.

Truth or Consequences is also a major service center for Sierra County, whose nine thousand residents are ranchers, chile farmers, retirees, or workers in the recreation industry so important to the region. Historically, ranching was the primary activity for those who lived in Sierra County. Ranches were immense, spreading across the Jornada del Muerto for miles. Cowboys brought cattle to the railroad stop at Engle, and then enjoyed the mineral baths in Hot Springs. While ranching still flavors the life in Sierra County, chile farming, especially in the Arrey and Derry areas, has also become important. Farmers plant hundreds of acres of chile, from the hottest varieties to those that even the most timid of eastern palates can enjoy. From late July into November, you can purchase fresh green chile in grocery stores in T or C or in the agricultural communities south of town. And there is a new industry in Sierra County. A French concern bought twenty-one thousand acres of land near Engle from the Pedro Armendaris Grant in 1980, successfully negotiated water rights, and began planting varieties of grapes that now produce an award-winning champagne.

Recreation, however, seems to be what brings people to Sierra County and T or C. Some people come here to soak in the mineral baths at the bathhouses around town. Most visitors come to nearby Elephant Butte Lake, a reservoir that holds as many as 2.2 million acre feet of the Rio Grande. A concrete dam at the south end of the lake just above T or C, built in 1911–16, holds back water that can irrigate eighty-eight thousand acres in New Mexico and sixty-seven thousand acres in Texas. Farmers and ranchers downstream need Elephant Butte Lake for agricultural purposes. College students on spring break, families over

15

summer weekends, and sailors come year-round to Elephant Butte Lake to slake their thirst for water in the desert. You can also play golf, visit the Ralph Edwards Park along the river, or attend one of the many annual events that T or C hosts.

It might be fun to take a brief detour out of T or C. You can drive to Engle at the edge of the Jornada del Muerto to visit the Domaine Cheurlin Vineyards and Winery and then backtrack to the west side of Elephant Butte Lake and I-25. Going north on Date Street, take N.M. 51 east out of town, first passing the small homes and trailer parks that make up most of T or C, and then the dam itself. Past the dam, climb uphill, and soon the vast Jornada del Muerto lies before you. The Jornada was a shortcut for pre-twentieth-century travelers, who sometimes preferred this passage to the river route via present-day T or C. Try to imagine what it must have been like for the first Spanish settlers who trudged across this desolate, almost waterless land on their way to unknown territory in the north. Then picture the Spanish as they fled south in 1680, crossing the same unyielding landscape to escape the bloody Pueblo Revolt. Engle, about fifteen miles ahead, is as close as you can get to the Jornada; White Sands Missile Range now encompasses most of it.

Cross the high desert, look for winery signs after about fifteen minutes, and then follow the most well-beaten of all the dirt paths for about three miles to a tall, metal building. This is the winery, incongruously surrounded by vineyards, yucca, and roaming cattle. Here, a French family with roots in Celles-sur-Ource, France, makes a New Mexico sparkling wine by the *méthode Champenoise.* The vintners will take you through their vineyards and the winery, explaining how the grapes pass from the vine through the large stainless-steel vats and into the cooled rooms where hundreds of bottles await turning, bubbles, and perfection.

Return to Elephant Butte Lake via N.M. 51, taking N.M. 179 east to N.M. 195, which leads to Elephant Butte Park and Marina, right on the shore. The butte that gave the lake its name is before you, a massive shape that only resembles an elephant if you can picture a head and a trunk, both of which are now submerged. As you drive along the lake, you will come upon a number of separate parcels of the state park, some just picnic areas, some camping spots, some boat landings. You will also notice that there is little shade, a factor to consider when camping in the summer. Stay on N.M. 195 and it will take you along the lake shore and then west to I-25 and your return to Socorro.

Those who frequently drive on I-25 between T or C and Socorro tend to find this stretch of road boring. It need not be. You have mountains on three sides and the Rio Grande to the east. Old mines, ghost towns, working ranches, even an old fort are within a few miles of the busy Interstate. Just north of T or C, for example, you can drive west on N.M. 52, a paved road, to Cuchillo, an old village where the stage once stopped and where fossil hunters have found prehistoric treasures in the nearby canyons. Beyond Cuchillo, N.M. 52 extends to the real ghost towns of Winston and Chloride, and then becomes a dirt road as it crosses the Black Range and the Mogollons to the Catron County town of Mogollon. Take this route only if the weather is good, you are familiar with four-wheel-drive terrain, and you have no need of services. You can also take the N.M. 52 turnoff to visit two small villages, Placitas and Monticello, which are just up N.M. 142 along the Alamosa River.

At exit 124, you can drive east three miles on gravel toward a forbidding mesa and the remains of San Marcial, where there is definitely more past than present. This was Senecu, an agricultural community of the Piro Indians long before the Spanish arrived. When the Spanish came, missionaries built the San Antonio Mission and a *reducido*, a school where the Indians were taught catechism, cooking, crafts, and music in Spanish. After an Apache raid in 1675, followed closely by the Spanish Revolt in 1680, the Piro went north to Socorro. When the Spanish resettled Socorro, a few colonists ventured south and developed El Paraje, later changed to La Mesa de San Marcial, on the east side of the river. After a flood, the town moved back across to the west side of the Rio Grande. The Santa Fe Railroad came in 1880, and the town grew and prospered. At the turn of the century, there were a thousand people, a roundhouse, repair shops, and soon a bridge across the river so that the railroad could head straight across the

1

Jornada toward Las Cruces. The San Marcial of the 1920s was a busy place, with a Fred Harvey restaurant, stores and shops to serve the surrounding ranches, and several thousand residents. During that decade, one flood buried many buildings. A second flood in 1929 completely destroyed the city. And that was the end of San Marcial. Everything was buried, except the cemetery.

Also accessible from exit 124 are more ruins, those of Fort Craig, built in 1854 to protect American settlers from Apache raids. Fort Craig also played an important role during the Civil War when Union troops set off from here to fight the Confederates in the Battle of Valverde (near San Marcial) in 1862. The Union soldiers from Fort Craig lost this battle. But the same Confederate troops, after marching northward and securing Albuquerque and Santa Fe without a fight, lost to the Union at Glorieta a few weeks later. The presence of Fort Craig not only provided a deterrent against the Apaches, it also brought growth to this region of New Mexico. By the time Fort Craig was decommissioned in 1885, the Socorro area was a lively place with an economy based on mining, cattle, and railroad industries. It is not easy to reach the ruins at Fort Craig, and once you get there, you will only see stabilized foundations that outline what was once a large fort. We suggest that you call the U.S. Bureau of Land Management (BLM) in Socorro to get directions for finding Fort Craig.

Snow Geese

Your last stop before Socorro will be the Bosque del Apache National Wildlife Refuge. Although the refuge is a treat any time of the year, do visit the bosque in the winter months, when thousands of birds, including snow geese, mallards, bald eagles, sandhill cranes, whooping cranes, and egrets have migrated to this feeding and resting area along the Rio Grande. Plan your winter visit for dawn or dusk to watch immense flocks of flapping, squawking birds fly onto the ponds at feeding time. From I-25, you can take either the San Marcial exit and drive ten miles north to the bosque along N.M. 1 (quiet and less traveled) or the San Antonio exit to U.S. 380 and then N.M. 1.

The visitor center provides information about the Bosque del Apache, established in 1939 by the U.S Fish and Wildlife Service as a place for the refuge and breeding of different kinds of wild birds. You will learn some of the history, both physical and historical, of the region. And you will be treated to the foster family story of the bird world. The whooping crane, the tallest bird in North America (with a wingspan of up to seven feet), was almost extinct in the early 1940s, when only seventeen such birds were counted. Wildlife specialists planted whooping crane eggs within a flock of sandhill cranes, establishing a kind of foster parent program between the two birds. Now when you watch large flocks of birds swoop in at feeding time, you can occasionally spy the larger whooping crane amid his sandhill friends. Biologists must next ensure that the whoopers will mate with each other. About 295 different bird species have been counted at the refuge. There are a number of animals—deer, snakes, turtles, porcupines—which are protected here, and you will find them if you come during the daytime and take one of the loop walks.

Bosque del Apache

The bosque is arranged so that you stop first at the visitor center and then take a twelve-mile auto tour along marshes and through areas planted in corn, sorghum, winter wheat, and millet for the migrating birds. If time is an issue, take the shorter of the two loops. Stop at observation towers built close to some of the more popular feeding spots. Refuge rangers will provide guided tours for groups if you make arrangements ahead of time. As the sun sets behind the San Mateo and Magdalena mountains to the west and the sky becomes dark and dramatic, a caravan of cars drives slowly along the embankments near the feeding areas. Families walk quietly along paths through the high marsh grass to watch in awe as thousands of birds flock to the water. You and your fellow humans are definitely in the minority.

If it is dinnertime for people, drive north on

N.M. 1 to San Antonio to the Owl Bar, a favorite gathering spot, where you can have a green chile cheeseburger alongside other birders, local townspeople, students from New Mexico Tech, truck drivers, and scientists from the White Sands Missile Range. The Owl Bar, listed as a State Historical and Cultural Property, is not San Antonio's only claim to fame. This is also the place where Conrad Hilton was born and where his father, Augustus, was trader, merchant, and hotelkeeper in the late nineteenth century.

People have settled in this spot along the Rio Grande for hundreds, maybe thousands of years. The village was certainly the site of a Piro pueblo, and later home to a community of Spanish settlers who cultivated grain, beans, chile, onions, and grapes in irrigated farms along the river. Because of its location on the route between Chihuahua and Santa Fe, the community expanded to include a stage line east to White Oaks and west to Magdalena, a coal mine and coke oven, and then, when the Santa Fe Railroad arrived, a railroad station and more stores and a hotel. San Antonio is smaller than it was in its prime, but it retains the flavor of a stopping-off place for travelers, and many of its older buildings, including the Crystal Palace and private homes, are being restored. In San Antonio, travelers will find a bed-and-breakfast inn, an RV park, and gas and grocery services.

And now it is time to complete this immense circle at its starting point, the plaza in Socorro. The fifteen-minute drive north on I-25 will probably be completed as darkness falls. If it is summer, the Socorro plaza may be filled with families out for a walk or old people chatting as they sit in the cool of the evening. In winter, the plaza will be empty, the trees bare, perhaps lit with garlands of Christmas lights. Whatever the time of year, after so long and satisfying a journey, the plaza is a welcome sight.

TOUR
SIXTEEN
CAVERNS
AND SANDS

16

Places:	Albuquerque, Clines Corners, Roswell, Artesia, Carlsbad, Carlsbad Caverns National Park, Cloudcroft, White Sands, Valley of Fires State Park, Albuquerque
Suggested travel time:	Three days to one week
Mileage:	Approximately 712 miles, excluding side trips
Highways:	I-40, U.S. 285, U.S. 60, N.M. 2, N.M. 137, U.S. 62/180, N.M. 7, U.S. 82, N.M. 6563, U.S. 70, U.S. 54, U.S. 380, I-25
Accommodations:	Motels or hotels in Roswell, Artesia, Carlsbad, Whites City, Cloudcroft, Alamogordo, and Carrizozo
Camping:	Carlsbad, Whites City, Cloudcroft, White Sands (for the hardy), Oliver Lee State Park, Three Rivers, and Valley of Fires State Park

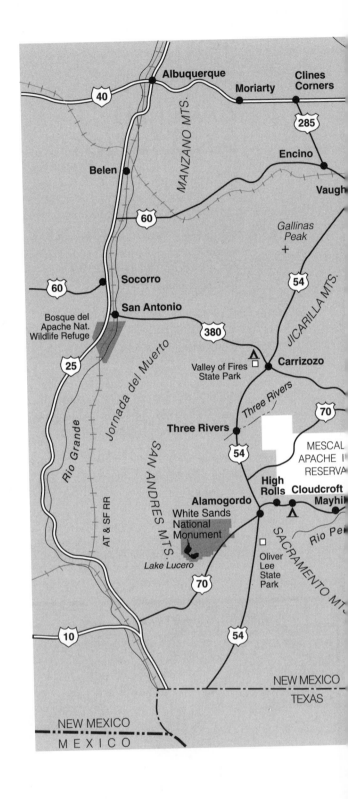

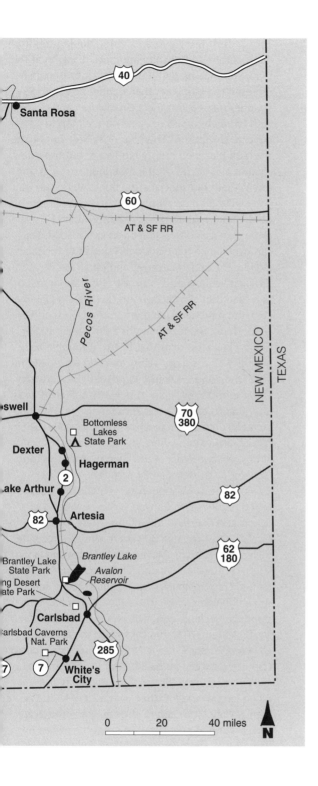

16

Santa Rosa

40

60

AT & SF RR

Pecos River

AT & SF RR

NEW MEXICO

TEXAS

swell

Bottomless
Lakes
State Park

70
380

Dexter

Hagerman

2

ake Arthur

82

82

Artesia

Brantley Lake

62
180

Brantley Lake
State Park

Avalon
Reservoir

ng Desert
ate Park

Carlsbad

arlsbad Caverns
Nat. Park

285

7

7

White's
City

0   20   40 miles

N

Tour Sixteen takes you on a long, looping trip from Albuquerque to Carlsbad and back. Looking at the map, you may be daunted by the unbroken lines representing highways that wander across huge counties named Torrance, Guadalupe, and Chaves, with hardly a square or circle on the map to indicate civilization. This tour does take you across the high plains on empty highways, but those few squares and circles on the map indicate cities and towns that hold special attractions. Along the way you can visit a fine art museum in Roswell, an observatory high in the sky near Cloudcroft, and a living desert and riverside parks in Carlsbad. You can experience the wide-open spaces of the plains, explore the fabled caverns, and picnic on the dazzling White Sands. You will also travel a mountain road that climbs through the Lincoln National Forest to a picturesque town in the clouds and then twists down the mountain to a dry valley, and a narrow blacktop road that passes through a lava flow and across a dry valley touched by the atomic age. On a long weekend you could visit Carlsbad Caverns and White Sands, but with side trips and attention to all the attractions along the way Tour Sixteen could take a week or more. Besides the natural attractions, there are community festivals almost every month of the year, making this tour ideal for an in-state family vacation.

As you leave Albuquerque you will drive east on I-40 through Tijeras Canyon, a gap between the Sandia and Manzano mountains. These mountains in centuries past reached upward to almost three times their present height. Movement between and along faults, constant weathering, and other processes have formed crags, pinnacles, and granite blocks, and strewn boulders about the canyon. If you had time to stop for a geologic walk, you would find fossils of snails and ferns from the days when this area was covered by a shallow sea. Note the sign for Carnue or Carnuel, a settlement dating back to 1819, when Governor Facundo Melgares granted thirty-five Albuquerque residents their own tract of land. Known then as Cañon de Carnue, the site was home to an earlier group of people in 1763. Apache raiders on their way to Albuquerque persuaded these first settlers to leave their homes in 1771. By the early 1800s, however, the Spanish were in control of the area, making land grants there practicable. Thus, the grants of San Miguel and San Antonio de Carnue were established in 1819. The older Indian settlement of Portozuelo (little door) may have been the home of the ancestors of the modern Isletans. Its remains are hidden among the rocks and boulders that litter the canyon. Present-day inhabitants have built their homes in a variety of styles on the craggy canyon floor.

If you are taking your trip in the winter, pay attention to weather reports. Often a storm that has little effect on Albuquerque will fill the canyon with high winds, snow, and ice, making travel through the canyon and on I-40 eastward difficult or impossible. As you continue eastward you cannot help but notice the suburban sprawl. The older towns of Tijeras and Moriarty are now joined by newer developments like Edgewood as more and more people are escaping Albuquerque's increased population to build new homes in the eastern foothills and out onto the high plains. Views of the Sangre de Cristo to the north, the Sandias and Manzanos on either side of the highway, and the Estancia Valley to the east explain the movement to this area from the metropolitan scene. Older farms and small settlements maintain the rural nature of the east mountain area.

The town of Moriarty skirts the Interstate. A service area for cross-country travelers and area ranches, Moriarty was named after one of the first Anglo settlers in this part of the Estancia Valley. Some readers of Sherlock Holmes have seized upon the name and made Moriarty the site of an annual, or almost annual, gathering in November to celebrate their antihero, Professor James Moriarty, supposedly born on a Friday the thirteenth. The group calls itself the Brothers Three after Moriarty and his two brothers.

North and south of Moriarty lies the Estancia Valley, called "pinto bean country" when dry farms used to dot the landscape. The drought years of the 1930s and people leaving the valley for war work in factories are the reasons cited for the decline of pinto bean farming. Nonetheless, the pinto bean is still celebrated in local festivals, a reminder of its days of glory, and some farmers still grow beans. Today the valley is worked mostly by

16

farmers and ranchers with large holdings and a variety of crops that depend on irrigation rather than fickle nature to water the land.

From Moriarty on, large signs heralding Clines Corners litter the highway, despite the best intentions of the Highway Beautification Act. Rest areas at exit 208 provide facilities for livestock as well as pets. Clines Corners is the classic interstate rest stop, with a gas station, gift shop filled with collectibles of every description, and a restaurant to serve you. It has serviced travelers almost since old Route 66 was built through this part of the country. Roy Clines bought the property in 1935 and sold gas to the early tourists and people going west. Modern freeway travelers welcome its location when winter storms close down I-40, a not uncommon occurrence on the wide-open road where there are no natural barriers to slow the storms.

At this crossroads of I-40 and U.S. 285, you head southeast to Encino, into what seems to be emptiness, broken only to the southwest by Pedernal Peak, part of the Pedernal (flint) Mountains to the west. This small range—forming part of the southern tip of the Sangre de Cristos and therefore the southernmost part of the Rockies— separates the Estancia Valley to the west from the area drained by the Pecos River. Pedernal Peak rises 7,565 feet from the high plain; it is named for flint deposits found at its base. A spring beneath the peak drains into nearby Pintada Creek, the eastern boundary of Pueblo culture in New Mexico in the 1200s. Past Pedernal, the road stretches out straight ahead of you, and fenced pastures on both sides are a home to sheep and cattle, and the ranchers who tend them. Just outside of Encino, U.S. 285 intersects with U.S. 60.

The tiny village of Encino is shrinking; many of its homes have been boarded up and the motel has been closed. The RV park, however, provides hookups, and a shiny new gas station and general store are there to meet travelers' needs. Take U.S. 60/285 east out of town. The road follows the Santa Fe Railroad tracks to Vaughn. Founded at the busy crossroads of the Southern Pacific and the Belen Cutoff of the Santa Fe Railroad, Vaughn today is also losing population. In its heyday, the railroad employed a large work force, and stores and businesses catered to the sheep and cattle ranchers who chose the fertile plains around Vaughn for raising their animals. That prosperity is evident in the old commercial buildings still standing on streets north of the highway and the People's Store, an old-style general store, and other small businesses that optimistically remain open. Southern Pacific as well as Atchison, Topeka, and Santa Fe freight trains still stop in Vaughn to ship cattle and sheep. Tourist accommodations and several homestyle cafés provide livelihoods for some Vaughn residents. If your children need a break here, visit the park and playground at the western edge of town. The next stop will be Roswell, ninety-five miles down the road.

South of Vaughn, U.S. 25 rolls across high plains. This stretch of blacktop is considered bleak by many people, but it does not have to be. An interested traveler can watch for flora and fauna on the landscape, like the many varieties of desert wildflowers, sometimes almost indistinguishable against the plain, at others a riot of color. The keen-eyed observer, perhaps aided by a handy guidebook, will be able to identify grama grasses, cholla cactus, and other native shrubs. Often, herds of pronghorn antelope graze in the distance. Closer to Roswell, you may spot some prairie chickens. Plan to drive this section before darkness, keeping in mind the thick fog that sometimes comes up in winter and spring and the dangers associated with two-lane driving.

No settlements break the trip between Vaughn and Roswell. Ramon and Mesa are made up of only a few houses each, but they do warrant a mention on most maps. Past Mesa and the intersection with N.M. 20, you enter the wide plain of the Pecos Valley, drained by the Pecos River, west of which there was no justice back in the wild and woolly 1800s. All along the east side of the valley are formations containing "Pecos diamonds," not the Tiffany variety, but crystals of the quartz variety. Rockhounds can look for these crystals in gypsum beds from Dunlap to just south of Artesia. Beyond Mesa, underlying a huge area, is the Artesian Basin, whose wells bring up cold, pure water from the limestone strata just under the topsoil. The water comes from heavy rains and melting snows, together with drainage from the streams emptying into the Pecos River. The porous limestone is honeycombed with channels, which catch the water as it runs down the east side of the Sacramento and other mountains to the valley floor. Water from artesian wells is pumped to the surface, making farming possible on otherwise arid land.

Traveling south on U.S. 285, far to the east you can see the Llano Estacado, which rise sometimes a thousand feet above the plain, paralleling the Pecos River. As the ancient Pecos cut its way through the caprock of the area, it created the irregular bluffs and "breaks" described by early explorers as "estacado" or "staked." To the west the Front Range breaks the sweep of the plain; from many points along the road, weather cooperating, you can see the peaks of the Gallinas, Capitan, Sacramento, and Guadalupe mountains. As you draw closer to Roswell, orchards and fields of cotton, corn, and alfalfa are irrigated by an extensive system of ditches that is fed by the abundant underground water.

Make time for a stop in Roswell. As the site of a major crossroads, this modern and attractive city has no shortage of places to stay and eat. Tour the Chaves County Museum and walk the surrounding historic district, whose gracious old homes were built by the pioneers of Roswell. Browse through the art museum and enjoy the works of Luis Jimenez, Georgia O'Keeffe, Andrew Dasburg, and Peter Hurd, as well as a replica of the workshop of J. R. Goddard, "Father of the Space Age." Drive around old Chihuahuita, one of the earliest settlements in eastern New Mexico, before you have a picnic in the Spring River Park. Northeast of the city is the Bitter Lakes National Wildlife Refuge, winter home to thousands of birds, and to the south is Bottomless Lakes State Park, both of which are popular recreation areas. Tour Seventeen fully describes Roswell and its surroundings.

Past the crenelated buildings of the New Mexico Military Institute, down Main Street, U.S. 285 takes you quickly out of town by way of Southeast Main Street. The old air force base now houses a branch of Eastern New Mexico University, the New Mexico Rehabilitation Center, and several manufacturing plants. Continuing on U.S. 285, it is a fairly direct thirty-nine miles to Artesia, named after the underground water.

Old Dexter Highway, N.M. 2, is a longer, meandering route through Dexter, Hagerman, and Lake Arthur, farming communities for crops like alfalfa, cotton, and chile. The old road parallels the Pecos River, once a watering source for huge herds of cattle driven up the river by cattle barons Charles Goodnight, Oliver Loving, and the "King," John Chisum. The vast cattle ranches that grew up around those trails are smaller now. In Dexter you can picnic at the Lake Vann Park and visit the National Fish Hatchery, where threatened species of desert fish are spawned, reared in ponds, and studied extensively before being introduced to the wild. A diminutive visitor center features some of these fish, from the larger squawfish to the tiny Gila top minnow, and explains how they have come to be endangered.

Along the Pecos River, you will notice the abundant tamarisk that has sprung up and tries to crowd out other, less pesky, plants. Just north of Artesia, on N.M. 2, history buffs may enjoy wandering among the old gravestones at the tiny Seven Rivers Cemetery, now part of Twin Oaks Memorial Park. Look at your map, where the name Seven Rivers appears considerably to the south of Artesia. You may well wonder what the cemetery is doing so far from Seven Rivers. The U.S. Bureau of Reclamation moved the old Boot Hill to its new site before Seven Rivers was flooded with the waters of Brantley Lake. Forty-five deceased inhabitants of Seven Rivers now rest near Twin Oaks, the violent deaths of several of the men hinting at the town's rough past.

Anyone in a hurry may stay on the main highway, U.S. 285, which is the more direct though less interesting route to Artesia. Where not watered for agricultural purposes, the desert stretches unbroken on both sides of the road. This part of the Pecos Valley had no permanent settlement by Spanish colonists, although early Indian groups had lived in the valley from A.D. 1000 to the thirteenth century. By the time the Spanish arrived in the sixteenth century, the area had become part of the Mescalero Apaches' huge hunting ground.

In 1582, Antonio de Espejo's exploration party followed the Pecos River up into the new territory; in 1590 Gaspar Castaño de Sosa and a group of would-be settlers traveled this way in the first wheeled vehicles to come into the new lands. Sr. Castaño de Sosa's group settled briefly farther north, until he was sent back to Mexico in chains for colonizing without the crown's permission.

Not until the middle of the nineteenth century did permanent settlements take root in the valley. John Truitt, a Union soldier, is credited with being the first permanent settler, homesteading at Chisum Springs Camp near what is now Artesia's business district. John Chisum, after driving his cattle along the Chisum Trail, was attracted to the fertility of the Pecos Valley, and his huge ranch extended from Fort Sumner to the Texas border. In the 1890s other homesteaders moved into the area, naming their settlement Miller's Siding after the Pecos Valley Railroad reached the area, and later Stegman. After the fabulous artesian wells were tapped, the little town became Artesia in 1903.

Refinery

Oil was discovered in the huge Abo oil field under Artesia in the spring of 1923; natural gas fields later added to Artesia's prosperity. Businessman Robert O. Anderson came out from Chicago in 1942 and bought a small refinery. Over the years he increased the value of his holdings; he bought, sold, and merged until he created the corporate giant ARCO, the state's largest oil producer and seventh largest extractor of natural gas. Since the 1920s, refineries have been the largest employers in Artesia, and the Navajo refinery dominates the town. Past the refinery, services attendant upon the oil and gas industries line the road, but just off the highway, Artesia has much more to offer.

Turn west off the highway onto Main Street, a wide, Western main drag. Here you can learn a condensed version of the city's history from bright murals along Heritage Walkway, near the corner of Roselawn Avenue. Two blocks south is the public library, and a couple of blocks west on Richardson are the museum and art center. The historic Moore-Ward cobblestone home is a museum, crammed with mementos from Artesia's past, from collections of arrowheads, barbed wire, and Pecos diamonds to photos of early oil gushers and schoolchildren. Upstairs you can view vintage clothes and furniture. The museum guide will be happy to supplement descriptions of the artifacts and memorabilia with an oral history of the area. By the time you leave, you will have a good grasp of how Artesia grew. Next door, the art center shows the works of local painters.

The Abo School on Center Street, described as the first underground school in the free world, reminds you of the time when the threat of atomic warfare led to a boom in bomb shelters. Even though you know the school is underground, the total absence of buildings is startling; the site looks like an ordinary playground. Three entrances lead from a small building on the playground down into the school, which is open to visitors on school days.

Wide streets, tree-lined parks, and sports facilities are evidence that Artesia is preoccupied with more pleasant activities nowadays. The Jaycees Park outside of town is one of the larger parks, with a playground and other facilities for a rest stop. An urban renewal project planted grass and trees in the Eagle Draw (which once drew water and often flooded) to make a parkway with playgrounds and lots of space to run and walk. Although declining fortunes in the oil and gas industries, as well as depressed farm prices, often bring hardship to Artesia, it is an optimistic little city and has recently attracted new employers like the Veterans Administration, whose satellite clinic will serve southeastern New Mexico, and the Federal Law Enforcement Training Center, housed in the old Christian College.

South of Artesia the highway continues its hypnotic route to Carlsbad, with abandoned farming equipment and skipjacks pumping oil silhouetted against the sky. The Atchison, Topeka, and Santa Fe railroad tracks that have been paralleling the highway cut farther east here. From the turnoff to Lakewood, the highway continues to approximate the route of the Pecos River as it meanders through the valley to Carlsbad.

Twelve miles north of Carlsbad the new Brantley

Dam State Park offers picnic spots for the day tripper, spaces for overnight camping, facilities for people with disabilities, and a visitor center. The first turnoff to Brantley leads to the day area, where you can launch your sailboat and have a picnic. To get to the buildings on the other side of the lake, go back to the highway and take the second entrance, which takes you along a rough road past the new dam to the visitor center and camping areas. You can launch boats here, too. Because Brantley was built for irrigation purposes, its water level will vary depending on the time of year, but there is enough water for boaters, swimmers, and fishermen. Like other manmade lakes in New Mexico, Brantley has no trees or vegetation for shelter from the sun. The Carlsbad Reclamation Project, an intricate system of dams, canals, and ditches, carries water from Brantley Lake and Lake Avalon south throughout the valley, allowing farmers to plant miles of cotton, alfalfa, and other crops.

Just opposite the lower entrance to Brantley is the turnoff to Sitting Bull Falls, a popular site open from April to November. The paved road to the falls, N.M. 137, winds through Rocky Arroyo, leaving behind the desert as it cuts through a canyon and climbs along the hillside. Turn off at Forest Road 276. About eight miles on, you arrive at the parking area for Sitting Bull Falls. Sheltered tables with grills are convenient eating spots, but for a more scenic picnic, pack in your food over the short trail to the falls. Along the way, vegetation changes from cactus to lush trees and plants nourished by the stream. Interpretive signs explain the micro environment and the process that forms caves within the Guadalupe Mountains. What they do not explain is the origin of the name of the falls. (Contrary to legend, Sitting Bull did not refresh himself here, nor do the cliffs resemble his profile.) Relax by the emerald-green pools or cool off in them before hiking up to the source of the falls along a steep but well-maintained trail that leads out of the parking area.

Back at the junction with N.M. 137, a right turn will take you on a short detour to the Queen ruins, a somewhat grandiose name for the chimney stack that marks the remains of the little town of Queen. The name comes from the Queen brothers, who supplied the town's first owner with water. A new grocery and coffee shop sells food, gas, and other supplies and provides RV hookups. New Mexico 137 continues for thirty-five miles through lovely country, most of the way on a paved road, to Dog Canyon, where a National Park Service campground offers tent sites and RV spaces but no hookups.

Backtrack toward Highway 285. A few miles down the road you can take a shortcut to Carlsbad Caverns, leaving a visit to the town of Carlsbad for later. Look for a sign indicating the Dark Canyon turnoff. Although some maps do not even show this route (and others mark it as a gravel road), this is a good, twenty-two-mile paved road through isolated ranching country. Watch for groups of slow-moving cattle and the occasional flock of sheep crossing the road; you will meet little vehicular traffic. As the road dips through arroyos, signs warn that water may accumulate after a rain. Closer to Whites City (you cannot miss it because rows of signs proclaim its proximity) you can see the headlands of the Guadalupe Mountains, which end abruptly in Texas. At the junction of U.S. 285, you are only a few miles from Whites City, where you can camp at a KOA or stay at a motel. You can also head straight for the caverns on N.M. 7.

This road winds up the ancient Capitan Reef with several pull-offs for enjoying the vistas, descriptive markers, and short nature trails. Look for deer among the spiky yucca and ocotillo; prickly pear, *pitaya,* and strawberry cactus also hug the limestone palisade. During the Permian age, 250 million years ago, this area was covered by a shallow sea, a perfect environment for lime-secreting algae. The remains of generations of algae built up to form a lime reef more than a mile across and hundreds of feet thick.

At the top of the limestone reef, the visitor center orients you to the cavern tours. There are a couple of ways to see the caverns. The long tour takes about three hours; you enter the caverns through the natural entrance on foot and descend 830 feet—eighty-three stories—and then climb eighty more feet before reaching the underground lunchroom. Or you can take the elevator 750 feet down to the Big Room; from here the tour takes one and a half hours. Everyone returns to the

surface by elevator. People in wheelchairs or families with strollers can take the elevator and traverse a portion of the Big Room. Wear warm clothes (the temperature is a damp and constant 56°) and good walking shoes. If you brought along the family pet, you may drop it off in the kennel, and you may leave younger children in the nursery.

Be sure to pick up a guidebook or pamphlet describing the caverns and read the remarkable story of their formation before you start your tour. Remember the drive up to the caverns through the remains of an ancient reef that existed in the inland sea once covering the region. Changes in the climate caused the sea to evaporate, and the reef became covered with sediment. Natural erosion and uplift in the area uncovered the buried reef. Cracks in the reef were widened, as rainwater seeped down over eons and dissolved the limestone. Some geologists believe that the rainwater mixed with salty water deep in the cracks and formed sulfuric acid, which acted even more quickly on the limestone to form the huge passageways of the caverns.

Early Indians probably knew of the cave's existence, judging from drawings left behind. In the 1800s, settlers in the area discovered the riches of bat guano in the entrance of the cave, and mined it as fertilizer. In 1901, one of the "miners," Jim White, began exploring deeper inside the cave. His explorations revealed a fantastic world, which he described to anyone who would listen. People dismissed his stories as fanciful until a photographer, Ray Davis, verified them with his black-and-white photos. Later exploration by government officials convinced the Department of the Interior to declare the caverns a national monument in 1923 and led to President Hoover's designation of the area as a national park in 1930.

Visitors today can trace Jim White's trail through the cave mouth down past smaller "rooms" to the Big Room, an enormous opening whose wondrous rock formations are highlighted by artificial lights. Traces of iron and other mineral matter in the limestone have produced colorful tinting in the stalagmites and stalactites. Constant saturation with water causes the brilliant and translucent appearance of still-growing formations; the dull and dry stones are regarded as "dead." Over the years, park officials have labeled the limestone formations; visitors file past the King's Palace with its "throne" and other royal accoutrements, gaze at the Temple of the Sun with its delicate ceiling of stalactites and pagodalike rocks, and feel appropriate reverence for the monolithic Rock of Ages. The trail down to and including the Big Room is the only section of the cave open to tourists, although experienced cavers continue to discover spectacular new rooms.

While visiting the Caverns, you can take the Walnut Canyon Desert Drive, a 9.5-mile loop tour through the Chihuahua Desert that surrounds the cave. Pick up a guidebook at the visitor center before taking the self-guided tour along the Guadalupe Ridge and then down into Upper Walnut Canyon and back to the cavern. Billed as a scenic tour, the drive (posted for fifteen mph) will probably only interest those of you particularly desirous of learning the geology and ecology of the desert. A short nature walk near the cave entrance might be better for youngsters—and some oldsters. A trail to Rattlesnake Canyon is accessible to hikers about halfway through the loop drive.

There are thirty-nine other caves in the park. You can visit these undeveloped caves with permission of the superintendent of the park, and take overnight hiking trips with special permits available at the visitor center. Some caves are only open to experienced cavers. Lechuguilla Cave received unwelcome publicity when a caver broke a leg while exploring it and had to be rescued in a tricky operation. More than fifty miles of trails lead to the backcountry of the park, providing glimpses of the desert, canyons, and mountains that relatively few visitors get to see.

At the end of the day, May through October, you can watch hundreds of thousands of bats spiral out of the cave for their nightly hunt for insects. During the winter months the bats migrate to Mexico. Park naturalists give talks on the bats and their habits before the nightly bat flight. They will tell you, for example, that five species of bat live in the cave, but the most numerous is the Mexican freetail. You will be sobered to learn that thousands of bats die after ingesting pesticides. Once a year, the Bat Flight Breakfast provides a different experience, permitting a viewing of the return of the bats before dawn as they swoop back into the cave looking for sleeping space. The breakfast is a special occasion, hosted each August by the Employees' Association of Carlsbad Caverns. Be warned, however, that on at least one occasion the bats have been known to show up earlier than planned and early risers have been disappointed. Over the years that the bats inhabited the cave, before Jim White espied them, their droppings, or guano, grew to be many feet thick. Guano makes a rich fertilizer, and the Carlsbad Bat Guano Company for years sent fertilizer to California for use on fruit groves.

You can re-create Jim White's experience with a visit to Slaughter Canyon Cave, sixteen miles from Whites City via U.S. 62/180 and County Road 418. Slaughter Canyon Cave is actually millions of years old, but it was called "New" to differentiate it from the cave found by Jim White. In 1937 Tom Tucker's goats wandered into a cave, and Tucker followed them. Realizing the worth of the bat guano that lined the cave, Tucker filed a mineral claim so that he could mine the guano. Tucker and his partners stayed in business for twenty years, until chemical fertilizers replaced the natural stuff. The Park Service opened up Slaughter Canyon Cave to visitors in 1973 but left it fairly undeveloped. The entrance is reached after a half-mile steep hike up the mountain; again, good walking shoes or hiking boots are a must, and you must bring your own flashlight and water to take the 1.25-mile walk through the cave. (Plan on up to two and a half hours for the tour, including forty-five minutes for the strenuous hike from the parking lot up to the cave entrance.)

A ranger leads you through the darkened cave. The formations are unlit—you view them much as the early explorers did. Advance reservations are required, and the number of visitors to this site is restricted. Tours are only offered on weekends from September through May, daily during the summer months. Along the road up to Slaughter Canyon Cave you can stop and picnic at beautiful Rattlesnake Springs, an ancient water source for Indians, American soldiers, and pioneers. The spring is still a primary source of water for the caverns. An entirely new area opens up even farther south in the Guadalupe Mountains National Park, covered in detail in Tour Eighteen.

Continue up to Carlsbad on National Parks Highway or U.S. 62/180, and acquaint yourself with the town on the Discover Carlsbad Driving Tour. The Chamber of Commerce at Canal and Greene streets provides detailed maps, and bright blue signs will be your guideposts. The tour begins at the Bataan Bridge and continues north along the river. As the Pecos River flows through Carlsbad, it becomes Lake Carlsbad, sectioned off for speedboats, swimmers, and fishermen. All along its banks, Riverfront Park is a fine place for picnics or strolling among the tall shade trees. In June, the beach area hosts the Art Affair and makes a big splash on July 4 with entertainment, a boat parade, and a huge fireworks display. Across the river, President's Park provides a harbor for a paddleboat and a pontoon boat that ply the river in the summer months. An old carousel, bumper cars, and the Abe Lincoln train also attract summer visitors.

The Discover Carlsbad tour next takes you to the Pecos Flume, not an amusement park ride but a picturesque old aqueduct, part of a system that carries water from the Pecos River throughout the river valley. The spring that prompted the town of Eddy to change its name to Carlsbad (after the famous European health resort) bubbles just south of the flume. Continue the tour on Skyline Drive through the Ocotillo Hills. Down below, fields of alfalfa, which is Carlsbad's main cash crop, show up bright green in the summer. Carlsbad celebrates Alfalfafest in October with the world's biggest hayride and the Farm Olympics.

Living Desert State Park, a zoo and botanical garden off Skyline Drive, re-creates in a small space the Chihuahua Desert with its wonderful variety of plant and animal life. The visitor center introduces you to the area with exhibits on animal life, minerals, insects, archaeology, and history. The park displays more than a hundred species of desert birds, beasts, and plants in a natural setting of dry gypsum hills,

Prairie Dog

arroyos, and sand dunes. It will take you about an hour and a half to wander through the park on a paved trail, easily maneuvered by wheelchairs, checking out the javelina, a special exhibit for nocturnal creatures, and the lobo. At the end of the trail a huge greenhouse is filled with desert and tropical cactus and succulents. A special activity in the park during the full moon in May recreates a mescal roast; members of the Mescalero Apache tribe demonstrate how their ancestors roasted the heart of the agave and sotol plants and explain the ceremonial aspects of the ritual.

Returning to downtown Carlsbad, you can take a shortcut via Church Street, park your car near Mermod Street, and walk through the historic section, part of the National Main Street program. You will pass City Hall, designed by New Mexico architect John Gaw Meem, and across the street, the public library, museum, and art center. The imposing county courthouse sits back on a lawn at the corner of Canal and Mermod streets. Look for the cattle brands carved into the wood at the west entrance; ranching has been important to the area

since cattlemen Goodnight and Loving drove their cattle through here during the 1860s. Western Days every July celebrate ranching with a rodeo, barbecues, a chile cookoff, street dances, and fiddle contests.

The Waste Isolation Pilot Plant Visitor Center on Greene Street is an attraction of a different sort. The Waste Isolation Pilot Plant is the controversial site for the storage of nuclear waste in underground salt beds. Tourists may not visit the site itself, located 2,150 feet under the earth off N.M. 128, but the center has tried to re-create the salt tunnels, providing information on the facility.

Leaving Carlsbad, you return to Artesia, where U.S. 82 heads west to Cloudcroft, through open range country covered with coarse grass and occasional cactus. As the road begins to climb through the foothills of the Sacramento Mountains, Lombardy poplars, cottonwoods, and orchards signal that you are leaving the high desert and entering the mountains. You pass through the tiny outposts of Hope, Lower Peñasco, and Elk before reaching the top of the mountain at Cloudcroft.

Minutes from Cloudcroft, off U.S. 82, Ski Cloudcroft has an average annual snowfall of eighty-nine inches and maintains runs for beginning and intermediate skiers. The area draws a number of visitors, who not only take advantage of the downhill skiing but enjoy cross-country skiing, snowmobiling, and inner-tubing.

Cloudcroft (elevation 8,864 feet) is aptly named, because at this altitude clouds sometimes sweep through the town, obscuring landmarks and the views of the Tularosa basin below. The little town began when the El Paso and Northeastern Railroad built a steep narrow-gauge line up the side of the mountain to reach the timber it needed to make railroad ties. Taking advantage of an ideal vacation spot, the railroad also constructed a lodge in 1899 as a summer resort. A vacation village grew up around it. The lodge provided a focus for the town, which has continued to attract tourists escaping the heat of the summer and looking for sports areas in the winter.

Cloudcroft's main street, Burro Avenue, may be short, but it has all the amenities for a traveler: gas, food, and lodging; old-fashioned shops; and the Sacramento Mountains Historical Museum. The little museum is packed with photographs and antiques from an earlier time. Off the main street is the rustic Cloudcroft Inn. Perched even higher, at 9,200 feet, is the Lodge. The original building burned in a huge blaze in 1909, but its owners rebuilt it in the Bavarian style typical of many mountain retreats. Besides offering spectacular views—clouds permitting— and meticulously maintained Victorian rooms with a resident ghost, the Lodge owns a nine-hole golf course, the highest and the second oldest in the United States. In winter you can cross-country ski on the fairways. The wooden cabins along the way up to the lodge date from the turn of the century.

Several festivals draw large crowds: the Mayfest over Memorial Day weekend, with hayrides and an arts and crafts show; the July Jamboree featuring Western gunfighters and old-fashioned entertainment; and the Aspencade, on the first weekend in October. Thousands jam the small community for the latter festival, which offers a fair, country-western dancing, and a motorcycle race, in addition to the natural attraction of the turning of the aspen trees. Other monthly festivals are also popular: the Western Roundup in June, spiritual singing in August, and Railroad Days in September. Cloudcroft's picture-book scenery encourages an elaborate Christmas celebration with old-fashioned caroling and a live Nativity scene, a snow queen, and an ice-sculpture contest. Residents and visitors alike enjoy the pleasures of a natural skating rink in the winter and miles of hiking trails and campgrounds in the summer.

Two miles south of Cloudcroft on N.M. 130 you can take a side trip (about seventeen miles each way) via N.M. 6563 (the number refers to the wavelength of the red spectral line of hydrogen) to Sunspot, home of a solar observatory. Through the world's largest coronagraph and under some of the world's clearest skies, astronomers study the sun's corona, its gaseous outer envelope, and sunspots. The observatory welcomes visitors and allows you to take self-guided tours. For information on the guided tours, held Saturday afternoons, May through October, contact the observatory before you get there. The views from the observatory of the Tularosa and Hueco basins are spectacular. On the way back to the highway from Sunspot, you will pass campgrounds, the remains of a logging railway, Nelson Canyon Vista Trail (with an unobstructed view of the Tularosa Basin and White Sands), and closer to Cloudcroft, a sign to La Pasada Encantada, a trail for the visually impaired, where markers are in Braille as well as print.

From Cloudcroft, the trip follows a remarkable stretch of road that drops sharply down into Alamogordo. Highway 82 here approximates the route of the cog railway from the logging camps of Russia Canyon to Alamogordo. On your way out of Cloudcroft, be looking for remains of the old railroad trestle on your left. As you maneuver the paved road down the mountainside, you can imagine the twists and turns the track had to make The drop in altitude is so abrupt that the route takes in several vegetative zones of North America, from the Hudson Bay Zone in the high Sacramentos to the lower Sonoran Zone in the Tularosa basin. The Canadian Zone covers only 2 percent of the state; the Cloudcroft area takes up a lot of it. Soon you are into High Rolls and Mountain Park country, where the cool temperatures encourage orchards that grow peaches, pears, apples, and cherries and provide a livelihood for the area's growers. Nearby Fresnal Creek gave High Rolls its name, referring to the rapids on the creek.

October is a good time to tour this region, for then you can enjoy the bounty of the area while experiencing the beauty of the aspens. Many growers sell their produce—jams, honey, berries, fruits, and pumpkins—at roadside stands. The twin communities sponsor an apple festival in October. Past High Rolls, turn on your headlights before entering the highway tunnel. The view from the rest stop is breathtaking—White Sands and the Tularosa Basin stretching to the far western mountains. At this point, you leave the green zones behind. The rest of the highway twists down through rugged mountains, where hardy junipers, piñons, pine trees, and gambel oaks cling to the hillsides. As you approach the plain, you will notice a definite Lower Sonoran desert influence: mesquite, creosote, and cacti including the prickly pear, stick, and elk horn, and a variety of grasses that manage to survive the punishing heat.

Alamogordo is described in Tour Eighteen. Now follow U.S. 82 to its intersection with U.S. 70. Turn left, following the signs to White Sands National Monument, about fifteen miles west of Alamogordo. You cannot avoid the presence of huge Holloman Air Force Base on the way to the monument; jets practice dips and rolls in the sky, and acres of base housing spread out across the desert. Other obtrusive signs of modern civilization line the sides of the highway. You may wish that you were approaching White Sands a hundred years earlier, before signs and billboards diverted your attention.

The visitor center, an attractive adobe building, sits right at the edge of the sands. Turn off here, and check out the exhibits on the history and geology of the area. Rangers schedule different interpretive events throughout the year: daily patio talks at the center, evening strolls on the sands, and slide shows in the picnic area. On full-moon nights during the summer, rangers offer special programs, and once a month you can take a half-day guided tour to Lake Lucero (the source of the white sand). You can also take your own loop drive through the monument, sixteen miles round-trip.

White Sands National Monument was established in 1933. Resulting from eons of erosion of the gypsum rock peculiar to the area, the monument takes up nearly 230 square miles of pure white sand dunes. It is one of New Mexico's most impressive sights. As you begin the drive into the dunes, you notice only glimmers of white sand among the fourwing saltbush that flourishes on the low dunes lining the road. Soon the scrub lessens and the dunes get higher. Now you begin to understand why White Sands is a national monument. About three miles in, there is parking at the trailhead for the Big Dune Trail. The trail skirts the edge of the dunes and then leads you up to the top of one of the highest dunes. Stretching out around you are waves of brilliant white sand.

WHITE SANDS

The sands are part of the Tularosa Basin, which was created millions of years ago by massive shifts in the earth's crust. As the basin sank, it left the San Andres Mountains to the west and the Sierra Blanca to the east. Both ranges contain layers of gypsum rock. Over the years, rain and melting snow have worked away at the gypsum deposits, carrying them down to Lake Lucero at the lowest part of the basin. As the hot sun evaporates the water, gypsum crystals collect on the dry lake bed. The wind then does its work on the crystals, which disintegrate into fine white sand and pile up as dunes. The dunes actually move away from the lake and the alkali flats toward the north, some as much as twenty feet a year, and new ones take their place.

As you continue your drive, look for marked guideposts. For example, post 6 points out gypsum pedestals, formed as the plant roots bond grains of sand together, which then are left behind as the sand dune moves on. At post 8 you enter the heart of the dunes. You may park only at designated spots, but take advantage of these, and climb the dunes to look out on a vast, white sea. Kids especially, but grownups too, will be tempted to slide on these waves of sand.

Somewhere out there, just outside the north-western corner of the monument, is the White Sands Space Harbor, an alternate site for space shuttle landings. The harbor is actually Northrup Strip, located on Alkali Flat, whose baked, hard sand makes a natural runway. Unfortunately, it can be treacherous when winds kick up a sandstorm like the one that once delayed a shuttle landing for a day. The area has been used for military training and weapons testing for forty years. In the 1960s, NASA was allowed about ninety-four square miles for its experiments and tests, including shuttle landings. Back in March 1982, it was raining at the principal landing site at Edwards Air Force Base in California where the shuttle *Columbia* was sched-uled to land. Rerouted to Northrup, the shuttle was further delayed by a fierce sandstorm. In honor of that landing, the strip was renamed White Sands Space Harbor, a far more romantic title. No other shuttles have used the harbor since.

Camping is not permitted on the sands except at a primitive campsite for backpackers one-third of a mile off the road. Because the White Sands Missile Range borders on the monument, you may find this campsite temporarily closed. Check at the visitor center for information on closings. You can always enjoy a picnic on the sands, either at the picnic areas set up at the end of the drive, or near one of the designated parking areas out on the dunes for a hotter, sandier lunch. During the summer months, when the monument is open late on moonlit nights, a picnic on the sands is an occasion to remember. White Sands is open all year except Christmas Day.

When you leave White Sands, the tour is almost over. Driving straight to Albuquerque would take about four hours nonstop. Depending on your timing, you may want to spend the night at one of Alamogordo's motels or camp at Oliver Lee State Park or Three Rivers (see Tour Eighteen). However, you should plan on making at least one more sightseeing stop at the Valley of the Fires State Park, where camping is available in the park and nearby Carrizozo provides motel rooms. Returning to U.S. 54 you will drive north through Alamogordo and Tularosa, past the Three Rivers turnoff and tiny Oscuro (indeed *oscuro,* or obscure) into Carrizozo.

16

Five miles west, the sign to Valley of Fires State Park invites you to leave the road and explore the malpais, easily accessible here. Valley of Fires Park provides a unique opportunity to learn some geology while stretching your legs after the ride from White Sands. The huge lava beds, contrasting with the brilliant white sands you just left, stretch from Three Rivers north across U.S. 380, but for most of the way the lava is too far from the road to be visible. Highway 380 runs right through the lava bed, however; the road was built in the 1930s to replace an old wagon road that led travelers across the sharp lava rock.

An Indian legend describes the site as an ancient valley of fire spewed from a volcano west of Carrizozo. The modern park takes its name from the old story. As you enter the park, the malpais nature walk wanders off on the right. The trail is rough, but an intrepid person in a sturdy wheelchair will be able to maneuver it. Pick up a pamphlet to help answer questions about plant and animal life and the violent processes that formed rugged malpais.

The Carrizozo Lava Flow is thought to be the youngest lava flow in the lower forty-eight states, scorching through the area only 1,500 years ago, leaving behind an inhospitable land. Prospectors hoping to find valuable minerals here were disappointed, but the desolate area is home to a variety of wildlife. Biologists have found deer, badgers, coyotes, and rattlesnakes. Even tiny fish, descended from those that swam in ancient oceans, inhabit the pools at the lower end of the lava flow. You will probably only see lizards as you make your way through the lava beds. But prickly pear, cholla, sotol, and saltbrush seem to flourish here and even provide color in late spring when the cactus are in bloom.

The park provides campsites, barely noticeable against the black rock and scrub, and spots for daytrippers to picnic under cover. A group shelter is also available. Restrooms, a dump site and electric hookup for RVs, and a playground for children make a stay in this "bad country" a little more comfortable. However, apart from the picnic shelters, there is no shade.

Past Valley of the Fires, the highway takes you on

a lonely route across the upper Tularosa Valley and the forbidding Jornada del Muerto to I-25. At night this part of the route can be frightening. In the daytime, it is easier to navigate the narrow, twisting road. There are many roadside stops along the way, offering barely more than a table and garbage can. Colorful wildflowers on the side of the road, an old windmill and a corral, and the blue mountains stretched out in the distance break up the dry landscape. A steep drop out of the Oscura Mountains takes you down into ranching country, where cattle drowse around water holes.

To the south, the land is restricted to visitors. This is the White Sands Missile Range, confiscated by the army in 1944 for testing the atom bomb. About one hundred ranchers, some of whom still fight the government for the right to return, were evicted from their land. In 1982, Dave McDonald, eighty-one, and his niece, defied the army, moved back onto McDonald's ranch, and erected a fence around the homestead. The army won that confrontation, and the McDonalds moved out peacefully, never having used the rifles with which they were armed. At Bingham, a rough road leads to Claunch and Gran Quivira. About fifteen miles south and a little west of Bingham, Trinity Site still fascinates tourists. Here, on July 16, 1945, scientists from Los Alamos tested the first atomic bomb in an awesome explosion that lit up the early morning sky as far away as Albuquerque. Three weeks later, two bombs were dropped on Japan. Trinity does not look impressive today; the only remains of the tower in which the bomb was suspended is a bit of concrete. Nevertheless, twice a year the site is opened to visitors, who must be escorted in a caravan from an entrance in Alamogordo or from the Stallion Gate entrance off U.S. 380. A road sign here points to the White Sands Missile Range and the Stallion Range Center Installation, whose white buildings can be seen from the road.

Soon after passing Stallion Gate, you approach the outskirts of San Antonio. Just before the bridge over the Rio Grande, look very carefully for a primitive road leading seventeen miles south to Val Verde, the scene of one of New Mexico's Civil War battles. Because little remains of the battlefield, only die-hard Civil War buffs will want to make a detour here. The rest of us may be content to know that the battle, won by the Confederates, occurred in 1862.

San Antonio is the gateway to the Bosque del Apache National Wildlife Refuge and home of the Owl Bar and Cafe and the birthplace of Conrad Hilton (see Tour Fourteen). From here I-25 parallels the Rio Grande to Albuquerque. To the east the Manzanos limit the valley, whose farms and small ranches are watered by the river. The Sevilleta National Wildlife Refuge and the La Joya State Game Refuge, south of Bernardo, provide safe places for animals and birds. The names of the refuges are taken from the old town of Sevilleta, an important settlement of the Piro Indians, who built pueblos in the area. The town was abandoned in 1680 and recolonized in 1800. Later the name was changed to La Joya (jewel) de Sevilleta, and then simply La Joya.

Soon highway signs indicate that Albuquerque and the end of the tour are near. Your heads are full of the contrasting images of this trip, of long drives across plains and over mountains, into caverns and to an observatory, to shining white sands and black lava beds, to an amusement park and a living museum.

TOUR SEVENTEEN
THE CAPITAN MOUNTAINS

Places: Roswell, Hondo, Ruidoso, Mescalero, Tularosa, Carrizozo, Lincoln, Hondo, Roswell

Mileage: Approximately 240 miles, excluding side trips

Suggested travel time: One or two days

Highways: U.S. 70/380, U.S. 70, N.M. 48, U.S. 54, U.S. 380, N.M. 409

Accommodations: Ruidoso, Mescalero, Tularosa, Carrizozo, Capitan, Lincoln, and Roswell

Camping: Ruidoso, Three Rivers, Capitan, and Lincoln

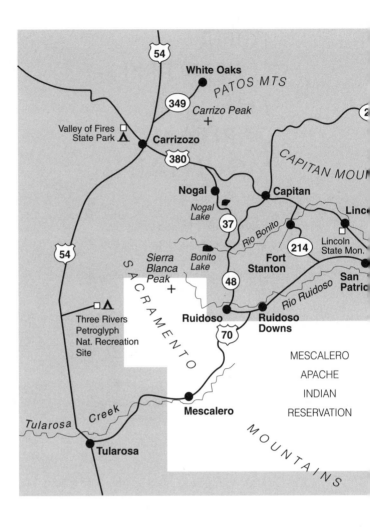

El Capitan dominates Roswell's western horizon. Tour Seventeen explores the environs of this majestic mountain—its slopes and parks, the plains that surround it, and the rivers, villages, and recreation sites it shares with Sierra Blanca, its mountain neighbor to the southwest. The tour will also extend you a cordial invitation to explore Roswell and experience the historic districts, the museums, and the parks of southeastern New Mexico's principal city.

For the first fifty miles west from Roswell you will follow U.S. 70/380 and the Rio Hondo up toward its source high in the mountains. Most of the land on this tour is ranch country, flat or broken, open or wooded. Innovative ranchers throughout the region are now using sheep, cattle, and goats to

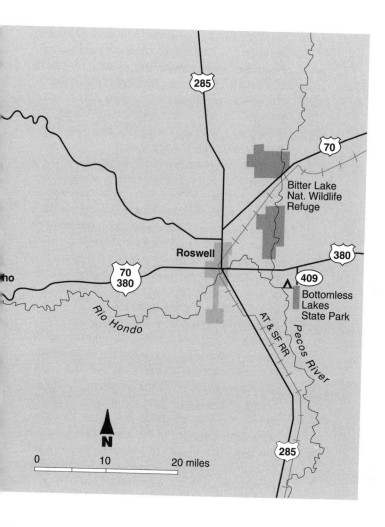

heal erosion, to reestablish native perennial grasses,
and to return the vigorous and healthy grasslands,
woodlands, and watersheds that attracted settlers
to the area in the 1860s. This reclamation is
accomplished by imitating the habits of the wild
grazers—elk, bison, and pronghorn antelope—that
once roamed the region in great herds. Elk and
antelope have survived and are making a come-
back. Especially in open country, keep a lookout for
the white rumps of the pronghorns—delicate,
tough, and exquisitely adapted to their home on
the shortgrass plains.

You will explore three of southeastern New
Mexico's largest counties, Chaves, Lincoln, and
Otero, at one time in the Territorial period a single,
colossal county whose only post office was Fort

Stanton. About twenty-five miles west of Roswell, we enter Lincoln County, named for the slain president, but known far and wide for the trouble that erupted here in the late 1870s called the Lincoln County War. The tour visits all the important sites of this conflict and its best-known protagonist, Michael Henry McCarty, alias William Bonney, alias Billy the Kid.

Thirty-five miles west of Roswell, you will begin to see some of the first indications of the settlements that have existed in this valley for nearly a century and a half. The road soon begins a sharp ascent up Picacho Hill, whose steep grades once challenged drivers on the Butterfield Stage mail route. After offering a view of the canyon to the south from near the summit, the highway makes a long, curving descent to join the cottonwoods and irrigated farms of the Hondo Valley.

Hispanic settlers from the Rio Grande, hoping to avoid the big river's floods, arrived in the Hondo Valley around 1865 and began the combination of fruit and vegetable growing and livestock grazing still popular in these sheltered valleys. By 1875, Charles Goodnight, John Chisum, and other Anglo newcomers from the Texas plains had added large-scale cattle ranching to the life of the region. On this tour, in fact, you are following the celebrated Chisum Trail between Roswell and Tularosa. Here in Picacho, you can try to imagine the adobe building that once housed a store, a post office, a Butterfield Stage stop, and a hotel for travelers between Roswell and Lincoln Courthouse.

The main attraction of Tinnie, five miles farther west, is a landmark that has survived to the present, the old Tinnie Mercantile Company. Dating back to the 1870s, when it began as a store and post office, the building has a complex past. One of its owners enlarged the store and named it, and the town, after his daughter Tinnie. Robert O. Anderson of Roswell bought the old Mercantile Company in 1959 and immediately began a careful renovation of the old building. He added the porch, the tower, and the pavilion, and opened the Silver Dollar Bar and Steak House, which has served guests ever since.

Today you can dine in the restaurant, enjoy views of the valley from the pavilion, visit with the friendly and informative staff, and study old photographs that show past and present uses of this remarkable structure. The old bar has been restored, the stables were converted into a lovely gift shop, and the original store survives as a special banquet room. John Meigs, the artist from San Patricio who planned the additions, gathered the old artifacts you have probably been admiring, including furniture, artwork, ornate doors, and stained-glass windows believed to have come from a Frank Lloyd Wright house.

Hondo sits at the confluence of two rivers. The highways divide here, U.S. 70 following the Rio Ruidoso (noisy river), while U.S. 380 branches off along the Rio Bonito (pretty river) toward Lincoln and Capitan. It is a difficult decision: which river to choose. This tour follows the Ruidoso upriver toward the southwest, and later returns down the Bonito from the northwest. Roadside stands will tempt you all along both valleys—cherries, peaches, and cherry cider in the summer; apples, melons, cider, and pumpkins in the fall. Enterprises associated with fruit and vegetable growing—packing sheds, a refrigeration service, and a trucking company—are now the mainstay of Hondo's economy. There is a picture-book horse ranch just west of town.

The next little town offers one of the best chances to get a feel for the beauty and tranquillity of the Hondo Valley. The Irish priest who built the church here named it for his patron, Saint Patrick, and the villagers decided upon San Patricio for the name of their town. One of its first postmasters was William Brady, grandson of Sheriff Brady who was killed in the Lincoln County War. The town thrived in the early years of the twentieth century, and welcomed such newcomers as the Hurd family, who migrated here from Boston for health reasons. San Patricio shrank during and after World War II and then found itself left below the new highway, rerouted to higher ground in the 1950s. Three old white buildings—the school (now a community center), the church, and the post office—greet you when you loop off onto the old main street. Turn toward the river to see the fields, modest old houses, and the magnificent cottonwoods that enchant visitors today as they must have a century ago.

Since its beginnings, San Patricio has attracted well-known people. Former residents include Billy the Kid, actress Helen Hayes, author Paul Horgan, and artist Henriette Wyeth. It is home today of artist Peter Hurd's studio, La Rinconada, of "Fort Meigs" (John Meigs's gallery), of sculptor Luis Jimenez's spread (near Hondo) as well as of southeastern New Mexico's only polo grounds. Visitors confused by such incongruities soon catch on to San Patricio's good-natured mimicry of the pretentiousness of artist colonies elsewhere. You are welcome here. The galleries display fine artwork to the public.

Members of the Coe clan, one of the early pioneering families in Lincoln County, homesteaded Glencoe in 1880. The original place is now the Bonnell Ranch. From A.D. 900 to 1200, pit-house villages of the archaeological "Glencoe Phase" occupied this area. Glencoe's town center has moved several times, owing to flooding of the Ruidoso and to changes in the routing of U.S. 70.

A site just a few miles upriver shares some of the antiquity of Glencoe but also has a thoroughly contemporary ring. The famous racetrack Ruidoso Downs first called itself Palo Verde and later that name's translation, Green Tree. Hale Spring, at the base of the mountain just to the south, was the reason for Palo Verde's existence and, centuries before, for a settlement of prehistoric people.

By the 1930s, there were gardens, orchards, two water-driven sawmills, and a population of five hundred people nestled here against the mountainside. Across the road, meanwhile, the Ruidoso Downs Race Track grew from hosting contests between friends and visitors into a nationally known track that features the All-American Quarter Horse Futurity, richest horse race in the country.

Racing season runs from early May to the famous Futurity on Labor Day, with races Thursdays through Sundays. You can tour the track and the stables and observe practice sessions all summer long. The three-day All-American Quarter Horse Yearling Sale attracts thousands of prospective buyers and curious visitors at the end of each season.

To visit Ruidoso (the recreation mecca for southeastern New Mexico and West Texas), turn off on N.M. 37 two miles west of the racetrack. The town is named Ruidoso (noisy) after the stream running through town, not for the flow of tourist traffic. The river powered a mill, now south of the highway, which inspired the town's first name, Dowlin's Mill, in 1882. Present buildings consist primarily of vacation homes and a myriad of recreation facilities. The twenty-four-hour Chamber of Commerce information center tells of the golf courses, both in town and nearby; of opportunities to swim, skate, eat, and play tennis; of art fairs and plays; and of movies at the architecturally incongruous "castle." Several parks and a library round out the recreational opportunities in town. Immediately beyond its boundaries, you can enjoy the town's spectacular setting while picnicking, hiking, skiing, riding, or fishing.

If you are heading for Ski Apache or Bonito Lake, turn north on Mechem Drive (N.M. 48). A twenty-mile drive high up the slopes of Sierra Blanca brings you to Ski Apache, run by the Mescalero people and open to the public for skiing November through March. Farther north, the beautiful waters of Bonito Lake attract trout fishers from far and wide and cover the 1880s silver mining town of old Bonito. Those people wishing an abbreviated tour of the area can turn northeast on N.M. 48, rejoin the main tour at Capitan, and return to Roswell via U.S. 380.

To continue on the main tour, follow N.M. 48 back east through Ruidoso. Turn right at the Y on Junction Road a short distance to U.S. 70. Immediately southwest of Ruidoso, the tour enters the Mescalero Apache Reservation and soon leaves tributaries of the Ruidoso and begins to follow the Rio Tularosa down toward the town of Tularosa, thirty miles to the southwest. The Mescalero Reservation was established in 1872 and eventually comprised 460,177 acres between the Sacramento and the White mountains. With timbered slopes, rich pastures, and two thousand acres of cropland, the Mescalero Reservation ranks among the best-endowed in the nation. The Mescaleros manage hunting and fishing preserves and the ski area, and also operate a luxury resort, the Inn of the Mountain Gods.

The Mescalero Apache were not always so well-off, however. They once ranged over the vast region between the present-day Texas Panhandle and Chihuahua, living in the mountains during the summers and wintering on the plains. Their name comes from the mescal, an agave or "century" plant they prepared as a staple food. This is the way they did it. In late spring small bands of the tribe would find several dozen of the large plants and chop off and discard the larger leaves and the roots. They threw the bulbs into a heated, rock-bottomed pit, covered them with grass, dirt, and rocks, and "pressure cooked" them until a syrupy feast was uncovered hours later. What was not eaten on the spot was spread in thin sheets, dried on flat rocks, and taken home for storage. The Apaches also used fibers of the mescal plant for making sandals and bags. A hallucinogen derives from the plant, as does a distilled beverage, but neither of these products is particularly associated with the Mescalero Apaches.

Beginning in the 1600s but intensifying in the mid-1800s, the Apaches' nomadic way of life increasingly clashed with the interests of the newer Hispanic and Anglo settlers. After years of raids and reprisals, hardship, and internment at Fort Stanton, the Mescaleros were finally settled on the reservation mapped out for them by the Bureau of Indian Affairs. There they had to try to live on a tiny fraction of their former territory and to depend for food upon government contracts for meat and cornmeal awarded to rival Lincoln merchants—merchants whose feuding eventually resulted in the Lincoln County War.

The Apaches welcome visitors to the reservation headquarters, located at the town of Mescalero. Today the tribe numbers about two thousand people, maintains its own police force and game and fish agency, and educates elementary school children, sending high school students to Tularosa and Ruidoso.

The Mescaleros especially invite neighbors and tourists to their four-day ceremonial, held annually in early July. This ceremony combines the celebration of the coming of age of young women, the coming forth of the mountain spirits for the healing of the tribe, and typical Fourth of July festivities. Cooking areas, booths, and tepees all are decorated with pine boughs, symbolizing the spirit of the mountains. Women serve dried mescal and mescal "pudding." Visitors are advised that dances during daylight hours usually are for fun and have no ceremonial intent. The sacred part of the event begins when celebrants dressed as mountain spirits light the bonfire at dark. Groups of "spirits" then begin their dancing and ritual clowning. The puberty ceremony culminates when the young women, dressed in beaded buckskin, with sacred yellow pollen on their cheeks and foreheads, dance and await the rising sun in front of their special tepee, which faces east. The last day of the celebration normally falls on the Fourth and is purely for entertainment. As is true with American Indian ceremonials all over the country, it is often difficult in one visit to appreciate all that this festival means to the Mescaleros.

Leaving Mescalero, you will continue down the Rio Tularosa, wooded canyons gradually giving way to rugged desert slopes. Whenever the road allows a view to the west, the sparkle of the White Sands far below catches the eye. As you get closer you can see that the white splotch is a tiny ripple in a vast intermountain basin that stretches across to the wall on the west and south as far as the eye can see. This is the Tularosa Valley. The Sierra Blanca and the Sacramento Mountains (to your right and left, respectively) form the eastern rim here, and you can look over to the San Andres and Organ mountains that enclose it on the west. In the geologic past, downfaulting of a huge block of the earth's crust created a large hole here, which the elements have been filling up ever since with material washed or blown in from the flanking mountains. Some of that debris has been gypsum, which washes down from both sides, collects in shallow lakes (there is no drainage out of this valley), and when the water evaporates, dries out and moves on the prevailing southwesterly winds, creating dunes of pure white gypsum.

After a sharp fifteen-mile descent that carries you from the near-alpine summits down through successively warmer and drier biological zones, Tularosa, the green jewel of the valley, awaits you. Here is a 130-year-old town that has managed to survive as a beautiful little city and to have elicited the admiration and praise of two worthy chroniclers. Eugene Manlove Rhodes grew up here and set several novels and numerous short stories in the region. "Oasis" was his name for the Tularosa that figures in many of them. Later, C. L. Sonnichsen

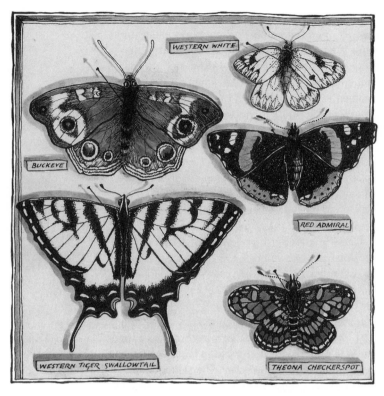

WESTERN WHITE

BUCKEYE

RED ADMIRAL

WESTERN TIGER SWALLOWTAIL

THEONA CHECKERSPOT

(who also wrote an excellent account entitled *The Mescalero Apaches*) wrote his classic *Tularosa: Last of the Frontier West* (1963). Block-long adobe structures (Rhodes's "recumbent skyscrapers") line the streets shaded by dense cottonwoods. Ditches branch through the town carrying Rio Tularosa water to gardens and fruit trees. Older sections, including the forty-nine blocks registered since 1979 as an historic district, lie west of U.S. 54; a handsome school is to the east. As was common in New Mexico, when the railroad came in 1898, it missed Tularosa. A small center sprang up around the station a mile and a half to the west, but because of the moderate expansion of the community, the two towns never grew together.

Three festivals celebrate Tularosa's history and unite residents and visitors. Although the city and river were named for the reedy places hereabouts (*tule* means reed; a *tular* is a reedy place), Tularosa is known as the "City of Roses" and holds a Rose Festival annually the first weekend in May. The Rose Queen, an old-timers' picnic, and arts and crafts exhibits help celebrate the blossoming of the flowers, which do grow well here. The following weekend is usually the St. Francis de Paola Fiesta, commemorating the building of the first church after a showdown with the Apaches at nearby Round Mountain in 1868. On Christmas Eve candlelit paper lanterns glow on the church and the plaza, and along U.S. 54 for almost two miles through the village. Tularosans are invited to share Fourth of July with their former rivals, the Apaches, at the Mescalero Festival.

Hispanic farmers founded Tularosa during the Civil War when nearby Fort Stanton offered some promise of peace with the Mescaleros. The new village thrived on the precious liquid that the Rio Tularosa brought down from the mountains. Soon, however, the little valley had to accommodate two additional groups of settlers: former Union soldiers who liked what they saw of New Mexico during the war and returned to stay, and Texans who began arriving with herds of cattle. Tularosa survived the cattle wars and political feuding that threatened to tear the town apart in the 1880s, and has since managed to escape being abandoned, destroyed, or made to look like someplace else. The pecans, pistachios, and alfalfa growing in the surrounding valley testify to the continuing importance of agriculture and the everlasting value of the water that nourishes it.

The next leg of the tour follows U.S. 54 for forty-five miles north toward Carrizozo. The vegetation here is characteristic of the Chihuahuan desert: creosote bush, large yuccas, and flowering sotol mix with prickly pear, smaller cacti, frail tentacles of ocotillo, and precious native grass. Travelers who observe that the landscape is gouged by arroyos and dominated by woody brush will require some imagination to picture the lush stands of bunchgrass that lured successive waves of settlers into this valley. They might take comfort in knowing that the deterioration, which began with the elimination of wild grazers and the enclosure of domestic ones, can be reversed by use of domestic herds and careful management.

Three Rivers, seventeen miles north, was the rail station for the Three Rivers Ranch, established in the 1870s by Patrick Coghlan, "King of Tularosa." Among other profitable ventures here, Coghlan fenced cattle stolen by Billy the Kid. After the killing of William McSween during the Lincoln County

War, his widow, Susan McSween Barber, acquired part of the valley above Coghlan's ranch and became known as "The Cattle Queen of New Mexico." By 1915, Senator Albert B. Fall had bought out both Pat Coghlan and Susan Barber. The ranch, now translated as Tres Ritos, became a desert paradise under Emma Fall's horticultural care. The Falls enlarged Coghlan's mansion, and this was the scene, in 1921, of discussions that created the Teapot Dome Scandal. Was Fall (then U.S. Secretary of the Interior) guilty of accepting a bribe from his business associates, Doheny and Sinclair, in return for granting them oil-drilling contracts in the Elk Hills Reserve in Wyoming? Or was he a scapegoat who paid for the low public morality of the times? This is a still-debated issue. Fall, broken and ailing, spent six months in prison in 1931.

Thomas Fortune Ryan was the next to be captivated by Three Rivers. He acquired the ranch in 1941, tore down all of Fall's mansion except the library, and built a Spanish-style house surrounded by poplar and cottonwood trees.

Despite its magnificent setting—the broad Tularosa Valley below, clear creek water underfoot, and Old Baldy towering over all—an aura of sinister mystery hangs over this "magic valley." Murders, suicides, unexplained corpses, hair-raising tales, and ruined millionaires have been a part of the ranch ever since the 1870s.

When you turn east up Forest Road 1447 from the now abandoned Three Rivers station, you will first see Ryan's house and then Susan McSween Barber's "rock house" about eight miles in. Near the eastern limits of the ranch, Ryan built a hunting lodge for survivors of the Bataan March. The nearby chapel of Santo Niño is dedicated to the memory of all the New Mexicans who fought the Japanese in the Philippines during World War II. The White Mountain Wilderness begins at the campground where the road ends. A hiking trail follows the stream up amid huge walnut and juniper trees, past rocky promontories to the alpine summit of Sierra Blanca. If such an ascent calls to you, the strenuous thirteen-mile round-trip can be done in a full day.

The Department of the Interior recently opened the Three Rivers Petroglyph Site on the same forest

Juniper

road five miles up the valley from U.S. 54. Here, on a ridge between the mountains and the Tularosa Basin, a mile-long marked trail winds among the more than five hundred beautiful and intricate rock pictures, which are at least one thousand years old. You can also see partially reconstructed pueblo and pit-house dwellings dating from A.D. 1000 to 1350 along the trail. The petroglyph site has water and facilities for picnicking and camping.

Continuing north of Three Rivers Station on U.S. 54, you will soon spot the blackness of the "Valley of Fires" lava flow to the west and beyond that, through notches in the near-lying ridge, the Oscura Mountains. It was on the far side of the Oscura range that the first atomic bomb was exploded, on July 16, 1945. This event, which changed the course of history, also signaled that this remote valley would never again be the same. Although the entire area is closed to the public, tours of the Trinity Site, the spot at which the blast occurred, are conducted twice a year by the army, usually in April and October. The Alamogordo Chamber of Commerce provides up-to-date information.

Carrizozo is named for the carrizo grass that is native to the plain and foothills here. Highway 54 has been following the route of the Southern Pacific Railway, which in 1900 connected El Paso to Chicago. The town of Carrizozo owes its existence to the fact that the railroad built a roundhouse and repair shops here. Soon a sizable city sprang up, which became the trading center for a wide area and the new seat of Lincoln County.

A railroad strike in the 1920s and subsequent advances in railroad technology dampened Carrizozo's robust growth. The last passenger train ran through in 1968. Today, Carrizozo boasts county offices, a medical clinic, a library, several parks, a weekly newspaper, and an inviting soda fountain and ice-cream store, restored to its original 1920s appearance. The children's park just east across the tracks is judged by people aged three to sixteen to be one of the most fun in the state. Pushing kids on the swings, feeding the ducks, and watching sunlight sparkle on the pond, you feel the presence of the encircling mountains here as at few other spots on this vast, quiet plain.

Before turning east on U.S. 380, consider taking two short side trips.

Side Trip to White Oaks

Twelve miles north off U.S. 54, N.M. 349 leads to Carrizozo's early rival, the recently reclaimed ghost town of White Oaks. Gold discoveries near the springs between the Patos and Carrizo mountains in 1879 inspired a city of over 2,500 inhabitants. White Oaks soon became a stop on the stage line from San Antonio (on the Rio Grande) to Roswell, as well as on the Las Vegas stage road to old Mesilla and El Paso. The new railroad bypassed the town in 1898, however, and it steadily lost ground to Carrizozo. By the time the town faded away in the 1950s, it had served as trading center, school, and post office for such mountain and farming communities as Raventon, Texas Park, Vera Cruz, Encinoso, and Jicarilla.

Now you drive up a paved road and at the old townsite see stores on Main Street and once stately mansions of the 1890s (some now being refurbished) on top of the surrounding hills. Cattle queen Susan McSween Barber lived here for a time, as did former governors, congressmen, and Lincoln County War refugees. Annually in early August a "pony express" horse race covers the forty-one miles from Capitan Gap to White Oaks. Emerson Hough, a reporter for a Lincoln paper, set his 1903 novel *Heart's Desire* in the high time of White Oaks.

Side Trip to Valley of Fires

The Valley of Fires State Park lies a few miles west of Carrizozo where U.S. 380 crosses what is believed to be the youngest lava flow in the continental United States. Tour Sixteen tells you what to expect from a visit to these badlands.

The tour now follows U.S. 380 east from Carrizozo, over the Southern Pacific tracks, past the children's park and the golf course, and past the turnoff on N.M. 37 to Nogal, and Bonito Lake in the Sierra Blancas. Here the road begins a serious climb, between Nogal Peak to the south and Vera Cruz Mountain on the north, up toward the Capitan Mountains. The highway parallels an old railroad built in 1899 by the Phelps Dodge Company to haul coal from the Capitan area down to Carrizozo. Old railway cuts are still visible. At Indian Divide, you leave the Tularosa Valley behind and head straight for Smokey Bear's home in Capitan.

As soon as you get into town, you will see the Smokey Bear Museum and the Smokey Bear Motel and Café on your left. The story of Smokey goes back to a day in May 1950. It was then, after a five-day fire that burned seventeen thousand acres in the Capitan Mountains, that firefighters found a small bear cub and nicknamed him Hot Foot Teddy. The bear, renamed Smokey, was flown to Santa Fe for medical care and later to Washington, D.C. He soon became the most famous bear in the country, as a survivor of a devastating fire that had been started by a careless person and as a symbol of the nation's concern about the protection of our forests. The town of Capitan built the Smokey Bear Motel and Café and constructed a log museum to tell the story of the cub's beginnings. At about the time when a state park was created in 1976 (to include the museum, a picnic spot, a nature trail, and a playground), the original Smokey died at the National Zoo in Washington. He was buried at the new Smokey Bear State Park. A second Capitan Mountains bear, Smokey Junior, took over the role of representing fire prevention to the country.

Capitan offers complete tourist facilities, a rodeo ring, and the magnificent setting of a small mountain valley surrounded by imposing peaks. This small crossroads town takes its name from El Capitan Peak, which rises to 10,083 feet just to the east. The Capitan Mountains are among the few ranges in the country that extend east and west rather than north and south. They are also one of the few without a major stream. New Mexico 246, unpaved, curves north and east around them. It once connected the towns of Encinoso, Richardson,

Spindle, and Arabela with the outside world; it now serves ranches and recreation areas. New Mexico 48 heads southwest from Capitan as a paved road back toward the fishing, hunting, and resort areas of Angus, Alto, Nogal, and Ruidoso.

Four miles east of Capitan, N.M. 214 leads to Fort Stanton, located 2.5 miles south of U.S. 380 on the banks of the Rio Bonito. The fort was established in 1855 to encourage settlement in this part of New Mexico. The Mescaleros, who signed a treaty with the United States in 1852, were quartered here for a short time, but they soon set out on their own and eventually resettled on their present reservation thirty miles to the southwest. Union forces burned the fort in 1861 upon the advance of General Sibley's Texas troops. Volunteers under Kit Carson reoccupied the post in 1863. Fort Stanton was rebuilt in 1868 and for thirty years served as both a military post and a social and economic center for the region.

By 1898 the army no longer needed the military post, and Fort Stanton became a U.S. Marine Hospital for tubercular patients. It later served as a public health hospital, a state hospital for the tubercular and, since 1966, a state institution for people with mental retardation. A project now in the planning stage could restore this remarkable old fort as an educational and tourist attraction.

Just beyond the Fort Stanton turnoff, the road leaves the high ridge and begins to follow the Rio Bonito back down toward Hondo. Irrigated fields and orchards reappear, as do adobe farmhouses, fruit stands, valley pastures, and meadows. After a few miles you enter old Lincoln town, still the center of this little valley and still very much a part of it. Here among historic buildings and sites where acts of blood and passion were played out, you can stop, relax, and walk about in a serenity quite at odds with the violent reputation of this village's much discussed little war of a century ago.

The town was first settled in 1849 by Hispanic villagers from the east side of the Manzano Mountains. Until the creation of Lincoln County in 1869 and its designation as county seat, the new village was called Las Placitas (little settlements) del Rio Bonito. The establishment of nearby Fort Stanton in 1855 encouraged more settlers to come during the 1850s and 1860s. A chapel dedicated to San Juan became the center of an area of small farms up and down the river, with sheep herding in the adjacent mountains.

Since the 1870s, however, Lincoln's story has been the one of honor and revenge immortalized by its best-known figure, Billy the Kid. The Lincoln County War began as a commercial rivalry between mercantile houses, but it eventually engulfed all the main groups of the region: Texas cowboys, former Union soldiers, Hispanic settlers, and Mescalero Apaches. First came a falling out, then a murder and a delay of justice, next the assassination of a sheriff, then pitched gun battles that culminated in a five-day shootout here in Lincoln, July 15–19, 1878, which took the lives of several of the combatants and nearly destroyed the town.

His faction was routed in the shootout, but Billy the Kid escaped and, with his gang of a handful of men, continued the blood feud. He swore his intention of visiting justice upon all those (now firmly in power in the county) whom he held responsible for the original murder. To contain the young desperado, Lincoln County installed a new sheriff, Pat Garrett, and the Territory of New Mexico installed a new governor, Lew Wallace. U.S. Army regulars arrived to patrol Lincoln. Garrett captured Billy the Kid, who was tried and sentenced to be hanged. But Billy shot his way out of the Lincoln County jail and assured himself a place in history. Finally, a bullet from Pat Garrett's gun ended Billy the Kid's short career on July 15, 1881. Legends about his exploits sprang up almost immediately. Was he a hero who died fighting the crooked establishment, or a ruthless killer? Later generations have been asked to decide. Playwright Don McAlavy has created a historical drama of Billy's life that plays June through August evenings at the Caprock Amphitheater near San Jon. (Refer to Tour Seven for details.)

Lincoln celebrates Billy the Kid's jailbreak during an annual pageant held on the first weekend of August; a parade, fiddlers' contest, arts-and-crafts fair, and pony express race from Capitan Gap to White Oaks attract thousands of visitors each year. More and more of the buildings from the 1880s have been carefully restored and are open to the public. The Murphy Store, which was converted in 1880 into the courthouse and jail from which Billy escaped, is now a museum. (The guides here are a great source of Lincoln County lore, and can point out such details as the bullet holes from the jailbreak.) The Tunstall Store, at the east end of town, also survives, and contains many original stock items from the nineteenth century. The Wortley Hotel, across from the old courthouse, burned in the 1930s but was faithfully restored in 1960. It is now open as an inn, furnished in the style of the late 1880s, and noted for fine home cooking. Juan Patron's old store, at the east end of town, has recently become a bed-and-breakfast.

Ten more miles of the sparkling Rio Bonito, alfalfa fields, orchards, and steep valley walls bring you back to Hondo and the return to Roswell via U.S. 70/380. Now is your chance to get to know Roswell. Tall buildings pinpoint the downtown area at the crossroads of U.S. 285 and U.S. 380, Main and Second streets, respectively. From this spot the Roswell Historic District (and the Chaves County Museum) lies to the west, the Chihuahuita Historic District to the southeast. North on Main Street is an extraordinary museum and art center. The city has created several pleasant parks along the arroyos that carry water down from the mountains toward the Pecos River.

Apaches had frequented the region for a long time and Spanish colonizing expeditions passed by what is now Roswell in the 1590s, but "permanent" settlement of the area came only in the mid-nineteenth century with the migration of Hispanic farmers and herders into the Bonito and Hondo valleys and the cattle drives from West Texas. Nearby settlements of Rio Hondo, Missouri Plaza, and El Berrendo date from the 1860s. Roswell got its present name only in 1873. By then Main Street had been laid out, and the central commercial zone had begun to take shape. The lush valley here, meanwhile, had become a major stopover for cattle drivers moving up the Pecos toward military forts to the north. Texas cattlemen Goodnight, Loving, Chisum, and Lea all left their names hereabouts: Charles Goodnight and Oliver Loving to the series of cattle trails that followed the Pecos upriver and branched out over northeastern New Mexico and southern Colorado; John Chisum to a cattle trail from Roswell to Las Cruces (paralleled by the first half of this tour); and Lea to the southeasternmost county in the state. Chisum settled here and headquartered his ranch six miles south of Roswell, at South Spring. It became an important social and political center for southeastern New Mexico. The South Spring Ranch, now owned by the Robert O. Anderson family, has been maintained as it was in the early years of this century. (You can make arrangements at the Historical Society to visit it.) Captain Joseph C. Lea built a cattle empire northwest of Roswell. His family were leaders in turning the new settlement into an important trading center.

Over the years, Roswell struggled with drought and flood, but attracted a steady stream of newcomers who sought refuge from the devastation of the Civil War, and then good weather for their health. By the first decade of this century, the coming of the railroad, together with the discovery of artesian water in the area, led to a population boom. By then Anglos outnumbered the early Hispanic settlers. Military-related work during the Second World War, and the boom in oil and gas production that followed, brought new waves of settlers here in the 1940s and 1950s. Today you can see all these influences in Roswell. A day walking the historic districts, browsing in the museums, picnicking in a park, or visiting nearby scenic spots is highly recommended.

An excellent walking tour of the downtown Roswell Historic District begins at the Chaves County Historical Museum at the corner of Second and Lea. J. B. White built this house in 1910, when he was a partner in the Littlefield Cattle Company. The building reflects the importance of its owner, with its many rooms, gracious staircase and front hall, and extensive porch. Donated to the public by White's descendants, the museum is furnished as a home would have been at the turn of the century. Children will especially enjoy the kitchen, where volunteers describe how all the odd-looking implements are used. The museum provides copies of walking (or driving) tours of sections of the historic district.

Once the main residential section of Roswell—until expansion in the 1940s pushed dwellers out onto the plains and outskirts of town—the Downtown District was placed on the National Register of Historic Places in 1985. The architecture here represents styles popular from the 1890s to the 1930s: Prairie style, Mission Revival, Hipped Box (referring to the hipped roof), the decorative and gabled Queen Anne, the simple Bungalow (an early California transplant), and the Southwest, or Pueblo, style.

One of the earliest settlements in eastern New Mexico, the Chihuahuita Historic District dates from the 1850s, when this valley attracted Hispanic newcomers from northern New Mexico, Texas, and Mexico. A brief tour of Chihuahuita will reveal other architectural styles that reflect these origins as well as the care and individuality expressed in details of stuccoed exteriors, gardens, shrines, fences, and walls. It will also take you past two community gathering places, St. John's Church and El Tapatio Bakery. You will find this intriguing enclave by turning south off Second Street onto Garden or Elm street.

Just north of downtown on Main Street, it is hard to miss the lighted dome and huge columns of the neo-Classical Chaves County Courthouse. Farther north on Main Street, the Roswell Museum and Art Center emphasizes both Southwestern art and the space sciences. The permanent collection contains works by Georgia O'Keeffe, Marsden Hartley, Stuart Davis, John Marin, Ernest Blumenschein, and Andrew Dasburg. The museum also features many pieces by the late Roswell native Peter Hurd, best known as a regional landscape painter and portraitist who worked in the medium of egg tempera. Among many other works, Hurd is remembered for a commissioned portrait of President Lyndon B. Johnson, which LBJ did not like and refused to accept. The museum's artist-in-residence program provides grants that bring innovative young artists to the area for residencies of up to one year. The Goddard Wing of the museum houses an exact 1931 replica of Dr. Robert Goddard's liquid-fuel rocket workshop. New Mexico's moon-walking former senator, Harrison Schmitt, donated his astronaut equipment to the museum. These exhibits are complemented by a planetarium.

Another popular attraction for children is the Spring River Park and Zoo. A local artisan has

restored the fine wooden animals on the popular carousel, and a small lake provides fishing and duck watching. The annual Eastern New Mexico State Fair in September, a tradition since 1892, brings crowds to the Roswell Fairgrounds to show off or to admire the agricultural products of the region. Visitors also swarm to the midway, food booths, and the exciting rodeos.

The Lea family can claim credit for convincing a commandant of the Fort Worth Military University to locate a military school in Roswell. The New Mexico Military Institute is now a state-supported coeducational preparatory school and junior college housed in handsome, buff brick buildings on a spacious campus at what was once the north edge of town.

In the 1970s, Roswell attracted national attention by its successful experiment with conversion from a military to a civilian-based economy. After the removal of Walker Air Force Base, many expected the city would shrivel and decay. Citizens and community leaders rallied, however, and turned the old air base into an industrial park, which houses a branch of Eastern New Mexico University, a bus manufacturing plant, an office complex, a hospital, an airport, and a rehabilitation center.

The beauty and natural history of two bodies of water within a short distance of Roswell, Bitter Lake and Bottomless Lakes, have for a long time attracted both residents and visitors. You will find Bitter Lake National Wildlife Refuge by turning east on the old Roswell-Clovis highway at the north edge of Roswell and driving nine miles to the headquarters building. The lakes and bottomland here are seasonal home to snow geese, ducks, sandhill cranes, and other marsh birds. During the spring and fall, hundreds of white pelicans stop over at the lakes on their migratory flights up and down the Pecos. Gravel trails for cars, hikers, and joggers follow dikes and levees into the recesses of this watery hostel. Fishing is permitted on certain lakes after most of the birds have gone north. Bitter Lake, a natural and highly alkaline lake, has long been a roosting area for the magnificent sandhill cranes. At dusk, the large birds wade into the water to seek safety from such local predators as bobcats, foxes, badgers, and coyotes.

For a water experience of a different kind, follow U.S. 380 and N.M. 409 for sixteen miles southeast of Roswell to Bottomless Lakes, New Mexico's first state park. The deepest of these bodies of water, Lea Lake, has good facilities for fishing, picnicking, camping, scuba diving, and boating. A network of nature trails leads you by the high red bluffs that tower above each of the lakes, formed when the roofs of underground cavities collapsed, and the resulting holes filled with water. The lakes are not truly bottomless, and range in depth from seventeen to ninety feet. Despite local legends of lake monsters and long underground passageways, the true wonders of these lakes are probably the rare species of animals that live here. The tiny cricket frog, which can jump up to eighty-four times its length, is one of the park's remarkable inhabitants, as are two endangered species, the two-inch-long Pecos pupfish and the eastern barking frog. Deer, skunks, snakes, and jackrabbits are plentiful, but they try to avoid visitors.

Upon returning to Roswell, you may relax in one of the city's fine motels, shop for old treasures in the antique mall on North Main, picnic in a city park, or browse in bookstores, the historical museum, or the public library to understand more about the remarkable people, places, and events mentioned in this tour.

TOUR
EIGHTEEN
OASES

Places: Whites City, Guadalupe Mountains, Hueco Tanks, El Paso, Ciudad Juárez, Las Cruces, Aguirre Springs, Oliver Lee State Park, Alamogordo

Mileage: Approximately 260 miles, excluding side trips

Suggested travel time: Two days

Highways: U.S. 62/180, I-10, U.S. 70, U.S. 54

Accommodations: Whites City, El Paso, Ciudad Juárez, Las Cruces, and Alamogordo

Camping: Guadalupe Mountains National Park, Hueco Tanks State Historical Park, Aguirre Springs National Recreational Park, and White Sands National Monument, Oliver Lee State Park

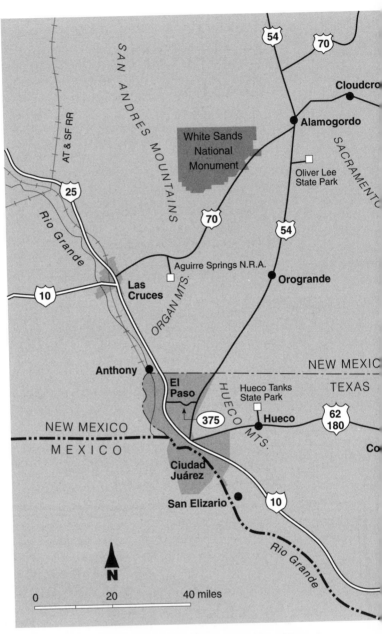

The "Oases Tour" is intended for visitors to
Carlsbad Caverns and White Sands who want to
experience more of the attractions in the region
where New Mexico, Texas, and Mexico come
together. It will introduce you to the semiarid
triangle of Texas that lies west of the Pecos River
and has had such a long and close association with
New Mexico.

You will see the highest point in Texas, the

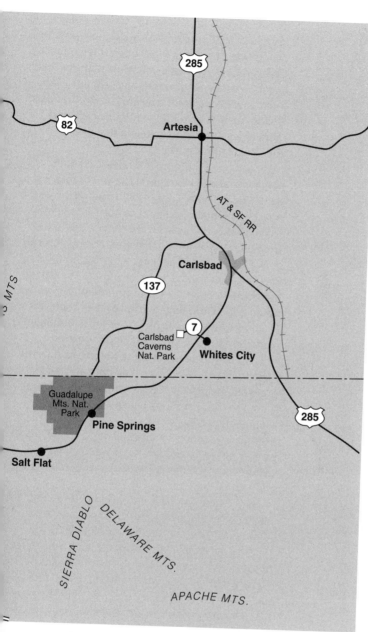

fourth largest city in Mexico, and the miles of salt
flats and desert plain along which the Butterfield
Stage once made its way. You are also invited to
explore a vast and seldom visited region of scattered and rugged mountains whose cool forested
peaks, secluded canyons, and precious springs
teeming with life have lured adventurers since
before the Apaches came.

We also recommend this tour as a shorter loop

in its own right for "weekend" travelers beginning from Roswell, Carlsbad, Las Cruces, or Alamogordo. Your journey begins at Whites City, the entrance to Carlsbad Caverns. Within a few miles at the Texas line it becomes an interstate tour and finally an international one upon crossing the Rio Grande at El Paso. After El Paso, the tour loops back past yet more life-giving waters to rejoin the main part of Tour Sixteen in Alamogordo.

As you head south from Whites City, the panorama ahead helps persuade you to follow U.S. 62/180 into Texas. On the southern horizon lie the Apache Mountains, distant cousins to those from which Carlsbad Caverns were carved. Down the west side stretch the Guadalupes, ending abruptly at El Capitan Peak. The horseshoe-shaped Capitan Reef once encircled a huge inland sea. The part of the barrier reef off the western shore of the sea late became the Guadalupes. The Apache Mountains (and the Glass Mountains farther to the southeast) mark the southern rim of the ancient basin.

Up until the late 1800s, the Mescalero Apaches hunted and gathered over the entire area and prepared their staple food from the mescal plant. Although they have long considered the White Mountains of New Mexico their main home, the Mescaleros also lived in the Guadalupes and nearby smaller ranges, seeking warmer weather and mature mescal bulbs at lower elevations during the winter months.

By the time you have crossed into Texas, you will be able to distinguish features of the Guadalupe Mountains. Two hundred fifty million years ago, this was the edge of a shallow sea, with a huge reef of algae on its western shore. The mountains before you are that old reef, which was buried by sediment as the ancient sea evaporated, and later was raised up by geologic forces that exposed parts of the reef and left others underground. Meanwhile, the climate here changed from humid subtropical to the semiarid conditions of the recent past millennia. Despite the revolutionary change, isolated remnants of ancient plant communities have survived in the protection afforded by mountain canyons. This kind of miraculous mix-up is most evident in McKittrick Canyon, which slices eastward across the ancient reef, carrying a spring-fed stream.

One of the most recently established parks in the federal park system (1972), Guadalupe Mountains National Park has introduced and interpreted to the public these remarkable mountains, their deep canyons, and the surrounding desert. The park offers two main entrances for highway travelers, each with a visitor center. You will reach the McKittrick Canyon Gate first, then the Pine Springs Campground, where there are trailheads for hikes to the high peaks. If you want to visit McKittrick Canyon, drive on to the main visitor center first for maps, books, conversation with park rangers, and a brief slide presentation. Then backtrack the short distance to McKittrick Canyon, judged by many people as the most beautiful spot in Texas. Named by Captain Felix McKittrick in 1869, the spirit of the place later captivated Wallace Pratt, a petroleum geologist. Pratt established a ranch in the canyon in the 1930s and built a stone slab cabin three miles upstream from the present McKittrick Canyon Visitor Center. Pratt's donation of the ranch in 1959 set the wheels in motion for the creation of the national park.

As you walk in the canyon, you can easily understand why he so loved the region and was dedicated to its preservation.

Although most of the trails in the national park are steep and rugged, the walk to Pratt Cabin is over a gentle grade, and inspires admiration and wonder at the surrounding beauty. The canyon provides protection from the harsh extremes of the desert, and the stream nourishes an abundance of plant and animal life. A geologic circumstance adds further enchantment; dissolved limestone from the springs leaves white deposits all along the stream-bed, creating dozens of small dams across the path of the water. Your walk takes you from pool to white pool, each level of vegetation changing gradually from desert to canyon woodland to highland forest, and in many spots there are strange intermixtures of all three.

As if the canyon itself were not enough, the drive up to the McKittrick Canyon Visitor Center offers the opportunity to explore the Permian Reef Geology Trail. This takes you up along the canyon wall to clefts and outcroppings in the old reef and, if you are so inclined, up across the ridge back into New Mexico. The entire canyon region is open to the public only during daylight hours. No camping is permitted here, and the gate to the highway closes each night.

The Pine Springs Campground is north of the highway just west of the main visitor center. The campground features RV hookups, water, restrooms, and tent sites. Trails to all the high-country peaks branch out from the campground. One goes to El Capitan, the three-thousand-foot promontory at the end of the reef. Another switchbacks its way through a bewildering variety of vegetation and exposed rock to Guadalupe Peak (8,749 feet), the highest point in Texas. Others lead to Bush Mountain, Blue Ridge, McKittrick Ridge, The Bowl, and Dog Canyon. (Backcountry camping is allowed on these trails.) Dog Canyon, not to be confused with the Dog Canyon in the Sacramentos later on this tour, is also accessible by vehicles from the Carlsbad side via N.M. 137 and El Paso Gap.

A few hundred yards from the campground, you will find ruins of the Pinery, a Butterfield Stage station built of the same limestone layers that visitors can trace in the ridges and up and down the trails. For westbound passengers on the transcontinental mail route during the 1860s and 1870s, the sighting of El Capitan meant fresh springwater and the beginning of the mountains. Journals relate that travelers watched the landmark loom ahead for days, rested at its base, and then slowly left it behind as they headed for El Paso across the salt flats.

As you exit the national park, the highway climbs up Guadalupe Pass right under El Capitan, then quickly descends to the basin below. From your vantage point on the slope, several of the dozen small mountain ranges of Trans Pecos Texas come into view. The Delaware Mountains stretch to the south; and beyond them to the southwest are the Sierra Diablo (devil's range), featuring Victorio Canyon and the site of the final battle in 1881 between the Texas Rangers and Chief Victorio of the Mescalero Apaches. Ahead to the west lie the Cornudas (horned) Mountains, with Cerro Diablo hugging the New Mexico border.

Soon after passing the turnoff to Van Horn on Texas 54, U.S. 62/180 eases down onto the Guadalupe Salt Flats. This saline depression has been highlighted in the history of West Texas more often than other more attractive sites because of a war fought over its control—the El Paso Salt War of 1877. Although little of the action of that conflict actually occurred here on the salt, as you coast along elevated pilings across the basin you may be interested in some of the region's history.

It goes back to post–Civil War El Paso, where the settlement on the Texas side was finally beginning to rival her Mexican sister city, which dated from early colonial days. A new breed of Southern Democrats sought to wrest power and influence away from the Republican/Hispanic interests that had long predominated in the American city. One commercial prize would be control of Guadalupe salt.

In the spirit of the Boston Tea Party, villagers from several Rio Grande towns below El Paso defied claims by Anglo newcomers that would have ended generations of common use of this salt under Spanish grant. By December 1877, tensions had escalated to the point that the armed villagers prepared to resist the combined might of the Texas Rangers and U.S. Army. At San Elizario, sixty miles southwest of here, a bloody battle erupted. That confrontation involved a number of prominent names in El Paso history and left several people dead on both sides, but failed to settle the issue of ownership of the salt beds.

Miles of plain, isolated mountains, and a few tiny crossroad hamlets now accompany you on the way into El Paso. The town of Salt Flat has a café; Dell Junction has a gas station; Cornudas, proclaiming the law west of the Pecos, boasts a convenience store, a restaurant, a post office, and a municipal center all housed in a single building; and Hueco offers tourist services. Since the MacGregor Missile Range closed off access from the New Mexico side, these Texas towns provide the only entry points for hunters, hikers, and explorers to the Cornudas and Hueco mountains that straddle the Texas–New Mexico line.

Once you are well past the salt basin, you may become aware of a change in vegetation. The woody brush that has dominated almost since Whites City gradually gives way to the grassy slopes and yucca-spiked plains with dark mountains in the background that photographers love to capture as the essence of West Texas. Shy, but curious and relatively unafraid of people, pronghorn antelope thrive here. Elk and bighorn sheep have been reintroduced to the high, remote ridges. In this spare and demanding country it is nearly impossible for modern people, who must bring in everything we need in order to live here, to believe that this was really home for the Mescaleros. Anthropologists have learned about how they must have lived and about their social system, which reflects humor and mutual assistance. But what about the predecessors of the Mescaleros—the people who faced the same climatic challenge and left remains of corn, baskets, pictographs, and paintings by the thousand, which have been found in the Guadalupe, the Sierra Diablo, and the Hueco mountains? Similarly forbidding landscapes in other parts of the world have nurtured strange adaptations.

On this immense crossing, the mountains and mesa surround you. Antelope abound. Yucca and cactus fruit mature in season. Jackrabbits, gophers, hawks, and eagles thrive. Hidden springs nourish green-leafed trees, rushes, and flowers. What verse, what song helps travelers relate to this landscape: the Psalms, Woody Guthrie, "Waltzing Across Texas," Mozart? Or is it Marty Robbins singing of Rosa's Cantina "out in the West Texas town of El Paso"?

About forty miles out of El Paso, the steep and

rugged Hueco Mountains come into view. Ranch Road 2775 takes you eight miles north to Hueco Tanks State Historical Park. "Hueco" here refers to a pool of trapped rainwater, several of which nestle amid the strange-shaped stone formations. The willow-lined banks of these emerald oases have over the centuries supplied water for wildlife, for prehistoric farmers and hunters, and for the Butterfield stagecoaches. The 860-acre park also protects cave and rock formations, as well as petroglyphs and ruins of the ancient people who lived here. The state park maintains picnic areas and improved campsites with facilities for the disabled.

After Hueco, a long descent, bands of exposed rock, and more grassy hills bring you to the outskirts of El Paso. Quarries and gravel pits, and then auto salvage yards mark the beginnings of the huge metropolitan area. Of all the many routes into the city, the one chosen by this tour is probably the humblest. Before the highway turns into a multilane commercial strip inside the city limits, you can almost imagine being that cowboy, alone in the dark, riding down from New Mexico, and sighting the lighted bar with horses tied in back and a small sign identifying Rosa's Cantina.

The Franklin Mountains, the last of the desert ranges shared by Texas and New Mexico, thrust deep into El Paso from the north, nearly bisecting the town and squeezing the main business center into a narrow neck between the foothills and the Rio Grande. You need not be especially concerned about finding your way there, because geography channels all the major roads toward downtown and the nearby bridges to Ciudad Juárez, Mexico. By now U.S. 62/180 will have become Montana Street. Interstate 10 (from Van Horn and San Antonio) angles in from the southeast. This is the direction toward San Elizario of the Salt War, as well as the old missions at Ysleta and Socorro, which were displaced from New Mexico during the 1680 Pueblo Revolt. U.S. 54 (to Alamogordo and White Sands) joins from the north. If you stay on city streets (several besides Montana will do) you will travel through miles of barrios, industrial areas, shopping centers, and older neighborhoods.

For the trip into Mexico, proceed into downtown El Paso and watch for Stanton Street or Santa

Mariachi band

Fe Street and signs for Juárez. Two one-way bridges connect the centers of the two cities. Southbound Stanton Street connects with Avenida Lerdo on the Mexican side; then northbound Avenida Juárez completes the loop back into the United States to Santa Fe Street. For a brief visit or an overnight stay in Juárez, most travelers find it easier not to drive. They thus avoid problems of insurance and liability (certain automobile policies cover border Mexico, others do not) and the long lines of traffic (especially on weekends) waiting to pass through U.S. Customs on the way back. If you plan on walking across, you can use either bridge. We recommend proceeding to Santa Fe Street, turning left (south) and finding one of several reliable parking lots near the bridge.

If you have come into town on I-10, you will notice an exit to Mexico 2.5 miles east of the downtown bridges. This is the newer Chamisal crossing commemorating the peaceful settlement of a long-standing land dispute between the two countries. Although you will find shops, hotels, and restaurants there, many United States visitors interested in walking on Mexican soil and experiencing something of Mexican life still prefer the downtown crossings. However, if you are driving farther into Mexico (to Chihuahua or beyond) you will need to use this entrance to get the required permits for yourself and your car.

Once across the Rio Grande, what you see for the first several blocks along Avenida Juárez is partly explained by the proximity of the huge military installation at Fort Bliss northeast of El Paso, and the fact that soldiers are accustomed to using weekend passes for R and R in Juárez. After a little while, the gaudier attractions give way to a variety of mercantile houses with great selections of items, small restaurants, bakeries, and grocery stores. A half mile's walk will take you to the 16 de Septiembre, the principal east-west artery through central Juárez. A few blocks to the right you will see the old restored cathedral and its plaza; beyond that a huge market area awaits anyone interested in seeing something of the trading life of the city: foodstuffs, herbs and spices, housewares, ceramics, hardware, and tinware. The City Market (Mercado Juárez), which caters more to tourists, is located five short blocks to the left (east) of the intersection of Avenida Juárez and 16 de Septiembre. Here you will find groceries, housewares, and handcrafts downstairs, stalls of rugs, clothing, leather, metal work, glassware, and woodwork upstairs, with mercantile houses, and meat and fish markets on surrounding streets. Because products from all over the republic are shipped here, Ciudad Juárez is an ideal place to shop for Mexican handcrafts—better, in some cases, than shopping in the regions where they came from. You can find several clean but modest hotels within a few blocks of the City Market.

Is Juárez Mexico? Is El Paso the United States? These questions may occur to visitors. Taken together, the two cities act in many ways as a single international metropolis. They share drinking water, languages, the dollar, the labor force, and industrial capital. Both El Paso and Juárez dispute New Mexico's original allocation of groundwater. In this largest and most industrial of the border cities, thousands find jobs in the twin plants (*maquiladores*) that dominate large sections of Juárez. These are shops where labor-intensive assembly work is performed (mainly by women) before products are shipped back into the United States. Recent heavy migration from other parts of Mexico challenges efforts of the metropolis to keep up with city services.

One way to gain an idea of the Mexican nature

of Ciudad Juárez is to look at the street signs. Even in the small sector between the cathedral, the market, and the downtown bridges, there are enough heroes, localities, and historical events named to give a clear picture of what is important to the Mexican national identity. Moctezuma, the last of the Aztec rulers, met his death in 1520 at the time of the Spanish conquest; and his heir, Cuauhtemoc, led a resistance movement against Spanish rule. Bartolome de las Casas championed rights of the Indians in the early Colonial period. The 16th de Septiembre commemorates Padre Hidalgo's famous cry for independence from Spain in 1810. Chapultepec and the Niños Heroes commemorate the military academy in Mexico City and the young cadets overwhelmed there by American forces in 1846 during the Mexican War. Cinco de Mayo, a Mexican holiday increasingly popular in New Mexico, celebrates the defeat of Napoleon III's French forces by Mexican troops in the city of Puebla in 1863.

The French captured Puebla on their second try, and soon Mexico City and most of the rest of the nation. They chased President Benito Juárez all the way up to the border outpost here at El Paso del Norte, where the seat of government remained for a time until Juárez could return south. The "El Paso" on the Mexican side later changed its name to "Juárez" to commemorate the president's residence here during the French occupation.

Visitors returning from Mexico are reminded that retail quantities of most items can be brought duty free into the United States. However, many foods, including most fresh fruits, cannot be imported. Any liquor you bring back is subject to Texas state tax. Please check with U.S. Customs on your way into Juárez.

Once you are back on the United States side of the border, you will have a chance to explore some of the highlights of El Paso. Pick up a walking tour brochure at the Paso del Norte Hotel for a stroll around the historical downtown area, beginning and ending at San Jacinto Plaza at Oregon and Main streets. You will see a lively interest in the city's colorful past—El Pasoans seem especially fond of displays of old photographs. You will also experience a vibrant commercial downtown district, where banks, hotels, stores, and the Civic

Center commingle with plaques commemorating past visitors to the city: travelers on the old Camino Real, Butterfield Stage drivers, gunslingers Wyatt Earp and John Wesley Harding, and Pancho Villa.

A short drive north of the downtown section along Mesa Street, the University of Texas at El Paso (UTEP) offers a wide variety of academic programs, specializing in regional literature, archaeology, and natural history. Farther to the northeast, the McKelligon Canyon Amphitheater attracts audiences on summer evenings to the outdoor historical pageant called ¡Viva El Paso!

For your return to New Mexico you must make a choice. One option is to retrace your steps back through eastern El Paso and follow U.S. 54 north toward Alamogordo. This direct route slices across the White Sands Missile Range past the old gold-mining town of Orogrande and the turnoff to Oliver Lee State Park on the outskirts of Alamogordo. The present tour, however, follows a more populous route northwest into Las Cruces, then over the San Agustin Pass, and across the missile range to White Sands National Monument and Alamogordo.

Take I-10 west out of El Paso. The Rio Grande will be on your left and the steep western slopes of the Franklin Mountains on your right. The exit for Transmountain Road invites you to El Paso's favorite scenic drive. With views of both cities and the Rio Grande, Transmountain Road climbs past rugged desert scenery to Smugglers Gap before descending to connect with U.S. 54 in northeast El Paso. The road (Texas Loop 375) also offers the cool shade of the Tom Mays Unit of Franklin Mountains State Park.

Back on I-10, the bistate town of Anthony marks your reentry into New Mexico. The fertile Rio Grande Valley, once renowned for its wines, now shows off pecan groves, chile fields, and large dairies. Freeway signs direct you to Old Mesilla, to New Mexico State University, and to downtown Las Cruces. Tour Fourteen describes the attractions and facilities of the Las Cruces metropolitan area, second in size only to Albuquerque among New Mexico cities. The Organ Mountains (named for the series of spires resembling organ pipes) demarcate the valley on the east. Las Cruceños enjoy picnicking and hiking at Dripping Springs

Agave

and Conklin Cave up on the western slopes of these mountains.

The trip to Alamogordo takes you on U.S. 70 through the 5,719-foot San Agustin Pass between the Organs and the San Andres Mountains to the north. Just beyond the summit of the gentle and open passage lies the turnoff to another favorite oasis, Aguirre Springs National Recreation Area. The 5.5-mile road into the springs gives excellent views of the craggy heights on the back side of the towering organ pipes, an abundance of desert vegetation (prickly cactus and long-spiked agaves), together with mountain-slope trees and grasses, and the White Sands Missile Range headquarters. Aguirre Springs offers camping and picnic sites and trails of various lengths. For hikers of modest ambition, the Pine Tree Trail offers graded pathways winding among boulders, small trees, and seasonal flowers. The trail up the steep mountainside to Baylor Pass beckons to the more adventurous.

Back on U.S. 70, the tour begins the long descent into the Tularosa Valley, the immense mountain-enclosed basin that stretches east across to Sierra Blanca and the Sacramento ranges. With clear skies you will soon see the sparkle of the White Sands down at the bottom. Since the Second World War, the U.S. government has reserved this entire valley for testing missiles and rockets. Access is strictly controlled, and U.S. 70 is occasionally closed during brief periods of firing. Tour Sixteen describes the amenities available at White Sands National Monument and the wonder of the sands themselves. Best visited in the evenings or early mornings, the stark white dunes and multicolored sky and mountains engage all our sensibilities: the athletic, the artistic, the playful, the contemplative.

Surrounded by the wonders of White Sands and the mountains to the east, Alamogordo can be an excellent stopping place. Without leaving the highway (White Sands Boulevard), you will find a wide variety of places to eat and stay the night. On the west side of the boulevard, you will see the long cottonwood-shaded Alameda Park, with its zoo (at Tenth Street), the Toy Train Depot, and the Chamber of Commerce Welcome Cottage. The attractive campus of the New Mexico School for the Visually Handicapped is on the opposite side.

One block east along New York Avenue (one-way south between Tenth and Eighth Streets), there are shops and stores from the original downtown district.

For Alamogordo's newest attractions, signs point you east along the Scenic Drive or up Indian Wells Road to the Space Center. There you will have the opportunity of visiting the Clyde W. Tombaugh Planetarium and Omnimax, a dazzling multimedia array of earthly and cosmic experiences. Farther up the hill, on appropriately numbered N.M. 2001, the "Golden Cube" houses space exhibits and hands-on activities for all ages, in addition to portraits and histories of the dozens of space pioneers from all over the world who have been inducted into the International Space Hall of Fame.

Leaving Alamogordo you must again make a choice. "Caverns and Sands" (Tour Sixteen) will return you north toward Socorro and Albuquerque. The Capitan Tour (Tour Seventeen) introduces you to Mescalero, Ruidoso, and other spots in the Sierra Blanca and Capitan Mountains. Or, if you are completing a loop back toward Roswell or Carlsbad, Tour Sixteen also will escort you east across the mountains on U.S. 82.

The present tour, that of vast deserts and life-giving waters, ends at Oliver Lee State Park, eight miles south of Alamogordo. The short road into the park reveals Dog Canyon cutting midway through the thirty five-mile-long Sacramento Range. One of the most remarkable lines of demarcation in the state, this escarpment abruptly separates the cool, pine-clad uplands from the sun-baked plains just a few miles (but nearly 4,500 feet) below.

Oliver Lee was an early settler whose politically important family later donated this land to the state. He had come here in 1884 and built the ranch house, not yet acquired by the state, that can be seen just to the south. Although the park took Oliver Lee's name, the spirit of Jean Jacques Rochas lives on at the mouth of the canyon here. The rock walls he built up the steep slopes remain apparently as he left them. Visitors find it hard to resist tracing the outlines of his orchards and gardens and studying the ruin of his simple cabin for clues to his daily life. Nicknamed "Frenchy," Rochas arrived at Dog Canyon in the mid-1880s, set out fruit trees, built up a herd of cattle, and

Windows of the Space Center's Golden Cube

watered crops from an irrigation flume, which he and Oliver Lee built together. But Frenchy was killed in front of his cabin on Christmas Day, 1894, as a result, it is supposed, of a dispute over cattle and water. People interested in the solitary Frenchman later contacted his relatives in the old country and learned something about what his life was before he arrived in New Mexico. Almost one hundred years later, a French relative, fascinated by the strange land his ancestor chose and the rude but appealing life he made for himself here, became one of the first visitors to the newly established park.

The visitor center includes displays of the plant and animal life of the canyon that thrives in comparative ease here amid the harsh extremes of the surrounding desert, artifacts from prior Indian cultures, and examples of Frenchy's works. A nature trail leads down the steps and along the boardwalk at the bottom, pointing out species of trees, flowers, and herbs naturally favored by the steep canyon walls and the perennial stream. The Dog Canyon Trail (admired and respected by hikers far and wide) begins just behind the visitor center and makes the 3,500 foot ascent to the high ridges in four and a half miles. An early morning start, water, and plenty of time for the round trip are recommended for this experience.

We hope you have enjoyed the tour and have heard the voice of this unusual corner of the world—in the bustle of Juárez, in the quiet of the plain, in the wind atop a mountain peak, or in the babble of a secluded spring. If you have, we imagine you are already thinking of coming back and staying longer the next time.

GLOSSARY

The origin of these terms is Spanish unless noted. Definitions were drawn from *A Dictionary of New Mexico and Southern Colorado Spanish,* by Ruben Cobos (Museum of New Mexico Press, Santa Fe, 1983), and *Cassell's Spanish-English Dictionary,* by Anthony Gooch and Angel Garcia de Paredes (Macmillan, New York, 1978).

acéquia—irrigation ditch

alcalde—mayor

algodón—cotton

anasazi (from the Navajo: the old ones)—generally refers to the ancient Indians such as those at Chaco Canyon or Bandelier, who were possibly ancestors of today's Pueblo Indians

bizcochito—New Mexico's state cookie; a sugar cookie flavored with anise

bosque—wooded area fringing a body of water, such as a lake or river

brujo—witch

bulto—statue, usually religious and made of wood

burrito—food, often including meat or beans (frijoles) enclosed in a flour tortilla

cacique—Pueblo Indian chief and political leader

caprock—thick layer of rock that underlies the high plains

carne adovada—meat, usually pork, marinated in red chile

carreta—ox cart, such as the wooden cart used by the Penitentes and by Doña Sebastiana, a figure of death

chamisa—rabbitbrush, large round plant with narrow leaves, covered in yellow flowers in late summer

cholla—a variety of thin, tall, spiky cactus found in the Lower Sonoran zone

colcha—bedspread or homemade embroidered coverlet often used as a tapestry, or the kind of embroidery used in making such an item

comanchero—itinerant merchant in colonial and Territorial periods who traded with Plains Indians

convento—convent: either a nunnery or monastery

corbel—architectural member projecting from within a wall to support a weight above

entrada—entrance; in New Mexico, often refers to an exploring or reconnoitering military expedition, such as the Entrada of Coronado

farolito—a kind of festive light, especially of the candle-in-a-bag variety (this word has traditionally been used throughout Hispanic New Mexico; in some parts of the state these lanterns are called *luminarias.*)

fonda—inn

genízaro—non–Pueblo Indian captive rescued, ransomed, or kidnapped from various nomadic tribes (also spelled *jenizaro*)

grito—cry or scream, as in the famous Grito de Dolores, a shouted slogan that proclaimed the beginning of Mexico's War of Independence from Spain

heishi—small beads, usually cut by hand, with a drilled hole, strung as beads for necklaces in Pueblo jewelry

hermano—brother

hermano mayor—older brother; the presiding brother of a Penitente brotherhood

hogan (Navajo)—traditional circular home

kachina (from Hopi)—one of the deified ancestral spirits believed to visit the pueblos (especially Hopi and Zuni) at intervals, or a doll or human impersonator of these deities

kiva (from Hopi)—Pueblo structure used as ceremonial, council, work, or lounging place, usually by men; often round and partially or completely below the ground

Koshare (from Keres)—one of a Pueblo Indian clown society, representing ancestral spirits

latilla—small peeled poles used as lath in beamed ceilings (also spelled *latia*)

llano—plains

luminaria—traditionally the bonfire lit on the feast and saint days that help celebrants find their way around the village or pueblo; see *farolito*

malpais—"bad land"; refers to a lava flow or badlands with little vegetation

manta—shawl or straight-sided dress

maquiladores—American-owned factories in which parts are assembled or completed across the Mexican border

matachines—old Spanish ritual dance with traditional European and Moorish overtones, introduced in New Spain by early settlers; modified by clergy to include aspects of Aztec rituals and the clash of Spanish and Mexican Indian cultures

mayordomo—ditch boss; foreman or overseer; patron or sponsor of annual church fiesta

morada—penitente chapel

nacimiento—crèche or manger scene

ocotillo—thorny desert shrub

paraje—camping ground or encampment; a stop along the trail

penitentes or *hermanos penitentes*—those who do penance; members of a Roman Catholic brotherhood of Indo-Hispanic origin, which observes certain rites related to the Passion of Christ; these rites include fasting, flagellation, enactment of the Last Supper and scenes from the Passion, as well as the singing of *alabados*, religious songs.

placita—settlement; court; patio

portal—covered porch usually at the front or rear of a house

posada(s)—inn(s); *Las Posadas* are an enactment of Joseph and Mary's search for lodging on the night of Christ's birth.

posole—hominy stew

presidio—group of citizens armed for defense; location where such a group is stationed

reducido—Catholic religious school where youngsters are taught catechism

reredos (from French)—screen or partition wall, usually ornamental, located behind an altar

ristra—string (in New Mexico, usually a string of chiles)

sala—hall; drawing room; parlor

santero—one who carves *santos,* or religious statues

santo—a saint; or a statue of a saint

santuario—sanctuary

sopaipilla—fritter made of bread dough cut in squares or triangles and fried in deep fat so that it puffs up

terrones—sod squares held together by plant roots, used in house construction; similar to adobe bricks

tinaja—a depression in a rock in which water collects

torreón—a round tower built for defense

trazo—Spanish street design in which small buildings with interior courtyards and common walls form a continuous facade facing the street

viga—roof beam

zaguán—entrance or vestibule, often wide and sheltered

Explanation of some terms relating to New Mexico's Indian tribes

There are two major groups of Indians in New Mexico, the *Athapaskan* and the *Pueblo.* Athapaskans include the *Navajo* in the northwest corner of the state (as well as in Arizona and Utah) and the *Apaches,* who are divided into two New Mexican groups, the *Jicarilla* Apaches in the north and the *Mescalero* Apaches in the south. Pueblo Indians are usually designated by language groups, including the *Hopi* in Arizona and the *Zuni* in northwestern New Mexico. The *Rio Grande* Pueblo tribes live in northern and central New Mexico along the Rio Grande and several of its tributaries. The *Tiwas* occupy the north and the south, at *Taos, Picuris, Isleta,* and *Sandia* pueblos. The *Towa* language group has only one representative, *Jemez.* The *Tewas* are in the area north of Santa Fe, at *Santa Clara, San Ildefonso, San Juan, Pojoaque, Nambe,* and *Tesuque* pueblos. A small group of their descendants occupy Tewa Village on the Hopi Reservation in Arizona. Tewa, Tiwa, and Towa groups together are called the *Tanoan* language grouping. Finally, the *Keres* language is spoken in *Cochiti, Santo Domingo, Zia, Santa Ana, Acoma,* and *Laguna,* all south and west of Santa Fe.

PERSONAL
ENTRADAS

August 1962. I was twenty years old and looking for adventure. So I transferred from a midwestern college to a university I had never seen in a state where I had never been. I arrived in Albuquerque on the Santa Fe Chief, unloaded my bags, and wondered where to go. A kindly stationmaster called his friend Benny, who picked me up in his blue pickup truck and deposited me at Hokona Hall, my dormitory on the University of New Mexico campus. A group of greeters dressed in cowboy clothes welcomed me and ushered me to my room. The next morning I awoke to the chatter of gardeners working beneath my window. I tried to understand what they were saying, and only later realized that they were speaking Keres, a Pueblo language. I fell in love with New Mexico within twenty-four hours of my arrival. In 1968, I left the state. When I returned to New Mexico six years later with my husband and our three children, we were towing a U-Haul behind our Volkswagen van. We had no jobs awaiting us, and we questioned the wisdom of our decision. But as we drove west from Tucumcari at dusk, the cold winter sky opened up and a warm New Mexico sunset dazzled the kids and assured the adults that we were, indeed, home.

—POLLY ARANGO

A childhood family camping trip took me into the Santa Fe plaza on the very day of the conquistador parade. The crowd's faces and the fiesta colors made a profound impression on me. When my husband and I returned to New Mexico a dozen years later for his work in the Public Health Service, it was again faces and the colors of the earth and sky that charmed me. Our first child was born in the Gallup Indian Hospital and made our family semi-native. Getting to know the people behind the faces made me a New Mexican, too.

—KATHY CHILTON

The Atchison, Topeka, and Santa Fe Railroad took me through New Mexico thirty years ago on a big southern swing from Chicago to San Francisco, but my impressions of what was to become my home really began in 1970 when my wife and I arrived as teacher and physician to care for Indian children in Gallup. We had come from Seattle's cool, damp weather and western Washington's green-wooded mountains. We continued to look for green woods when we came to New Mexico. The large patches of brown punctuated by a piñon here and a juniper there seemed ugly at first, so we sought solace in the San Juan mountains in southern

Colorado or the Sangre de Cristos north of Santa Fe. The high desert has grown on us, however; to bicycle in spring around Albuquerque's volcanoes or to walk in the Sandia Mountains is now a cherished experience.

But it was New Mexico's people that drew us back after a short absence. Waiting in Denver's Stapleton Airport for a flight to the north, I watched passengers board a flight to Albuquerque. The diversity of New Mexico's people struck me as never before; we have since come home for good.

—LANCE CHILTON

My father's collection of Western stories by Eugene Manlove Rhodes opened my teenage eyes to things New Mexican at a time when nobody in my family had ever been here. Later, as a history student in Mexico City, I read again about that remote province of Nuevo Mexico far to the north. When I finally came here, in my twenties, I arrived by crossing the Great Plains, like traders on the Santa Fe Trail, and my fascination with the state continued to grow as my ignorance

of its climate, history, landforms, and people began to diminish.

By now I have spent twenty-four years trying to become a knowledgeable citizen of my adoptive state. During that time I have also married, helped raise a family, and worked to persuade New Mexico's high school students to study mathematics.

—JIM DUDLEY

Unlike many other newcomers to New Mexico, I arrived reluctantly. Like many other wives, I followed my husband to a new job. I grew up outside of the United States; we had been living in San Francisco; and I had only a dim notion of where New Mexico was. A short trip to the state reinforced my impression of a dusty, empty place. Where were the ethnic restaurants? The street festivals and Victorian houses? Worse, there was no ocean. Two travel books and seventeen years later, I have come to love the desert and mountains, vast distances, multiple cultures and experiences, and green chile.

—PATRICIA STELZNER

INDEX